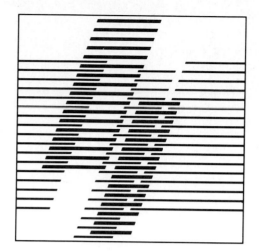

THIRD EDITION

STRATEGIC MANAGEMENT

D0520164

Thomas L. Wheelen
University of South Florida

J. David Hunger
Iowa State University

ADDISON-WESLEY PUBLISHING COMPANY

Reading, Massachusetts · Menlo Park, California
New York · Don Mills, Ontario · Wokingham, England
Amsterdam · Bonn · Sydney · Singapore · Tokyo
Madrid · San Juan

Sponsoring Editor: Mary Fischer
Senior Production Supervisor: Kazia Navas
Production Administrators: Sarah Hallet, Loren Hilgenhurst Stevens
Text Designer: Deborah Schneck
Cover Designer: Marshall Henrichs
Technical Art Consultant: Dick Morton
Copyeditor: Fannie Toldi
Permissions Editor: Mary Dyer
Manufacturing Media Supervisor: Lu Anne Piskadlo
Software Production: Glenn Hoffman

ISBN 0-201-50825-7

EFGHIJ—DO—943210

To

Kathy, Richard,
and Tom

Betty
Kari, Suzi, Lori, Merry

Preface

The corporate world is becoming a very different place. Mergers and acquisitions have transformed the landscape. International boundaries have faded as businesses take on a more global perspective, and the technology of the "Information Age" has telescoped the time it takes to communicate and make decisions. Strategic management takes a panoramic view of this changing corporate terrain and dares to ask *why*.

As a capstone course, strategic management, or business policy, unites the various departments, majors, and subdisciplines usually found in a school of business. Other courses deal in depth with procedures and activities designed to answer *how* corporations exist. Because strategic management itself is in a constant state of flux, and because the course takes a holistic approach, business policy is often a difficult course to teach and to take. Consequently, this book is organized around a strategic management model, which prefaces each chapter and provides a structure for content and for complex case analyses by students. Our goal was to make the text as comprehensive and useful as possible while addressing the following AACSB concerns described in the 1988 report of the "Futures Project" by Porter and McKibbin (published by McGraw-Hill as *Management Education and Development: Drift or Thrust into the 21st Century):* balanced coverage of internal and external environments; a global perspective; cross-functional integration; and attention to the information/service society.

This text was originally part of a hardcover book titled *Strategic Management and Business Policy,* 3rd ed., published in 1989 by Addison-Wesley. The hardcover book includes the twelve chapters of this text plus thirty-eight comprehensive policy cases. Given the strong demand for the hardcover book, we decided to publish the text alone in a soft-cover version. This gives policy instructors the opportunity to continue using the textural material with cases or a simulation from another source. The same instructor's manual originally prepared for the hardcover book can be used with this text. For a softcover casebook, which can be used in conjunction with this text, try *Cases in Strategic Management and Business Policy,* 2nd ed., by Wheelen and Hunger and published by Addison-Wesley.

NEW TO THIS EDITION

This edition includes many of the same features and content that helped make previous editions successful. In addition to updating and fine-tuning these tested features, there are a number of additions to make the book more useful to students and professors, and more representative of the rapidly growing field of strategic management and business policy:

- A *new chapter*—"Strategic Issues in Entrepreneurial Ventures and Small Businesses"—has been included to reflect the increasing interest in innovation and entrepreneurship in today's world.

- Recent developments in the management of *technology* and *organizational innovation,* as well as research and development, receive expanded coverage in Chapters 5 and 8.

- An *integrative case* dealing with a successful company (CSX Corporation) operating in a rapidly changing, deregulated industry (transportation) follows Chapters 1 through 10 in a series of ten discrete segments. Each segment of the integrative case relates to the content discussed in the preceding chapter. The case thus gives the reader an opportunity to apply the concepts and techniques discussed in each chapter to CSX Corporation's particular situation.

- Increased emphasis is placed on *industry analysis* by including, as an appendix to Chapter 4, Michael Porter's now-classic *Harvard Business Review* article "How Competitive Forces Shape Strategy." In addition, *strategic groups* and *mobility barriers* are discussed in Chapter 6.

- A totally revised section on *corporate strategies* is added to Chapter 7 in order to more clearly explain the many corporate-level strategies and how they differ from business and functional strategies.

- A strengthened and expanded section on *scenario construction* in Chapter 7 now enables the reader to actually develop optimistic, pessimistic, and most likely scenarios for each strategic alternative under consideration. This ties in directly with the new software, Financial ANalyzer (FAN) available with our casebook, *Cases in Strategic Management and Business Policy.*

- *The concepts of strategic control* and the *hierarchy of control* are discussed in Chapter 9 as a natural extension of the well-accepted hierarchy of strategy.

- Work by Kenichi Ohmae, the "Peter Drucker of Japan," on the importance of the *triad countries,* and by Michael Porter, on the significance of *multidomestic* versus *global industries,* expands the discussion of multinational corporations in Chapter 10.

- An enhanced supplements package is available with the new edition. A detailed description of this expanded package is provided on page vii of this Preface.

OBJECTIVES

This book focuses on the following objectives, typically found in most business policy and strategic management courses:

- To develop *conceptual skills* so that a student is able to integrate previously learned aspects of corporations.
- To develop a *framework of analysis* to enable a student to identify central issues and problems in complex, comprehensive cases; to suggest alternative courses of action; and to present well-supported recommendations for future action.
- To develop an understanding of strategic management *concepts, research,* and *theories.*
- To develop an understanding of the *roles* and *responsibilities* of the Board of Directors, Chief Executive Officer, and other key managers in strategic management positions.
- To develop the ability to analyze and evaluate the *performance* of the people responsible for strategic management.
- To bridge the gap between theory and practice by developing an understanding of when and how to apply *concepts* and *techniques* learned in earlier courses on marketing, accounting, finance, management, and production.
- To improve the *research capabilities* necessary to gather and interpret key environmental data.
- To develop a better understanding of the *present and future environments* within which corporations must function.
- To develop and refine *analytical and decision-making skills* for dealing with complex conceptual problems.

This book achieves these objectives by presenting and explaining concepts and theories useful in understanding the strategic management process. It provides studies in the field of strategy and policy in order to acquaint the student with the literature of this area and to help develop the student's research capabilities. It also describes the people who manage strategically and suggests a model of strategic management. It recommends a strategic audit as one approach to the systematic analysis of complex organization-wide issues. The book focuses on the business corporation because of its crucial position in the economic system of the free world.

STRUCTURE

Part I is an overview of the subject, surveying the basic skills and competencies needed to deal with strategic issues in modern corporations. Chapter 1 presents a descriptive model as well as key terms and concepts that will be used throughout the book. Chapter 2 focuses on the development of the skills necessary for understanding and applying strategic concepts to actual situations.

Part II discusses important concepts that arise from both the external and internal environments of a corporation. It also describes key people in the corporation who are responsible for strategic management. Chapter 3 discusses the role and importance of a corporation's board of directors and top management in the strategic management process. Chapter 4 discusses both the task and societal environments of a corporation and suggests environmental scanning and forecasting as key corporate tasks. Michael Porter's article on competitive forces is included as an appendix to Chapter 4 to emphasize the importance of industry analysis. Chapter 5 examines the importance of a corporation's structure, culture, and resources to its strategic management.

Part III deals with strategy formulation. It emphasizes long-range planning and the development of alternative courses of action at both the corporate and business levels. Chapter 6 discusses situational analysis. Chapter 7 examines the many possible corporate, business, and functional strategies.

Part IV considers the implementation of strategies and policies, as well as the process of evaluation and control, with continued emphasis on corporate and division-level strategic management. Chapter 8 explains strategy implementation in terms of programs, budgets, and procedures. It describes the people in charge of implementation, what they need to do, and how they should do it. Chapter 9 focuses on evaluation and control. It considers the monitoring of corporate processes and the accomplishment of goals, as well as various methods and criteria used in evaluating performance.

Part V summarizes and examines strategic concerns in particular types of organizations. Chapter 10 looks at strategic issues in multinational corporations and deals with the implications of operating within an international environment. Chapter 11 examines the not-for-profit organization and explains how it differs from the typical business firm. Chapter 12, *a new addition to the text,* discusses strategic issues in entrepreneurial ventures and small businesses.

FINANCIAL ANALYZER (FAN) DECISION-SUPPORT DISKETTES

Financial ANalyzer (FAN)™ was specially developed for students of strategic management and business policy. This software allows the instructor to introduce students to meaningful *computer-assisted strategic and financial analysis.* Financial ANalyzer (FAN) consists of two disks that contain the software plus balance sheets and income statements from over 20 cases in the book, *Cases in Strategic Management and Business Policy,* 2nd ed., by Wheelen and Hunger. The disks are to be used with the Lotus 1-2-3® spreadsheet program on IBM-compatible (MS-DOS) personal computers with two drives. FAN is "user friendly" and requires minimal knowledge of Lotus 1-2-3, programming, or microcomputers beyond the basic knowledge of "booting up." The student can learn to use FAN in less than one hour. Step-by-step instructions are provided for the student so that the instructor need not be involved.

FAN is the most comprehensive software package available for students of strategic management and will enhance the student's knowledge of financial and strategic management analytical techniques. It links the classroom with the methods that strategic managers use in their companies.

Financial ANalyzer (FAN) helps students to more quickly and easily complete *on their own* the financial analysis of complex strategy/policy cases. It uses historical financial information in the form of balance sheets and income statements from the cases to generate:

- Balance sheets in 1967 constant dollars (see pages 37–39).
- Income statements in 1967 constant dollars (see pages 37–39).
- 27 financial ratios plus Altman's Z-value (see Table 2.1 and pages 33–37).
- Common-size balance sheets (see page 36).
- Common-size income statements (see page 36).
- Scenario construction box which enables the students to develop *pro forma* projected financial statements to accompany their recommendations (see pages 227–229). *A special feature of this box is that it interacts directly with Lotus 1-2-3 for ease of operation.*

In addition, as a special feature, FAN automatically calculates financial ratios and develops common-size balance sheets and income statements for the *pro forma* projections generated by the students in their scenario construction. This enables the student to check to see if the recommendation is feasible and in general agreement with the historical ratios and relationships. Contact Addison-Wesley Publishing Company for further information about FAN and the casebook, *Cases in Strategic Management and Business Policy*, 2nd ed.

SUPPLEMENTS

Instructor's Manual

A comprehensive Instructor's Manual has been carefully constructed to accompany *Strategic Management and Business Policy*, 3rd ed., the hardcover version of this text which includes cases. Except for the part dealing with cases, the Manual can be used in conjunction with this softcover text. It is composed of suggested course outlines, teaching aids, lists of key concepts/terms, suggested answers to discussion questions, multiple-choice questions, and transparency masters.

Computerized Testing

Multiple choice questions from the Instructor's Manual are available free to adopters in a computerized test bank.

Transparency Acetates

Acetates of the transparency masters from the Instructor's Manual are available free to adopters of the text.

FAN Decision-Support Disk

As described earlier, FAN is specially prepared software for use with IBM-compatible (MS-DOS) personal computers. The disks include balance sheet and income statements from selected cases in the book plus a program that uses Lotus 1-2-3 to *calculate financial ratios*. This feature should allow students to reduce time spent on calculations and increase time spent on case analysis. The FAN disks are available packaged with *Cases in Strategic Management and Business Policy*, 2nd ed. by Wheelen and Hunger.

Student Edition of Lotus 1-2-3

Available separately from Addison-Wesley, the Student Edition is a full-function version of Lotus 1-2-3 with a 64 column × 256 row spreadsheet. The Student Edition is compatible with the decision-support disk available with the text.

ACKNOWLEDGMENTS

We are grateful to the many people who reviewed drafts of the various editions of this book for their constructive comments and suggestions. Their thought and effort has resulted in a book far superior to our original manuscript.

Ivan Abel, *Baruch College, CUNY*
Sol Ahiarah, *University of Pittsburgh at Johnstown*
Sumer Aggarwal, *University of Massachusetts, Boston*
William Boulton, *University of Georgia*
Barry Baysinger, *Texas A&M University*
Richard Castaldi, *San Diego State University*
William Crittenden, *Northeastern University*
T. K. Das, *Baruch College, CUNY*
Keith Davis, *Arizona State University*
Richard Deane, *Georgia State University*
Donald Del Mar, *University of Idaho*
Cathy Enz, *Indiana University*
Roger Evered, *Naval Postgraduate School*
Jerry Geisler, *Sangamon State University*
Fred Haas, *Virginia Commonwealth University*
Kathryn Harrigan, *Columbia University*
R. Duane Ireland, *Baylor University*
Rose Knotts, *North Texas State University*
Bruce Lamont, *Texas A&M University*
William Litzinger, *University of Texas at San Antonio*

John Logan, *University of South Carolina*
John Mahon, *Boston University*
Martin Marsh, *California State University at Bakersfield*
Stan Mendenhall, *Eastern Montana College*
James Miller, *Georgia State University*
Thomas Navin, *University of Arizona*
Henry Odell, *University of Virginia*
Neil Snyder, *University of Virginia*
Jeffrey Susbauer, *Cleveland State University*
Natalie T. Taylor, *Babson College*
James Thurman, *George Washington University*
John P. van Gigch, *California State University*
Robert Viches, *Old Dominion University*
William Warren, *College of William and Mary*
Carl Zeithaml, *Texas A&M University*

Our special thanks go to Janis Jackson Hill, Connie Spatz, Cindy Johnson, Jim Heitker, Susan Badger, and Mary Fischer who served in turn as editors for the three editions of this text. We are extremely grateful to Mary Clare McEwing, Kazia Navas, and Fannie Toldi for their careful copyediting. The valuable contributions of these people at Addison-Wesley Publishing Company are reflected in the overall quality of the book and in the fact that it was published on time—every time!

We thank Betty Hunger for her cheerful typing of the text revisions and for her work in indexing. We are also grateful to Kari Hunger and Kathy Wheelen for their help in proofreading page proofs. Kim Hammonds and Karen Jackson were invaluable in helping us produce the Instructor's Manual accompanying this book.

In addition, we express our appreciation to Dr. Charles B. Handy, Dean, and to Dr. Thomas Chacko, Management Department Chairman, of Iowa State's College of Business Administration for their provision of the resources so necessary to write a textbook. A note of thanks is also given to Dr. James L. Pappas, Dean, and to Dr. Alton Bartlett, Management Department Chairman, of the University of South Florida's College of Business Administration.

Both of us also acknowledge our debt to the University of Virginia and specifically to Dr. William Shenkir, Dean of the McIntire School of Commerce, for the provision of a work climate most supportive to the development of this textbook. A special note of thanks is offered to Dr. Frank S. Kaulback, Jr., former Dean of Virginia's McIntire School of Commerce, for encouraging the faculty to pursue individual research and consulting interests. His emphasis on quality teaching as a top priority and his willingness to let faculty experiment in teaching and in research enabled people to develop their talents in ways that helped both them and the school.

Lastly, to the many policy instructors and students who have moaned to us about their problems with the policy course: We have tried to respond to your problems as best we could by providing a comprehensive yet usable text. To you, the people who work hard in the policy trenches, we acknowledge our debt. This book is yours.

Tampa, Florida   T. L. W.
Ames, Iowa   J. D. H.

About the Authors

J. David Hunger, Ph.D. (Ohio State University), is Professor of Management at Iowa State University. Previously he was with George Mason University and the University of Virginia. His research interests lie in strategic management, conflict management, and leadership. He has worked in management positions for Procter & Gamble, Lazarus Department Store, and the U.S. Army. He has been active as consultant and trainer to business corporations, as well as to state and federal government agencies. He has written numerous articles and cases appearing in the *Academy of Management Journal, Journal of Management, Case Research Journal, Journal of Management Case Studies, Human Resource Management,* and *SAM Advanced Management Journal,* among others. Dr. Hunger is a member of the Academy of Management, Midwest Society for Case Research, North American Case Research Association, and Strategic Management Society. He presently serves as Vice President of the Midwest Society for Case Research and on the Board of Directors of the Midwest Management Society and on the editorial review boards of the *SAM Advanced Management Journal* and the *Journal of Management Case Studies.* He is coauthor of *Strategic Management and Business Policy,* Third Edition, and *Cases in Strategic Management,* Second Edition.

Thomas L. Wheelen, D.B.A. (George Washington University), is a Professor of Strategic Management, University of South Florida, and was formerly the Ralph A. Beeton Professor of Free Enterprise at the McIntire School of Commerce, University of Virginia. He was Visiting Professor at both the University of Arizona and Northeastern University. He has worked in management positions for General Electric and the U.S. Navy. He has been active as a consultant and trainer to business corporations, as well as to federal and state government agencies. He served on the editorial boards of the *Journal of Management* and the *Journal of Retail Banking.* He is currently serving on the boards of the *Journal of Management Case Studies, SAM Advanced Management Journal,* and *Case Research Journal.* He is Associate Editor of *SAM Advanced Management Journal,* coauthor of *Strategic Management and Business Policy,* Third Edition, and *Cases in Strategic*

Management, Second Edition, as well as coeditor of *Developments in Management Information Systems* and *Collective Bargaining in the Public Sector.* He has authored 35 articles appearing in such journals as *Journal of Management, Business Quarterly, Personnel Journal, SAM Advanced Management Journal, Journal of Retailing,* and *International Journal of Management.* His cases appear in 25 management textbooks, plus the *Journal of Management Case Studies* and *Case Research Journal.* He has served on the Board of Directors of the Southern Management Association, as Vice President at Large for the Society for the Advancement of Management, and as President of the North American Case Research Association. He is a member of the Academy of Management, Southern Management Association, North American Case Research Association, Society for Advancement of Management, Institute for Decision Sciences, Midwest Society for Case Research, Strategic Management Association and Strategic Planning Society. He is serving as Vice President for Strategic Management for the Society for the Advancement of Management.

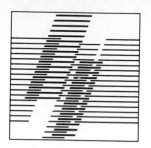

Contents*

*Chapter Summary and Discussion Questions follow each chapter.

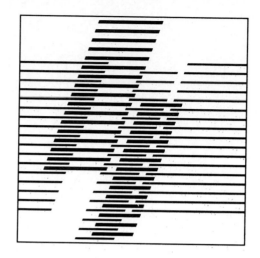

THIRD EDITION

STRATEGIC MANAGEMENT

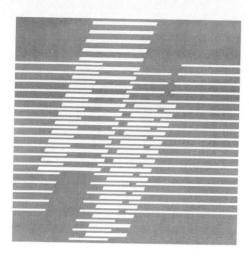

CHAPTER 1

INTRODUCTION

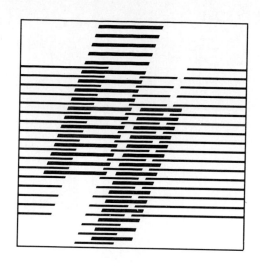

PART ONE

INTRODUCTION TO STRATEGIC MANAGEMENT

STRATEGIC MANAGEMENT MODEL

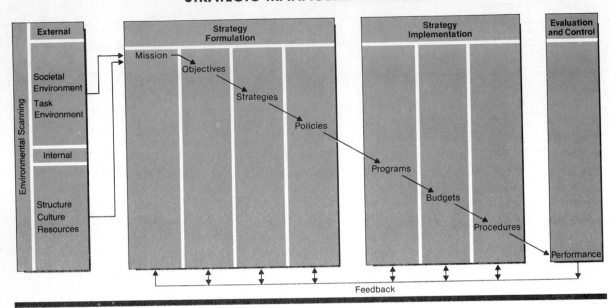

W ho remembers Beaunit Mills, Hercules Powder, or Liebmann Breweries? These companies, along with 250 others that appeared in the first Fortune 500 list of top business corporations in 1955, have vanished from the major ranks of American industry. Why did so many fail to thrive? Although some of the changes are due to mergers and acquisitions, most of the turnover can be attributed to the company's inability to adapt to changing conditions.[1] One example of such a failure to adapt is the vacuum tube industry. During the first half of the twentieth century, the vacuum tube was a key electronic part of radios and televisions. Most televisions in the 1950s contained around ten to twenty vacuum tubes. They worked well, but took up a lot of space and gave off a large amount of heat—significant drawbacks for their use in early computers. One would assume that once the transistor was invented, most vacuum tube manufacturers would convert to the new technology. Surprisingly, that did not occur. Instead manufacturers spent more money in attempts to improve their current vacuum tube technology. As a result, the top ten manufacturers of vacuum tubes in 1955 gave way to other firms exploiting semiconductor technology and are no longer market leaders in this industry.[2]

With an 80% share of the market, National Cash Register (NCR) of Dayton, Ohio dominated the U.S. mechanical cash register business in 1971. NCR's management had invested millions of dollars in a highly sophisticated manufacturing facility. Also in 1971, Data Terminal Systems introduced the first electronic cash register in the U.S.A. This was the product of the future.

NCR, however, continued to emphasize its tried and true mechanical products until its profits turned to losses. In a frantic effort to recover its lost sales, the company fired 80% of its top managers and destroyed its expensive manufacturing facility to make room for a new plant. Despite the introduction of NCR's own electronic cash register, NCR's market share dropped from 80% in 1971 to 25% in 1978. It never regained industry dominance.[3]

These examples show how a leading company can quickly become an also-ran because of its failure to adapt to change or, even worse, its failure to create change. Current predictions are that the environment will become even more complex and turbulent as the world enters the twenty-first century. A recent report prepared by the American Assembly of Collegiate Schools of Business and the European Foundation for Management Development states, "Living with uncertainty is likely to be management's biggest challenge."[4]

Strategic management is a quickly developing field of study that has emerged in response to this environment of increasing turbulence. This field of study looks at the corporation as a whole and attempts to explain why some firms develop and thrive while others stagnate and go bankrupt. Strategic management typically focuses on analyzing the problems and opportunities faced by people in top management. Unlike many decisions made at lower levels in a corporation, **strategic decisions** deal with the long-run future of the entire organization and have three characteristics:

1. *Rare:* strategic decisions are unusual and typically have no precedent to follow.
2. *Consequential:* strategic decisions commit substantial resources and demand a great deal of commitment.
3. *Percursive:* strategic decisions set precedents for lesser decisions and future actions throughout the organization.[5]

Because strategic decisions have these characteristics, the stakes can be very high. For instance, the strategic decision made after World War II by Sears, Roebuck and Company to expand from catalog sales into retail stores and insurance gave Sears many years of successful profits. A similar decision made independently during the 1960s by the top managements of General Motors, Ford, and Chrysler to emphasize the production of large, powerful automobiles over small, fuel-efficient ones resulted in their low profits and even the threat of bankruptcy in the early 1980s.

Another example of a strategic decision was that made by the top management of International Rectifier Corporation (IR) in the mid-1980s. Founded in 1947 by Lithuanian immigrant Eric Ludlow and subsequently managed by Ludlow and his two sons, Alex and Derek, the company attempted to transform itself from a small firm in the U.S. microchip industry to an industry leader. From 1985 to 1987, top management poured $82 million into a state-of-the-art chipmaking plant designed to cut production costs in half, slash production time from eight weeks to one, and boost the yield of quality semiconductor silicon wafers. If the plant proved to be successful, the resulting output per worker would be $350,000 annually—more than double the industry's average.

Industry analysts criticized management's decision to build a plant at a cost that was more than half of International Rectifier's annual revenues and greater than the company's current book value of $55 million—especially when the semiconductor industry was in a prolonged slump. "There's no way a niche player like IR can use up new capacity," commented Adam Cuhney, vice-president for research at Kidder, Peabody and Company. Paul White, a vice-president of marketing at Motorola warned: "If they don't pull it off, they're going to sink." Nevertheless, the Ludlows remained confident in their decision. They pointed to experts' prediction that the world consumption of microchips would soar from $160 million in 1986 to $450 million by 1990. Accepting the fact that the company was deeply in debt after struggling with losses for three of the past five years, Alex Ludlow admitted that this was a strategic gamble: "We're putting everything on the line. We're betting we can produce a high-volume item in the U.S. better than anywhere else in the world."[6]

Alex Ludlow's comment suggests why the managers of today's business corporations must manage firms strategically. They cannot make decisions based on long-standing rules, policies, or standard operating procedures. Instead, they must look to the future as they plan organization-wide objectives, initiate strategy, and set policies. They must rise above their training and experience in such functional/operational areas as accounting, marketing, production, or finance, and grasp the overall picture. They must be willing to ask these key strategic questions:

1. Where is the corporation now?

2. If no changes are made, where will the corporation be in one year, two years, five years, ten years? Are the answers acceptable?

3. If the answers are not acceptable, what specific actions should the corporation undertake? What are the risks and payoffs involved?

1.1

STUDY OF STRATEGIC MANAGEMENT AND BUSINESS POLICY

Most business schools offer a strategic management or business policy course. Although this course typically serves as a capstone or final integrative class in a business administration program, it—also typically—takes on some of the characteristics of a separate discipline.

In the 1950s the Ford Foundation and the Carnegie Corporation sponsored investigations into the business school curriculum.[7] The resulting Gordon and Howell report, sponsored by the Ford Foundation, recommended a broad business education and a course in business policy to "give students an opportunity to pull together what they have learned in the separate business fields and utilize this knowledge in the analysis of complex business problems."[8] The report also suggested the content that should be part of such a course:

> The business policy course can offer the student something he [or she] will find nowhere else in the curriculum: consideration of business problems which are not prejudged as being marketing problems, finance problems, etc.; emphasis on the development of skills in identifying, analyzing, and solving problems in a situation which is as close as the classroom can ever be to the real business world; opportunity to consider problems which draw on a wide range of substantive areas in business; opportunity to consider the external, nonmarket implications of problems at the same time that internal decisions must be made; situations which enable the student to exercise qualities of judgment and of mind which were not explicitly called for in any prior course. Questions of social responsibility and of personal attitudes can be brought in as a regular aspect of this kind of problem-solving practice. Without the responsibility of having to transmit some specific body of knowledge, the business policy course can concentrate on integrating what already has been acquired and on developing further the student's skill in using that knowledge.[9]

By the late 1960s most business schools included such a business policy course in their curriculum. But since that time the typical policy course has evolved to one that emphasizes the total organization and strategic management, with an increased interest in business social responsibilities and ethics. This evolution is in line with a recent survey of business school deans that reported that a primary objective of undergraduate business education is to develop an understanding of the political, social, and economic environment of business.[10] This increasing concern with the effect of environmental issues on the management of the total organization has led leaders in the field to replace the term *business policy* with the more comprehensive *strategic management*.[11] **Strategic management** is that set of managerial decisions and actions that determines the long-run performance of a corporation. It includes strategy formulation, strategy implementation, and evaluation and control. The study of strategic management therefore emphasizes the monitoring and evaluating of environmental opportunities and constraints in light of a corporation's strengths and weaknesses. In contrast, the study of **business policy,** with its integrative orientation, tends to look inward. By focusing on the efficient utilization of a corporation's assets, it thus emphasizes the formulation of general guidelines that will better accomplish a firm's mission and objectives. We see, then, that strategic management incorporates the concerns of business policy with a heavier environmental and strategic emphasis.

1.2

RESEARCH ON THE EFFECTIVENESS OF STRATEGIC MANAGEMENT

Many of the concepts and techniques dealing with long-range planning and strategic management have been developed and used successfully by business corporations such as General Electric and the Boston Consulting Group, among others. Nevertheless, not all organizations use these tools or even attempt to manage strategically. Many are able to succeed for a while with unstated objectives and intuitive strategies. American Hospital Supply Corporation (AHS) was one such organization until Karl Bays became chief executive in 1971 and introduced strategic planning to a sales-dominated management. Previously, the company's idea of long-range planning was "Maybe in December we should look at next year's budget," recalled a former AHS executive.[12]

From his extensive work in the area, Bruce Henderson of the Boston Consulting Group concluded that intuitive strategies cannot be continued successfully if (1) the corporation becomes large, (2) the layers of management increase, or (3) the environment changes substantially.[13] Research suggests that the increasing risks of error, costly mistakes, and even economic ruin are causing today's professional managers to take strategic management seriously in order to keep their company competitive in an increasingly volatile environment.[14] Research by Gluck, Kaufman, and Walleck proposes that, as top managers attempt to better deal with their changing world, strategic planning evolves through *four sequential phases:*

Phase 1. *Basic financial planning:* seeking better operational control through the meeting of budgets.

Phase 2. *Forecast-based planning:* seeking more effective planning for growth by trying to predict the future beyond the next year.

Phase 3. *Externally oriented planning:* seeking increased responsiveness to markets and competition by trying to think strategically.

Phase 4. *Strategic management:* seeking to manage all resources to develop competitive advantage and to help create the future.[15]

Concern about external as well as internal factors seems to be increasing in today's large corporations. Research conducted by Henry indicates that the planning systems of fifty large companies are becoming increasingly sophisticated. For example, there is more effort to formulate, implement, and evaluate strategic plans. There is also a greater emphasis on strategic factors in the evaluation of a manager's performance.[16] Gordon Brunton, president of Britain's International Thomson Organisation, Ltd. emphasized this point when he made the following statement:

All International Thomson senior managers now understand that unless they demonstrate their ability to think strategically, their future career potential will be limited accordingly.[17]

William Rothschild, staff executive for business development and strategy at General Electric (GE), notes the current trend to push strategic management duties down the organizational hierarchy to operating line managers. He observes that at GE, "over half of our managers are strategic thinkers. Another 20 percent to 25 percent lean that way. The rest don't understand it, and if they're fortunate enough to be in the right business where there is a stable environment, it doesn't matter too much."[18]

Many researchers have conducted studies of corporations to reveal whether organizations that engage in strategic planning outperform those that do not. One analysis of five companies with sales ranging from $1 billion to $17 billion reports that the impact of strategic planning has been to

- help the companies sort their businesses into "winners and losers,"
- focus attention on critical issues and choices, and
- develop a strategic frame of mind among top and upper-level managers.

The study concludes that management should expect strategic planning to improve a company's competitive position and long-term profits, plus yield growth in earnings per share.[19]

Research studies attempting to measure objectively this anticipated connection between a corporation's use of formal strategic planning and its performance have found mixed results.[20] Rhyne, however, explains these contradictory findings as resulting from the use of varying measures for planning and performance plus a typical failure to consider industry effects. When he controlled for industry variation, focused only on the total return to stockholders, and considered strategic planning as being different from less-evolved stages of planning (such as budgeting or annual planning), Rhyne found a positive relationship between strategic planning and performance. He concluded that "these results provide assurance that the prescriptions of strategic management theory are indeed valid."[21] Research by Smith and Grimm on the impact of deregulation upon the U.S. railroad industry adds further support to Rhyne's conclusion. The study reveals that those railroads that changed their strategy as their environment changed out-performed those railroads that did not change.[22]

From this evidence we can conclude that a knowledge of strategic management is very important for business performance to be effective in a changing environment. The use of strategic planning and the selection of alternative courses of action based on an assessment of important external and internal factors are becoming key parts of a general manager's job.

1.3

HIERARCHY OF STRATEGY

The typical large, multidivisional business firm has three levels of strategy: (1) corporate, (2) business, and (3) functional.[23]

Corporate strategy explores the ways in which a firm can develop a favorable "portfolio strategy" for its many activities. It is the pattern of decisions regarding the types of businesses in which a firm should be involved, the flow of financial and other resources to and from its divisions, the relationship of the corporation to key groups in its environment, and the ways in which a corporation can increase its return on investment (ROI). Corporate strategy may be one of stability, growth, or retrenchment.

Business strategy, in contrast, usually occurs at the divisional level, and emphasizes improvement of the competitive position of a corporation's products or services in the specific industry or market segment served by the division. A division may be organized as a **Strategic Business Unit** (SBU) around a group of similar products, such as housewares or electric turbines. Top management usually treats an SBU as a semi-autonomous unit with, generally, the authority to develop its own strategy within corporate objectives and strategy. A division's business strategy probably would stress the increasing of its profit margin in the production and sales of its products and services. Business strategies also should integrate various functional activities so that divisional objectives are achieved. Sometimes called **competitive strategy,** business strategy may be one of overall cost leadership, differentiation, or focus.

The principal focus of **functional strategy**, is the maximizing of resource productivity.[24] Within the constraints of the corporate and business strategies around them, functional departments develop strategies in which their various activities and competencies are pulled together for the improvement of performance. For example, a typical strategy of a marketing department might center on developing the means to increase the current year's sales over those of the previous year. With a *market development* functional strategy, the department would attempt to sell current products to different customers in the current market or to new customers in a new geographical area. Examples of R&D functional strategies are *technological followership* (imitate the products of other companies) and *technological leadership* (pioneer an innovation).

The three levels of strategy—corporate, business, and functional—form a **hierarchy of strategy** within a large corporation. They interact closely with each other and must be well integrated if the total corporation is to be successful. As depicted in Fig. 1.1, each level of strategy forms the strategic environment of the next level in the corporation. (The interaction among the three levels is depicted later in the chapter in Fig. 1.5.)

1.4

DESCRIPTIVE MODEL OF STRATEGIC MANAGEMENT

The process of strategic management involves four basic elements: (1) **environmental scanning,** (2) **strategy formulation,** (3) **strategy implementation,** and (4) **evaluation and control.** Figure 1.2 shows how these four elements interact. We will discuss these interactions later in this section.

At the corporate level, the strategic management process includes activ-

FIGURE 1.1
Hierarchy of Strategy.

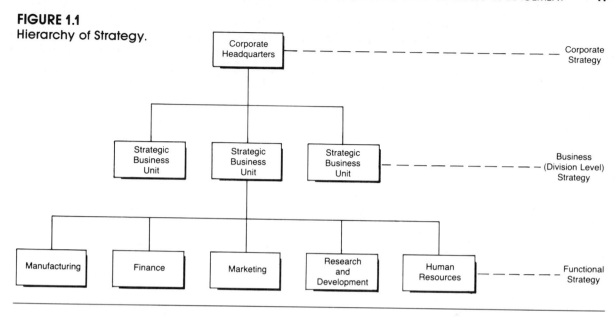

ities that range from environmental scanning to the evaluation of performance. Top management scans both the external environment for opportunities and threats, and the internal environment for strengths and weaknesses. The factors that are most important to the corporation's future are referred to as strategic factors and are summarized with the acronym **S.W.O.T.,** standing for **S**trengths, **W**eaknesses, **O**pportunities, and **T**hreats. Once these are identified, top management then evaluates the strategic factors and determines corporate mission. The first step in the formulation of strategy, a statement of mission leads to a determination of corporate objectives, strategies, and policies. These strategies and policies are implemented through programs, budgets, and procedures. Finally performance is evaluated, and information is fed back into the system so that adequate control of organizational activities is ensured. Figure 1.3 depicts this process as a continuous one. It is an expansion of the basic model presented in Fig. 1.2.

The model in Fig. 1.3, with minor changes, also reflects the strategic management process at both divisional and functional levels of the corporation. A division's external environment, for example, includes not only task and societal variables, but also the mission, objectives, strategy, and policies of corporate headquarters. Similarly, both corporate and divisional constraints form the external environment of a functional department. The model depicted in Fig. 1.3 therefore is appropriate to any strategic level of a corporation.

FIGURE 1.2
Basic Elements of the Strategic Management Process.

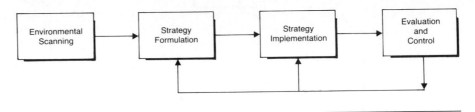

Environmental Scanning: External

The *external environment* consists of variables (**O**pportunities and **T**hreats) that are outside the organization and not typically within the short-run control of top management. These variables form the context within which the corporation exists. The external environment has two parts: task environment and societal environment. The **task environment** includes those elements or groups that directly affect and are affected by an organization's major operations. Some of these are stockholders, governments, suppliers, local communities, competitors, customers, creditors, labor unions, special

FIGURE 1.3
Strategic Management Model.

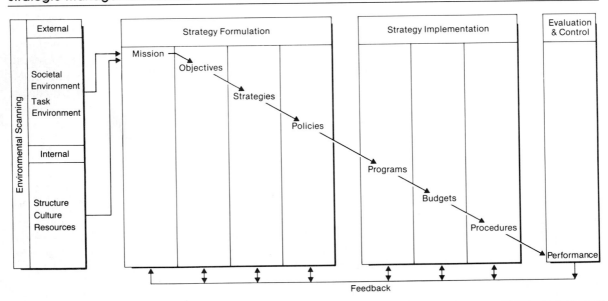

interest groups, and trade associations. The task environment of a corporation is often referred to as its *industry*. The **societal environment** includes more general forces—ones that do not directly touch the short-run activities of the organization but that can, and often do, influence its long-run decisions. Such economic, sociocultural, technological, and political-legal forces are depicted in Fig. 1.4 in relation to a firm's total environment. (These external variables are discussed in more detail in Chapter 4.)

Environmental Scanning: Internal

The *internal environment* of a corporation consists of variables (**Strengths** and **Weaknesses**) that are within the organization itself and are not usually within the short-run control of top management. These variables form the context in which work is done. They include the corporation's structure, culture, and resources. The **corporate structure** is the way a corporation is organized in terms of communication, authority, and workflow. It is often referred to as the "chain of command" and is graphically described in an

FIGURE 1.4
Environmental Variables.

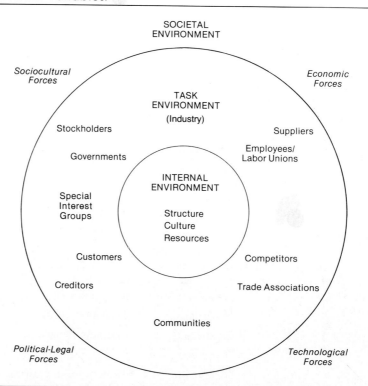

organization chart. The **corporation's culture** is that pattern of beliefs, expectations, and values shared by the corporation's members. In a firm norms typically emerge that define the acceptable behavior of people from top management down to the operative employees. **Corporate resources** are those assets that form the raw material for the production of an organization's products or services. These assets include people and managerial talent as well as financial assets, plant facilities, and the skills and abilities within functional areas. (These internal variables in a firm's environment are discussed in more detail in Chapter 5.)

Strategy Formulation

Strategy formulation is the development of long-range plans for the effective management of environmental opportunities and threats, in light of corporate strengths and weaknesses. It includes defining the corporate mission, specifying achievable objectives, developing strategies, and setting policy guidelines.[25]

Mission

The corporate mission is the purpose or reason for the corporation's existence. For example, the mission of a savings and loan association might be to provide mortgage money to people of the community. By fulfilling this mission, the S&L would hope to provide a reasonable rate of return to its depositors. A mission may be narrow or broad in scope. A **narrow mission** clearly limits the scope of the corporation's activities in terms of product or service offered, the technology used, and the market served. The above-mentioned S&L has the narrow mission of providing mortgage money to the people of the community. The problem with such a narrow statement of mission is that it might restrict the use of future opportunities for growth. A **broad mission** widens the scope of the corporation's activities to include many types of products or services, markets, and technologies. A broad mission of the same S&L might be to offer financial services to anyone, regardless of location. The problem with such a broad statement of mission is that it does not clearly identify which area the corporation wishes to emphasize and might confuse employees and customers. Other examples of narrow and broad missions are shown here.

NARROW SCOPE	BROAD SCOPE
Railroads	Transportation
Insurance	Financial services
Typewriters	Office equipment
Television	Telecommunications

Objectives

The corporate mission, as depicted in Fig. 1.3, determines the parameters of the specific objectives to be defined by top management. These objectives are listed as the end results of planned activity. They state *what* is to be accomplished by *when* and should be quantified if possible. (The term *goal* is often confused with *objective*. In contrast to an objective, a *goal* is an *open-ended* statement of what one wishes to accomplish with *no* quantification of what is to be achieved and *no* time criteria for completion.[26] For example, a goal of an S&L might be to increase its rate of return—a rather vague statement.) The achievement of corporate objectives, however, should result in a corporation's fulfilling its mission. An S&L, for example, might set an objective for the year of earning a 10% rate of return on its investment portfolio.

Strategies

A strategy of a corporation forms a comprehensive master plan stating *how* the corporation will achieve its mission and objectives. It maximizes competitive advantage and minimizes competitive disadvantage. For example, to achieve its objective of a 10% rate of return, an S&L could increase demand for its mortgages by offering special terms to a particular market segment, such as young professional people who can't meet the normal down-payment requirements. In order to increase the amount of money deposited in savings accounts that fund the mortgages, the S&L might offer large depositors special privileges and interest rates not available from other financial institutions. A different strategy would be to offer financial services so that the S&L's income becomes less dependent on mortgages.

Policies

Flowing from the strategy, policies provide broad guidance for decision making throughout the organization. Policies are thus broad guidelines which serve to link the formulation of strategy with its implementation. In attempting to increase the amount of mortgage loans as well as the amount of deposits available for mortgages, an S&L might set policies of always evaluating a mortgage candidate on the basis of *potential* rather than on current or historical income and of developing *creative* incentives for savings depositors. (Strategy formulation is discussed in detail in Chapters 6 and 7).

Strategy Implementation

Strategy implementation is the process by which strategies and policies are put into action through the development of programs, budgets, and procedures. This process might involve changes within the overall culture, structure, and/or management system of the entire organization. Except when such drastic corporate-wide changes are needed, however, the implementation of strategy is typically conducted by middle- and lower-level managers with review by top management. Sometimes referred to as operational planning, strategy implementation often involves day-to-day decisions in resource allocation.

Thus working under the guidance of top management, division and/or functional managers will fully develop the programs, budgets, and procedures that will be used to achieve the objectives of the corporate strategy. At the same time, these managers are involved in strategy formulation at the divisional or functional level. If, for example, the corporate strategy for an automobile manufacturer is to grow through international expansion through joint ventures, the business-level strategy of a particular division of the corporation might be to form a joint venture with a Brazilian auto firm in order to build the lowest-priced auto for sale in South America. Although this strategy formulation is at the business level of the corporation, it can also be viewed by top management as a program that implements its corporate strategy of international expansion through joint ventures.

Programs

A program is a statement of the activities or steps needed to accomplish a single-use plan. It makes the strategy action-oriented. For instance, to implement its strategy and policies, an S&L might initiate an advertising program in the local area, develop close ties with the local realtors' association, and offer free silverware with every $1,000 savings deposit.

Budgets

A budget is a statement of a corporation's programs in dollar terms. Used in planning and control, it lists the detailed cost of each program. The S&L might thus draw up separate budgets for each of its three programs: the advertising budget, the public relations budget, and the premium budget.

Procedures

Sometimes termed Standard Operating Procedures (SOP), procedures are a system of sequential steps or techniques that describe in detail how a particular task or job is to be done. They typically detail the various activities that must be carried out for completion of the corporation's program. The S&L, for example, might develop procedures for the placement of ads in newspapers and on radio. They might list persons to contact, techniques for the writing of acceptable copy (with samples), and details about payment. They might establish detailed procedures concerning eligibility requirements for silverware premiums. (Strategy implementation is discussed in more detail in Chapter 8.)

Evaluation and Control

Evaluation and control is the process in which corporate activities and performance results are monitored so that actual performance can be compared with desired performance. Managers at all levels use the resulting information to take corrective action and resolve problems. Although evaluation and control is the final major element of strategic management, it also can pinpoint weaknesses in previously implemented strategic plans and thus stimulate the entire process to begin again.

For evaluation and control to be effective, managers must obtain clear, prompt, and unbiased feedback from the people below them in the corporation's hierarchy. The model in Fig. 1.3 indicates how feedback in the forms of performance data and activity reports runs through the entire management process. Using this feedback, managers compare what is actually happening with what was originally planned in the formulation stage.

For example, the S&L management would probably ask its internal information systems people to keep track of both the number of mortgages being made and the level of deposits at the end of each week for each S&L branch office. It might also wish to develop special rewards for loan officers who increase their mortgage lending.

To monitor and evaluate broad-scale results, top management of large corporations typically uses periodic reports dealing with key performance indicators, such as return on investment, net profits, earnings per share, and net sales. From what these reports indicate, top management takes further action. For example, it might see a need to emphasize rewards for long-term performance improvement and thereby alter the corporation's current incentive system. To help managers pinpoint those areas with performance problems, corporations are sometimes structured with profit centers, investment centers, expense centers, cost centers, and revenue centers. (These are discussed in detail in Chapter 9.)

Activities are much harder to monitor and evaluate than are performance results. Because of the many difficulties in deciding which activities to monitor and because of the bias inherent in evaluating job performance, some firms now manage by objectives. Management By Objectives (MBO) has been criticized, however, for ignoring many of the intermediate activities that can lead to the desired results. To counter this criticism, consulting firms have developed management "audits," which assess key organizational activities and provide in-depth feedback to consultants and managers. Management audits complement standard measures of performance and help complete the picture of the corporation's activities. (We discuss an example of a comprehensive audit in Chapter 2.)

1.5

STRATEGIC MANAGEMENT MODEL IN ACTION

Most major corporations are structured on both a divisional and a functional basis. As depicted in Fig. 1.5, the corporate level goes through all three stages of the strategic management process. Top management *with input from the divisions* formulates strategies and makes plans for implementation. These implementation plans stimulate the strategy formulation process at the divisional level. To accomplish the corporate programs, each division formulates its own objectives, strategies, and policies. For example, a corporate-level program of CSX Corporation (a multidivisional major transportation company) in 1986 was to dispose of unproductive and marginal assets. To implement this program, the railroad business segment (or division) formulates an objective specifying how many miles of track would be abandoned or/and sold during the coming year and develops a strategy for accomplishing that objective. Then, as the division acts on its strategy, it feeds its evaluation and control information upward to the corporate level for its use in evaluation and control.

Responding to each division's programs for implementation, separate functional departments within each division begin to formulate their own objectives and strategies. For example, American Commercial Lines (ACL), CSX's barge subsidiary, might set an objective of increasing its barge tonnage by 10% over the previous year and propose this business strategy: to differentiate its service from that of the competition, it will guarantee fewer losses in transit. In response to this strategy, each functional department—such as operations and marketing—develops its own objectives and strategies. ACL's operations department would set an objective for loss reduction

FIGURE 1.5
Strategic Management Process at Three Corporate Levels.

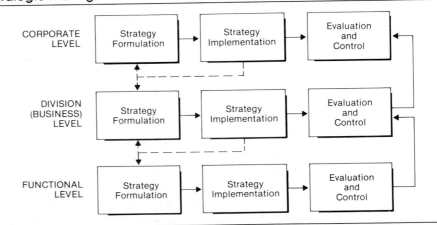

and begin formulating a strategy for the reduction of damage to goods being transported. ACL's marketing department would also set objectives specifying how many new customers will have to be attracted and how much tonnage from its current customers will have to be increased, to fulfill ACL's overall objective. Marketing would then formulate the appropriate advertising and promotion strategies. In this way each level of the corporation develops its own objectives, strategies, policies, programs, budgets, and procedures to complement those of the level above.

The specific operation of the hierarchy of strategy may vary from one corporation to another. The one described here of CSX Corporation is an example of **top-down strategic planning,** in which corporate-level top management initiates the strategy formulation process and calls upon divisions and functional units to formulate their own strategies as ways of implementing corporate-level strategies. Another approach is *bottom-up* strategic planning, in which the strategy formulation process is initiated by strategic proposals from divisional or functional units. This approach is shown by the arrows pointing upward in Fig. 1.5; strategy formulation leads from the functional level to the divisional level and from the divisional to the corporate level. Bechtel Group, the largest construction and engineering company in the U.S., uses bottom-up strategic planning because it uses autonomous divisions as independent profit centers.[27] Although an *interactive approach* is sometimes proposed as a third approach to strategic planning,[28] it is clear that in most companies the origin of the formulation process is not as important as the resultant interaction between levels. The process involves a lot of negotiation between levels in the hierarchy so that the various objectives, strategies, policies, programs, budgets, and procedures fit together and reinforce each other. It is a continuous process of adjustment between the formulation and implementation of each level of strategy.[29]

1.6
ILLUSTRATION OF THE CHAPTER: INTRODUCTION TO THE INTEGRATIVE CASE

To illustrate the strategic management model presented in this chapter, we will discuss CSX Corporation, a large multidivisional business corporation based in the United States. This example will also serve as an integrative case for the rest of the textbook. Each of the remaining chapters—except Chapters Eleven and Twelve, which cover special issues in strategic management—will include a part of the CSX Corporation case as an illustration of that chapter's content. By showing each part of the strategic management process as it operates within the same company, we can thus offer a consistent, integrated view of strategy formulation, strategy implementation, and evaluation and control.

The part of the integrative case at the end of this chapter presents a brief introduction to the CSX Corporation. It illustrates the strategic management model by providing the company's mission, objectives, strategies, policies, programs, budgets, procedures, and evaluation and control reports. Each of the following chapters will present an additional piece of the CSX case. Use the case to apply some of the concepts discussed in each chapter. Since the concepts are not applied for you (except for that part following Chapter One), the integrative case can be used for in-class discussions following each chapter. In this manner, the integrative case of CSX Corporation illustrates some of the many factors that need to be considered when a corporation is being managed strategically.

SUMMARY AND CONCLUSION

This chapter sets the stage for the study of strategic management and business policy. It explains the rationale for including the subject in a business school curriculum. In addition to serving as a capstone to integrate the various functional areas, the course provides a framework for the analysis of top management's decision process and the effects of environmental issues on the corporation. Research generally supports the conclusion that corporations that manage strategically perform at higher levels than do those firms that do not. Strategic management is thus an important area of study for anyone interested in organizational productivity.

Our model of strategic management includes environmental scanning, strategy formulation and implementation, plus evaluation and control. The mission of a corporation derives from the interaction of internal and external environmental factors, as modified by the needs and values of top management. A precise statement of mission guides the setting of objectives and the formulation of strategies and policies. Strategies are implemented through specific programs, budgets, and procedures. Management continuously monitors and evaluates performance and activities on the basis of measurable results and audits of key areas. These data feed back into the corporation at all phases of the strategic management process. If results and activities fail to measure up to the plans, managers may then take the appropriate actions.

Although top management and the board of directors have primary responsibility for the strategic management process, many levels of the corporation conduct strategy formulation, implementation, and evaluation and control. Large multidivisional corporations utilize divisional and functional levels that integrate the entire corporation by focusing their activities on the accomplishment of the corporate mission.

DISCUSSION QUESTIONS

1. What differentiates strategic decisions from other types of decisions?

2. How does strategic management typically evolve in a corporation? Why?

3. What is meant by the hierarchy of strategy?

4. Does every business firm have business strategies? Explain.

5. What information is needed for the proper formulation of strategy? Why?

6. What are the pros and cons of *bottom-up* as contrasted with *top-down* strategic planning?

NOTES

1. W. Shanklin, "Fortune 500 Dropouts," *Planning Review* (May 1986), pp. 12–17.

2. S. R. Craig, "Seeking Strategic Advantage with Technology? Focus on Customer Value!" *Long Range Planning* (April 1986), pp. 50–51.

3. Craig, p. 53.

4. J. Robertson, "The Changing Expectations of Society in the Next Thirty Years," in *Management for the XXI Century*, edited by the AACSB and EFMD (Boston/TheHague/London: Kluwer-Nijhoff Publishing, 1982), p. 5.

5. D. J. Hickson, R. J. Butler, D. Cray, G. R. Mallory, and D. C. Wilson, *Top Decisions: Strategic Decision-Making in Organizations* (San Francisco: Jossey-Bass, 1986), pp. 26–42.

6. R. Neff, "The Riverboat Gamblers of the Chip Business," *Business Week* (December 15, 1986), pp. 96–98.

7. R. A. Gordon and J. E. Howell, *Higher Education for Business* (New York: Columbia University Press, 1959).
F. C. Pierson et al., *The Education of American Businessmen* (New York: McGraw-Hill, 1959).

8. Gordon and Howell, p. 206.

9. Gordon and Howell, pp. 206–207.

10. J. D. Hunger and T. L. Wheelen, *An Assessment of Undergraduate Business Education in the United States* (Charlottesville, Va.: McIntire School of Commerce Foundation, 1980). Also summarized in "A Performance Appraisal of Undergraduate Business Education," *Human Resource Management* (Spring 1980), pp. 24–31.

11. M. Leontiades, "The Confusing Words of Business Policy," *Academy of Management Review* (January 1982), p. 46.

12. B. Lancaster, "American Hospital's Marketing Program Places Company Atop a Troubled Industry," *Wall Street Journal* (August 24, 1984), p. 19.

13. B. D. Henderson, *Henderson on Corporate Strategy* (Cambridge, Mass.: Abt Books, 1979), p. 33.

14. R. Lamb, *Advances in Strategic Management*, Vol. 2 (Greenwich, Conn.: Jai Press, Inc., 1983), p. x.

15. F. W. Gluck, S. P. Kaufman, and A. S. Walleck, "The Four Phases of Strategic Management," *The Journal of Business Strategy* (Winter 1982), pp. 9–21.

16. H. W. Henry, "Evolution of Strategic Planning in Major Corporations," *Proceedings, American Institute of Decision Sciences* (November 1980), pp. 454–456.
H. W. Henry, "Then and Now: A Look at Strategic Planning Systems," *Journal of Business Strategy* (Winter 1981), pp. 64–69.

17. G. C. Brunton, "Implementing Corporate Strategy: The Story of International Thomson," *Journal of Business Strategy* (Fall 1984), p. 14.

18. P. Pascarella, "Strategy Comes Down to Earth," *Industry Week* (January 9, 1984), p. 51.

19. W. B. Schaffir and T. J. Lobe, "Strategic Planning: The Impact at Five Companies," *Planning Review* (March 1984), pp. 40–41.

20. C. B. Shrader, L. Taylor, and D. R. Dalton, "Strategic Planning and Organizational Performance: A Critical Appraisal," *Journal of Management* (Summer 1984), pp. 149–179.
G. E. Greenley, "Does Strategic Planning Improve Company Performance?" *Long Range Planning* (April 1986), pp. 101–109.
J. A. Pearce II, E. A. Freeman, and R. B. Robinson, Jr., "The Tenuous Link Between Formal Strategic Planning and Financial Performance," *Academy of Management Review* (October 1987), pp. 658–675.

21. L. C. Rhyne, "The Relationship of Strategic Planning to Financial Performance," *Strategic Management Journal* (September-October 1986), p. 435.

22. K. G. Smith and C. M. Grimm, "Environmental Variation, Strategic Change and Firm Performance: A Study of Railroad Deregulation," *Strategic Management Journal* (July-August 1987), pp. 363–376.

23. Some theorists propose a fourth level of strategy called "enterprise," which seeks to position an organization within its broader environment. See R. E. Freeman and P. Lorange, "Theory Building in Strategic Management," in *Advances in Strategic Management, Volume 3*, edited by R. Lamb and P. Shrivastava (Greenwich, Conn.: Jai Press, 1985), p. 20. We chose, however, to include these broad environmental concerns with other factors considered in the development of corporate level strategy. See K. R. Andrews, *The Concept of Corporate Strategy*, Third Edition (Homewood, Illinois: Irwin, 1987), p. 13.

24. C. W. Hofer and D. Schendel, *Strategy Formulation: Analytical Concepts* (St. Paul, Minn.: West Publishing Co., 1978), p. 29.

25. Although some theorists propose that *both* objective setting and the consideration of competitive methods are a part of strategy, we agree with those who contend that objectives and strategy are separate means and ends considerations. See G. G. Dess, "Consensus on Strategy Formulation and Organizational Performance: Competitors in a Fragmented Industry," *Strategic Management Journal* (May-June 1987), pp. 259–260.

26. M. D. Richards, *Setting Strategic Goals and Objectives*, 2nd edition (St. Paul, Minn.: West Publishing Co., 1987), p. 12.

27. D. M. Slavick, "Planning at Bechtel: End of the Megaproject Era," *Planning Review* (September 1986), p. 20.

28. B. Ho Rho, "A Comparison of Long-Range Planning in South Korea, Japan, and the U.S.," *Planning Review* (March-April 1987), pp. 32–36.

29. M. E. Naylor, "Regaining Your Competitive Edge," *Long Range Planning* (February 1985), pp. 33–34.
R. G. Hamermesh, *Making Strategy Work* (New York: Wiley and Sons, 1986), p. 47.

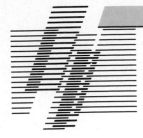

CSX CORPORATION

CSX Corporation is a major transportation company formed as a result of a merger in 1980 between two major railroad systems in the eastern United States and part of Canada. Through a series of acquisitions, CSX was by 1986 heavily involved in railroads, trucking, barge operations, and pipelines, and had real estate and managerial interests in coal mines and resort hotels. At that time, in order to integrate their five-year financial projection into the company's operating strategic plans, top management initiated formal strategic management. Statements from top management, published in media accounts and in CSX annual reports, infer that the following process occurred.

To begin the strategic management process described in Fig. 1.3, CSX top management first scanned the external environment for relevant information about opportunities and threats. As 1986 began, the U.S. government's deregulation of the transportation industries continued to be a strategic factor—deregulation opened the opportunity for mergers across traditional lines, such as railroads, trucking, and barge operations. Another external factor was the nation's economic health. The only depressed parts of the country were those dependent on agriculture and petroleum; otherwise, the economy was healthy and growing.

Top management also scanned its internal environment and assessed the strengths and weaknesses of its business units and functional areas. Corporate structure and culture continued to be a strategic factor as CSX attempted to integrate its many activities and manage its diverse assets in an effective and efficient manner. This environmental scanning provided the data for the formulation, implementation, and evaluation and control stages of strategic management. As depicted in Integrative Case Example 1.1, CSX top management begins with defining its mission and ends with developing a feedback system for evaluation and control.

INTEGRATIVE CASE EXAMPLE 1.1

Strategic Management at CSX Corporation (Corporate Level—Early 1986)

STRATEGY FORMULATION

Mission

Broad: become a national multimodal transportation system.

Narrow: become an intermodal, one-stop freight transportation provider in the eastern United States.

Objectives

1. To reach and exceed a 15% return on invested capital by 1990.

2. Continue in the coming years to outperform the peer group and Standard and Poor's 500 in terms of stock price and earnings per share.

Strategies

1. Grow by *merging* with and *acquiring* other transportation companies whose transportation systems complement that of CSX.

2. Improve corporate productivity by *streamlining* the CSX transportation system and *divesting* those assets unrelated to the corporation's strategic mission.

Policies

1. Integrate the activities of the various transportation systems so that reliable, one-stop service is achieved and transportation efficiency is improved.

2. Expand only into those areas having long-term growth opportunity and promising a rate of return substantially exceeding the cost of capital.

3. Respect the history and traditions of the companies that comprise CSX so as to be a "partnership of equals."

4. Delegate responsibility for day-to-day operations to the divisions. The corporate office should be small and should focus on the three Ps—Policy, Planning, and Policing—while emphasizing finance.

STRATEGY IMPLEMENTATION

Programs

1. Initiate an acquisition program of finding a company that will complement current transportation businesses.

2. Restructure the corporation into four major business units—transportation, energy, technology, and properties.

3. Dispose of unproductive and marginal assets in all business units, especially railroads.

4. Reduce the number of rail employees through a buy-out program for contract and noncontract workers.

5. Institute a long-term incentive program to link management compensation to corporate financial performance.

6. Integrate the marketing and sales departments of the transportation business units so as to present the customer with a single representative of the corporation's many transportation modes.

Budgets

Prepare budgets showing a cost–benefit analysis of each planned program and a statement of how much the corporation can afford to spend for each program.

Procedures

1. Develop procedures for the sale of bonds or stock in quantities sufficient to finance the acquisition of a new transportation business.

2. Develop procedures for the reorganization in terms of accounting practices and personnel relocation.

3. Develop criteria to be used to determine asset productivity.

4. Develop the specifics of the early retirement program.

5. Develop the details of the long-term incentive program.

(Continued)

INTEGRATIVE CASE EXAMPLE 1.1

(Continued)

6. Develop procedures for combining the various transportation marketing and sales departments and handling human resources issues.

EVALUATION AND CONTROL

Require business units to provide monthly status reports on the following items:

1. Tonnage of originated coal by category (steam and metallurgical) and export coal dumpings.

2. Principal rail commodities (coal, automotive, chemicals, etc.) by carload and by revenues.

3. Miles of rail installed, ties laid, and track surfaced as well as track abandoned or sold.

4. Amount of principal barge commodities (coal, grain, liquids, etc.) by tons and by revenues.

5. Barge ton-miles traveled.

6. Average cost and average sales price of natural gas transmitted.

7. Sources of gas supply and volume transmitted.

8. Average revenue and volume of natural gas and oil condensate produced and sold.

Require business units to provide additional annual reports on the following items:

1. Operating revenues.

2. Operating costs and expenses for labor and fringe benefits, materials and supplies, fuel, equipment rental, and depreciation.

3. Identifiable assets in dollars plus property additions and deletions.

4. Number of rail employees.

SOURCE: Developed from "CSX Corporation" by J. D. Hunger, B. Ferrin, H. Felix-Gamez, and T. Goetzman in *Cases in Strategic Management and Business Policy* by T. L. Wheelen and J. D. Hunger (Reading, Mass.: Addison-Wesley Publishing Co., 1987), pp. 91–123 and from the 1985 Annual Report of CSX Corporation, published in early 1986. The above statements were developed by the authors strictly as pedagogical examples and were inferred from CSX publications and statements by CSX management.

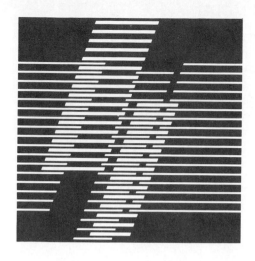

CHAPTER 2

DEVELOPING CONCEPTUAL SKILLS: THE CASE METHOD AND THE STRATEGIC AUDIT

STRATEGIC MANAGEMENT MODEL

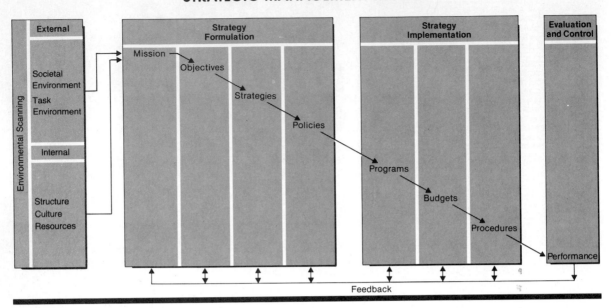

An analysis of a corporation's strategic management calls for a top-down view of the organization. In our analysis we view the corporation as an entity composed of interrelated units and systems, such as accounting, marketing, and finance. We examine the interrelationships of these units in light of the opportunities and threats in the corporation's environment. We carry out our analysis through the use of complex cases or management simulations. These techniques will give you the opportunity to move from a narrow, specialized view to a broader, less precise analysis of the overall corporate picture. Consequently, the emphasis in case analysis is on developing and refining conceptual skills, which are different from the skills you developed in your technical and function-oriented courses. As you will see, conceptual skills are vital to successful performance in the business world.

2.1

IMPORTANCE OF CONCEPTUAL SKILLS IN BUSINESS

Many have attempted to specify the characteristics necessary for a person to successfully advance from an entry-level position to one in top management. Few of these studies have been successful.[1] But Robert L. Katz has suggested one interesting approach. He focused on the skills successful managers exhibit in performing their jobs; this approach negates the need to identify specific personality traits.[2] These skills imply abilities that can be developed and are manifested in performance.

Katz suggests that effective administration rests on three basic skills: technical, human, and conceptual. He defines them as follows:[3]

- **Technical skills** pertain to *what* is done and to working with *things*. They comprise one's ability to use technology to perform an organizational task.
- **Human skills** pertain to *how* something is done and to working with *people*. They comprise one's ability to work with people in the achievement of goals.
- **Conceptual skills** pertain to *why* something is done and to one's view of the corporation as a *whole*. They comprise one's ability to understand the complexities of the corporation as it affects and is affected by its environment.

Katz further suggests that the optimal mix of these three skills varies at the different corporate levels:

At lower levels, the major need is for technical and human skills. At higher levels, the administrator's effectiveness depends largely on human and conceptual skills. At the top, conceptual skill becomes the most important of all for successful administration.[4]

Results of a survey of 300 presidents of *Fortune*'s list of the top fifty banking, industrial, insurance, public utility, retailing, and transportation firms support Katz's conclusion regarding the different skill mixes needed at the different organizational levels.[5] As shown in Fig. 2.1, the need for technical skills decreases and the need for conceptual skills increases as a person moves from first-line supervision to top management.

In addition, when executives were asked, "Are there certain skills necessary to move from one organizational level to another?", 55% reported conceptual skills to be the most crucial in movement from middle to top management.[6] Similar results concerning accountants in CPA firms have been reported.[7] Most theorists therefore agree that conceptual work carried out by an organization's leaders is the heart of strategy-making.[8]

The strategic management and business policy course attempts to develop conceptual skills through the use of comprehensive cases or complex simulations. Of course, you also need technical skills in order to analyze various aspects of each case. And you will use human skills in team presentations, study groups, or team projects. But in this course, by focusing on strategic

FIGURE 2.1
Optimal Skill Mix of a Manager by Hierarchical Level.

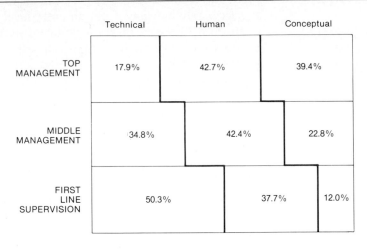

	Technical	Human	Conceptual
TOP MANAGEMENT	17.9%	42.7%	39.4%
MIDDLE MANAGEMENT	34.8%	42.4%	22.8%
FIRST LINE SUPERVISION	50.3%	37.7%	12.0%

Source: T. L. Wheelen, G. K. Rakes, and J. D. Hunger, "Skills of an Executive," a paper presented to the Academy of Management, Kansas City, Mo., August 1976.

issues, you will primarily develop and refine your conceptual skills. Concentrating on strategic management processes forces you to develop a better understanding of the political, social, and economic environment of business, and to appreciate the interactions of the functional specialties required for corporate success.

2.2

AUDITS

Consulting firms, management scholars, boards of directors, and practicing managers suggest the use of audits of corporate activities.[9] An audit provides a checklist of questions, by area or issue, that enables a systematic analysis of various corporate activities to be made. It is extremely useful as a diagnostic tool to pinpoint problem areas and to highlight strengths and weaknesses.

Management Audit

The National Association of Regulatory Utility Commissioners analyzed thirty-one management audits that had been completed or were in progress. The report concluded that the regulatory agencies using management audits were pleased with the results and intended to continue using them. In general, these audits recommended changes in the operating practices of management and suggested areas where substantial reductions in operating costs could be made. The audits gave the boards of directors and management the opportunity to establish new priorities in their objectives and planning, and provided specific recommendations that had impact on the "bottom line."[10]

Typically, the term **management audit** is used to describe a list of questions that forms the basis for an in-depth analysis of a particular area of importance to the corporation. Examples are the sales-force management audit, the social audit, the stakeholder audit, the forecasting audit, the technology audit, the strategic-marketing audit, the culture audit, and the human-resource-management audit.[11] Rarely, however, does it include consideration of more than one issue or functional area. The **strategic audit** is, in comparison, a *type of management audit* that takes a corporate-wide perspective and provides a comprehensive assessment of a corporation's strategic situation. Most business analysts predict that the use of management audits of all kinds will increase. As corporate boards of directors become more aware of their expanding duties and responsibilities, they should call for more corporate-wide management audits to be conducted.

Strategic Audit

As contrasted with the typically more specialized management audit, the strategic audit considers external as well as internal factors and includes alternative selection, implementation, and evaluation and control. It therefore covers the key aspects of the strategic management process and places them within a decision-making framework. This framework is composed of the following eight interrelated steps:

1. **Evaluation of a corporation's current performance results**, in terms of (a) return on investment, profitability, etc., and (b) the current mission, objectives, strategies, and policies.

2. **Examination and evaluation of a corporation's strategic managers**—its board of directors and top management.

3. **A scan of the external environment**, to locate strategic factors that pose opportunities and threats.

4. **A scan of the internal corporate environment**, to determine strategic factors that are strengths and weaknesses.

5. **Analysis of the strategic factors**, to (a) pinpoint problem areas, and (b) review and revise the corporate mission and objectives as necessary.

6. **Generation, evaluation, and selection of the best alternative strategy** in light of the analysis conducted in step 5.

7. **Implementation** of selected strategies, via programs, budgets, and procedures.

8. **Evaluation** of the implemented strategies via feedback systems, and the **control** of activities to ensure their minimum deviation from plans.

This strategic decision-making process, depicted in Fig. 2.2, basically reflects the approach to strategic management being used successfully by corporations such as Warner-Lambert, Dayton Hudson, Avon Products, and Bechtel Group, Inc.[12] Although some research suggests that this type of "normative" approach might not work so well for firms in very unstable environments,[13] a recent survey of 956 corporate long-range planners reveals that actual business practice agrees generally with the model presented in Fig. 2.2.[14] This strategic decision-making process is made operational through the strategic audit.

The audit presents an integrated view of strategic management in action. It describes not only how objectives, strategies, and policies are formulated as long-range decisions, but also how they are implemented, evaluated, and controlled by programs, budgets, and procedures. The strategic audit, therefore, enables a person to better understand the *ways* in which various functional areas are interrelated and interdependent, as well as the *manner* in which they contribute to the achievement of the corporate mission.

FIGURE 2.2
Strategic Decision-making Process.

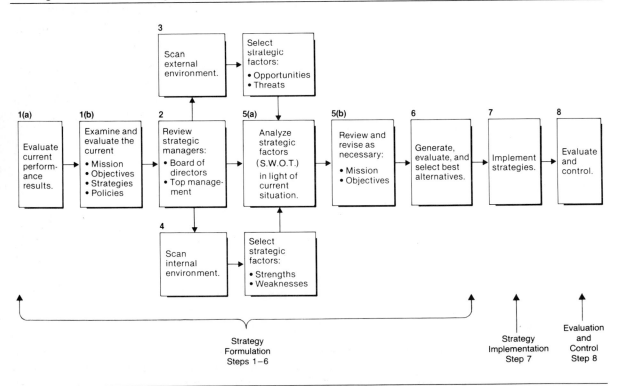

Consequently, the strategic audit is very useful to those people, such as boards of directors, whose jobs are to evaluate the overall performance of a corporation and its management.

Appendix 2.A (at the end of this chapter) is an example of a strategic audit proposed for use in the analysis of complex business policy cases and for strategic decision-making. The questions in the audit parallel the eight steps depicted in Fig. 2.2, the strategic decision-making process. It is *not* an all-inclusive list, but it presents many of the critical questions needed for the strategic analysis of any business corporation. You should consider the audit as a guide for analysis. Some questions or even some areas might be inappropriate for a particular case; in other cases, the questions may be insufficient for a complete analysis. However, each question in a particular area of the strategic audit can be broken down into an additional series of subquestions. It is up to you to develop these subquestions when they are needed.

A strategic audit fulfills three major *functions* in a case-oriented strategy and policy course:

1. It serves to highlight and review important concepts from previously studied subject areas.

2. It provides a systematic framework for the analysis of complex cases. (It is especially useful if you are unfamiliar with the case method.)

3. It generally improves the quality of case analysis and reduces the amount of time you might spend in learning how to analyze a case.

Students also find the audit helpful in their organizing a case for written or oral presentation and in seeing that all areas have been considered. The strategic audit thus enables both students and teachers to maximize their efficiency, both in analyzing why a certain area is creating problems for a corporation, and in considering solutions to the problems.

2.3

CASE METHOD

The analysis and discussion of case problems has been the most popular method of teaching strategy and policy for many years.[15] Cases present actual business situations and enable you to examine both successful and unsuccessful corporations. For example, you might be asked to critically analyze a situation in which a manager had to make a decision of long-run corporate importance. This approach gives you a feel for what it is like to work in a large corporation and to be faced with making a business decision.

Case Analysis and Presentation

There is no one best way to analyze or present a case report. Each instructor has personal preferences for format and approach. Nevertheless, we present one suggested approach for both written and oral reports in Appendix 2.B, at the end of the chapter. This approach provides a systematic method for successfully attacking a case.

The presentation of case analysis can be organized on the basis of a number of frameworks. One obvious framework to follow is the strategic audit as detailed in Appendix 2.A. Another is the McKinsey 7-S Framework, composed of the seven organizational variables of *structure, strategy, staff, management style, systems and procedures, skills,* and *shared values.*[16] Regardless of the framework chosen, be especially careful to include a complete analysis of key environmental variables—especially of trends in the industry and of the competition.

The focus in case discussion is on critical analysis and logical development of thought. A solution is satisfactory if it resolves important problems and is likely to be implemented successfully. How the corporation actually dealt with the case problems has no real bearing on the analysis, because its management might have analyzed its problems incorrectly and implemented a series of flawed solutions.

Researching the Case

You should undertake outside research into the environmental setting of the case. Check each case to find out when the case situation occurred and then screen the business periodicals for that time. This background will give you an appreciation for the situation as it was experienced by the people in the case. A company's annual report from that year can be very helpful.[17] An understanding of the economy during that period will help you avoid making a serious error in your analysis—for example, suggesting a sale of stock when the stock market is at an all-time low or taking on more debt when the prime interest rate is over 15%. Information on the industry will provide insights on its competitive activities. Some resources available for research into the economy and a corporation's industry are suggested in Appendix 2.C at the end of the chapter.

If you are unfamiliar with these business resources we urge you to read *How to Use the Business Library: With Sources of Business Information,* 5th ed., by H. W. Johnson, A. J. Faria, and E. L. Maier (Cincinnati: South-Western Publishing Co., 1984).

Financial Analysis: A Place To Begin

A review of key financial ratios can help you assess the company's overall situation and pinpoint some problem areas. Table 2.1 lists some of the most important financial ratios. Included are (1) **liquidity ratios,** which measure the corporation's ability to meet its financial obligations, (2) **profitability ratios,** which measure the degree of the corporation's success in achieving desired profit levels, (3) **activity ratios,** which measure the effectiveness of

TABLE 2.1
Financial Ratios

	FORMULA	HOW EXPRESSED	MEANING
1. Liquidity Ratios			
Current ratio	$\dfrac{\text{Current assets}}{\text{Current liabilities}}$	Decimal	A short-term indicator of the company's ability to pay its short-term liabilities from short-term assets; how much of current assets are available to cover each dollar of current liabilities.
Quick (acid test) ratio	$\dfrac{\text{Current assets} - \text{Inventory}}{\text{Current liabilities}}$	Decimal	Measures the company's ability to pay off its short-term obligations from current assets, excluding inventories.
Inventory to net working capital	$\dfrac{\text{Inventory}}{\text{Current assets} - \text{Current liabilities}}$	Decimal	A measure of inventory balance; measures the extent to which the cushion of excess current assets over current liabilities may be threatened by unfavorable changes in inventory.
Cash ratio	$\dfrac{\text{Cash} + \text{cash equivalents}}{\text{Current liabilities}}$	Decimal	Measures the extent to which the company's capital is in cash or cash equivalents; shows how much of the current obligations can be paid from cash or near-cash assets.
2. Profitability Ratios			
Net profit margin	$\dfrac{\text{Net profit after taxes}}{\text{Net sales}}$	Percentage	Shows how much after-tax profits are generated by each dollar of sales.
Gross profit margin	$\dfrac{\text{Sales} - \text{Cost of goods sold}}{\text{Net sales}}$	Percentage	Indicates the total margin available to cover other expenses beyond cost of goods sold, and still yield a profit.
Return on investment (ROI)	$\dfrac{\text{Net profit after taxes}}{\text{Total assets}}$	Percentage	Measures the rate of return on the total assets utilized in the company; a measure of management's efficiency, it shows the return on all the assets under its control regardless of source of financing.
Return on equity (ROE)	$\dfrac{\text{Net profit after taxes}}{\text{Stockholders equity}}$	Percentage	Measures the rate of return on the book value of stockholder's total investment in the company.

(Continued)

NOTE: In using ratios for analysis, calculate ratios for the corporation and compare them to the average ratios for the particular industry. Refer to Standard and Poor's and Robert Morris Associates for average industry data. For an in-depth discussion of ratios and their use, refer to J. F. Weston and E. F. Brigham, *Essentials of Managerial Finance*, 8th ed. (Chicago, Ill.: Dryden Press, 1987), pp. 240–259. Special thanks to Dr. Moustafa H. Abdelsamad, Dean of Southeastern Massachusetts University, for his writing of the meanings of these ratios.

TABLE 2.1 (Continued)

	FORMULA	HOW EXPRESSED	MEANING
Earnings Per Share (EPS)	$\dfrac{\text{Net profit after taxes} - \text{Preferred stock dividends}}{\text{Average number of common shares}}$	Dollar per share	Shows the after-tax earnings generated for each share of common stock.
3. Activity Ratios			
Inventory turnover	$\dfrac{\text{Net sales}}{\text{Inventory}}$	Decimal	Measures the number of times that average inventory of finished goods was turned over or sold during a period of time, usually a year.
Days of inventory	$\dfrac{\text{Inventory}}{\text{Cost of goods sold} \div 365}$	Days	Measures the number of one day's worth of inventory that a company has on-hand at any given time.
Net working capital turnover	$\dfrac{\text{Net sales}}{\text{Net working capital}}$	Decimal	Measures how effectively the net working capital is used to generate sales.
Asset turnover	$\dfrac{\text{Sales}}{\text{Total assets}}$	Decimal	Measures the utilization of all the company's assets; measures how many sales are generated by each dollar of assets.
Fixed asset turnover	$\dfrac{\text{Sales}}{\text{Fixed assets}}$	Decimal	Measures the utilization of the company's fixed assets (i.e., plant and equipment); measures how many sales are generated by each dollar of fixed assets.
Average collection period	$\dfrac{\text{Accounts receivable}}{\text{Sales for year} \div 365}$	Days	Indicates the average length of time in days that a company must wait to collect a sale after making it; may be compared to the credit terms offered by the company to its customers.
Accounts receivable turnover	$\dfrac{\text{Annual credit sales}}{\text{Accounts receivable}}$	Decimal	Indicates the number of times that accounts receivable are cycled during the period (usually a year).
Accounts payable period	$\dfrac{\text{Accounts Payable}}{\text{Purchases for year} \div 365}$	Days	Indicates the average length of time in days that the company takes to pay its credit purchases.
Days of cash	$\dfrac{\text{Cash}}{\text{Net sales for year} \div 365}$	Days	Indicates the number of days of cash on hand, at present sales levels.
4. Leverage Ratios			
Debt to asset ratio	$\dfrac{\text{Total debt}}{\text{Total assets}}$	Percentage	Measures the extent to which borrowed funds have been used to finance the company's assets.
Debt to equity ratio	$\dfrac{\text{Total debt}}{\text{Stockholders' equity}}$	Percentage	Measures the funds provided by creditors versus the funds provided by owners.

Ratio	Formula	Unit	Description
Long-term debt to capital structure	$\dfrac{\text{Long-term debt}}{\text{Stockholders' equity}}$	Percentage	Measures the long-term component of capital structure.
Times interest earned	$\dfrac{\text{Profit before taxes} + \text{Interest charges}}{\text{Interest charges}}$	Decimal	Indicates the ability of the company to meet its annual interest costs.
Coverage of fixed charges	$\dfrac{\text{Profit before taxes} + \text{Interest charges} + \text{Lease charges}}{\text{Interest charges} + \text{Lease obligations}}$	Decimal	A measure of the company's ability to meet all of its fixed-charge obligations.
Current liabilities to equity	$\dfrac{\text{Current liabilities}}{\text{Stockholders' equity}}$	Percentage	Measures the short-term financing portion versus that provided by owners.
5. Other Ratios			
Price/Earning ratio	$\dfrac{\text{Market price per share}}{\text{Earnings per share}}$	Decimal	Shows the current market's evaluation of a stock, based on its earnings; shows how much the investor is willing to pay for each dollar of earnings.
Dividend payout ratio	$\dfrac{\text{Annual dividends per share}}{\text{Annual earnings per share}}$	Percentage	Indicates the percentage of profit that is paid out as dividends.
Dividend yield on common stock	$\dfrac{\text{Annual dividends per share}}{\text{Current market price per share}}$	Percentage	Indicates the dividend rate of return to common stockholders at the current market price.

NOTE: In using ratios for analysis, calculate ratios for the corporation and compare them to the average ratios for the particular industry. Refer to Standard and Poor's and Robert Morris Associates for average industry data. For an in-depth discussion of ratios and their use, refer to J. F. Weston and E. F. Brigham, *Essentials of Managerial Finance*, 8th ed. (Chicago, Ill.: Dryden Press, 1987), pp. 240–259. Special thanks to Dr. Moustafa H. Abdelsamad, Dean of Southeastern Massachusetts University, for his writing of the meanings of these ratios.

the corporation's use of resources, and (4) **leverage ratios,** which measure the contributions of owners' financing compared with creditors' financing.

In your analysis do *not* simply make an exhibit including all the ratios, but select and discuss only those ratios that have an impact on the company's problems. For instance, external resources, accounts receivable, and inventory may provide a source of funds. If receivables and inventories are double the industry average, reducing them may provide needed cash. In this situation, the case report should include not only sources of funds, but also the number of dollars freed for use.

A typical financial analysis of a firm would include a study of the operating statements for five or ten years, including a trend analysis of sales, profits, earnings per share, debt/equity ratio, return on investment, etc., plus a ratio study comparing the firm under study with industry standards. To begin, scrutinize historical income statements and balance sheets. These two basic statements provide most of the data needed for analysis. Compare the statements over time if a series of statements is available. Calculate changes that occur in individual categories from year to year, as well as the total change over the years. Determine the change as a percentage as well as an absolute amount, and determine the amount *adjusted for inflation* (constant dollars). Examination of this information may reveal developing trends. Compare trends in one category with trends in related categories. For example, an increase in sales of 15% over three years may appear to be satisfactory until you note an increase of 20% in the cost of goods sold during the same period. The outcome of this comparison might suggest that further investigation into the manufacturing process is necessary.

Another approach to the analysis of financial statements is to convert them into **common-size statements.** Convert every category from dollar terms to percentages. For the balance sheet, give the total assets or liabilities a value of 100%, and calculate all other categories as percentages of the total assets or liabilities. For the income statement, net sales represent 100%: calculate the percentage of each category so that the categories sum to the net sales percentage (100%). When you convert statements to this form, it is relatively easy to note the percentage that each category represents of the total. Comparisons of these percentages over the years can point out areas for additional analysis. To get a proper picture, however, make comparisons with industry data, if available, to see if fluctuations are merely reflecting industry-wide trends. If a firm's trends are generally in line with those of the rest of the industry, there is a lower likelihood of problems than if the firm's trends are worse than industry averages. These statements are especially helpful *in developing scenarios and pro forma statements,* since they provide a series of historical relationships (for example, cost of goods sold to sales, interest to sales, and inventories as a percent of assets).

If the corporation being studied appears to be in poor financial condition, calculate its "Z-value." Developed by Edward Altman, the formula com-

ILLUSTRATIVE EXAMPLE 2.1

The Altman Bankruptcy Formula

Edward I. Altman developed a formula to predict a company's likelihood of going bankrupt. His system of multiple discriminate analysis is used by stockholders to determine if the corporation is a good investment. The formula was developed from a study of thirty-three manufacturing companies with assets averaging $6.4 million that had filed Chapter X bankruptcies. These were paired with thirty-three similar but profitable firms with assets between $1 million and $25 million. The formula is:

$$Z = 1.2x_1 + 1.4x_2 + 3.3x_3 + 0.6x_4 + 1.0x_5$$

where

x_1 = Working capital divided by total assets.

x_2 = Retained earnings divided by total assets.

x_3 = Earnings before interest and taxes divided by total assets.

x_4 = Market value of equity divided by book value of total debt.

x_5 = Sales divided by total assets.

Z = Overall index of corporate fiscal health.

The range of the Z-value for most corporations is -4 to $+8$. According to Altman:

- Financially strong corporations have Z values above 2.99.
- Corporations in serious trouble have Z values below 1.81.
- Corporations between 1.81 and 2.99 are question marks that could go either way.

The closer a firm gets to bankruptcy, the more accurate is the Z value as a predictor.

SOURCE: M. Ball, "Z Factor: Rescue by the Numbers," *INC.* (December 1980), p. 48. Reprinted with permission, *INC.* magazine, (December, 1980). Copyright © 1980 by INC. Publishing Company, 38 Commercial Wharf, Boston, MA 02110.

bines five ratios by weighting them according to their importance to a corporation's financial strength (see Illustrative Example 2.1). The formula predicts the likelihood of the company going bankrupt. Firms in serious trouble have Z values below 1.81.

Adjusting for Inflation

Many of the cases in business policy/strategy textbooks take place during a period of inflation. When analyzing these cases, you should calculate sales and profits in constant dollars in order to perceive the "true" performance of the corporation in comparison with that of the industry, or of the economy in general. Remember that chief executive officers wish to keep their jobs and that some will tend to bias the figures in their favor. Sales stated in current dollars may seem to show substantial growth, but when they're converted to constant dollars, they may show a steady decline.

The return-on-investment ratio is doubly susceptible to distortion. Because net income is generally measured in current dollars, it rises with inflation. Meanwhile, investment (generally valued in historical dollars) effectively falls. Thus ROI may appear to be rising when it is actually stable, or appear to be stable when it is actually falling.[18]

To adjust for general inflation, most firms use the Consumer Price Index (CPI), as given in Table 2.2. The simplest way to adjust financial statements for inflation is to divide each item by the CPI for that year. This changes each figure to 1967 constant dollars. The CPI uses 1967 as the base year (with a CPI of 100.0) against which all other year's prices are compared. Remember that the CPI for each year is a percentage. For example, to convert 1985 reported sales of $950,000 to constant (1967) dollars, divide 950,000 by the CPI for 1985 (3.222); 1985 sales are thus converted to constant (1967) dollars of $294,848. This conversion displays the fact that, in terms of general purchasing power, a U.S. dollar in 1985 was worth only 32 cents in 1967 dollars.

For a comparison of recent financial statements, it might help to use a more recent base year than 1967 in the adjustment for inflation. For example, in Table 2.3 selected figures are taken from CSX Corporation's annual reports for 1982 through 1984. Instead of using 1967 as the base year for these comparisons, one may use 1982. To do so, divide the CPIs for 1983 and 1984 (as provided in Table 2.2) by the CPI for 1982; the appropriate adjustment factors are found to be 1.032 for 1983 and 1.076 for 1984. Table 2.3 shows operating revenue and net earnings figures first as reported (in 1983 and 1984 dollars) and second, divided by each year's adjustment factor, to result in 1982 constant dollars. Once this conversion is done, the impact of inflation on a firm's revenues and earnings can be clearly seen. Note, for example, that reported operating revenue increased by 62% from 1982 to 1984. In constant 1982 dollars, however, they increased only 50%. Although net earnings as reported in 1984 increased 12% from 1982, they increased only 4% when they are considered in constant dollar terms.

Another helpful aid in the analysis of cases in business policy is the chart

TABLE 2.2
Consumer Price Index for All Items (1967 = 100.0)

YEAR	CPI	YEAR	CPI
1974	147.7	1981	272.4
1975	161.2	1982	289.1
1976	170.5	1983	298.4
1977	181.5	1984	311.1
1978	195.4	1985	322.2
1979	217.4	1986	328.4
1980	246.8	1987	340.4

SOURCE: U.S. Department of Commerce, *1987 Statistical Abstract of the United States,* 107th edition, Chart no. 774, p. 463. *Monthly Labor Review* (March, 1988), p. 83.

TABLE 2.3

General Price Level Adjustment for Inflation Using Consumer Price Index

(In Millions of Dollars)

	1984	1983	1982
Operating Revenue, as reported	$7,934	$5,891	$4,909
% increase (decrease) over 1982	62%	20%	—
Operating Revenue			
Constant (1982) dollars	7,374	5,708	4,909
% increase over 1982	50%	16%	—
Net Earnings, as reported	465	272	414
% increase (decrease) over 1982	12%	(66%)	—
Net Earnings			
Constant (1982) dollars	432	263	414
% increase (decrease) over 1982	4%	(63%)	—
CPI Adjustment Factor (1982 = 100%)	1.076	1.032	1.000
$\dfrac{198x\ \text{CPI}}{1982\ \text{CPI}}$	$\left(\dfrac{311.1}{289.1}\right)$	$\left(\dfrac{298.4}{289.1}\right)$	$\left(\dfrac{289.1}{289.1}\right)$

SOURCE: Selected reported figures taken from CSX Corporation, *1984 Annual Report,* p. 20.

on prime interest rates given in Table 2.4. For better assessments of strategic decisions, it can be useful to note the level of the prime interest rate at the time of the case. A decision to borrow money to build a new plant would have been a good one in 1977, but somewhat foolhardy in 1981.

TABLE 2.4

Changes in Prime Interest Rates*

YEAR	LOW	HIGH	YEAR	LOW	HIGH
1974	8¾	12	1981	15¾	20½
1975	7	10½	1982	11½	17
1976	6¼	7¼	1983	10½	11½
1977	6½	7¾	1984	10¾	12¾
1978	6	11¾	1985	9½	10¾
1979	11½	15¾	1986	8	9½
1980	11	21½	1987	8	9¾

SOURCE: D. S. Benton, "Banking and Financial Information," Table 1.1, p. 2 in *Thorndike Encyclopedia of Banking and Financial Tables,* Revised Edition, *1987 Yearbook* (Boston, Mass.: Warren, Gorham & Lamont, 1987).

*The rate of interest that banks charge on the lowest-risk loans they make.

SUMMARY AND CONCLUSION

The strategic management/business policy course is concerned with developing the conceptual skills that successful top management needs. The emphasis is therefore on improving your analytical and problem-solving abilities. The case method develops those skills and gives you an appreciation of environmental issues and the interdependencies among the functional units of a large corporation. The strategic audit is one recommended technique for the systematization of the analysis of fairly long and complex policy cases. It also provides a basic checklist for the investigation of any large corporation. Nevertheless, the strategic audit is only one of many techniques with which you can analyze and diagnose case problems. We expect consultants, managers, and boards of directors to increasingly employ the audit as an analytical technique.

DISCUSSION QUESTIONS

1. Should people be selected for top management positions primarily on the basis of their having a particular combination of skills? Explain.

2. What are the strengths and weaknesses of the strategic audit as a technique for assessing corporate performance?

3. What value does the case method hold for the study of strategic management/business policy?

4. Why should one begin a case analysis with a financial analysis? When are other approaches appropriate?

5. Reconcile the strategic decision-making process depicted in Fig. 2.2 with the strategic management model depicted in Fig. 1.3.

6. Analyze the financial statements of CSX Corporation as provided in Tables 2.5 and 2.6 in the Integrative Case at the end of this chapter. What can you conclude?

NOTES

1. B. M. Bass, *Stogdill's Handbook of Leadership* (New York: Free Press, 1981), p. 73.

2. R. L. Katz, "Skills of an Effective Administrator," *Harvard Business Review* (January–February 1955), p. 33.

3. Katz, pp. 33–42. These definitions were adapted from the material in this article.

4. Katz, p. 42.

5. T. L. Wheelen, G. K. Rakes, and J. D. Hunger, "Skills of an Executive" (Paper presented at the Thirty-Sixth Annual Meeting of the Academy of Management, Kansas City, Mo., August 1976).

6. Wheelen, Rakes, and Hunger, p. 7.

7. W. G. Shenkir, T. L. Wheelen, and R. H. Strawser, "The Making of an Accountant," *CPA Journal* (March 1973), p. 219.

8. E. E. Chaffee, "Three Models of Strategy," *Academy of Management Review* (January 1985), pp. 89–90.
D. Norburn, "GOGOs, YOYOs and DODOs: Company Directors and Industry Performance," *Strategic Management Journal* (March–April 1986), p. 112.
B. C. Reimann, "Doers as Planners," *Planning Review* (September 1986), p. 45.

9. T. L. Wheelen and J. D. Hunger, "Using the Strategic Audit," *SAM Advanced Management Journal* (Winter 1987), pp. 4–12.
R. B. Buchele, "How to Evaluate a Firm," *California Management Review* (Fall 1962), pp. 5–16.
J. Martindell, *The Appraisal of Management* (New York: Harper & Row, 1962).
R. Bauer, L. T. Cauthorn, and R. P. Warner, "Management Audit Process Guide," (Boston: Intercollegiate Case Clearing House, no. 9-375-336, 1975).
J. D. Hunger and T. L. Wheelen, "The Strategic Audit: An Integrative Approach To Teaching Business Policy" (Paper presented at the Forty-Third Annual Meeting of the Academy of Management, Dallas, Texas, August 1983).
M. Lauenstein, "The Strategy Audit," *Journal of Business Strategy* (Winter 1984), pp. 87–91.

10. T. Barry, "What a Management Audit Can Do for

You," *Management Review* (June 1977), p. 43.

11. A. J. Dubinsky and R. W. Hansen, "The Sales Force Management Audit," *California Management Review* (Winter 1981), pp. 86–95.

A. B. Carroll and G. W. Beiler, "Landmarks in the Evolution of the Social Audit," *Academy of Management Journal* (September 1975), pp. 589 599.

R. E. Freeman, *Strategic Management: A Stakeholder Approach* (Boston: Pitman Publishing, 1984), p. 111.

J. S. Armstrong, "The Forecasting Audit," in S. Makridakis and S. C. Wheelwright (eds.), *The Handbook of Forecasting* (New York: Wiley and Sons, 1982), pp. 535–552.

D. Ford, "The Management and Marketing of Technology," in *Advances in Strategic Management, Vol. 3,* edited by R. Lamb and P. Shrivastava (Greenwich, Conn.: Jai Press, 1985), pp. 107–109.

M. P. Mokwa, "The Strategic Marketing Audit: An Adoption/Utilization Perspective," *Journal of Business Strategy* (Spring 1986), pp. 88–95.

J. W. Lorsch, "Strategic Myopia: Culture as an Invisible Barrier to Change," in *Gaining Control of the Corporate Culture,* edited by R. H. Kilmann, M. J. Saxton, and R. Serpa (San Francisco: Jossey Bass, 1985), pp. 97–98.

C. J. Fombrun, M. A. Devanna, and N. M. Tichy, in *Strategic Human Resources Management,* edited by C. J. Fombrun, N. M. Tichy, and M. A. Devanna (New York: John Wiley and Sons, 1984), pp. 235–248.

12. E. E. Tallett, "Repositioning Warner-Lambert as a High-Tech Health Care Company," *Planning Review* (May 1984), pp. 12–16, 41.

K. A. Macke, "Managing Change: How Dayton Hudson Meets the Challenge," *Journal of Business Strategy* (Summer 1983), pp. 78–81.

D. M. Slavick, "Planning at Bechtel: End of the Megaproject Era," *Planning Review* (September 1986), pp. 16–22.

H. Waldron, "Putting a New Face On Avon," *Planning Review* (July 1985), pp. 18–23.

13. J. W. Fredrickson, "The Comprehensiveness of Strategic Decision Processes: Extension, Observation, Future Directions," *Academy of Management Journal* (September 1984), pp. 445–466.

14. P. M. Ginter and A. C. Rucks, "Relative Emphasis Placed on the Steps of the Normative Model of Strategic Planning by Practitioners," *Proceedings, Southern Management Association* (November 1983), pp. 19–21.

15. C. Boyd, D. Kopp, and L. Shufelt, "Evaluative Criteria in Business Policy Case Analysis: An Exploratory Study," *Proceedings, Midwest Academy of Management* (April 1984), pp. 287–292.

16. T. J. Peters and R. W. Waterman, Jr., *In Search of Excellence* (New York: Harper & Row, 1982), pp. 9–12.

17. A survey of 6,000 investors and analysts in the United States, United Kingdom, and New Zealand, revealed a strong belief in the importance of annual reports, especially the financial statement sections, for investment decisions. See L. S. Chang and K. S. Most, "An International Study of the Importance of Financial Statements," *International Journal of Management* (December 1985), pp. 76–85.

18. M. J. Chussil, "Inflation and ROI," *The Pimsletter on Business Strategy, Number 22* (Cambridge, Mass.: The Strategic Planning Institute, 1980), p. 1.

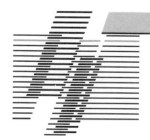

INTEGRATIVE CASE

CSX CORPORATION'S FINANCIAL STATEMENTS

Tables 2.5 and 2.6 are the consolidated financial statements of CSX Corporation for the years 1982 through 1984. As explained earlier, a detailed analysis of these statements first includes an adjustment for inflation. A *second* step is to convert the income statement (Table 2.5) and the balance sheet (Table 2.6) into common-size statements. To do this, convert operating revenue, total assets, and total liabilities into 100%, and list the other entries as percentages of each total. This will show, for example, if accounts receivable as a percentage of total assets had increased or decreased from 1982 to 1984. Dividing the accounts receivable for 1982 through 1984, as shown in Table 2.7, by the total assets for each of the three years, indicates that accounts receivable increased from 7.9% of total assets in 1982 to 10.7% in 1983 to 10.1% in 1984. Further analysis would be needed to ascertain if accounts receivable were mismanaged in 1983 or if the increase in accounts receivable in 1983 reflected a downturn in the economy.

The *third* step in initial case analysis is to calculate the financial ratios listed earlier in Table 2.1. Keep in mind that sometimes one has to make some decisions about which categories to lump together, so that one can ascertain the data needed in the calculation of a particular ratio. These decisions can explain why two people can calculate different ratios from the same financial statements—and yet both be correct, on the basis of different underlying assumptions. Also remember that not every ratio can be calculated for every case. In Tables 2.5 and 2.6, some of the needed data has been left out. That is why N.A. for Not Available is listed for certain ratios in Table 2.7.

TABLE 2.5
Consolidated Statement of Earnings and Retained Earnings: CSX Corporation
(In Millions of Dollars, Except Per-Share Amounts)

	YEARS ENDED DECEMBER 31		
	1984	**1983**	**1982**
Operating revenue	$7,934	$5,891	$4,909
Operating expense	6,916	5,255	4,432
Income from operations	1,018	636	447
Other income (mostly interest)	64	45	273[1]
Interest expense	242	215	171
Earnings before taxes and minority interest	840	466	579
Income taxes	344	165	138
Minority interest (in subsidiaries)	31	29	27
Net earnings	$ 465	$ 272	$ 414
Retained earnings—January 1	2,809	2,670	2,376
Dividends	154	133	120
Retained earnings—December 31	$3,120	$2,809	$2,670
Average common shares outstanding (thousands)	147,608	131,078	125,368
Common shares outstanding at year-end (thousands)	149,556	146,023	126,648
Per-share amounts			
Net earnings	$ 3.15	$ 2.07	$ 3.30
Dividends—common	$ 1.04	$ .99	$ .95

SOURCE: *1984 Annual Report*, CSX Corporation, p. 20.

NOTE: [1]Includes $171 million for sales of publishing and cable television subsidiaries plus $32 million from MCI for communications line right of way.

TABLE 2.6

Consolidated Statement of Financial Position: CSX Corporation

(In Millions of Dollars)

	DECEMBER 31		
	1984	1983	1982
Assets			
Current assets			
Cash and short-term investments	$ 377	$ 314	$ 528
Accounts receivable	1,178	1,175	728
Inventories	458	424	251
Other current assets	142	153	111
Total current assets	2,155	2,066	1,618
Investments			
Properties	9,143	8,589	7,257
Affiliates and other companies	137	115	96
Other assets	201	234	228
Total investments	9,481	8,938	7,581
Total assets	$11,636	$11,004	$9,199
Liabilities			
Current liabilities			
Accounts payable and other current liabilities	$ 1,663	$ 1,542	$1,229
Current maturities of long-term debt	261	282	167
Total current liabilities	1,924	1,824	1,396
Claims and other long-term liabilities	343	343	355
Deferred income taxes (due to investment tax credits)	1,828	1,511	1,321
Long-term debt	2,302	2,466	1,866
Redeemable preferred stock and minority interest	330	334	316
Common shareholders' equity			
Common stock	150	146	42
Other capital	1,639	1,571	1,233
Retained earnings	3,120	2,809	2,670
Total common shareholders' equity	4,909	4,526	3,945
Total liabilities and shareholders' equity	$11,636	$11,004	$9,199

SOURCE: CSX Corporation, *1984 Annual Report*, p. 24.

TABLE 2.7
Financial Ratio Analysis: CSX Corporation

	1984	1983	1982
Liquidity ratios			
Current	1.12	1.13	1.16
Quick	.88	0.90	0.98
Inventory to net working capital	1.98	1.75	1.13
Cash ratio	0.20	0.17	0.38
Profitability ratios			
Net profit margin	5.9	4.6	8.4
Gross profit margin	N.A.	N.A.	N.A.
ROI	4.0	2.5	4.5
ROE	9.5	6.0	10.5
EPS	3.15	2.07	3.30
Activity ratios			
Inventory turnover	17.3	13.9	19.6
Days of inventory	N.A.	N.A.	N.A.
Net working capital turnover	34.35	24.3	22.1
Asset turnover	0.7	0.5	0.5
Fixed asset turnover	0.9	0.7	0.7
Average collection period	54.2	72.8	54.1
A/R turnover	N.A.	N.A.	N.A.
Accounts payable period	N.A.	N.A.	N.A.
Days of cash	17.3	19.5	39.3
Leverage ratios			
Debt to asset	57.8	58.9	57.1
Debt to equity	137.0	143.1	133.2
L.-t. debt to capital structure	46.9	54.5	47.3
Times interest earned	N.A.	N.A.	N.A.
Coverage of fixed charges	N.A.	N.A.	N.A.
Current liabilities to equity	39.1	40.3	35.4
Other ratios			
Price/earnings	N.A.	N.A.	N.A.
Dividend payout	33.0	47.8	28.8
Dividend yield	N.A.	N.A.	N.A.
Net working capital (in $ millions)	231	242	222

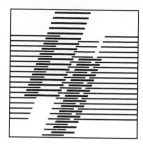

APPENDIX 2

AIDS FOR CASE ANALYSIS AND PRESENTATION

APPENDIX 2.A
STRATEGIC AUDIT OF A CORPORATION

I. Current Situation

A. How is the corporation performing in terms of return on investment, overall market share, profitability trends, earnings per share, etc.?

B. What are the corporation's current mission, objectives, strategies, and policies?

 1. Are they clearly stated or are they merely implied from performance?

 2. *Mission:* What business(es) is the corporation in? Why?

 3. *Objectives:* What are the corporate, business, and functional objectives? Are they consistent with each other, with the mission, and with the internal and external environments?

 4. *Strategies:* What strategy or mix of strategies is the corporation following? Are they consistent with each other, with the mission and objectives, and with the internal and external environments?

 5. *Policies:* What are they? Are they consistent with each other, with the mission, objectives, and strategies, and with the internal and external environments?

II. Strategic Managers

A. Board of Directors

 1. Who are they? Are they internal or external?

 2. Do they own significant shares of stock?

 3. Is the stock privately held or publicly traded?

 4. What do they contribute to the corporation in terms of knowledge, skills, background, and connections?

 5. How long have they served on the board?

 6. What is their level of involvement in strategic management? Do they merely rubber-stamp top management's proposals or do they actively participate and suggest future directions?

B. Top Management

 1. What person or group constitutes top management?

 2. What are top management's chief characteristics in terms of knowledge, skills, background, and style?

 3. Has top management been responsible for the corporation's performance over the past few years?

 4. Has it established a systematic approach to the formulation, implementation, and evaluation and control of strategic management?

 5. What is its level of involvement in the strategic management process?

 6. How well does top management interact with lower-level management?

 7. How well does top management interact with the board of directors?

 8. Is top management sufficiently skilled to cope with likely future challenges?

III. External Environment: Opportunities and Threats (S.W.O.T.)

A. Societal Environment

 1. What general environmental factors among the sociocultural, economic, political-legal, and technological forces are currently affecting both the corporation and the industries in which it competes? Which present current or future threats? Opportunities?

2. Which of these are currently the most important (that is, are **strategic factors**) to the corporation and to the industries in which it competes? Which will be important in the future?

B. Task Environment

1. What forces in the immediate environment (that is, threat of new entrants, bargaining power of buyers, threat of substitute products or services, bargaining power of suppliers, rivalry among competing firms, and the relative power of unions, governments, etc.) are currently affecting the level of competitive intensity within the industries in which the corporation offers products or services?

2. What key factors in the immediate environment (that is, customers, competitors, suppliers, creditors, labor unions, governments, trade associations, interest groups, local communities, and stockholders) are currently affecting the corporation? Which present current or future threats? Opportunities?

3. Which of these forces and factors are the most important (that is, are strategic factors) at the present time? Which will be important in the future?

IV. Internal Environment: Strengths and Weaknesses (S.W.O.T.)

A. Corporate Structure

1. How is the corporation presently structured?
   a) Is decision-making authority centralized around one group or decentralized to many groups or units?
   b) Is it organized on the basis of functions, projects, geography, or some combination of these?

2. Is the structure clearly understood by everyone in the corporation?

3. Is the present structure consistent with current corporate objectives, strategies, policies, and programs?

4. In what ways does this structure compare with those of similar corporations?

B. Corporate Culture

1. Is there a well-defined or emerging culture composed of shared beliefs, expectations, and values?

2. Is the culture consistent with the current objectives, strategies, policies, and programs?

3. What is the culture's position on important issues facing the corporation (that is, on productivity, quality of performance, adaptability to changing conditions)?

C. Corporate Resources

1. Marketing
   a) What are the corporation's current marketing objectives, strategies, policies, and programs?
      i) Are they clearly stated, or merely implied from performance and/or budgets?
      ii) Are they consistent with the corporation's mission, objectives, strategies, policies, and with internal and external environments?
   b) How well is the corporation performing in terms of analysis of market position and marketing mix (that is, of product, price, place, and promotion)?
      i) What trends emerge from this analysis?
      ii) What impact have these trends had on past performance and how will they probably affect future performance?
      iii) Does this analysis support the corporation's past and pending strategic decisions?
   c) How well does this corporation's marketing performance compare with those of similar corporations?
   d) Are marketing managers using accepted marketing concepts and techniques to evaluate and improve product performance? (Consider product life cycle, market segmentation, market research, and product portfolios.)
   e) What is the role of the marketing manager in the strategic management process?

2. Finance
   a) What are the corporation's current financial objectives, strategies, policies, and programs?
      i) Are they clearly stated or merely implied from performance and/or budgets?

ii) Are they consistent with the corporation's mission, objectives, strategies, policies, and with internal and external environments?

b) How well is the corporation performing in terms of financial analysis? (Consider liquidity ratios, profitability ratios, activity ratios, leverage ratios, capitalization structure, and constant dollars.)

   i) What trends emerge from this analysis?

   ii) Are there any significant differences when statements are calculated in constant versus reported dollars?

   iii) What impact have these trends had on past performance and how will they probably affect future performance?

   iv) Does this analysis support the corporation's past and pending strategic decisions?

c) How well does this corporation's financial performance compare with that of similar corporations?

d) Are financial managers using accepted financial concepts and techniques to evaluate and improve current corporate and divisional performance? (Consider financial leverage, capital budgeting, and ratio analysis.)

e) What is the role of the financial manager in the strategic management process?

3. Research and Development (R&D)

a) What are the corporation's current R&D objectives, strategies, policies, and programs?

   i) Are they clearly stated, or implied from performance and/or budgets?

   ii) Are they consistent with the corporation's mission, objectives, strategies, policies, and with internal and external environments?

   iii) What is the role of technology in corporate performance?

   iv) Is the mix of basic, applied, and engineering research appropriate given the corporate mission and strategies?

b) What return is the corporation receiving from its investment in R&D?

c) Is the corporation technologically competent?

d) How well does the corporation's investment in R&D compare with the investments of similar corporations?

e) What is the role of the R&D manager in the strategic management process?

4. Operations (Manufacturing/Service)*

a) What are the corporation's current manufacturing/service objectives, strategies, policies, and programs?

   i) Are they clearly stated, or merely implied from performance and/or budgets?

   ii) Are they consistent with the corporation's mission, objectives, strategies, policies, and with internal and external environments?

b) What is the type and extent of operations capabilities of the corporation?

   i) If product-oriented, consider plant facilities, type of manufacturing system (continuous mass production or intermittent job shop), age and type of equipment, degree and role of automation and/or robots, plant capacities and utilization, productivity ratings, availability and type of transportation.

   ii) If service-oriented, consider service facilities (e.g., hospital, theater, or school buildings), type of operations systems (continuous service over time to same clientele or intermittent service over time to varied clientele), age and type of supporting equipment, degree and role of automation and/or use of mass communication devices (e.g., diagnostic machinery, videotape machines), facility capacities and utilization rates, efficiency ratings of professional/service personnel, availability and type of transportation to bring service staff and clientele together.

c) Are manufacturing or service facilities vulnerable to natural disasters, local or national

---

*Research suggests that the strategic approach developed for manufacturing companies is very useful for service firms. See H. M. O'Neill, "Do Strategic Paradigms Work in Service Industries?" in *Handbook of Business Strategy, 1986/87 Yearbook,* edited by W. D. Guth (Boston: Warren, Gorham, and Lamont, 1986), pp. 19.1–19.14.

strikes, reduction or limitation of resources from suppliers, substantial cost increases of materials, or nationalization by governments?

d) Is operating leverage being used successfully with an appropriate mix of people and machines, in manufacturing firms, or of support staff to professionals, in service firms?

e) How well does the corporation perform relative to the competition? Consider costs per unit of labor, material, and overhead; downtime; inventory control management and/or scheduling of service staff; production ratings; facility utilization percentages; and number of clients successfully treated by category (if service firm), or percentage of orders shipped on time (if product firm).

   i) What trends emerge from this analysis?

   ii) What impact have these trends had on past performance and how will they probably affect future performance?

   iii) Does this analysis support the corporation's past and pending strategic decisions?

f) Are operations managers using appropriate concepts and techniques to evaluate and improve current performance? Consider cost systems, quality control and reliability systems, inventory control management, personnel scheduling, learning curves, safety programs, engineering programs, that can improve efficiency of manufacturing or of service.

g) What is the role of the operations manager in the strategic management process?

5. Human Resources Management (HRM)

a) What are the corporation's current HRM objectives, strategies, policies, and programs?

   i) Are they clearly stated, or merely implied from performance and/or budgets?

   ii) Are they consistent with the corporation's mission, objectives, strategies, policies, and with internal and external environments?

b) How well is the corporation's HRM performing in terms of improving the fit between the individual employee and the job? Consider turnover, grievances, strikes, layoffs, employee training, quality of work life.

   i) What trends emerge from this analysis?

   ii) What impact have these trends had on past performance and how will they probably affect future performance?

   iii) Does this analysis support the corporation's past and pending strategic decisions?

c) How does this corporation's HRM performance compare with that of similar corporations?

d) Are HRM managers using appropriate concepts and techniques to evaluate and improve corporate performance? Consider the job analysis program, performance appraisal system, up-to-date job descriptions, training and development programs, attitude surveys, job design programs, quality of relationship with unions.

e) What is the role of the HRM manager in the strategic management process?

6. Information Systems (IS)

a) What are the corporation's current IS objectives, strategies, policies, and programs?

   i) Are they clearly stated, or merely implied from performance and/or budgets?

   ii) Are they consistent with the corporation's mission, objectives, strategies, policies, and with internal and external environments?

b) How well is the corporation's IS performing in terms of providing a useful database, automating routine clerical operations, assisting managers in making routine decisions, and providing information necessary for strategic decisions?

   i) What trends emerge from this analysis?

   ii) What impact have these trends had on past performance and how will they probably affect future performance?

   iii) Does this analysis support the corporation's past and pending strategic decisions?

c) How does this corporation's IS performance and stage of development compare with that of similar corporations?

d) Are IS managers using appropriate concepts and techniques to evaluate and improve corporate performance? Do they know how to build and manage a complex data-base, conduct system analyses, and implement interactive decision-support systems?

    e) What is the role of the IS manager in the strategic management process?

V.   Analysis of Strategic Factors

A. What are the key internal and external factors (<u>S</u>.<u>W</u>.<u>O</u>.<u>T</u>.) that strongly affect the corporation's present and future performance?

    1. What have been the key historical strategic factors for this corporation?

    2. What are the key short-term (0–1 year) strategic factors for this corporation?

    3. What are the key intermediate-term (1–3 year) strategic factors for this corporation?

    4. What are the key long-term (3–10 year) strategic factors for this corporation?

B. Are the current mission and objectives appropriate in light of the key strategic factors and problems?

    1. Should the mission and objectives be changed? If so, how?

    2. If changed, what will the effects on the firm be?

VI.   Strategic Alternatives

A. Can the current or revised objectives be met by the simple, more careful implementing of those strategies presently in use (for example, fine tuning the strategies)?

B. What are the major feasible alternative strategies available to this corporation? What are the pros and cons of each? Can *scenarios* be developed and agreed upon?

    1. Consider stability, growth, and retrenchment as corporate strategies.

    2. Consider cost leadership, differentiation, and focus as business strategies.

    3. Consider any functional strategic alternatives that might be needed for reinforcement of an important corporate or business strategic alternative.

VII.   Recommendation

A. Specify which of the strategic alternatives you are recommending for the corporate, business, and

functional levels of the corporation. Do you recommend different business or functional strategies for different units of the corporation?

B. Justify your recommendation in terms of its ability to resolve both long- and short-term problems and effectively deal with the key strategic factors.

C. What policies should be developed or revised to guide effective implementation?

VIII.   Implementation

A. What kinds of programs (for example, restructuring the corporation) should be developed to implement the recommended strategy?

    1. Who should develop these programs?

    2. Who should be in charge of these programs?

B. Are the programs financially feasible? Can *pro forma* budgets be developed and agreed upon? Are priorities and timetables appropriate to individual programs?

C. Will new standard operating procedures need to be developed?

IX.   Evaluation and Control

A. Is the current information system capable of providing sufficient feedback on implementation activities and performance?

    1. Can performance results be pinpointed by area, unit, project, or function?

    2. Is the information timely?

B. Are adequate control measures, to ensure conformance with the recommended strategic plan, in place?

    1. Are appropriate standards and measures being used?

    2. Are reward systems capable of recognizing and rewarding good performance?

APPENDIX 2.B
SUGGESTED TECHNIQUES FOR CASE ANALYSIS AND PRESENTATION

A. Case Analysis

1. Read the case rapidly, to get an overview of the nature of the corporation and its environment. Note the date on which the case was written so that you can put it into proper context.

2. Read the case a second time, and give it a detailed analysis according to the strategic audit (see Appendix 2.A) when appropriate. The audit will provide a conceptual framework for the examination of the corporation's objectives, mission, policies, strategies, problems, symptoms of problems, and issues. You should end up with a list of the salient issues and problems in the case. Perform a financial analysis.

3. Undertake outside research, when appropriate, to uncover economic and industrial information. Appendix 2.C suggests possible sources for outside research. These data should provide the environmental setting for the corporation. Conduct an in-depth analysis of the industry. Analyze the important competitors. Consider the bargaining power of suppliers, as well as buyers that might affect the firm's situation. Consider also the possible threats of future competitors in the industry, as well as the likelihood of new or different products or services that might substitute for the company's present ones.

4. Marshal facts and evidence to support selected issues and problems. Develop a framework or outline to organize the analysis. Your method of organization could be one of the following:

   a) The case as organized around the strategic audit.

   b) The case as organized around the key individual(s) in the case.

   c) The case as organized around the corporation's functional areas: production, management, finance, marketing, and R&D.

   d) The case as organized around the decision-making process.

   e) The case as organized around the seven variables (McKinsey 7-S Framework) of structure, strategy, staff, management style, systems and procedures, skills, and shared values.

5. Clearly identify and state the central problem(s) as supported by the information in the case. Use the S.W.O.T. format to sum up the key **strategic factors** facing the corporation: Strengths and Weaknesses of the company; Opportunities and Threats in the environment.

6. Develop a logical series of alternatives that evolve from the analysis to resolve the problem(s) or issue(s) in the case.

7. Evaluate each of the alternatives in light of the company's environment (both external and internal), mission, objectives, strategies, and policies. For each alternative, consider both the possible obstacles to its implementation and its financial implications.

8. Make recommendations on the basis of the fact that action must be taken. (Don't say, "I don't have enough information." The individuals in the case may have had the same or even less information than is given by the case.)

   a) Base your recommendations on a total analysis of the case.

   b) Provide the evidence gathered in step A4 to justify suggested changes.

   c) List the recommendations in order of priority—those to be done immediately and those to be done in the future.

   d) Show clearly how your recommendations deal with each of the *strategic factors* that were mentioned earlier in step A5. How do they build upon corporate *Strengths* to take advantage of environmental *Opportunities*? How do they deal with environmental *Threats* and corporate *Weaknesses*?

   e) Explain how each recommendation will be implemented. How will the plan(s) deal with anticipated resistance?

   f) Suggest feedback and control systems, to ensure that the recommendations are carried out as planned and to give advance warning of needed adjustments.

B. Written Presentation

1. Use the outline from step A4 to write the first draft of the case analysis. Follow steps A5 through A8.

   a) Don't rehash the case material; rather, supply the salient evidence and data to support your recommendations.

b) Develop exhibits on financial ratios and other data for inclusion in your report. The exhibits should provide meaningful information. Mention key elements of an exhibit in the text of the written analysis. If you include a ratio analysis as an exhibit, explain the meaning of the ratios in the text and cite only the critical ones in your analysis.

2. After it is written, review your case analysis for content and grammar. Remember to compare the outline (step A4) with the final product. Make sure you've presented sufficient data or evidence to support your problem analysis and recommendations. If the final product requires rewriting, do so. Keep in mind that the written report is going to be judged not only on *what* is said but also on the *manner* in which it is said.

3. If your written or oral presentation requires *pro forma* statements, you may wish to develop a scenario for each quarter and/or year in your forecast. A well-constructed scenario will help improve the accuracy of your forecast. Chapters 4 and 7 suggest methods for the development of scenarios.

C. Oral Presentation by Teams

1. The team should first decide upon a framework or outline for analysis, as mentioned in step A4. Although teams often divide the analysis work among team members, it is helpful if each team member also follows steps A5 through A8 in developing a preliminary analysis of the entire case to share and compare with team members.

2. The team should combine member input into one consolidated team audit, including S.W.O.T. analysis, alternatives, and recommendation(s). Gain agreement on the strategic factors and the best alternative(s) to support.

3. Divide, among the team's members the further development and presentation of the case analysis and recommendation(s). Agree upon responsibilities for the preparation of visual aids and handouts.

4. Modify the team outline, if necessary, and have one or two rehearsals of the presentation. If there is a time constraint for the final presentation, apply it to the practice presentation. If exhibits are used, make sure to allow sufficient time for their explanation. Critique one another's presentations and make the necessary modifications to the analysis.

5. During the class presentation, if a presenter misses a key fact, either slip a note to him or her, or deal with it in the summary speech.

6. Answer the specific questions raised by the instructor or classmates. If one person acts as a moderator for the questions and refers the questions to the appropriate team member, the presentation runs more smoothly than it will if everyone (or no one!) tries to deal with each question.

APPENDIX 2.C
RESOURCES FOR CASE RESEARCH

A. Company Information

1. Annual Reports
2. *Moody's Manuals on Investment* (a listing of companies within certain industries, that contains a brief history and a five-year financial statement of each company)
3. Securities and Exchange Commission Annual Report Form 10-K
4. *Standard and Poor's Register of Corporations, Directors, and Executives*
5. *Value Line Investment Survey*

B. Economic Information

1. Regional statistics and local forecasts from large banks
2. *Business Cycle Development* (Department of Commerce)
3. Chase Econometric Associates' publications
4. Census Bureau publications on population, transportation, and housing
5. *Current Business Reports* (Department of Commerce)
6. *Economic Indicators* (Joint Economic Committee)
7. *Economic Report of the President to Congress*
8. *Long-Term Economic Growth* (Department of Commerce)
9. *Monthly Labor Review* (Department of Labor)
10. *Monthly Bulletin of Statistics* (United Nations)
11. "Survey of Buying Power," *Sales Management*

12. Standard and Poor's Statistical Service
13. *Statistical Abstract of the United States* (Department of Commerce)
14. *Statistical Yearbook* (United Nations)
15. *Survey of Current Business* (Department of Commerce)
16. *U.S. Industrial Outlook* (Department of Defense)
17. *World Trade Annual* (United Nations)
18. *Overseas Business Reports* (published by country, by U.S. Department of Commerce)

C. Industry Information
   1. Analyses of companies and industries by investment brokerage firms
   2. *Annual Report of American Industry* (a compilation of statistics by industry and company, published by *Fortune*)
   3. *Business Week* (provides weekly economic and business information, and quarterly profit and sales rankings of corporations)
   4. *Fortune Magazine* (publishes listings of financial information on corporations within certain industries)
   5. *Industry Survey* (published quarterly by Standard and Poor Corporation)

D. Directory and Index Information
   1. *Business Information: How to Find and Use It*
   2. *Business Periodical Index*
   3. *Directory of National Trade Associations*
   4. *Encyclopedia of Associations*
   5. *Funk and Scott Index of Corporations and Industries*
   6. *Thomas's Register of American Manufacturers*
   7. *Wall Street Journal Index*
   8. *Where to Find Business Information*

E. Ratio Analysis Information
   1. *Almanac of Business and Industrial Ratios* (Prentice-Hall)
   2. *Annual Statement Studies* (Robert Morris Associates)
   3. *Dun's Review* (Dun and Bradstreet: published annually in September-December issues)
   4. *Industry Norms and Key Business Ratios* (Dun and Bradstreet)
   5. *How to Read a Financial Report* (Merrill Lynch, Pierce, Fenner and Smith, Inc.)
   6. *Quality of Earnings: The Investor's Guide to How Much Money a Company Is Really Making* (T. L. O'Glove, Free Press, 1987)

F. General Sources
   1. *Commodity Yearbook*
   2. *U.S. Census of Business*
   3. *U.S. Census of Manufacturers*
   4. *World Almanac and Book of Facts*

G. Business Periodicals
   1. *Business Week*
   2. *Forbes*
   3. *Wall Street Journal*
   4. *Fortune*
   5. Industry-specific periodicals (e.g., *Oil and Gas Journal*)

H. Academic/Practitioner Journals
   1. *Harvard Business Review*
   2. *Journal of Business Strategy*
   3. *Long-Range Planning*
   4. *Strategic Management Journal*
   5. *Planning Review*
   6. *Academy of Management Review*
   7. *SAM Advanced Management Journal*

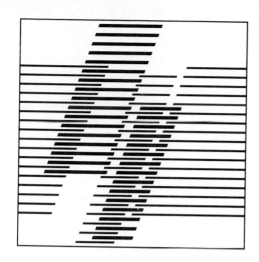

PART TWO

SCANNING THE ENVIRONMENT

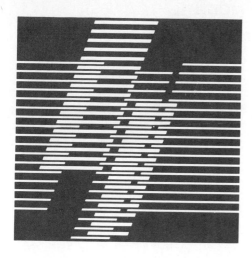

CHAPTER 3

STRATEGIC MANAGERS

STRATEGIC MANAGEMENT MODEL

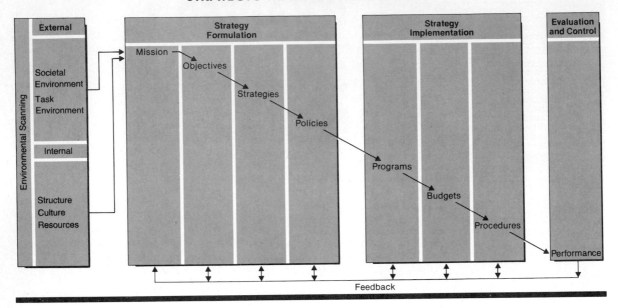

Strategic managers are the people in a corporation who are involved in the strategic management process. They are the people who scan the internal and external environments, formulate and implement objectives, strategies, and policies, and evaluate and control the results. The people with direct responsibility for this process are the board of directors and top management. The chief executive officer (CEO), the chief operations officer (COO) or president, the executive vice-president, and the vice-presidents in charge of operating divisions and functional areas typically form the top management group. Traditionally, boards of directors have engaged in strategic management only to the extent that they passively approved proposals from top management and hired and fired their CEOs. Their role, however, is changing dramatically. The strategic management process, therefore, is also changing.

3.1

CORPORATE BOARD OF DIRECTORS

Directors conduct a far different meeting from those in the past. Pressures—from regulatory agencies, shareholders, lenders, and the public—have practically forced greater awareness of directors' responsibilities. The board as a rubber stamp or a bastion of the "old-boy" selection system has largely been replaced by more active, more professional boards.[1]

Even in the recent past, boards of directors functioned rather passively. Members were selected because of their prestige in the community, regardless of their knowledge of the specific functioning of the corporation they were to oversee. Traditionally, members of the board were requested to simply approve proposals by top management or the firm's legal counsel, and the more important board activities generally were conducted by an executive committee composed of insiders.[2] Even now, the boards in some family-owned corporations are more figureheads than overseers; they exist on paper because the laws of incorporation require their presence, but rarely, if ever, do they question management's plans.

Lee Iacocca describes how such a situation existed at the Ford Motor Company under Henry Ford II.

> The Ford Motor Company had gone public in 1956, but Henry never really accepted the change. As he saw it, he was like his grandfather, the rightful owner—Henry Ford, Prop. (Proprietor)—and the company was his to do [with] as he pleased. When it came to the board, he, more than most CEO's, believed in the mushroom treatment—throw manure on them and keep them in the dark. That attitude, of course, was fostered by the fact that Henry and his family, with only 12% of the stock, held on to 40% of the voting rights.[3]

Over the past decade, stockholders and various interest groups have seriously questioned the role of the board of directors. A recent survey by the National Association of Corporate Directors, for example, revealed that almost half of stockholders believe that directors ignore stockholder interests when considering a merger.[4] As a result of these and other doubts, the general public has become more aware and more critical of many boards' apparent lack of responsibility for corporate activities. Who is responsible for radioactive leaks in nuclear power plants? For the manufacture and sale of unsafe toys? For not properly safeguarding employees from hazards in the workplace? For bribery attempts by corporate officers? Can boards, especially those of multinational corporations, realistically monitor the decisions and actions of corporate employees in countries halfway around the world? What are the legal liabilities of a board for the actions taken by the corporation?

Responsibilities of the Board

At this time, there are no national standards defining the accountability or responsibility of a board of directors. The law offers little guidance on this question. Specific requirements of directors vary, depending on the state in which the corporate charter is issued. According to Conference Board reports authored by Bacon and Brown, "State corporation laws give boards of directors rather sweeping powers couched in general language that does not specify to whom they are accountable nor clarify what it is they are accountable for."[5] There is, nevertheless, a developing consensus concerning the major responsibilities of a board.

The board of directors of a corporation is appointed or elected by the stockholders for the following purposes:

- To oversee the management of the corporation's assets;
- To establish or approve the corporation's mission, objectives, strategy, and policies;
- To review management's actions in light of the financial performance of the corporation; and
- To hire and fire the principal operating officers of the corporation.

In a legal sense, the board is required to direct the affairs of the corporation but not to manage them. It is charged by law to act with "due care." As Bacon and Brown put it, "Directors must act with that degree of diligence, care and skill which ordinarily prudent men would exercise under similar circumstances in like positions."[6] If a director or the board as a whole fails to act with due care and, as a result, the corporation is in some way harmed, the careless director or directors can be held personally liable for the harm done.

For example, after the Federal Deposit Insurance Corporation (FDIC) put together a $4.5 billion package to rescue the failing Continental Illinois Bank of Chicago in 1984, it dismissed nine of the bank's sixteen directors. Two other directors resigned. Even though each director had sworn the Joint Oath of the National Bank Directors to "diligently and honestly administer the affairs" of the bank, the FDIC contended that the directors should have monitored more carefully what was happening at Continental Illinois.[7] Another example was provided in 1986: A federal court in Delaware fined directors of Trans Union Corporation, a railcar-leasing company, for negligence in connection with the sale of the company.[8]

The increasing popularity of personal liability insurance for board members suggests that a number of people on boards of directors are becoming very concerned that they might be held personally responsible not only for their own actions but also for the actions of the corporation as a whole. This concern is reinforced by the requirement of the Securities and Exchange Commission (SEC) that a majority of directors must sign the Annual Report Form 10-K. A recent survey found that of 606 major U.S. corporations, 51% go beyond the SEC requirement by requiring that *all* directors sign the 10-K.[9]

Directors must make certain, in addition to these duties, that the corporation is managed in accordance with the laws of the state in which it is incorporated. They must also ensure management's adherence to laws and regulations, such as those dealing with the issuance of securities, insider trading, and other conflict-of-interest situations. They must also be aware of the needs and demands of constituent groups, so that they can achieve a judicious balance among the interests of these diverse groups while ensuring the continued functioning of the corporation. For example, the Delaware Supreme Court in 1986 concluded that when Revlon's directors authorized management to negotiate the sale of the company, the legal duties of the directors changed. In the court's words, the directors' role became that of "*auctioneers* charged with getting the best price for the stockholders in the sale of the company!"[10]

Role of the Board in Strategic Management

In terms of strategic management, a board of directors has three basic tasks.[11]

- **To initiate and determine.** A board can delineate a corporation's mission and specify strategic options to its management. Most boards still leave this task to top management.
- **To evaluate and influence.** A board can examine management's proposals, decisions, and actions; agree or disagree with them; give advice and offer suggestions; outline alternatives.
- **To monitor.** By acting through its committees, a board can keep abreast of developments both inside and outside the corporation. It can thus bring to management's attention developments it might have overlooked.

Even though every board will be composed of people with varying degrees of commitment to the corporation, we can make some generalizations about a board of directors as a whole, in its attempt to fulfill these three basic tasks. We can characterize a board as being at a specific point on a continuum, on the basis of its degree of involvement in corporate strategic affairs. As types, boards can range from phantom boards with no real involvement to catalyst boards with a very high degree of involvement. Highly involved boards tend to be very active. They take their tasks of initiating, evaluating and influencing, and monitoring very seriously; they provide advice when necessary and keep management alert. As depicted in Fig. 3.1, they can be deeply involved in the strategic management process. At Texas Instruments, for example, the board attends a four-day strategic planning conference each year, in which they discuss business opportunities of the next decade. Several members of the board also attend, during the following two days, management meetings attended by 500 managers from throughout the company.[12] Other corporations with active participation boards are Mead Corporation, Rohm and Haas, and Dayton-Hudson.[13]

As a board becomes less involved in the affairs of the corporation, it moves farther to the left on the continuum. On the far left are passive

FIGURE 3.1
Board of Directors Continuum.

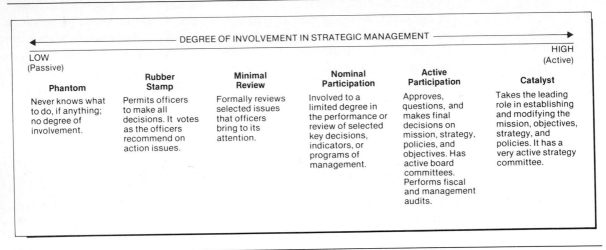

boards that typically *never* initiate or determine strategy unless a crisis occurs. For example, when Mellon Bank Corporation suffered its first loss in its 118-year history in 1987, stockholders claimed that the directors had failed in their responsibilities. "The officers (management) were determining policy and the directors were just sitting around uninformed," reported a former director who had resigned from Mellon's board in 1984.[14]

Generally, the smaller the corporation, the less active is its board of directors. The board tends to be dominated by directors who are also owner-managers of the company. Other directors are usually friends or family members. As the corporation grows and goes public, however, the boards become more active in terms of roles and responsibilities.[15]

Most large, publicly owned corporations probably have boards that operate at some point between nominal and active participation. Few have catalyst boards, except for those with major problems (that is, pending bankruptcies, mergers, or acquisitions).

A survey of the nation's 2,235 largest commercial banks by Egon Zehnder International, a management consulting firm, supports this characterization of boards of directors.[16] The chief executive officers were asked:

"What phrase best characterizes the role of your Board of Directors in the *strategic* success of your bank?" They responded as follows:

- Critical contributor to our strategic success (catalyst)   5%
- Very active contributor (active participation)   22%
- Somewhat active contributor (nominal participation)   45%

- Passive (minimal review)   21%
- Largely ceremonial (phantom/rubber stamp)   8%

Many CEOs and board members do not want the board to be involved in strategy matters at more than a superficial level. Kenneth Andrews, an authority on strategic managers, suggests why:

> Many chief executive officers, rejecting the practicality of conscious strategy, preside over unstated, incremental, or intuitive strategies that have never been articulated or analyzed—and therefore could not be deliberated by the board. Others do not believe their outside directors know enough or have time enough to do more than assent to strategic recommendations. Still others may keep discussions of strategy within management to prevent board transgression onto management turf and consequent reduction of executives' power to shape by themselves the future of their companies.[17]

Nevertheless, recent surveys of directors reveal that one of the most pressing concerns of directors is strategic planning.[18] "In the past," said one director, "strategic planning has been exclusively a management function. But now it has been intertwined with the role and functions of the board."[19] Therefore, board members are now coming to think of themselves as participants in the corporation's strategic management.[20]

Board Membership: Inside versus Outside Directors

The boards of most publicly owned corporations are comprised of both inside and outside directors. Inside directors are typically officers or executives employed by the corporation. The outside director may be an executive of another firm but is not an employee of the board's corporation. A recent survey of large corporations in manufacturing and service industries found outsiders to account for almost 70% of board membership. The majority of these outside directors owned fewer than 500 shares—a rather minuscule amount—of the corporations for which they served.[21] A survey of small companies found that outsiders comprise only 40% of the average board.[22]

A recent Hay Survey of Directors reported outside directors to be compensated for their work at an average rate of $26,095 by industrial companies and $22,468 by financial companies. However, some such as Allied Signal pay as much as $45,000 annually. Generally, the compensation is composed of an annual retainer fee plus board- and committee-meeting fees.[23] Almost 60% of smaller companies compensated their directors. The average retainer fee was $4,300 and the average meeting fee, $510.[24] Few, if any, insider (management) directors are paid for assuming this extra duty.

The American Law Institute, an association of 1,800 leading lawyers, judges, and law professors, proposes in its "Principles of Corporate Governance and Structure: Restatement and Recommendations" that all corporations be required to have outside directors form a majority of the membership of their boards of directors.[25] The Securities and Exchange Commission (SEC) now requires corporations whose stock is listed on the New York Exchange to have at least two outside directors. The ALI and the SEC apparently take the view that outside directors are less biased and more likely to evaluate objectively management's performance than are inside directors. This view is in agreement with **agency theory**—a theory which states that problems arise in corporations because the agents (top management) no longer bear the full results of their decisions unless they own a substantial amount of stock in the corporation. The theory thus suggests that a majority of a board needs to be from outside the firm, so that top management is prevented from acting selfishly to the detriment of the stockholders.[26] Vance, an authority on boards of directors, contends, however, that outside directors are less effective than are insiders because the outsiders have "questionable interest, availability, or competency."[27] Although research by Kesner supports Vance's argument, there is some evidence that the amount of stock owned by directors can also have some impact on a corporation's stock price and profits.[28] Research by Pearce found that the directors' orientation toward the external environment was more associated with corporate performance than was the ratio of outsiders to insiders.[29] Nevertheless, the general trend seems to be one of an increasing percentage of outsiders on the boards of U.S. corporations.

Surveys of manufacturing companies disclose that a majority of the outside directors are presidents, managing partners, or chairmen of the boards of other corporations. Outside directors come from a variety of organizations, some even from the ministry, but a majority of them come from the manufacturing, banking, law, and investment industries. With the current concern for productivity, there appears to be a movement toward having more executives on boards with strong operating experience and fewer investment bankers and attorneys.

In 1986, 44% of corporations surveyed had women on their boards; 30% had members from minority groups. White males held 92.1% of directors' positions in 1987 compared to 95.4% in 1982.[30]

A majority of the inside directors include the president, chairman of the board, and vice-presidents; the rest are key officers or former employees. Lower-level operating employees, including managers, form only 1% of the total employee board membership of the companies surveyed.[31]

Codetermination

The dearth of nonmanagement-employee directors on the boards of U.S. corporations may be changing. Codetermination, the inclusion of a corporation's workers on its board, began only recently in the United States. Critics raise the issue of conflict of interest. Can a member of the board, who is privy to confidential managerial information, function for example as a union leader whose primary duty is to fight for the best benefits for his members?

The addition of Douglas Fraser, President of the United Auto Workers, to the board of Chrysler Corporation in 1980 was a controversial move designed to placate the union while Chrysler was attempting to avoid bankruptcy. With the replacement of Fraser in 1984 by Owen Bieber, the newly elected president of the UAW, a seat for labor in the Chrysler boardroom appeared to become permanent. Eastern Airlines, Western Air Lines, and Wheeling-Pittsburgh Steel Corporation have also added representatives from employee associations to their boards. As did Chrysler, these corporations have appointed employee directors in concordance with an agreement with their unions, that the unions accept major pay concessions.

Research in fourteen other U.S. firms with workers on the board found that "worker board representation is no guarantee that workers will have an effective role in the governance of the organization."[32] The need to work for the corporation as a whole as well as to represent the workers creates role conflict and stress among the worker directors—thus cutting into their effectiveness.

While the movement to place employees on the boards of directors of U.S. companies is only just beginning, the European experience reveals an increasing acceptance of worker participation on corporate boards. The Federal Republic of Germany pioneered the practice with its Co-Determination Acts of 1951 and 1976, and Works Constitution Act of 1952. Worker representatives in the coal, iron, and steel industries were given equal status with management on policy-making boards. Management in other industries, however, retained a two-thirds majority on policy-making boards.

Other countries, such as Sweden, Denmark, Norway, and Austria have passed similar codetermination legislation. Belgium, Luxembourg, France, Italy, Ireland, and the Netherlands use worker councils to work closely with management, but are seriously considering moving closer toward the German model.

However, the British government in the 1960s established the codetermination concept in nationalized industries but found it to be a failure. It did not cause better labor-management relations.[33] And recent research on German codetermination found that legislation requiring firms to put employee representatives on their boards "lowered dividend payments, led to a more conservative investment policy, and reduced firm values."[34]

Interlocking Directorates

Boards that are primarily composed of outside directors will not necessarily be more objective than those primarily composed of insiders. CEOs may nominate for board membership chief executives from other firms, for the exchange of important information and a guarantee of the stability of key marketplace relationships. One or more individuals serving on the boards of directors of two or more corporations create an *interlocking directorate*. Although the Clayton Act and the Banking Act of 1933 prohibit interlocking directorates by U.S. companies competing in the same industry, interlocking continues to occur in almost all corporations, especially large ones.[35] Research has shown that the larger the firm, the greater the number of different corporations represented on its board of directors. Interlocking occurs because large firms have a large impact on other corporations; and these other corporations, in turn, have some control over the firm's inputs and marketplace. Interlocking directorates are also a useful method for gaining both inside information about an uncertain environment and objective expertise about a firm's strategy.[36] Family-owned corporations, however, are less likely to have interlocking directorates than are corporations with highly dispersed stock ownership, probably because family-owned corporations do not like to dilute their corporate control by adding outsiders to boardroom discussions.[37]

Corporations also have members of their management teams on the boards of other corporations. In 1985, 74% of inside board members of large companies sat on one or more boards besides their own.[38] General Motors, for example, has 284 connections (11 through ownership, 67 through direct interlocking, and 206 through indirect interlocking).[39]

Nomination and Election of Board Members

Traditionally, the CEO of the corporation decided whom to invite to board membership and merely asked the stockholders for approval. The chief criteria used by most CEOs in nominating board members were that the persons be compatible with the CEO and that they bring some prestige to the board.

There are some dangers, however, in allowing the CEO free reign in nominating directors. The CEO might select only board members who, in the CEO's opinion, will not disturb the company's policies and functioning. More importantly, directors selected by the CEO often feel that they should go along with any proposals made by the CEO. Thus, board members find themselves accountable to the very management they are charged to oversee. Because of the likelihood of these occurrences, there is an increasing tendency for a special board committee to nominate new outside board members. A survey by Heidrick and Struggles revealed that the percentage of Fortune 1000 corporations using nominating committees to select new directors rose from 9% in 1976 to 90% in 1986.[40]

Term of Office

A recent study by the Hay Group reports that 46% of U.S. corporations surveyed elect all directors annually for a one-year term of office. In contrast, 35% elect directors for a three-year term.[41]

Virtually every corporation whose directors serve terms of more than one year divide the board into classes and stagger elections so that only a portion of the board stands for election each year. Arguments in favor of this practice are that it provides continuity by reducing the chance of an abrupt turnover in its membership and that it reduces the likelihood of people unfriendly to management being elected through cumulative voting. Among the many companies recently attempting to switch from one-year terms to longer-term staggered elections to reduce the likelihood of a takeover are Beatrice Foods, Union Oil, Sterling Drug, and Quaker Oats.

Cumulative Voting

The practice of cumulative voting allows a stockholder to concentrate his or her votes in an election of directors. Cumulative voting is required by law in eighteen states and is mandatory on request or permitted as a corporate option in thirty-two other states or territories. Under cumulative voting, the number of votes allowed is determined by multiplying the number of voting shares held by the number of directors to be elected. Thus, a person owning 1,000 shares in an election of 12 directors would have 12,000 votes. These votes may then be distributed in any manner—for instance, divided evenly (or unevenly) between two directors or concentrated on one. This method is contrasted with straight voting in which the stockholder votes simply yes or no for each director to be elected.[42] Although few stockholders use the privilege of cumulative voting, it is a powerful way for them to influence a board of directors. For example, a minority of stockholders could concentrate their voting power and elect one or more directors of their choice. In contrast, straight voting allows the holders of the majority of outstanding shares to prevent the election of any director not to their liking.

Those in favor of cumulative voting argue that it is the only system under which a candidate not on the management slate can hope to be elected to the board. Otherwise, under straight voting, an entrenched management could insulate itself from criticism and use the board as a rubber stamp. Critics of cumulative voting argue that it allows the board to deteriorate into interest groups more concerned with protecting their own special concerns than in working for the good of the corporation. This could become a serious problem if the corporation is in danger of being bought or controlled by another firm. For instance, by purchasing some shares, another firm (such as a potential acquirer) could, through cumulative voting, elect enough board members that it could directly influence or even incapacitate the board. It is for this reason that a number of U.S. corporations have recently re-incorporated in the state of Delaware where cumulative voting is not mandatory.[43] Nevertheless, the practice of cumulative voting has been recommended as a way to achieve minority representation on the boards of directors of major corporations.

Organization of the Board

The size of the board is determined by the corporation's charter and its bylaws in compliance with state laws. Although some states require a minimum number of board members, most corporations have quite a bit of discretion in determination of board size. Surveys of U.S. business corporations reveal that the average *privately* held company has eight board members who meet four times a year, as compared to the average *publicly* held corporation with thirteen directors who meet seven times a year. In addition, there appears to be a direct relationship between company size as measured by sales volume and the number of people on the board.[44]

Chairman

A fairly common practice in U.S. corporations is to have the chairman of the board also serve as the chief executive officer. The CEO concentrates on strategy, planning, external relations, and responsibility to the board. The chairman's responsibility is to ensure that the board and its committees perform their functions as stated in their charter. Further, the chairman schedules board meetings and presides over the annual stockholders' meeting. In over 75% of the Fortune 500 corporations, the CEO also serves as chairman of the board.[45]

Committees

The most effective boards of large corporations accomplish much of their work through committees.[46] Although the committees do not have legal duties, unless detailed in the bylaws, most committees are granted full power to act with the authority of the board between board meetings. Typical standing committees are the executive committee, audit committee, compensation committee, finance committee, and nominating committee. The executive committee is formed from local directors who can meet between board meetings to attend to matters that must be settled quickly. This committee acts as an extension of the board and, consequently, may have almost unrestricted authority in certain areas. A recent survey reports that in 68% of industrial and 72% of financial corporations, the executive committee includes at least a majority of outside directors.[47] Other less common committees are the strategic planning, social responsibility, investments (pension funds), stock options, conflict-of-interest, and research/technology committees.[48]

Trends for the Future

The role of the board of directors in the strategic management of the corporation is likely to be a more active one in the future. Change is more likely to be evolutionary than radical or revolutionary. Different boards are at different levels of maturity and will not be changing in the same direction or at the same speed.[49] There are, nevertheless, some current overall trends that should continue into the near-term future. Some of these are the following:[50]

- Boards will be held to increasingly high standards of conduct. Society will pay more attention to the board as the corporation's overseer of ethical, legal, and social standards.

- Directors will increasingly recognize that they are responsible for the long-run best interests of the corporation as a whole, not merely the interests of the stockholders. Although a key concern of strategic managers today is "shareholder value," corporations will need to pay more attention to other concerned groups in their task environments.

- There will be fewer successful law suits against boards as the legal system makes liability laws more rational. Already many U.S. state legislatures, beginning with Delaware, have passed laws limiting a director's personal liability as long as he/she acts in good faith, follows laws, and avoids conflicts of interest.[51]

- The board will be increasingly active in the evaluation and development of strategies. Expect more boards in corporations of all sizes to create and use a strategic planning committee.

- Directors will fulfill their larger responsibilities without a corresponding increase in the time they spend on board business. Although the average outside director of a typical large corporation spends 145 hours annually on board business, this amount should stabilize and could even drop as information provided to board members is made more appropriate and timely.[52]

- Corporations will work harder to select and keep active, qualified board members. John Nash, President of the National Association of Corporate Directors, has proposed a certification program that ensures the selection of competent directors. Although it is currently a pilot program, Nash predicts broad acceptance of the concept by the mid-1990s.[53]

- Boards will become more assertive in their selections of directors. More boards will use nominating committees to select an increasingly diverse pool of qualified candidates. Expect an increasing use of "professional" directors who will take the time to get involved in corporate affairs, to keep the board current on company activities, and to probe into areas in which most outside directors would not normally be knowledgeable.

- Directors will become more independent of the CEO. Although there will continue to be a commonality of purpose, the board will become more sensitive to its responsibility of being objective and independent of top management.

The importance of the board of directors and its likely future is aptly summarized by James Worthy and Robert Neuschel in their study on corporate governance:

> Boards of directors will be importantly concerned with helping to achieve the balance (between the degree of freedom necessary for business to function profitably and the need for society to preserve other freedoms and institutions) in the years ahead. More and more, society will expect the board to provide the fine line between achieving the economic objectives of the corporation and meeting the broader needs of society.[54]

3.2

TOP MANAGEMENT

The top management function is usually conducted by the CEO of the corporation in coordination with the COO or president, executive vice-president, and vice-presidents of divisions and functional areas. As we mentioned earlier in this chapter, some corporations combine the office of CEO with that of chairman of the board of directors. Although this plan has the advantage of freeing the president or COO of the firm from many strategic responsibilities so that he or she can focus primarily on operational matters, it has been criticized because it gives the combined CEO/chairman too much power and serves to undercut the independence of the board.[55]

Responsibilities of Top Management

Top management, and especially the CEO, is responsible to the board of directors for the overall management of the corporation. It is tasked with getting things accomplished through and with others, in order to meet the corporate objectives. Top management's job is thus multidimensional and is oriented toward the welfare of the total organization. Specific top management tasks vary from firm to firm and are developed from an analysis of the mission, objectives, strategies, and key activities of the corporation. But all top managers are people who see the business as a whole, who can balance the present needs of the business against the needs of the future, and who can make final and effective decisions.[56] The chief executive officer, in particular, must successfully handle three responsibilities crucial to the effective strategic management of the corporation: (1) fulfill key roles; (2) provide corporate leadership; and (3) manage the strategic planning process.

Fulfill Key Roles

From five weeks of in-depth observation of five chief executives, Henry Mintzberg concluded that the job of a top manager contains ten interrelated *roles*. The importance of each role and the amount of time demanded by each probably varies from one job to another. These roles are as follows:

- **Figurehead:** Acts as legal and symbolic head; performs obligatory social, ceremonial, or legal duties (hosts retirement dinners, luncheons for employees, and plant dedications; attends civic affairs; signs contracts on behalf of firm).
- **Leader:** Motivates, develops, and guides subordinates; oversees staffing, training, and associated activities (introduces Management By Objectives [MBO], develops a challenging work climate, provides a sense of direction, acts as a role model).
- **Liaison:** Maintains a network of contacts and information sources outside top management, in order to obtain information and assistance (meets with key people from the task environment, meets formally and informally with corporate division managers and with CEOs of other firms).

- **Monitor:** Seeks and obtains information needed for understanding the corporation and its environments; acts as nerve center for the corporation (reviews status reports from vice-presidents, reviews key indicators of corporate performance, scans *Wall Street Journal* and key trade journals, joins select clubs and societies).

- **Disseminator:** Transmits information to the rest of the top management team and other key people in the corporation (chairs staff meetings, transmits policy letters, communicates five-year plans).

- **Spokesman:** Transmits information to key groups and people in the task environment (prepares annual report to stockholders, talks to the Chamber of Commerce, states corporate policy to the media, participates in advertising campaigns, speaks before congressional committees).

- **Entrepreneur:** Searches the corporation and its environment for projects to improve products, processes, procedures, and structures: then supervises the design and implementation of these projects (introduces cost reduction programs, makes plant trips to divisions, changes forecasting system, brings in subcontract work to level the work load, reorganizes the corporation).

- **Disturbance Handler:** Takes corrective action in times of disturbance or crisis (personally talks with key creditors, interest groups, congressional committees, union leaders; establishes investigative committees; revises objectives, strategies, and policies).

- **Resource Allocator:** Allocates corporate resources by making and/or approving decisions (reviews budgets, revises program scheduling, initiates strategic planning, plans personnel load, sets objectives).

- **Negotiator:** Represents the corporation in negotiating important agreements; may speak directly with key representatives of groups in the task environment or work through a negotiator; negotiates disagreements within the corporation by working with conflicting division heads (works with labor negotiator; resolves jurisdictional disputes between divisions; negotiates with key creditors, suppliers, and customers).[57]

Provide Corporate Leadership

People who work in corporations look to top management for leadership. Their doing so, says Drucker, reflects a need for standard setting and example setting.[58] According to Mintzberg, this is a key role of any manager.

Corporate leadership is important because it sets the tone for the entire corporation. In a survey of top investment analysts and money managers, almost half responded that their personal evaluation of top management is worth 60% of their total evaluation of the company.[59] This is in agreement with research reporting that individual CEOs have a strong impact on the strategic direction of their firms.[60]

Most middle managers look to their boss for guidance and direction and so tend to emulate the characteristics and style of successful top managers. People in an organization want to have a vision of what they are working toward—a sense of mission. Only top management is in the position to specify and communicate this sense of mission to the general work force. Top management's enthusiasm (or lack of it) about the corporation tends to be contagious.

For instance, a positive attitude characterizing many well-known industrial leaders—such as Alfred Sloan at General Motors, Ed Watson at IBM, Robert Wood at Sears, Ray Kroc at McDonald's, and Lee Iacocca at Chrysler—have energized their respective corporations. In their book *In Search of Excellence,* Peters and Waterman report that "associated with almost every excellent company was a strong leader (or two) who seemed to have a lot to do with making his company excellent in the first place."[61] A two-year study by McKinsey & Co. found the CEOs of midsized, high-growth companies to be "almost inevitably consummate salesmen who radiate enormous contagious self-confidence" and "take pains to communicate their strong sense of mission to all who come in contact with them."[62]

Chief executive officers with a clear sense of mission are often perceived as dynamic and charismatic leaders. They are able to command respect and to influence strategy formulation and implementation because they tend to have three key characteristics.

1. The CEO *presents a role* for others to identify with and to follow. The leader sets an example in terms of behavior and dress. The CEO's attitudes and values concerning the corporation's purpose and activities are clear-cut and constantly communicated in words and deeds.

2. The CEO *articulates a transcendent goal* for the corporation. The CEO's vision of the corporation goes beyond the petty complaints and grievances of the average work day. Because this vision puts activities and conflicts in a new perspective, it gives renewed meaning to everyone's work activities and enables them to see beyond the details of their own jobs to the functioning of the total corporation. As John W. Teets, CEO and Chairman of The Greyhound Corporation, states, "Management's job is to see the company not as it is . . . but as it can become."[63]

3. The CEO *communicates high performance standards* but also *shows confidence* in the followers' abilities to meet these standards. No leader ever improved performance by setting easily attainable goals that provide no challenge. The CEO must be willing to follow through by coaching people.[64]

Manage Strategic Planning

Top management must initiate and manage the strategic planning process. To specify the corporate mission, delineate corporate objectives, and formulate appropriate strategies and policies, it must take a very long-range view. As depicted in Fig. 3.2, the ideal time horizon for management's planning varies according to level in the corporate hierarchy. The president of a corporation, for example, should allocate the largest proportion of planning time to looking two to four years ahead. One reason given for the

FIGURE 3.2

"Ideal" Allocations of Time for Planning in the "Average" Company.

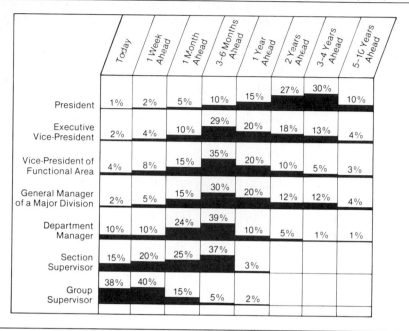

	Today	1 Week Ahead	1 Month Ahead	3-6 Months Ahead	1 Year Ahead	2 Years Ahead	3-4 Years Ahead	5-10 Years Ahead
President	1%	2%	5%	10%	15%	27%	30%	10%
Executive Vice-President	2%	4%	10%	29%	20%	18%	13%	4%
Vice-President of Functional Area	4%	8%	15%	35%	20%	10%	5%	3%
General Manager of a Major Division	2%	5%	15%	30%	20%	12%	12%	4%
Department Manager	10%	10%	24%	39%	10%	5%	1%	1%
Section Supervisor	15%	20%	25%	37%	3%			
Group Supervisor	38%	40%	15%	5%	2%			

Source: Reprinted with permission of The Free Press, a division of Macmillan, Inc. from *Top Management Planning* by G. A. Steiner. Copyright © 1969 by the Trustees of Columbia University in the City of New York.

worldwide economic success of many Japanese corporations is the reputed ability of their top managers to conceptualize corporate mission and strategy far into the future. Mr. Ishihara, President of Nissan, has been quoted as saying "In what I do now, I am thinking twenty or thirty years ahead."[65] A department manager, however, should put the heaviest proportion of planning time on looking only three to six *months* ahead.

To accomplish its tasks, top management must use information provided by three key corporate groups: a long-range planning staff, divisional or SBU managers, and managers of functional departments.

A **long-range planning staff** typically consists of six people, headed by a senior vice-president or director of corporate planning.[66] In order to generate data for strategic decisions by top management, it continuously monitors both internal and external environments. It also suggests to top management possible changes in the corporate mission, objectives, strategies, and policies. Although only one in five companies with sales under $100 million have a separate, formal planning department, nearly all corporations with sales of at least $2 billion have such departments.[67] The size of corporate planning staffs in large corporations is currently decreasing, however, as strategic planning responsibilities are being shifted to line managers.[68]

Divisional or SBU managers, with the assistance of the long-range planning staff and with input from their product managers, perform the strategic planning function for each division. These SBU managers typically initiate proposals for top management's consideration and/or respond to requests for such proposals by corporate headquarters. They may also be tasked to carry out strategies and policies decided upon at the corporate level for organization-wide implementation. These division managers typically work with the heads of various functional units within the division to develop the appropriate functional strategies for the implementation of planned business-level strategies.

Managers of functional departments (marketing, engineering, R&D managers, etc.) report directly either to divisional managers in a multidivision corporation or to top management if the corporation has no divisions. Although they may develop specific functional strategies, they generally do so within the framework of divisional or corporate strategies. They also respond to initiatives from above that ask them for input or require them to develop strategies for the implementation of divisional plans.

Characteristics of Top Management Tasks

Top management tasks have two characteristics that differentiate them from other managerial tasks.[69] First, *very few of them are continuous*. Rarely does a manager work on these tasks all day. The responsibilities, however, are always present, even though the tasks themselves are sporadic. And when the tasks do arise, they are of crucial significance, such as the selection of a person to head a new division.

Mintzberg reports that the activities of most executives are characterized by brevity, variety, and fragmentation: "Half of the observed activities were completed in less than nine minutes and only one-tenth took more than an hour. In effect, the managers were seldom able or willing to spend much time on any one issue in any one session."[70]

It is likely that serious objective-setting and strategy formulation will not occur in corporations if most top managers are as activity-oriented as those in the Mintzberg study. John De Lorean suggests as much in his comments about "The Fourteenth Floor" (the executive offices) of General Motors.

> I was trying to bring a set of new eyes to the job of group executive, as one only can do in the first few months in a new position. But I had no time to perform the real function of my position. Instead, I was being tied down and totally consumed by this constant parade of paperwork and meetings.[71]

The second characteristic of top management tasks is that *they require a wide range of capabilities and temperaments*. Some tasks require the capacity to analyze and carefully weigh alternative courses of action. Some require an awareness of and an interest in people, whereas others call for the ability to pursue abstract ideas, concepts, and calculations.

One effect of tasks having these two characteristics is that top managers are often drawn back into the functional work of the corporation. Because their activities are not continuous, people in top management often have unplanned free time. They tend therefore to get caught up in the day-to-day work in manufacturing, marketing, accounting, engineering, or in other operations of the corporation. They may find themselves constantly solving crises that could probably have been better handled by lower-level managers. These managers are also usually fond of protesting, "How can I be expected to drain the swamp when I'm up to my eyeballs in alligators!?"

A second effect of the tasks' characteristics is that top managers tend to perceive only those aspects and responsibilities of the top management function that are compatible with their abilities, experience, and temperaments. And, if the board of directors fails to state explicitly what it considers to be the key responsibilities and activities of top management, the top managers are free to define the job themselves. Therefore, important tasks can be overlooked until a crisis occurs.

Top Management Team

The typical chief executive officer of the largest publicly held U.S. business corporations is around fifty-six years old, draws an average annual salary of $651,000, and has been with the company twenty-three years. Nearly half of these CEOs have graduate degrees. A high proportion are firstborn children who learned early to be family caretakers and mediators.[72] Nevertheless, these top managers are finding the job of the CEO to be increasingly difficult and unpredictable. Therefore, many scholars and executives propose that strategic planning and top management is a job for a team rather than for one person.[73]

The top management team could be organized as a chief executive "office" in which a number of people serve as equals, each with an assigned area of responsibility. Corporations such as DuPont, Schering A. G., Standard Oil of New Jersey, Royal Dutch Shell, Eastman Kodak, and Unilever have taken this approach.

Or the team may consist of one person who carries the title of CEO and several colleagues, each of whom has clearly assigned authority and responsibility for a segment of the top management task. General Motors and Xerox Corporation use this structure. GM's team includes a chairman, a vice-chairman, a chairman of the executive committee, and a president. General Electric has taken a similar approach, although it refers to its four-man top management group as the Corporate Executive Office.

The use of top management teams has increased dramatically from only 8% of large U.S. corporations in the 1960s to 25% in the 1980s.[74] An advantage of the team approach to top management is the sharing of roles, responsibilities, and tasks, a sharing that depends on the strengths and weaknesses of the people involved. It makes more sense for large corporations to put together a top management team to achieve synergy, than to try to find the perfect person to be CEO. Certainly succession problems are minimized by the team approach; decisions can be made even though the CEO has resigned, is incapacitated, or is otherwise absent.

3.3
STRATEGIC MANAGEMENT STYLES

Just as boards of directors vary widely on a continuum of involvement in the strategic management process, so do top management teams. For example, a top management team with low involvement in strategic management will tend to be functionally oriented and will focus its energies on day-to-day operational problems; this type of team is likely either to be disorganized or to have a dominant CEO who continues to identify with his or her old division. In contrast, a top management team with high involvement will be active in long-range planning. It will try to get divisional managers involved in planning so that top management will have more time to scan the environment for challenges and opportunities.

Both the board of directors and top management can be placed on a matrix that reflects four basic styles of corporate strategic management. These styles are depicted in Fig. 3.3.

Chaos Management

When both the board of directors and top management have little involvement in the strategic management process, their style is referred to as chaos

FIGURE 3.3
Strategic Management Styles.

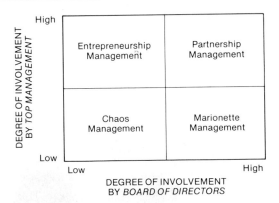

management. The board waits for top management to bring it proposals. Top management is operationally oriented and continues to carry out strategies, policies, and programs specified by the founding entrepreneur who died years ago. The basic strategic philosophy seems to be, "If it was good enough for old J. B., it's good enough for us." There is no strategic management being done here.

Entrepreneurship Management

A corporation with an uninvolved board of directors but a highly involved top management has entrepreneurship management. The board is willing to be used as a rubber stamp for top management's decisions. The CEO, operating alone or with a team, dominates the corporation and its strategic decisions. An example is Control Data Corporation under the leadership of its founder William C. Norris. For twenty-nine years, Norris dominated both the company's top management and its board of directors. Insisting that the company could profit by addressing "society's unmet needs," Norris directed corporate investments into the rejuvenation of ghettos and support of wind-powered generators and tundra farming, among other projects. Although these investments tended to result in losses, few people were willing to challenge his strategic decisions. Some employees even referred to him as "the Pope." A former Control Data executive noted, "More often than not, he's proven his critics wrong, so now his visions aren't challenged."[75]

Marionette Management

Probably the rarest form of strategic management styles, marionette management occurs when the board of directors is deeply involved in strategic decision making, but top management is primarily concerned with operations. Such a style evolves when a board is composed of key stockholders who refuse to delegate strategic decision making to the president. The president is forced into a COO role and can do only what the board allows him to do. This style also occurs when a board fires a CEO but is slow to find a replacement. The COO or executive vice-president stays on as "acting" president or CEO until the selection process is complete. In the meantime, strategic management is firmly in the hands of the board of directors.

This sequence occurred at Winnebago Industries in 1986 when the company's Board of Directors, chaired by its founder, 72-year-old John K. Hanson, took away Ronald Haugen's title as chief executive officer, but left him as company president. No new CEO was named. Hanson, whose family owned 46% of Winnebago's stock, had given up the CEO title in 1983 to President Haugen, a long-time employee. Outside observers noted that although Chairman Hanson did not also hold the title of CEO, he appeared to have taken on the CEO's responsibilities once again.[76]

Partnership Management

Probably the most effective style of strategic management, partnership management is epitomized by a highly involved board and top management. The board and the top management team work closely to establish the corporate mission, objectives, strategies, and policies. Board members are active in committee work and utilize strategic audits to provide feedback to top management on its implementations of agreed-upon strategies and policies. This appears to be the style emerging in a number of successful corporations such as Texas Instruments, Dayton Hudson Corporation, and General Electric Company.

SUMMARY AND CONCLUSION

The strategy-makers of a modern corporation are the board of directors and top management. Both must be actively involved in the strategic management process if the corporation is to have long-term success in accomplishing its mission.

An effective board is the keystone of the modern corporation. Without it, management would tend to focus on short-run problems and solutions or go off on tangents at odds with the basic mission. The personal needs and goals of executives would tend to overrule the interests of the corporation. Even the strongest critics of boards of directors are more interested in improving and upgrading boards than in eliminating them. An active board is critical in determining an organization's mission, objectives, strategy, and policies.

Top management, in contrast, is responsible for the overall functioning of the corporation. People in top management must view the cor-

poration as a whole rather than as a series of functional departments or decentralized divisions. They must constantly visualize and plan for the future, and set objectives, strategies, and policies that will allow the corporation to successfully realize that future. They must set standards and provide a vision not only of what the corporation is but also of what it is trying to become. They must develop working relationships with the board of directors, key staff personnel, and managers from divisions and functional areas.

The interaction between the board of directors and the top management of a corporation usually results in an overall strategic management style. The long-run success of a corporation is best ensured through a partnership style in which both the board and top management are genuinely involved in strategic issues.

DISCUSSION QUESTIONS

1. Does a corporation really need a board of directors? Why or why not?

2. What aspects of a corporation's environment should be represented on a board of directors?

3. Should cumulative voting for the election of board members be *required* by law in all political jurisdictions?

4. Do you agree that a chief executive officer

(CEO), in order to be effective, should fulfill Mintzberg's ten roles?

5. Is partnership management always the best style of strategic management?

6. What is your impression of the approach to strategic management being taken by the strategic managers of CSX Corporation in the Integrative Case following this chapter?

NOTES

1. W. L. Shanklin and J. K. Ryans, Jr., "Should the Board Consider This Agenda Item?" *MSU Business Topics* (Winter 1981), p. 35.

2. W. R. Boulton, "The Evolving Board: A Look at the Board's Changing Roles and Information Needs," *Academy of Management Review* (October 1978), p. 828.

3. L. Iacocca, *Iacocca: An Autobiography* (Toronto: Bantam Books, 1984), p. 104.

4. M. L. Weidenbaum, "The Best Defense Against the Raiders," *Business Week* (September 23, 1985), p. 21. This belief is supported by research reporting that the stockholders of an acquiring firm tend to lose in the transaction. See M. Weidenbaum and S. Vogt, "Takeovers and Stockholders: Winners and Losers," *California Management Review* (Summer 1987), pp. 157–168.

5. J. Bacon and J. K. Brown, *Corporate Directorship Practices: Role, Selection and Legal Status of the Board* (New York: The Conference Board, Report no. 646, 1975), p. 7.

6. Bacon and Brown, p. 75.

7. G. Smith, "Who Was Watching the Store?" *Forbes* (July 30, 1984), pp. 37–38.
"Rolling Heads," *Time* (December 17, 1984), p. 69.

8. "What's a Board For, Anyway?" *Business Week* (August 11, 1986), p. 84.

9. L. B. Korn and R. M. Ferry, *Board of Directors Ninth Annual Study* (New York: Korn/Ferry International, February 1982), p. 8.

10. L. A. Hamermesh, "The Director As Auctioneer," *Directors and Boards* (Winter 1987), p. 26.

11. Bacon and Brown, p. 15.

12. K. R. Andrews, "Corporate Strategy as a Vital Function of the Board," *Harvard Business Review* (November-December 1981), p. 175.

13. J. Rosenstein, "Why Don't U.S. Boards Get More Involved in Strategy?" *Long Range Planning* (June 1987), pp. 32–33.

14. C. Mitchell, "Mellon's Chairman Pearson Says Extent of Bad Loans Shocked Outside Directors," *Wall Street Journal* (April 21, 1987), p. 2.

15. C. N. Waldo, *Boards of Directors* (Westport, Conn.: Quorum Books, 1985), p. 2.
A. V. Bruno and J. K. Leidecker, "When to Convert From a Perfunctory Board or 'Staff Meeting' to an Operating Board of Directors," in *Handbook of Business Strategy, 1985/ 1986 Yearbook,* edited by W. D. Guth (Boston: Warren, Gorham, and Lamont, 1985), pp. 29.1–29.9.

16. *Third Annual Banking Survey of Chief Executive Officers* (Atlanta, Chicago, New York: Egon Zehnder International, Inc., 1984), p. 9.

17. K. R. Andrews, "Directors' Responsibility for Corporate Strategy," *Harvard Business Review* (November-December 1980), p. 30.

18. Annual survey of Korn/Ferry International as reported by A. Bennett, "Losing Ground? Surveyed Firms Report Fewer Women Directors," *Wall Street Journal* (July 17, 1987), p. 17.

19. T. R. Horton, "The Case for Planning Committees," *Directors & Boards* (Summer 1984), p. 26.

20. A. Tashakori and W. Boulton, "A Look to the Board's Role in Planning," *Journal of Business Strategy* (Winter 1983), pp. 64–70.

21. E. Mruk and J. Giardina, *Organization and Compensation of Boards of Directors* (New York: Financial Executives Institute, Arthur Young & Co., 1981), pp. 11 and 39.
A. Patton and J. C. Baker, "Why Won't Directors Rock the Boat?" *Harvard Business Review* (November-December 1987), p. 11.

22. R. J. Bronstein, "Good Pay on Small Boards," *Directors and Boards* (Spring 1987), pp. 36–37.

23. D. R. Simpson, "Board Fees and Benefits 1987," *Directors and Boards* (Spring 1987), pp. 33–37.

24. R. J. Bronstein, p. 36.

25. K. R. Andrews, "The American Law Institute's Proposals for Regulating Corporate Governance," *Harvard Business Review* (November-December 1982), p. 34.

26. R. D. Kosnik, "Greenmail: A Study of Board Performance in Corporate Governance," *Administrative Science Quarterly* (June 1987), pp. 163–185.
B. D. Baysinger and C. P. Zeithaml, "A Contingency Approach to Corporate Strategy and Board Composition: Theory and Empirical Research," Paper presented at the Annual Meetings of the Academy of Management, San Diego, August, 1985.

27. S. C. Vance, *Corporate Leadership: Boards, Directors, and Strategy* (New York: McGraw-Hill Book Company, 1983), p. 274.

28. I. F. Kesner, "Directors Stock Ownership and Organizational Performance: An Investigation of Fortune 500 Companies," *Journal of Management* (Fall 1987), pp. 499–507.
"A Little Ownership By Directors Is Good For Business," *Business Week* (December 8, 1986), p. 24.

29. J. A. Pearce, "The Relationship of Internal versus External Orientations to Financial Measures of Strategic Performance," *Strategic Management Journal* (December 1983), pp. 297–306.

30. P. Harrison, "On the Other Side of the Roadblock," *Directors and Boards* (Fall 1986), pp. 40–41; and *Wall Street Journal* (January 1, 1988), p. 1.

31. E. S. Buffa, "Making American Manufacturing Competitive," *California Management Review* (Spring 1984), p. 39.
J. Bacon, *Corporate Directorship Practices: Membership and Committees of the Board* (New York: The Conference Board, Report no. 588, 1973), pp. 28–29.

32. T. H. Hammer and R. N. Stern, "Worker Representation on Company Boards of Directors," *Proceedings, Academy of Management,* 1983, p. 368.

33. R. J. Kuhne, *Co-Determination in Business* (New York: Praeger Publishers, 1980), pp. 41–71.

34. L. H. Clark, Jr., "What Economists Say about Business—and Baboons," *Wall Street Journal* (June 7, 1983), p. 33. Article summarizes a research paper by G. Benelli, C. Loderer, and T. Lys presented to the Interlaken Seminar on Analysis and Ideology, Interlaken, Switzerland, 1983.

For further information on the German experience see articles by Thimm and by Thelen in the *California Management Review* (Spring 1987), pp. 115–148. The more radical Swedish approach is discussed by H. G. Jones in "Scenarios for Industrial Relations: Sweden Evolves a New Consensus," *Long Range Planning* (June 1987), pp. 65–76.

35. M. H. Bazerman and F. D. Schoorman, "A Limited Rationality Model of Interlocking Directorates," *Academy of Management Review* (April 1983), pp. 206–217.

M. Ornstein, "Interlocking Directorates in Canada: Intercorporate or Class Alliance?" *Administrative Science Quarterly* (June 1984), pp. 210–231.

36. R. S. Burt, "Cooptive Corporate Actor Networks: A Reconsideration of Interlocking Directorates Involving American Manufacturing," *Administrative Science Quarterly* (December 1980), p. 559.

L. B. Stearns and M. S. Mizruchi, "Broken-Tie Reconstitution and the Functions of Interorganizational Interlocks: A Reexamination," *Administrative Science Quarterly* (December 1986), pp. 522–538.

37. For a more in-depth discussion of this topic, refer to J. M. Pennings, *Interlocking Directorates* (San Francisco: Jossey-Bass, 1980), and M. S. Mizruchi, *The American Corporate Network 1904–1974* (Beverly Hills, Calif.: Sage Publications, 1982).

38. Patton and Baker.

39. Burt, p. 566.

40. G. R. Roche, "Committees Come to the Fore," *Directors and Boards* (Fall 1986), pp. 22–23.

41. R. C. Ochsner, "Directors Pay Develops Into a Dynamic Package," *Directors and Boards* (February 1986), p. 46.

42. Bacon, pp. 7–8.

43. A. C. Regan and A. Reichel, " 'Shark Repellents': How to Avoid Hostile Takeovers," *Long Range Planning* (December 1985), p. 62.

44. Korn and Ferry, p. 3; and Mruk and Giardina, p. 39.

45. I. F. Kesner, B. Victor, and B. T. Lamont, "Board Composition and the Commission of Illegal Acts: An Investigation of Fortune 500 Companies," *Academy of Management Journal* (December 1986), pp. 789–799.

46. J. C. Worthy and R. P. Neuschel, *Emerging Issues in Corporate Governance* (Evanston, Illinois: Northwestern University Press, 1983), pp. 15–18.

47. L. Barker, "Director Compensation 1984," *Directors & Boards* (Spring 1984), p. 39.

48. For further information on board committees, refer to Waldo, pp. 65–85; Roche, pp. 23–23; and J. R. Harrison, "The Strategic Use of Corporate Board Committees," *California Management Review* (Fall 1987), pp. 109–125.

49. Waldo, p. 173.

50. Taken from C. A. Anderson and R. N. Anthony, *The New Corporate Directors* (New York: John Wiley and Sons, 1986), pp. 221–241.

51. C. D. McCreesh, "Benchmark Changes in D & O Liability Statutes," *Directors and Boards* (Spring 1987), pp. 16–18.

52. W. E. Simon, "The Board Is at a Crossroad," *Directors and Boards* (Fall 1986), p. 4.

53. "Director Certification: Should You Prove Competence to Sit on a Board?" *Wall Street Journal* (February 17, 1987), p. 1.

54. Worthy and Neuschel, p. 100.

55. Bacon and Brown, p. 25.

Andrews, 1980, p. 36.

W. R. Boulton, "Effective Board Development: Five Areas of Concern," *Journal of Business Strategy* (Spring 1983), pp. 94–100.

H. S. Geneen, "Why Directors Can't Protect the Stockholders," *Fortune* (September 17, 1984), p. 29.

56. P. F. Drucker, *Management: Tasks, Responsibilities, Practices* (New York: Harper & Row, 1974), p. 613.

57. Adapted from H. Mintzberg, *The Nature of Managerial Work* (New York: Harper & Row, 1973), pp. 54–94.

58. Drucker, pp. 611–612.

59. T. H. Pincus, "A Crisis Parachute: Helping Stock Prices Have a Soft Landing," *Journal of Business Strategy* (Spring 1986), pp. 35–36.

60. R. P. Beatly and E. J. Zajac, "CEO Change and Firm Performance in Large Corporations: Succession Effects and Manager Effects," *Strategic Management Journal* (July-August 1987), p. 315.

61. T. J. Peters and R. H. Waterman, *In Search of Excellence* (New York: Harper & Row, 1982), p. 26.

62. A. Levitt, Jr., and J. Albertine, "The Successful Entrepreneur: A Personality Profile," *Wall Street Journal* (August 29, 1983), p. 12.

63. Advertisement in *Business Week* (October 23, 1987), pp. 118–119.

64. Adapted from R. J. House, "A 1976 Theory of Charismatic Leadership," *Leadership: The Cutting Edge*, eds. J. G. Hunt and L. L. Larson (Carbondale, Ill.: SIU Press, 1977), pp. 189–207.

This view of executive leadership is also referred to as *transformational leadership*. See *Emerging Leadership Vistas*, edited by J. G. Hunt, B. R. Baliga, H. P. Dachler, and C. A. Schriesheim (Lexington, Mass.: Lexington Books, 1988), pp. 5–84.

65. M. Trevor, "Japanese Decision-making and Global Strategy," in *Strategic Management Research: A European Perspective*, edited by J. McGee and H. Thomas (Chichester, U.K.: John Wiley and Sons, 1986), pp. 301.

66. S. Matlins and G. Knisely, "Update: Profile of the Corporate Planners," *Journal of Business Strategy* (Spring 1981), pp. 75 and 77.

67. C. D. Burnett, D. P. Yeskey, and D. Richardson, "New Roles for Corporate Planners in the 1980's," *Journal of Business Strategy* (Spring 1984), p. 67.

68. B. T. Houlden, "Developing a Company's Strategic Management Capability," *Long Range Planning* (October 1986), p. 92.

J. F. Orsini, "Artificial Intelligence: A Way Through the Strategic Planning Crisis?" *Long Range Planning* (August 1986), p. 71.

69. Drucker, pp. 615–617.

70. Mintzberg, p. 33.

71. J. P. Wright, *On a Clear Day You Can See General Motors* (Grosse Pointe, Mich.: Wright Enterprises, 1979), p. 28.

72. E. Ehrlich, "What the Boss Is Really Like," *Business Week* (October 23, 1987), pp. 37–44.

73. N. Gross, "Corporate Revitalization—Via Team Planning," in *Handbook of Business Strategy, 1985/1986 Year-book,* edited by W. D. Guth (Boston: Warren, Gorham and Lamont, 1985), pp. 24.1–24.15.

E. Ginzberg and G. Vojta, *Beyond Human Scale: The Large Corporation At Risk* (New York: Basic Books, 1985).

J. R. Galbraith and R. K. Kazanjian, *Strategy Implementation* (St. Paul: West Publishing Company, 1986), pp. 147–149.

74. R. F. Vancil, "How Companies Pick New CEOs," *Fortune* (January 18, 1988), p. 75.

75. R. Gibson, "Control Data's Comeback Faces Rough Road," *Wall Street Journal* (June 17, 1985), p. 6.

76. J. R. Healey, "Hanson Cracks the Whip at Winnebago," *Des Moines Register* (January 19, 1986), pp. 1F and 4F.

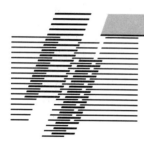

INTEGRATIVE CASE

CSX CORPORATION'S STRATEGIC MANAGERS

The first chairman of CSX was Prime F. Osborn, III, Chairman and CEO of Seaboard Coast Line Industries, Inc. Mr. Osborn acted as co-chief executive with Hays T. Watkins, who had served as Chairman and CEO of the Chessie System before the merger. From the very beginning of CSX, it was stressed that the corporation was to be a real partnership of equals. Even one year after the merger, *Business Week* reported that Osborn and Watkins "Practically make a fetish out of the partnership relationship of the two component railroads. Although one man is chairman and the other president, they insist they are truly co-chief executive officers."

This spirit of teamwork was embodied in the very name of the corporation. At the time of the merger, published reports quoted Hays T. Watkins as saying that the name CSX, originally chosen as a temporary working label, might become a permanent name. "Prime (Osborn) and I thought it up and like it because it's so anonymous and nondistinctive—the way we want the parent to be in relation to its operating railroads. . . . C is for Chessie, S is for Seaboard and X is for unknown, implying more," Watkins explained. One year after the merger, an article on CSX in *Business Week* carried the following statement, "Both Watkins and Prime F. Osborn, III, CSX's chairman, are fond of telling anyone who will listen that the 'X' in the name is the multiplication symbol, indicating that the company is much bigger than one plus one."

BOARDS OF DIRECTORS

To further reinforce this notion of a partnership, Osborn and Watkins adopted an interesting tactic: Chessie and Seaboard retained boards of directors that were distinct

---

SOURCE: Taken from "CSX Corporation" by J. D. Hunger, B. Ferrin, H. Felix-Gamez, and T. Goetzman in *Cases in Strategic Management and Business Policy* by T. L. Wheelen and J. D. Hunger (Reading, Mass.: Addison-Wesley, 1987), pp. 91–123.

from each other's and from the board of CSX. Watkins, who had been Chief Executive at Chessie, became Chairman of the Seaboard System board, while Osborn, who came from the Seaboard System, became Chairman of the Chessie board. "Flipping chairmanships is just one more device for cross-fertilization, for showing that this is a true partnership," said Watkins. Since the retirement of Osborn in 1982, Watkins assumed both roles of Chairman and CEO of CSX. The position of CSX President was assumed by Paul Funkhouser, who had been President and Chief Executive of the Seaboard System from the time of the merger until the retirement of Mr. Osborn.

The CSX Board was composed of twenty-seven members in 1985. (See Table 3.1.) Only five members of the Board were technically insiders, although a sixth (Mr. Osborn, the retired Chairman of the corporation) could have been considered an inside director. At the time of the merger creating the company, it was decided that Chessie and Seaboard would each have twelve seats on a twenty-four-person Board of Directors, even though the Seaboard shareholders wound up in control of slightly more stock in CSX than did the Chessie holders.

TABLE 3.1
CSX Board of Directors

Edward J. Boling*
President and Chief Executive Officer—The University of Tennessee, Knoxville, TN

Charles K. Cross, Sr.
Chairman of the Board and CEO—Barnett Bank of Central Florida, Orlando, FL

Frederick Deane, Jr.*
Chairman of the Board and CEO—Bank of Virginia Co., Richmond, VA

A. Paul Funkhouser*
President—CSX Corp., Richmond, VA

Richard A. Jay
Retired Vice-Chairman of the Board—Goodyear Tire and Rubber Co., Akron, OH

Clifford M. Kirtland, Jr.
Retired Chairman of the Board—Cox Communications, Inc., Atlanta, GA

John H. Lumpkin, Sr.
Honorary Chairman of the Board—South Carolina National Corp., Columbia, SC

William E. McGuirk, Jr.
Chairman of the Board—Mercantile Bankshares Corp., Baltimore, MD

Frank M. Northfleet
Chairman of the Board—Parts Industries Corp., Memphis, TN

Prime F. Osborn III
Retired Chairman of the Board—CSX Corp., Richmond, VA

Nicholas T. Camicia
Retired Chairman of the Board—The Pittston Co., Greenwich, CT

John T. Collinson
President and CEO—Chessie System Railroads, Cleveland, OH

John N. Dalton*
Senior Partner—McGuire, Woods & Battle, Richmond, VA

Alonzo G. Decker, Jr.
Honorary Chairman of the Board and Chairman of Executive Committee—The Black and Decker Mfr. Co., Baltimore, MD

Floyd D. Gottwald, Jr.
Chairman of the Board and CEO—Ethyl Corp., Richmond, VA

TOP MANAGEMENT

The role of the CSX parent was, according to Chairman and CEO Hayes Watkins, to coordinate operations, not to manage them. Major concerns of corporate management were to be finance, policy and shareholder relations, net income, and the company's progress against its major competitor, Norfolk Southern. According to Hays Watkins,

> Our management strategy . . . is to leave day-to-day operations largely with our subsidiaries. We at CSX . . . concentrate on what we call the three P's— Policy, Planning and Policing. We provide the broad policy and program guidance, and then we make sure that guidance is carried out. We at the CSX level also ensure that proper coordination is achieved among our various subsidiaries.
>
> We don't want to be an added bureaucracy that would run the organizations. We merely handle policy matters here. We're all overhead. We don't generate any mileage or freight. And we've been careful to keep our group small.

CSX and its subsidiaries were coordinated by a policy board composed of the top executives from each of the divisions plus the corporate office. Mr. Watkins reported,

Mary T. Kimpton
Economic Consultant to Business and Government, Chicago, IL

Richard L. Leatherwood
President and CEO—Texas Gas Resources Corp., Richmond, VA

Charles P. Lykes
Chairman of the Board and CEO— Lykes Bros., Inc., Tampa, FL

Steven Muller
President—The Johns Hopkins University, Baltimore, MD

James L. O'Keefe
Senior Partner—O'Keefe, Ashendon, Lyons & Ward, Chicago, IL

W. James Price
Managing Director—Alex, Brown & Sons, Inc., Baltimore, MD

Robert H. Radcliff
Chairman of the Board and CEO— Radcliff Marine Services, Inc., Mobile, AL

John K. Stevenson
Retired President—R.M. Stevenson Co., Bloomfield Hills, MI

Alvin W. Vogtle, Jr.
Retired Chairman of the Board— The Southern Co., Atlanta, GA

Richard D. Sandborn
President and CEO—Seaboard System Railroad, Inc., Jacksonville, FL

William B. Sturgill*
President—East Kentucky Investment Co., Lexington, KY

Hays T. Watkins*
Chairman of the Board and CEO— CSX Corp., Richmond, VA

SOURCE: *1984 Annual Report,* CSX Corporation, p. 44.
*Indicates Member of the Executive Committee.

TABLE 3.2

CSX Executive Officers

Hays T. Watkins Chairman of the Board and Chief Executive Officer	**Carl C. Hawk** Vice-President and Corporate Secretary
A. Paul Funkhouser President	**Kemper K. Hyers** Vice-President—Government Relations (State)
Robert L. Hintz Executive Vice-President	**Edward H. Latchford** Vice-President—Accounting and Financial Planning
John W. Snow Executive Vice-President	**James T. Lyon** Vice-President—Taxes
Gerald L. Nichols Senior Vice-President— Administration	**Woodruff M. Price** Vice-President—Government Relations
Josiah A. Stanley, Jr. Senior Vice-President—Audit	**Garth E. Griffith** General Counsel
Edwin E. Edel Vice-President—Corporate Communications	**Mark G. Aron** General Counsel—Special Projects
James Ermer Vice-President—Treasurer	
John H. Gobel Vice-President—Government Relations (State)	

SOURCE: *1984 Annual Report,* CSX Corporation, p. 15.

We meet at least once every other week and talk about policy matters. We also have three CSX staff people meeting with us regularly as members of the policy board; the senior vice-president of finance, the senior vice-president of corporate services (supervising the corporate secretary, public relations, the general counsel, and government affairs activities), and a recorder who is our office administrator.

Mr. Watkins emphasized the importance of finance at the corporate level. The financial person, according to Watkins, was "the key staff associate of CSX. He's the one that the president and I work with the most. . . . I guess we've had a culture around here for many years that the finance man is probably the single most important staff member of the company." This attitude was not surprising in view of Mr. Watkins's background, which included an M.B.A. from Northwestern University and a thirty-year career with the Chessie system in a variety of accounting and financial positions.

CSX corporate officers are listed in Table 3.2.

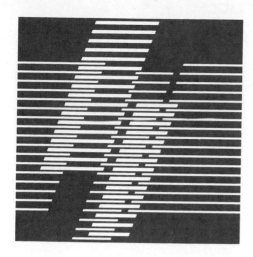

CHAPTER 4

THE EXTERNAL ENVIRONMENT

STRATEGIC MANAGEMENT MODEL

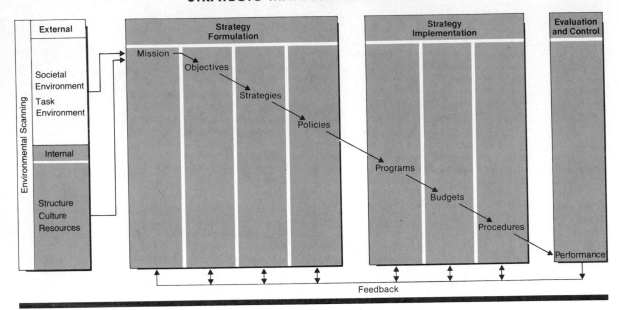

Business corporations do not exist in a vacuum. They arise out of society's need for a particular product or service and can continue to exist in freedom only so long as they acknowledge their role in the larger society. Therefore, corporations must constantly be aware of the key variables in their environment. These variables may be within a firm's task environment or in its larger societal environment (see Fig. 4.1). The **task environment** includes those elements or groups that directly affect the corporation and, in turn, are affected by it. These are governments, local communities, suppliers, competitors, customers, creditors, employees/labor unions, special interest groups, and trade associations. A corporation's task environment is the specific **industry** within which that corporation operates. The **societal environment** includes the more general forces that do not directly touch on the short-run activities of the organization but that can, and often do, influence its long-run decisions. These, also shown in Fig. 4.1, are as follows:

- **Economic forces** that regulate the exchange of materials, money, energy, and information.
- **Sociocultural forces** that regulate the values, mores, and customs of society.
- **Technological forces** that generate problem-solving inventions.
- **Political-legal forces** that allocate power and provide constraining and protecting laws and regulations.

All of these variables and forces constantly interact with each other. In the short run, societal forces affect the decisions and actions of a corporation

FIGURE 4.1
Key Environmental Variables.

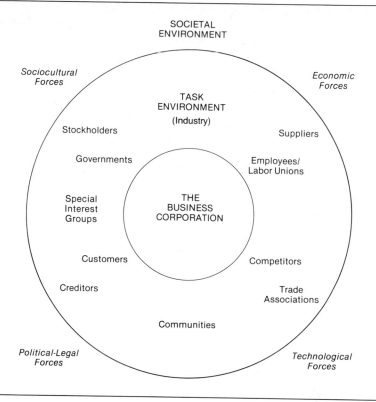

through the groups in its task environment. In the long run, however, the corporation also affects these groups through its activities. For example, the decision by a number of U.S. business corporations to relocate their manufacturing facilities to Asia and Latin America in order to reduce labor costs has increased the unemployment of U.S. blue-collar workers—and thus reduced union membership, adversely affected the country's balance of trade with other nations, and created economic depressions in those communities dependent for employment and tax revenue on the now-closed plants.

4.1

BUSINESS AND SOCIETY: A DELICATE RELATIONSHIP

For centuries, business corporations have lived in an uneasy truce with society. Exchange and commercial activities, along with laws governing them, are as old as recorded history. The Code of Hammurabi, established about 2000 B.C., provided guidelines for merchants and peddlers.[1] The Old Testament is filled with examples of commercial activity and the laws and regulations governing them. Greek philosophers, in general, regarded commercial activities as necessary but distasteful. The Romans, like the Greeks, were necessarily tolerant of commercial activity, but gave those so engaged a low status.[2] During the early years of the Middle Ages, the Roman Catholic Church held business and commercial activity in disdain and governed it through strict rules and limitations. Usury, the lending of money at interest, for instance, was decreed a mortal sin for Christians, who were forbidden the practice, although Jews were permitted to engage in it. Trade itself was of dubious purity, and the gathering of wealth was considered an action directly opposed to the charitable teachings of Jesus Christ. This view of trade and commerce and the associated accumulation of capital as necessary evils was commonly accepted in the Western world until the Protestant Reformation. The Eastern world, in contrast, was much more tolerant and accepting of business activities.

Development of the Capitalistic Ethic

With the end of the Middle Ages, values began to change in the West, and business activities were viewed more positively. Max Weber, noted economist and sociologist, postulated that changes in the religious ethic resulting from the Reformation and the Protestant movement provided an economic climate highly favorable for the development of capitalism.[3] A new spirit of individualism developed out of the Renaissance and was encouraged by humanism and Protestantism. Society placed a high value on frugality, thrift, and hard word—key elements of what is commonly referred to as the **Protestant ethic.**

Free trade was not, however, commonly accepted until much later. After the Reformation, kings and queens replaced the Church as earthly rulers. They established their right to regulate business activity through the concept of **mercantilism.** According to this concept, the individual was subordinate to the state, and all economic and business activity was dedicated to supporting the power of the state. Under mercantilism, Europeans set up organizations, such as the East India Company, to trade with the natives of distant lands and to return with goods valuable to crown and country.

In 1776, however, economist Adam Smith advanced a theory justifying capitalism in his book *An Inquiry into the Nature and Causes of the Wealth of Nations.* Smith argued that economic freedom would enable individuals through self-interest to fulfill themselves and would thereby benefit the total society. He used the term **laissez-faire** to suggest that government should leave business alone. The "invisible hand" of the marketplace would, through pure competition, ensure maximum benefit to society.

The doctrine of *laissez-faire*, as postulated by Smith and refined by others, called for society to give business corporations increasing autonomy so that they could accomplish their work—the production and sale of goods and services. In the rapidly changing world of the eighteenth and nineteenth centuries such work was considered worthwhile and valuable to society. For example, James Watt's development of a usable steam engine permitted muscle power to be replaced by an external power source and resulted in enormous increases in the production and distribution of scarce goods. Because of these benefits, governments relaxed many of their restrictions on commerce and trade, and allowed capital to accumulate and business to flourish.

Society Supports Free Enterprise

As changes in sociocultural values were fed by the benefits of new technology and *laissez-faire* economics, governments in the West began to support independent businesses. During much of the early part of the nineteenth century in the United States, government favored the development of commerce and industry. The Supreme Court, for example, ruled that the private corporation was a legal entity, and Congress passed tariff laws protecting business interests. In addition, the government provided vast sums of money and land for the rapidly expanding railroads.[4] As pointed out by McGuire,

> . . . the Federal government attempted to encourage business activities with a minimum of regulation and intervention. . . . Government's task in these years, it was thought by many politicians and businessmen, was to aid business enterprise in accord with the best principles of mercantilism and still leave business free to grow and develop without restraint, as set forth in the doctrine of *laissez-faire*. The tradition thus grew that businessmen in the United States could do what so few people were able to do—have their cake and eat it too.[5]

Beginnings of Regulation

In the late 1800s and early 1900s, the public began to find some business practices antisocial. This dissatisfaction was expressed increasingly. Karl Marx, who wrote *The Communist Manifesto* with Friedrich Engels in 1848 and *Das Kapital* in 1867, put into words much of this dissatisfaction. He, as well as many others, rejected the capitalistic ethic because of its many unsavory side-effects, such as child labor, unsafe working conditions, and subsistence wages. The development of monopolistic corporations and cartels caused various groups within the United States to demand some form of regulation. Although most U.S. citizens rejected the Marxist view, they challenged the *laissez-faire* concept and suggested that Adam Smith's economic system was based on a pure, competitive model that was ineffective in a system of entrenched monopolies and oligopolies. As a result, the U.S. federal government, to reclaim some of the freedom and autonomy it had granted business, enacted such legislation as the Interstate Commerce Act (1887), the Sherman Antitrust Act (1890), the Pure Food and Drug Act (1906), the Clayton Act (1914), and the Federal Trade Commission Act (1914). More restrictive laws were to follow.

A Question of Autonomy

The Great Depression of the 1930s, Keynesian economics, and the increasing popularity of socialism as a political force resulted in business losing even more of its autonomy to government. Governments all over the world assumed responsibility for their economies. In 1946, the U.S. Congress passed the Fair Employment Act, which states that the federal government has prime responsibility for the maintenance of full employment and full utilization of economic resources.[6] Through the decades of the 50s, 60s, and 70s, *laissez-faire*, if not dead, was certainly forgotten as people put their faith in a democratically elected central government rather than the self-interest of capitalists.

Consecutive years of profits earned by American big business during these prosperous decades suggested to a number of people that business was not truly paying its way in society. Increasingly, problems with product safety and environmental pollution were seen as the negative consequences of business peoples' selfish concern only with profits. Some of these feelings were expressed in 1962 by President Kennedy after the U.S. steel industry ignored his request to refrain from raising prices during a time of inflation.

> Some time ago I asked each American to consider what he would do for his country, and I asked steel companies. In the last 24 hours we had their answer. . . . My father always told me that all businessmen were sons of bitches, but I never believed it until now.[7]

Business people were increasingly constrained in their decision making by laws regarding air and water pollution, product safety, and employment practices, among others. In the United States, the number of federal agencies involved in regulating business activity increased from forty-nine in 1960 to eighty-three in 1970. Firms in the steel industry alone faced 5,600 regulations from twenty-seven federal agencies. The total cost of regulation to American business corporations in 1976 alone has been estimated at approximately $30 billion.[8] All around the world businesses were threatened by governments with more regulation or even by outright nationalization. Business autonomy was seriously threatened.

National Policy—Modern Mercantilism?

With the coming of the 1980s, the relationship between business and government changed. The labor productivity growth rate that had steadily increased in the United States for nearly two hundred years slowed and became negative during the period from 1978 to 1980.[9] Focusing upon high-volume standardized production, major Western firms found to their chagrin that companies in the developing nations had copied their technology. With lower production costs due to lower wages, among other factors, these companies in the third world were able to seriously erode the market share and profits of the business corporations in the industrialized countries of the West. Faced with serious problems of unemployment and balance of trade problems, governments of the United States, Great Britain, and other Western nations acted to reduce some of the constraints they had previously placed on business activity.

A number of people argued that not only should business be given more autonomy, but also that the national government should be an active supporter of business development. Stating that other nations with supportive industrial policies—such as Japan, Korea, and Singapore—had more competitive business corporations than did many Western nations, proposals for a sort of modern mercantilism were developed. Reich, in his influential book *The Next American Frontier,* contended that the federal government should develop a better system to help move U.S. industry more quickly out of high-volume standardized production into more flexible, quality-oriented systems of production using skilled labor.[10] National governments throughout the world were coming to think of business activity as the key to economic well-being. Questions of social responsibility were temporarily forgotten as people worried more about unemployment than pollution.

Unfortunately, by the latter half of the 1980s, problems of toxic waste, hazardous manufacturing plants, and unsafe products again became important topics for discussion as people once more became concerned about the disturbing side-effects of economic activity. Allegations of insider trading and other questionable activities in financial organizations around the world revealed some business people to have very low standards of ethics. Revelations in 1987 of automobile odometer tampering and the overexposure of workers to lead and arsenic in the workplace by Chrysler Corporation raised once again the issue of the extent to which business management is responsible to the society of which the organization is a part.[11]

4.2

SOCIAL RESPONSIBILITY

The concept that business must be socially responsible sounds appealing until one asks, "Responsible to whom?" As was shown in Fig. 4.1, the task environment includes a large number of groups with interest in a corporation's activities. These groups are referred to as **stakeholders** because they affect or are affected by the achievement of the firm's objectives.[12] Should a corporation be responsible only to some of these groups, or does business have a responsibility to all of them?

The corporation must pay close attention to its task environment, because its stakeholders are very responsive to the general trends in the societal environment and will typically translate these trends into direct pressure that affects corporate activities. Even if top management assumes the traditional *laissez-faire* stance that the major concern of its corporation is to make profits, it will find (often to its chagrin) that it must also be concerned with the effects of its profit-making on stakeholders within its task environment. Each stakeholder uses its own criteria to determine how well a corporation is performing, and each is constantly judging top management's actions in terms of their effect on itself. Therefore, top management must be aware not only of the key stakeholders in the corporation's task environment, but also of the criteria each group uses to judge the corporation's performance. The following is a list of some of these stakeholders and their probable criteria.

Stockholders	Price appreciation of securities. Dividends (How much and how often?).
Unions	Comparable wages. Stability of employment. Opportunity for advancement. Working conditions.
Governments	Support of government programs. Adherence to laws and regulations.
Suppliers	Rapidity of payment. Consistency of purchases.
Creditors	Adherence to contract terms. Dependability.
Customers/Distributors	Value given for the price paid. Availability of product or service.
Trade associations	Participation in association programs (time). Participation in association programs (money).
Competitors	Rate of growth (encroachment on their markets). Product or service innovation (source of new ideas to use).
Communities	Contribution to community development through taxes, participation in charitable activities, etc. Employment of local people. Minimum of negative side-effects (e.g., pollution).

Special interest groups   Employment of minority groups.
Contributions to urban improvement pro-
grams.
Provision of free services to the disadvan-
taged.

Priority of Concerns

In any one decision regarding corporate strategy, the interests of one stakeholder can conflict with another. For example, a business firm's decision to
build a plant in an inner-city location may have a positive effect on community relations but a negative effect on stockholder dividends. Which
group's interests have priority?

In a survey sponsored by the American Management Association, 6,000
managers and executives were asked to rate on a seven-point scale the
importance of a number of corporate stakeholders.[13] As shown in Table 4.1,
executives felt customers to be the most important concern. Employees were
also rated highly. Interestingly, the general public was felt to be of similar
importance as stockholders. Owners (presumably those who own large blocks
of stock), however, were rated as more important than either the public or
more typical stockholders. Government representatives were rated as least
important of all the groups considered.

Pressures on the Business Corporation

Because of the wide range of interests and concerns present in any corporation's task environment, one or more groups, at any one time, probably
will be dissatisfied with a corporation's activities. For example, consider
General Motors' decision in 1987 to close eleven of its manufacturing and
assembly plants located throughout Michigan, Illinois, and Ohio. The com-

TABLE 4.1
Importance to Executives of Various Stakeholders

STAKEHOLDER	RANK
Customers	6.40
Employees	6.01
Owners	5.30
General public	4.52
Stockholders	4.51
Elected public officials	3.79
Government bureaucrats	2.90

SOURCE: Adapted from B. Z. Posner and W. H. Schmidt, "Values and the American Manager:
An Update." Copyright © 1984 by the Regents of the University of California. Reprinted from
the *California Management Review*, Vol. 26, No. 3, p. 206. By permission of The Regents.

NOTE: The ranking is calculated on a scale of 7 (most important) to 1 (least important).

pany's profits and market share had seriously dropped and it could no longer pay the costs of excess capacity. One of the plants to be closed was in Norwood, Ohio, where GM employed 4,200 workers and paid nearly 40% of the city's taxes. Faced with the imminent loss of its primary employer, the city of Norwood needed financial aid to provide essential services to its citizens.

City officials asked the GM management for extra money to help cover the tax shortage, but were refused. Consequently, Norwood filed a lawsuit against GM asking for $318.3 million as "alimony" for "breach of contract." The city contended that it had gone out of its way to build schools, add police and fire protection, plus widen streets and build an underpass in response to GM's requests and promises of expansion. Norwood argued that the company had implied responsibilities to the city beyond its service simply as an employer and tax payer. GM's top management was in a situation of being damned by its stockholders if it failed to close the plants and damned by the cities if it did![14]

Another controversial issue was the presence of more than 300 United States business corporations in South Africa. Because of the apartheid policy of strict racial segregation and discrimination against non-whites of the South African government, many critics of apartheid have been urging U.S. firms to withdraw their business. American corporations controlled nearly 70% of South Africa's computer industry and half of its petroleum business in the early 1980s. Anti-apartheid spokespeople argued that the presence of such important firms as IBM, Exxon, G.E., GM, Kodak, Johnson and Johnson, Hewlett-Packard, and Ford, among others, gave tacit approval and financial support to a "racist" government. Calls for the *disinvestment* of American business in South Africa were criticized, however, by some black South Africans with a different point of view. Mangosutu Gatsha Buthelezi, hereditary Prime Minister of the Zulu nation, commented, "No one has proved to us that the suffering which will ensue within the black community as a result of disinvestment will actually force the regime to effect the fundamental changes all of us are clamoring for."[15] Torn between two conflicting demands, around 150 U.S. business corporations chose a compromise position in 1985. They remained in South Africa, but signed and followed the *Sullivan Code,* a set of equal-opportunity and fair-treatment principles drawn up by Leon H. Sullivan, minister of Philadelphia's Zion Baptist Church and a director of General Motors. A number of Canadian companies followed a voluntary Canadian government code for conducting business in South Africa. Nevertheless, in 1987 Sullivan repudiated his code because of its failure to end apartheid. He urged the total withdrawal of all business firms. Increasing numbers of U.S. and Canadian business organizations chose to close or sell their holdings in South Africa. Even then, many of them were criticized because they continued to supply parts to the then-South African-owned businesses.[16]

The previous examples indicate how easily a business corporation can run into problems—even when top management is trying to achieve the best outcome for all involved. There are other examples, however, of business firms engaging in very questionable, unethical, or even illegal actions. These examples reveal the dark side of corporate decision making and support those arguments in favor of increased governmental regulation and decreased business autonomy. There is no doubt that the top managements of some business firms have sometimes made decisions emphasizing short-term profitability or personal gain over long-term relations with governments, local communities, suppliers, and even customers and employees. For example, here are some of the questionable practices that have been exposed in recent years:

- Possible negligent construction and management practices at nuclear power and chemical plants (for example, nuclear plants at Three Mile Island and Diablo Canyon, and Union Carbide's chemical plant in Bhopal, India).[17]
- Improper disposal of toxic wastes (for instance, at Love Canal).[18]
- Production and sale of defective products (for example, A. H. Robbins' Dalkon Shield birth-control device).[19]
- Declaring bankruptcy to cancel a labor contract and cut wages (for instance, Wilson Foods and Continental Airlines).[20]
- Insufficient safeguarding of employees from exposure to dangerous chemicals and materials in the workplace (for instance, the asbestos problem at Manville Corporation and cyanide poisoning at Film Recovery Systems).[21]
- Continuous instances of fraud, bribery, and price fixing at corporations of all sizes and locations (for example, National Semiconductor's defrauding the Defense Department by failure to test electronic components properly, General Electric's illegal claims for more than $800,000 in cost overruns on Minuteman missile contracts, and E. F. Hutton's overdraft scheme that cost banks an estimated $8 million over a two-year period).[22]

Ethics: A Question of Values

Such questionable practices by business corporations run counter to the values of society as a whole and are justly criticized and prosecuted. Why are actions taken that so obviously harm important stakeholders in the corporation's task environment? Are business corporations and the people who run them amoral, or are they simply ignorant of the many consequences of their actions?

Cultural Differences

One reason for such behavior is that there is no worldwide standard of conduct for businesspeople. Cultural norms and values vary between countries and even between different geographic regions and ethnic groups within a country. One example is the use of payoffs and bribes to influence a potential customer's decision to buy from a particular supplier. Although this practice is considered illegal in the United States, it is deeply entrenched in many countries. In Mexico, for instance, the payoff, referred to as *la mordida* (the bite), is considered a fringe benefit or *propina* (a tip).[23]

Personal Differences

Another possible reason for a corporation's questionable practices lies in differences in values between top management and key stakeholders in the task environment. Some businesspeople might believe that profit maximization is the key goal of their firm, whereas concerned interest groups might have other goals, such as the hiring of minorities and women or the safety of their neighborhoods.

Economist Milton Friedman, in urging a return to a *laissez-faire* style of worldwide economy, argues against the concept of social responsibility. If a businessperson acts "responsibly" by cutting the price of the firm's product to prevent inflation, or by making expenditures to reduce pollution, or by hiring the hard-core unemployed, that person, according to Friedman, is spending the stockholder's money for a general social interest. Even if the businessperson has stockholders' permission or encouragement to do so, he or she is still acting from motives other than economic and can, in the long run, cause harm to the very society the firm is trying to help. By taking on the burden of these social costs, the business becomes less efficient; and either prices go up to pay for the increased costs, or investment in new activities and research is postponed. These results negatively affect—perhaps fatally—the long-term efficiency of a business. Friedman thus referred to the social responsibility of business as a "fundamentally subversive doctrine" and stated that "there is one and only one social responsibility of business— to use its resources and engage in activities designed to increase its profits so long as it stays within the rules of the game, which is to say, engages in open and free competition without deception or fraud."[24]

Friedman's stand on free enterprise has been both criticized and praised. Business people tend to agree with Friedman because his views are compatible not only with their own self-interests but also with their hierarchy of values. When tested on the six values measured by the Allport-Vernon-Lindzey "Study of Values" test (aesthetic, economic, political, religious, social, and theoretical), both U.S. and British executives scored high on economic and political values, and low on social and religious ones. Protestant ministers, in contrast, scored high on religious and social values, and very low on economic values.[25]

Imagine the controversy that would result if a group composed of ministers and executives had to decide the following strategy issues: Should business firms close on Sunday? Should the corporation hire handicapped workers and accept the increased training costs associated with their employment? In discussing these issues, the executive would probably be very concerned with the effects on the "bottom line" (profits), whereas the minister would probably be concerned with the effects on society and salvation (a very different bottom line).

This conclusion is supported by a study of 6,000 executives and managers who were asked to rate a representative sample of typical organizational goals, as depicted in Table 4.2. The results clearly show community service and public service ranked at the bottom of the list under organizational effectiveness and profit maximization.[26] This study generally agrees with previous studies that revealed a desire by businesspeople to limit their social responsibilities to those areas in which they can clearly see benefits to the corporation, in terms of reduced costs and less governmental regulation.[27] This very narrow view of businesses' responsibilities to society typically will cause conflicts between the business corporation and certain members of its task environment.

Types of Responsibilities

Carroll, in his research on social responsibility, suggests that in addition to the obvious economic and legal responsibilities, businesses have ethical and discretionary ones.[28]

The **economic responsibilities** of a business organization's management are to produce goods and services of value to society, so that the firm can repay its creditors and stockholders. **Legal responsibilities** are defined by governments in laws that management is expected to obey. The **ethical responsibilities** of an organization's management are to follow the generally held beliefs about how one should act in the surrounding society. For example,

TABLE 4.2

Importance to Executives of Various Organizational Goals

ORGANIZATIONAL GOAL	DEGREE OF IMPORTANCE
Organizational effectiveness	6.26
High productivity	6.16
High morale	6.01
Organizational efficiency	5.93
Profit maximization	5.44
Organizational growth	5.20
Organizational value to community	4.82
Service to the public	4.68

SOURCE: Adapted from B. Z. Posner and W. H. Schmidt, "Values and the American Manager: An Update." Copyright © 1984 by the Regents of the University of California. Reprinted from the *California Management Review,* Vol. 26, No. 3, p. 205. By permission of The Regents.

NOTE: The ranking is calculated on a scale of 7 ("very important to me") to 1 ("of little or no importance to me").

although there may be no law requiring an organization to discuss the closing of a plant with representatives of the local community, society generally expects the firm to work with the community in planning for a plant closing. As in the Norwood, Ohio example mentioned earlier, the affected people can get very upset if an organization's management fails to act according to generally prevailing ethical values. **Discretionary responsibilities,** in contrast, are the purely voluntary obligations that a corporation assumes. Examples are philanthropic contributions, training the hard-core unemployed, and providing day-care centers. The difference between ethical and discretionary responsibilities is that no one expects an organization to fulfill discretionary responsibilities, whereas many expect an organization to fulfill ethical ones.

The term "social responsibility" can thus be viewed as the combination of an organization's ethical and discretionary responsibilities. The discretionary responsibilities of today may become the ethical responsibilities of tomorrow. Carroll suggests that to the extent that business organizations fail to acknowledge discretionary or ethical responsibilities, society, through government, will act, and make them legal responsibilities. This action can be taken by government, moreover, without regard to an organization's economic responsibilities. Because of such an act, the organization may have greater difficulty in earning a profit than it would have had if it had initially assumed voluntarily some ethical and discretionary responsibilities. For example, it has been suggested by some people in the American automobile industry that the large number of safety and pollution regulations passed in the 1960s and 1970s were partially responsible for the poor health of the U.S. industry in the early 1980s.[29]

Nevertheless, studies in the area have *failed* to find any significant relation between a business corporation's social responsibility and its financial performance. Examples can be cited of both highly profitable and marginally profitable companies with both poor and excellent social records.[30] One interesting example is Control Data Corporation. Under the leadership of socially concerned William C. Norris as founder, Chairman, and CEO, Control Data had organized assembly plants in ghettos and prisons and spent millions of dollars on computer systems for use in education and training in schools and industry. Unfortunately, corporate earnings have fallen and Norris has been criticized for allowing his "pet businesses" to drain investment away from the company's profitable ventures. He was subsequently forced to resign from the company.[31]

Even with the finding that social responsibility has no relationship to profits, one conclusion seems clear. The **iron law of responsibility** applies: If business corporations are unable or unwilling to police themselves by considering their responsibilities to all stakeholders in their task environment, then society—usually in the form of government—will police their doing so, and once again governments will reduce business's autonomy via increased rules and regulations.[32] During the late 1980s, there was already some pressure building in the United States for government regulations to take away some of business' decision-making freedom in some industries. Table 4.3 indicates that although general attitudes toward U.S. business in 1987 were still favorable, people questioned managers' ethics and appeared to be more disposed toward a return to government regulation. For example, bills were being proposed in the U.S. Congress to subject airlines to new restrictions (primarily because of an increasing number of complaints by customers and local communities) and to require pre-notification of major plant closings.[33] In addition, sixteen states were considering rules on mandatory pregnancy leave for employees. Fifteen states had already passed such laws.[34]

TABLE 4.3
Recent U.S. Attitudes Toward Business*

1. Overall attitude toward business:

Favorable	*Unsure*	*Unfavorable*
72%	4%	24%

2. Has the federal regulation of business changed from being too strict to being too lax?

Yes	*Unsure*	*No*
50%	5%	45%

3. Has the deregulation of various industries brought positive results?

Yes	*Unsure*	*No*
46%	5%	49%

4. Overall ethical standards of business executives:

Excellent/Good	*Unsure*	*Fair/Poor*
40%	2%	58%

5. Should there be new laws restricting hostile takeovers of one business firm by another?

Yes	*Unsure*	*No*
64%	6%	30%

6. Should companies be required by law to notify their workers and the local community in advance that they are planning to shut down an operation?

Yes	*Unsure*	*No*
86%	1%	13%

SOURCE: Based on data reported by S. Jackson and H. Collingwood, "Business Week/Harris Poll: Is An Antibusiness Backlash Growing?" *Business Week* (July 20, 1987), p. 71.

*Nationwide survey of 1,250 adults in the U.S. conducted May 8–12, 1987, by Louis Harris & Associates for *Business Week*.

4.3

ENVIRONMENTAL SCANNING AND INDUSTRY ANALYSIS

Because they are a part of a larger society that constantly affects them in many ways, corporations must be aware of changes and potential changes within the key variables in their task and societal environments. In 1973, for example, the Arab oil embargo caught many firms completely by surprise, with the result that goods dependent on oil as a raw material or energy source could not be produced. The resulting shortages and price adjustments caused chaos throughout the world's economy. The top managements of many business corporations then realized just how dependent they were on seemingly unpredictable external events. It was at this time, in the early 1970s, that many corporations established for the first time formal strategic planning systems. By 1984, between 92% and 95% of the world's largest corporations were using planning departments to monitor the environment and to prepare forecasts.[35]

Before strategy makers can begin formulating specific strategies, they must scan the external environment to identify possible *opportunities* and *threats*. Environmental scanning is the monitoring, evaluating, and disseminating of information from the external environment to key people within the corporation.[36] It is a tool that a corporation uses to avoid strategic surprise and to ensure its long-run health. Waterman argues that one reason excellent companies are able to constantly "renew" themselves is because they "know more" and "treat information as their main competitive advantage."[37] Both the societal and task environments must be monitored so that strategic factors that are likely to have a strong impact on corporate success or failure can be detected.

Monitoring Strategic Factors

Strategic managers should engage in environmental scanning through use of a *Strategic Issues Management System*.[38] By monitoring for weak as well as strong environmental signals, such a system continuously scans for possible trends and future developments. As mentioned in Chapter 1, NCR paid little attention to the appearance of the first electronic cash register in 1971—an example of a weak signal. By 1978, however, NCR's market share had dropped from 80% to 25%—a rather strong signal!

When analyzed, environmental data form a series of **strategic issues**—those trends and developments that are very likely to determine the future environment. Insofar as a corporation's strategic managers are concerned, however, these strategic environmental issues must be further analyzed so that those of most importance to the corporation's own future are identified. A corporation's **strategic factors** are those environmental strategic issues that are judged to have a high probability of occurrence and a high probability of impact on the corporation. As shown in Fig. 4.2, an **issues priority matrix** can be used to help managers decide which strategic issues should be merely

FIGURE 4.2
Issues Priority Matrix.

Source: Adapted from L. L. Lederman, "Foresight Activities in the U.S.A.: Time for a Re-Assessment?" *Long-Range Planning* (June 1984), p. 46. Copyright © 1984 by Pergamon Press, Ltd. Reprinted by permission.

scanned (low priority) and which should be monitored as strategic factors (high priority). Those environmental issues judged to be a corporation's strategic factors are then categorized as *opportunities* and *threats,* and are included in strategy formulation.

Few firms, unfortunately, successfully monitor strategic issues.[39] The personal values of a corporation's top managers are likely to bias both their perception of what is important to monitor in the external environment and their interpretations of what they perceive. Therefore, different companies often respond differently to the same environmental changes because of differences in the ability of their strategic managers to recognize and understand strategic issues and factors.[40] For example, a study of presidents of savings and loan associations revealed that a president's perception of the environment strongly affected strategic planning. Those presidents who believed the present uncertain environment to be only temporary used no long-term planning staff or planning committees. They simply chose to wait for the "good old days" to return. In contrast, those presidents who believed the days of the stable, regulated environment to be long gone spent 30%–50% of their time considering long-range strategic issues and using planning staffs extensively.[41]

Societal Environment

The number of possible strategic factors in the societal environment is enormous. As noted in Table 4.4 large corporations categorize the societal

TABLE 4.4
Some Important Variables in the Societal Environment

SOCIOCULTURAL	ECONOMIC	TECHNOLOGICAL	POLITICAL-LEGAL
Lifestyle changes	GNP trends	Total federal spending for R&D	Antitrust regulations
Career expectations	Interest rates	Total industry spending for R&D	Environmental protection laws
Consumer activism	Money supply	Focus of technological efforts	Tax laws
Rate of family formation	Inflation rates	Patent protection	Special incentives
Growth rate of population	Unemployment levels	New products	Foreign trade regulations
Age distribution of population	Wage/Price controls	New developments in technology transfer from lab to marketplace	Attitudes toward foreign companies
Regional shifts in population	Devaluation/revaluation	Productivity improvements through automation	Laws on hiring and promotion
Life expectancies	Energy availability and cost		Stability of government
Birth rates	Disposable and discretionary income		

environment into four areas and focus their scanning in each area on trends with corporate-wide relevance. The economic area is usually the most significant, followed by the technological, political-legal, and sociocultural in decreasing order of importance.[42] Obviously, trends in any one area may be very important to the firms in one industry but of lesser importance to firms in other industries. For example, the demographic bulge in the U.S. population caused by the "baby boom" in the 1950s strongly affected the brewing industry, among others. As this demographic group became older during the 1980s, the percentage of the population that fell within the 18–25 years of age category—prime beer-drinking age—decreased. Thus sales and profits of breweries decreased and corporations like Anheuser-Busch found that they had to diversify if they were to stay profitable. In contrast, as the number of dual-career married couples in the 25–34 years of age category became larger, demand increased for day-care facilities like Kinder-Care Learning Centers.

Corporations throughout the developed nations of the world face some demographic societal pressures regardless of industry. The falling birth rates plus changing economic factors, for example, are leading to an aging of the workforce and to pressure for both men and women to have fulltime jobs. Because more than 60% of U.S. mothers with children under the age of 14 were actively employed in 1987 and there were predictions that the percentage would continue to rise, pressures were building on organizations to deal with the increasingly severe child-care dilemma facing their employees.[43] As the percentage of people in the U.S. workforce over 40 years of age increases from 37.8% in 1987 to nearly 50% in 2010, personnel practices and competitive strategies will be forced to change.[44] McDonald's fast-food chain has already begun to replace some of its teen aged employees with retired people. In attempts to change their offerings to match the changing lifestyles of their aging clientele, ski resorts are deemphasizing steep downhill slopes in favor of family-oriented lodges and scenic views.

John Naisbitt, in his influential book, *Megatrends,* states that America's present societal environment is turbulent because we are moving from one era to another. Having performed a content analysis of newspapers, he proposes that American society is being restructured by *ten broad influences* or "megatrends" that are defining the new society.

1. We are moving from an industrial to an information society.

2. We are moving from forced technology to a matching of each new technology with a compensatory human response ("Hi tech-hi touch").

3. We are moving from a national to a world economy.

4. We are moving from short-term to long-term considerations, with an emphasis on strategic planning.

5. We are moving from a period of centralization to decentralization of power.

6. We are shifting from reliance on institutional help to more self-reliance.

7. We are moving from representative democracy to more participative democracy, in politics as well as in the workplace.

8. We are giving up our dependence on traditional hierarchical structures in favor of informal networks of contacts.

9. We are moving geographically from the North to the South and West.

10. We are moving from a society with a limited number of personal choices to a multiple-option society.[45]

If Naisbitt is correct, these changes will have enormous impact not only upon American but also upon global society. To the extent that these trends are likely to have a strong impact on a particular corporation, they must be considered as strategic factors and be monitored closely by that firm's planners.

Task Environment/Industry Analysis

As was noted earlier, changes in the societal environment tend to be reflected in pressures on the corporation from task environment groups. As shown in Fig. 4.3, a corporation's scanning of the environment will include analyses of all the relevant elements in the task environment—interest groups, resources, the marketplace, competitors, suppliers, and governments. These analyses take the form of written reports, which, when boiled down to their essentials, act as a detailed list of strategic factors—those opportunities and

FIGURE 4.3
Scanning the External Environment.

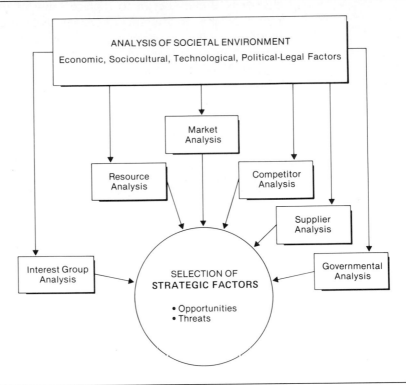

threats facing the corporation from its task environment. The task environment of a particular company is often referred to as its industry. Therefore, an examination of the task environment may also be called **industry analysis.** An *industry* is a group of firms producing a similar product or service, such as the automobile or soft drink industries.

Porter, an authority on competitive strategy, contends that a corporation is most concerned with the intensity of competition within its industry. The level of this intensity is determined by basic competitive forces, which are depicted in Fig. 4.4. "The collective strength of these forces," he contends, "determines the ultimate profit potential in the industry, where profit potential is measured in terms of long-run return on invested capital."[46] Although Porter mentions only five forces, a sixth—other stakeholders—is added to reflect the power of unions, governments, and other groups from the task environment on industry activities.

In carefully scanning the task environment, the corporation must assess the importance to its success of each of the following six forces.[47]

FIGURE 4.4
Forces Driving Industry Competition.

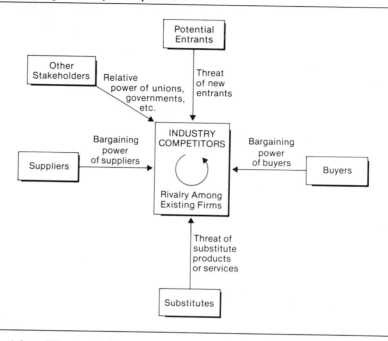

Source: Adapted/Reprinted with permission of The Free Press, a Division of Macmillan, Inc. from *Competitive Strategy: Techniques for Analyzing Industries and Competitors* by Michael E. Porter. Copyright © 1980 by The Free Press.

1. **Threat of New Entrants:** New entrants to an industry typically bring to it new capacity, a desire to gain market share, and substantial resources, and are, therefore, threats to an established corporation. The threat of entry depends on the presence of entry barriers and the reaction that can be expected from existing competitors. For example, there have been very few new automobile companies successfully established since the 1930s because of the high capital requirements to build production facilities and to develop a dealer distribution network.

2. **Rivalry among Existing Firms:** In most industries, corporations are mutually dependent. A competitive move by one firm can be expected to have a noticeable effect on its competitors and thus may cause retaliation or counter-efforts. For example, the entry of Philip Morris into the beer industry through the acquisition of Miller Brewing increased the level of competitive activity to such an extent that any introduction of a new product or promotion is now quickly followed by similar moves from other brewers.

3. **Threat of Substitute Products or Services:** In effect, all corporations within one industry are competing with other industries that produce substitute

products. According to Porter, "Substitutes limit the potential returns of an industry by placing a ceiling on the prices firms in the industry can profitably charge."[48] In the 1970s, for example, the high price of cane sugar caused soft drink manufacturers to turn to high-fructose corn syrup as a sugar substitute. Sometimes a difficult task, the identification of possible substitute products or services means searching for products or services that can perform the same *function*, even though they may not appear to be easily substitutable. Videotape recorders, for example, are becoming substitutes for home motion-picture projectors. The television screen thus substitutes for the portable projection screen.

4. **Bargaining Power of Buyers:** Buyers affect an industry through their ability to force down prices, bargain for higher quality or more services, and play competitors against each other. A buyer or a group of buyers is powerful if some of the following hold true:

   - It purchases a large proportion of the seller's product or service.
   - It has the potential to integrate backward by producing the product itself.
   - Alternative suppliers are plentiful.
   - Changing suppliers costs very little.

   For example, to the extent that General Motors purchases a large percentage of Firestone's total tire production, GM's purchasing department can easily make all sorts of demands on Firestone's marketing people. This would be the case especially if GM could easily get its tires from Goodyear or General Tire at no extra trouble or cost. Increasing demands by large manufacturing companies for "just-in-time delivery" means that, in order to get the orders, a small supplier dependent on the large firm's business must take over the warehousing functions previously handled by the large firm.

5. **Bargaining Power of Suppliers:** Suppliers can affect an industry through their ability to raise prices or reduce the quality of purchased goods and services. A supplier group is powerful if some of the following apply:

   - The supplier industry is dominated by a few companies, but sells to many.
   - Substitutes are not readily available.
   - Suppliers are able to integrate forward and compete directly with their present customers. An example was IBM's willingness in 1980 to open its own personal-computer stores instead of selling only through other established retailers.
   - A purchasing industry buys only a small portion of the supplier group's goods and services.

   For example, major oil companies in the 1970s were able to raise prices and reduce services because so many companies that purchased oil products had heavy energy needs and, in the short run, were unable to switch to substitute fuels, such as coal or nuclear power. Wishing to be less dependent on suppliers for the raw material so necessary to produce its synthetic materials, Dupont chose to buy Conoco, a major oil company.

6. **Relative Power of Other Stakeholders:** Freeman recommends adding this sixth force to Porter's list to include a variety of stakeholder groups from the task environment.[49] Some of these groups are governments, unions, local communities, creditors (if not included with suppliers), trade associations, special interest groups, and stockholders. The importance of these stakeholders will vary by industry. For example, environmental groups in Maine, Michigan, Oregon, and Iowa successfully fought to pass bills outlawing disposable bottles and cans, and thus deposits for most drink containers are now required. Although Porter contends that the government influences the level of competitive activity through the previously mentioned five forces, it is suggested here that governments deserve a special mention because of their strong relative power in all industries.

For additional information on industry analysis, refer to **"How Competitive Forces Shape Strategy"** by Michael E. Porter in Appendix 4.A at the end of this chapter.

Characterizing the Competition

In analyzing the level of competitive intensity within an industry, it is useful to characterize the competition for predictive purposes. According to Miles and Snow, competing firms within a single industry can be categorized on the basis of their general strategic orientation into one of four basic types: the Defender, the Prospector, the Analyzer, and the Reactor.[50] Each of these types has its own favorite strategy for responding to the environment, and has its own combination of structure, culture, and processes consistent with that strategy. This distinction helps explain why companies facing similar situations behave differently and why they continue to do so over a long period of time. These general types have the following characteristics:

- **Defenders** are corporations having a limited product line and focusing on improving the efficiency of their existing operations. This focus makes them unlikely to innovate in new areas. An example corporation is the Adolph Coors Company, which for so many years emphasized production efficiency in its one Colorado brewery and virtually ignored marketing.

- **Prospectors** are corporations having fairly broad product lines and focusing on product innovation and market opportunities. They tend to emphasize creativity over efficiency. An example would be the Miller Brewing Company, which successfully promoted light beer and generated aggressive, innovative advertising campaigns.

- **Analyzers** are corporations that operate in two different product-market areas, one stable and one changing. In the stable area, efficiency is emphasized. In the changing area, innovation is emphasized. An example would be Anheuser-Busch, which can take a defender orientation to protect its massive market share in beer and a prospector orientation to generate sales in its snack foods.

- **Reactors** are corporations that lack a consistent strategy-structure-culture relationship. Their (often ineffective) responses to environmental pressures tend to be piecemeal strategic changes. An example would be the Pabst Brewing Company, which, because of numerous takeover attempts, has been unable to generate a consistent strategy to keep its sales from dropping.

Dividing the competition into these four categories enables the strategic manager to not only monitor the effectiveness of certain strategic orientations, but also to develop scenarios of future industry developments (to be discussed later in this chapter).

Sources of Information

Studies have shown that much environmental scanning is done on an informal and individual basis. Information is obtained from a variety of sources, such as customers, suppliers, bankers, consultants, publications, personal observations, subordinates, superiors, and peers. For example, scientists and engineers working in a firm's R&D lab can learn about new products and competitors' ideas at professional meetings; someone from the purchasing department, speaking with supplier-representatives' personnel, may also uncover valuable bits of information about a competitor. A study of product innovation in the scientific instruments and machine tool industries found that 80% of all product innovations were initiated by the *customer* in the form of inquiries and complaints.[51] In these industries, the sales force and service departments must be especially vigilant.

Some of the main sources of information about an industry's environment are shown in Fig. 4.5. Because people throughout a corporation can obtain an extraordinary amount of data in any given month, top management must develop a system to get these data from those who obtained it to the people who can integrate it with other information to form a comprehensive environmental assessment.

As one would suspect, research suggests that corporations develop and implement more scanning procedures for following, anticipating, and responding to changes in the activities of *competitors* than of any other stakeholder in the environment.[52] At General Mills, for example, all members of the company have been trained to recognize and tap sources of competitive information. Janitors no longer simply place orders with suppliers of cleaning materials, they also ask about relevant practices at competing firms![53]

There is danger in focusing one's scanning efforts too closely on one's own industry, though. According to research by Snyder, "History teaches that most new developments which threaten existing business practices and technologies do not come from traditional industries."[54] For instance, **tech-**

FIGURE 4.5
Sources of Data for Industry Analysis.

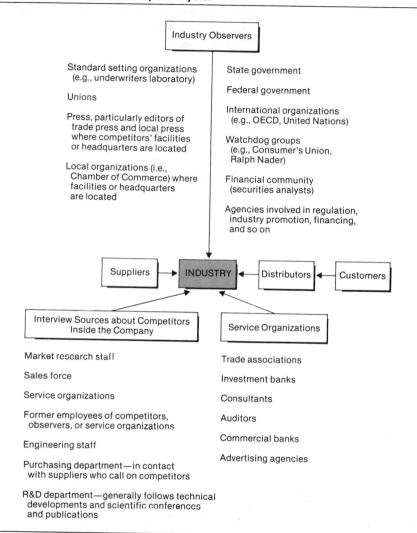

Source: Adapted/Reprinted with permission of The Free Press, a Division of Macmillan, Inc. from *Competitive Strategy: Techniques for Analyzing Industries and Competitors* by Michael E. Porter. Copyright © 1980 by The Free Press.

nology transfer, the process of taking new technology from the laboratory to the marketplace, has become an important issue in recent decades. Consider just one example. With the development of the integrated circuit, electronics firms, such as Texas Instruments, were able to introduce high-volume, low-cost electronic digital watches. These firms' entry into the watch-making industry took well-established mechanical watchmakers by surprise. Timex, Seiko, and especially the Swiss firms found that their market had changed overnight. Their production facilities, however, had not; and they spent a lot of money buying the new technology.

Most corporations rely on outside organizations to provide them with environmental data. Firms such as A. C. Nielsen Co. provide subscribers with bimonthly data on brand share, retail prices, percentages of stores stocking an item, and percentages of stock-out stores. These data can be used by management to spot regional and national trends as well as to assess market share. Information on market conditions, government regulations, competitors, and new products can be bought from "information brokers." Such firms as FIND/SVP, a New York company, and Finsbury Data Services, owned by Reuters in London, get their data from periodicals, reference books, computer data banks, directors, and experts in the area. Other firms, like Chase Econometrics, offer various data bases plus a software package that enables corporate planners to gain computer access to a large number of key indicators. Typically, the largest corporations spend from $25,000 to $30,000 per year for information services.[55] Close to 6,000 firms in the United States and Canada have established their own in-house libraries to deal with the growing mass of available information.[56]

Some companies, however, choose to use industrial espionage or other intelligence gathering techniques, to get their information straight from their competitors. For example, Hitachi Ltd., the large Japanese electronics firm, pleaded guilty in 1983 to conspiring to transport stolen IBM material to Japan.[57] In 1986, Kellogg Company closed its Battle Creek, Michigan, plant to public tours when it learned that industrial spies from two foreign competitors had gathered valuable information during visits. Experts report that modern "pirates" of information are inflicting billions of dollars worth of damage annually in missed sales and wasted R&D costs. Valuable information can slip out through managers, salespeople, and suppliers. Even cleaning workers have been caught selling trash to rival competitors![58]

4.4

FORECASTING

Once a business corporation has collected data about its current environmental situation, it must analyze present trends to learn if they will continue into the future. The strategic planning horizon for many large corporations is from five to ten years in the future. A long-term planning horizon is especially necessary for large, capital-intensive corporations, such as automobile or heavy-machinery manufacturers. In these corporations, moving from an accepted proposal to a finished product requires many years. Therefore, most corporations must base their future plans on a forecast, a set of assumptions about what that future will look like. These assumptions can be derived from an entrepreneur's vision, from a head-in-the-sand hope that the future will be similar to the present, or from the opinions of experts. Figure 4.6 depicts the role of forecasting in the strategy formulation process.

FIGURE 4.6
The Role of Forecasting.

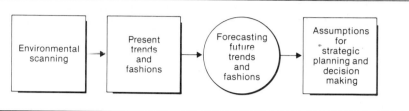

The Danger of Assumptions

A forecast is nothing more than a leap of faith into the future. Environmental scanning provides reasonably hard data on the present situation, but intuition and luck are needed to accurately predict the future. Faulty underlying assumptions appear to be the most frequent cause of forecasting errors.[59] Nevertheless, many managers who formulate and implement strategic plans have little or no realization that their success is based on a series of assumptions. Many long-range plans are simply based on projections of the current situation. One example of what can happen when a corporate strategy rests on the very questionable assumption that the future will simply be an extension of the present, is that of the Miller Brewing Company, a subsidiary of Philip Morris.

In 1980, Miller Brewing decided to construct a $412 million brewery in Trenton, Ohio. The decision was made after a decade of growth that saw Miller's beer volume increase 640% while that of the industry as a whole grew by only 40%. Miller's strategic managers assumed that with Philip Morris' marketing genius supporting the company, the sky was the limit for Miller beer. Unfortunately, that trend was not to continue. Of the total U.S. population, that percentage aged 18–25 years began to drop, and so did the overall demand for beer. The competition also increased its challenge: having been stung by Miller's marketing successes during the 1970s, Anheuser-Busch tripled its advertising budget and launched a $2 billion capital-expansion program. It became an aggressive competitor. Miller's Trenton brewery, completed in 1982, never opened. In 1986, the sales volume of Miller High Life (once the number two beer in America) had declined by 50% since the decade's beginning. Unable to reverse the trend, Miller took a $280 million writeoff on the Trenton brewery.[60]

Techniques

As depicted in Table 4.5, various techniques are used to forecast future situations. Each has its proponents and critics. A study of nearly 500 of the world's largest corporations revealed **trend extrapolation** to be the most

TABLE 4.5
Degree of Usage of Forecasting Techniques*

TECHNIQUE	TOP 1,000 U.S. INDUSTRIALS (n = 215)	TOP 100 U.S. INDUSTRIALS (n = 40)	TOP 300 U.S. NON-INDUSTRIALS (n = 85)	TOP 500 FOREIGN INDUSTRIALS (n = 105)
Trend extrapolation	73%	70%	74%	72%
Statistical modeling (i.e., regression analysis)	48	61	51	45
Scenarios	57	67	67	61
Relevance trees	5	3	7	4
Simulation	34	45	38	27
Brainstorming	65	61	69	52
Trend impact analysis	34	33	31	29
Expert opinion/Delphi	33	42	24	35
Morphological analysis	2	0	0	5
Signal monitoring	15	19	14	18
Cross-impact analysis	12	22	11	5

*Figures reflect the percentage of respondents indicating either "frequent" or "occasional" use. Respondents had been asked to classify their frequency of technique use as "not used," "rarely used," "used occasionally," or "used frequently."

SOURCE: H. E. Klein and R. E. Linneman, "Environmental Assessment: An International Study of Corporate Practices," *Journal of Business Strategy* (Summer 1984), p. 72. Copyright © 1984 by Warren, Gorham & Lamont, Inc. Reprinted by permission. All rights reserved.

widely practiced form of forecasting—over 70% use this technique either occasionally or frequently.[61] Simply stated, extrapolation is the extension of present trends into the future. As shown in the Miller Brewing example, it rests on the assumption that the world is reasonably consistent and changes slowly in the short run. Time-series methods are approaches of this type; these attempt to carry a series of historical events forward into the future. The basic problem with extrapolation is that a historical trend is based upon a series of patterns or relationships among so many different variables that a change in any one can drastically alter the future direction of the trend. As a rule of thumb, the further back into the past one can find relevant data supporting the trend, the more confidence one can have in the prediction. Nevertheless, even experts in forecasting admit: "Forecasts that cover a period of two years or more are typically very inaccurate."[62]

As shown in Table 4.5, brainstorming and statistical modeling are also very popular forecasting techniques. **Brainstorming** is a nonquantitative approach requiring simply the presence of people with some knowledge of the situation to be predicted. The basic ground rule is to propose ideas without first mentally screening them. No criticism is allowed. Ideas tend to build upon previous ideas until a consensus is reached. This is a good technique to use with operating managers who have more faith in "gut feel" than in more quantitative "number crunching" techniques.

Statistical modeling is a quantitative technique that attempts to discover causal or at least explanatory factors that link two or more time series together. Examples of statistical modeling are regression analysis and other econometric methods. Although very useful in the grasping of historic trends, statistical modeling, like trend extrapolation, is based on historical data. As the patterns of relationships change, the accuracy of the forecast deteriorates.[63]

Other forecasting techniques, such as *cross-impact analysis, trend impact analysis,* and *relevance trees* have not established themselves successfully as regularly employed tools. Research by Klein and Linneman reports that corporate planners found these techniques to be complicated, time-consuming, expensive, and academic. Usage was therefore concentrated among the very largest companies and there it was generally used to provide input for scenario-writing.[64]

Research further reports that **scenario-writing** appears to be the most widely used forecasting technique after trend extrapolation. Among corporations in the top Fortune 1,000 Industrials, the usage of scenarios increased from 22% in 1977 to 57% in 1981. Klein and Linneman predict that usage of this popular forecasting technique will increase, but point out that "most companies follow a very informal scenario-writing approach with little reliance on rigorous methodologies."[65] The scenario thus may be merely a written description of some future state, in terms of key variables and issues, or it may be generated in combination with other forecasting techniques.

A more complex version used by General Electric (depicted in Fig. 4.7) is based upon a Delphi panel of experts, a trend impact analysis, and a cross-impact analysis. The **Delphi technique** involves an anonymous panel of experts who are asked individually to estimate the probability of certain events' occurrence in the future. After seeing the anonymous responses from the other experts on the panel, each member of the panel is given several opportunities to revise his/her estimate. **Cross-impact analysis** (CIA), which is typically done on a computer, produces a matrix showing the interaction of the various likely developments that had been generated earlier by the Delphi panel. For example, in the lower right corner of Fig. 4.7, the CIA matrix indicates a prediction that the development of usable nuclear energy by the fusion (instead of the current fission) process will probably result in oil price-cuts by the members of OPEC and an increase in safety and environmental laws regarding the mining and burning of coal. **Trend-impact analysis** (TIA), in contrast, begins with an outside expert's or a Delphi panel's forecast of a trend or phenomenon. For example, if someone were interested in the future of cigarette smoking, one might use extrapolation to forecast a continuing downward trend in the number of smokers. Various possible influencing factors are then added to the forecast, and predictions

FIGURE 4.7
Scenario Construction at General Electric.

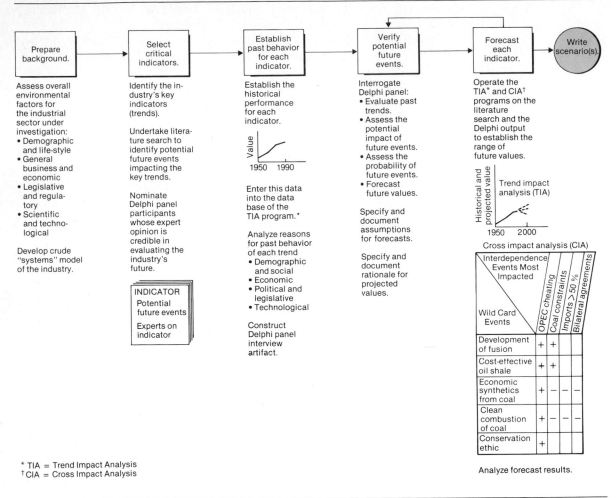

* TIA = Trend Impact Analysis
† CIA = Cross Impact Analysis

Source: General Electric Company. Used by permission.

of three or more alternative future trends result. For example, the likelihood that campaigns against public smoking will increase, might cause the trend in number of smokers to decline faster. The invention of smokeless tobacco might cause the trend to reverse its decline. The output from the Delphi panel, the cross-impact analysis, and the trend-impact analysis are then used in the development of a series of probable future scenarios.

In his book *Competitive Advantage,* Michael Porter strongly recommends the use of scenarios because they (1) allow a firm to move away from use of dangerous, single-point forecasts of the future in instances when the future cannot be predicted, and (2) encourage managers to make their assumptions explicit.[66] He recommends the use of **industry scenarios,** which utilize variables from the societal environment in terms of their effect on the key stakeholders in a corporation's task environment (industry). The process may operate as follows.[67]

1. **Examine possible shifts in the societal variables** (e.g., economic, socio-cultural, technological, and political-legal). Begin with the obvious variables listed in Table 4.4 and decide which of them might be changing so as to create a strategic issue. In order to identify those issues of most importance to the corporation and/or the industry, plot these variables on the issues-priority matrix depicted in Fig. 4.2.

2. **Identify uncertainties in each of the six forces from the task environment** (e.g., competitors, buyers, suppliers, likely substitutes, potential entrants, and other key stakeholders) as depicted in Fig. 4.4. Make sure that all the high-priority strategic issues identified in the first step are specified in terms of the appropriate forces in the task environment.

3. **Identify the causal factors behind the uncertainties.** These sources of uncertainty can be inside the industry (e.g., competitor behavior) or outside the industry (e.g., new regulations). It is likely that many of these causal factors were identified earlier when the societal environment was analyzed. It is also likely that new ones surfaced when the task environment was analyzed.

4. **Make a range of plausible assumptions about each important causal factor.** For example, if the price of oil is a causal factor, make reasonable assumptions about its future level in terms of high, low, and most probable price. A trend-impact analysis may be of some value here.

5. **Combine assumptions about individual causal factors into internally consistent scenarios.** Put various combinations of the assumptions together into sets of scenarios. Because one assumption may affect another, ensure that the scenarios are internally consistent. A simplified cross-impact analysis may be of some value in one's determining the interaction of likely trends. For example, if a scenario includes the assumptions of high oil prices and a low level of economic inflation, that scenario is not internally consistent and should be rejected. (It is an unlikely event because high oil prices tend to drive inflation upward.)

6. **Analyze the industry situation that would prevail under each scenario.** For example, if one scenario assumes that generic (no-name) drugs will be more in demand than brand-name drugs, the situation in the drug industry under that assumption will be very different than under the assumption that the demand for generic drugs will be negligible. For example, an industry dominated by generic drugs would have low profit margins for all firms and a very heavy degree of competition. It is likely that in that industry situation a few firms would leave the drug industry.

7. **Determine the sources of competitive advantage under each scenario.** For example, in an industry dominated by generic drugs, the combination

of low price backed up by low operating costs would provide competitive advantage to a firm. If brand-name drugs dominated, the combination of strong advertising, high-quality production, and heavy promotion would provide competitive advantage to the firm using them.

8. **Predict competitors' behavior under each scenario.** As the industry moves toward a particular scenario each competitor will make some adjustment. Some might leave the industry. New competitors might enter. Using each competitor's history and what is known about its management, estimate what each competitor is likely to do. Once this is done, management should be able to specify the *strategic factors* that are necessary for success (opportunities) as well as those that could cause failure (threats), in a variety of future scenarios. In order to choose the ones most likely to occur, one can also attach probabilities to each of the developed scenarios.[68]

Once management has scanned the external environment to identify strategic factors and forecasted their probable impact on future corporate activities, they must do the same for the corporation's internal environment, as will be shown next in Chapter 5.

SUMMARY AND CONCLUSION

Anyone concerned with how strategic decisions are made in large corporations should be aware of the impact of the external environment on top management and the board of directors. Long-run developments in the economic, technological, political-legal, and sociocultural aspects of the societal environment strongly affect the corporation's activities through the more immediate pressures in its task environment.

Business and commerce have lived an uneasy truce with society for centuries. Within societies that vacillate between heavy regulation and *laissez-faire* economics, business corporations are learning that they must be socially responsible if they are to operate with some autonomy. Top management and the board of directors must constantly balance the needs of one stakeholder in the corporation's task environment against the needs of another. They must ensure that the priorities of their corporation do not get too far away from those valued by society.

Before strategy can be formulated, strategy makers must scan the external environment for possible opportunities and threats. They must identify strategic issues to be monitored, as well as assess which are likely to affect the corporation in the future. Then they must analyze the resulting information and disseminate it to the people involved in strategic planning and decision making.

Just as environmental scanning provides an understanding of present trends in the environment, forecasting provides assumptions about the future that are crucial for strategic management. Most modern corporations use the techniques of trend extrapolation, scenario-writing, brainstorming, and statistical modeling to predict their future environment. Even if the predictions prove to be wrong, the very act of scanning and forecasting the environment helps managers take a broader perspective. These techniques also help prevent the development of reactive managers, who dare not take the time to plan for the future because they are caught up in the crises and problems of the present. Ward Hagan, Chief Executive Officer of Warner-Lambert, makes a strong argument in favor of environmental scanning and forecasting:

> Nobody can plan accurately, strategically, five years ahead. But the intellectual discipline that

it imposes on operating people once a year is the best possible medicine I know for clear, sequential thinking.[69]

DISCUSSION QUESTIONS

1. When business corporations close a facility, should they be required to pay some sort of compensation to the communities they are leaving?

2. How appropriate is the theory of *laissez-faire* in today's world?

3. Why should a business corporation be socially responsible?

4. What can a corporation do to ensure that information about strategic environmental factors gets to the attention of strategy makers?

5. To what extent do you agree with the conclusion that the ultimate profit potential of an industry depends on the collective strength of six key forces: the threat of new entrants, the rivalry among existing firms, the threat of substitutable products or services, the bargaining power of buyers, the bargaining power of

suppliers, and the relative power of other stakeholders? Defend your view.

6. If most long-term forecasts are usually incorrect, why bother doing them?

7. Compare and contrast trend extrapolation with the writing of scenarios, as forecasting techniques.

8. List and discuss the major stakeholders in CSX Corporation's task environment as discussed in the Integrative Case at the end of this chapter. What do each of them want from the company?

9. What are some of the most important opportunities and threats present in the external environment of CSX Corporation as mentioned in the following Integrative Case? Which of these should have a major impact in strategy formulation at the time of the case and in the future?

NOTES

1. E. C. Bursk, D. T. Clark, and R. W. Hidy, "The Oldest Business Code: Nearly 4000 Years Ago," *The World of Business,* vol. 1 (New York: Simon and Schuster, 1962), pp. 9–10.

2. F. E. Kast and J. E. Rosenzweig, *Organization and Management,* 2nd ed. (New York: McGraw-Hill, 1974), p. 28.

3. M. Weber, *The Protestant Ethic and the Spirit of Capitalism,* trans. Talcott Parsons (New York: Charles Scribner's Sons, 1958)

4. Kast and Rosenzweig, p. 35.

5. J. W. McGuire, *Business and Society* (New York: McGraw-Hill, 1963), p. 78.

6. Kast and Rosenzweig, pp. 37–39.

7. *New York Times* (April 23, 1962) as quoted by H. L. Gabel, G. A. Becker, and B. S. Seng, "Armco—The 1978 Wage and Price Guidelines," in T. L. Wheelen and J. D. Hunger, *Strategic Management and Business Policy,* 1st ed. (Reading, Mass.: Addison-Wesley, 1983), p. 397.

8. G. A. Steiner, *The New CEO* (New York: Macmillan Publishing, 1983), p. 6.
W. E. Deming, *Out of the Crisis* (Cambridge, Mass.: M.I.T. Center for Advanced Study, 1986), p. 153.

9. K. Hughes, *Corporate Response to Declining Rates of Growth* (Lexington, Mass.: Lexington Books, 1982), p. 14.

10. R. B. Reich, *The Next American Frontier* (New York: Times Books, 1983).

11. A. R. Karr, "Chrysler Agrees to Pay $1.6 Million Fine to Settle OSHA Health, Safety Charges," *Wall Street Journal* (July 7, 1987), pp. 3 and 8.

12. R. E. Freeman, *Strategic Management: A Stakeholder Approach* (Boston: Pitman Publishing Co., 1984), p. 25.

13. B. Z. Posner and W. H. Schmidt, "Values and the American Manager: An Update," *California Management Review* (Spring 1984), pp. 202–216.

14. J. M. Schlesinger, "GM Sued by Town for $318.3 Million Over Breakup of 64-Year 'Marriage,' " *Wall Street Journal* (August 21, 1987), p. 4.

15. "Kennedy, Zulu Leader Discuss Investments," *Ames Tribune* (United Press International) (Ames, Iowa, January 10, 1985), p. 20.

16. D. Kneale, "Sullivan Urges Firms to Quit South Africa," *Wall Street Journal* (June 4, 1987), p. 6.

"Half of Canadian Concerns in South Africa Pulled Out," *Wall Street Journal* (June 26, 1987), p. 6.

For an excellent review of the arguments for and against business involvement in South Africa, see "Divestment and Disinvestment from South Africa: A Reappraisal," by D. Beaty and O. Harari, *California Management Review* (Summer, 1987), pp. 31–50.

17. "Three Mile Island's Lingering Ills," *Business Week* (October 22, 1979), p. 75.

T. Redburn, "Stalled Nuclear Power Plant: PG&E Feels Powerless," *Los Angeles Times* (February 24, 1980), part 4, p. 1.

J. H. Dobrzynski, W. B. Glaberson, R. W. King, W. J. Powell, Jr., and L. Helm, "Union Carbide Fights for Its Life," *Business Week* (December 24, 1984), pp. 52–56.

18. "Who Will Be Liable for Toxic Dumping?" *Business Week* (August 28, 1978), p. 32.

19. C. P. Alexander, B. R. Leavitt, and R. Samghabadi, "Robbins Runs for Shelter," *Business Week* (September 2, 1985), pp. 32–33.

20. L. Sorenson, "Chapter 11 Filing by Wilson Foods Roils Workers' Lives, Tests Law," *Wall Street Journal* (May 23, 1983), p. 25.

J. Fierman, "Safe in Chapter 11," *Fortune* (March 5, 1984), p. 143.

21. S. Soloman, "The Asbestos Fallout at Johns-Manville," *Fortune* (May 7, 1979), pp. 197–206.

B. Richards and A. Kotlowitz, "Judge Finds 3 Corporate Officials Guilty of Murder in Cyanide Death of Worker," *Wall Street Journal* (June 17, 1985), p. 2.

22. "Test Case: A Defense Contractor Is Fined," *Time* (March 19, 1984), p. 47.

F. Schwadel, "General Electric Pleads Guilty in Fraud Case," *Wall Street Journal* (May 14, 1985), p. 119.

C. P. Alexander, A. Constable, and J. M. Nash, "Crime in the Suites," *Time* (June 10, 1985), pp. 56–57.

S. W. Gellerman, "Why 'Good' Managers Make Bad Ethical Choices," *Harvard Business Review* (July-August 1986), pp. 85–90.

23. W. M. Pride and O. C. Ferrell, *Marketing,* 2nd ed. (Boston: Houghton Mifflin, 1980), p. 720.

24. M. Friedman, "The Social Responsibility of Business Is to Increase Its Profits," *New York Times Magazine* (September 13, 1970), pp. 30, 126–127; and *Capitalism and Freedom* (Chicago: University of Chicago Press, 1963), p. 133.

25. M. Gable and P. Arlow, "A Comparative Examination of the Value Orientations of British and American Executives," *International Journal of Management* (September 1986), pp. 97–106.

W. D. Guth and R. Tagiuri, "Personal Values and Corporate Strategy," *Harvard Business Review* (September-October 1965), pp. 126–127.

26. Posner and Schmidt, pp. 203–205.

27. S. N. Brenner and E. A. Molander, "Is the Ethics of Business Changing?" *Harvard Business Review* (January-February 1977), p. 70.

28. A. B. Carroll, "A Three-Dimensional Conceptual Model of Corporate Performance," *Academy of Management Review* (October 1979), pp. 497–505.

29. L. Iacocca, *Iacocca: An Autobiography* (Toronto: Bantam Books, 1984), pp. 196–197.

30. K. E. Aupperle, A. B. Carroll, and J. D. Hatfield, "An Empirical Examination of the Relationship between Corporate Social Responsibility and Profitability," *Academy of Management Journal* (June 1985), p. 459.

A. A. Ullmann, "Data in Search of a Theory: A Critical Examination of the Relationship Among Social Performance, Social Disclosure, and Economic Performance of U.S. Firms," *Academy of Management Review* (July 1985), pp. 540–557.

31. "A Visionary Exits," *Time* (January 20, 1986), p. 44.

32. K. Davis, "The Meaning and Scope of Social Responsibility," in J. W. McGuire (ed.), *Contemporary Management: Issues and Viewpoints* (Englewood Cliffs, N.J.: Prentice-Hall, 1974), p. 631.

33. S. Kilman, "An Unexpected Result of Airline Decontrol Is Return to Monopolies," *Wall Street Journal* (July 20, 1987), p. 1.

R. W. Crandall, "Don't Cartelize the Steel Industry," *Wall Street Journal* (July 20, 1987), p. 16.

34. *Wall Street Journal* (July 21, 1987), p. 1.

35. H. E. Klein and R. E. Linneman, "Environmental Assessment: An International Study of Corporate Practices," *Journal of Business Strategy* (Summer 1984), p. 67.

36. N. H. Snyder, "Environmental Volatility, Scanning Intensity and Organization Performance," *Journal of Contemporary Business* (September 1981), p. 7.

37. R. H. Waterman, Jr., "The Renewal Factor," *Business Week* (September 14, 1987), p. 101.

38. J. E. Dutton and E. Ottensmeyer, "Strategic Issue Management Systems: Forms, Functions, and Contexts," *Academy of Management Review* (April 1987), pp. 355–365.

P. Lorange, M. F. S. Morton, and S. Ghoshal, *Strategic Control* (St. Paul: West Publishing Co., 1986), pp. 101–104.

39. P. V. Jenster, "Using Critical Success Factors in Planning," *Long Range Planning* (August 1987), p. 108.

40. J. E. Dutton and R. B. Duncan, "The Creation of Momentum for Change Through the Process of Strategic Issue Diagnosis," *Strategic Management Journal* (May-June 1987), pp. 279–295.

41. M. Javidan. "The Impact of Environmental Uncertainty on Long-Range Planning and Practices of the U.S. Savings and Loan Industry," *Strategic Management Journal* (October-December 1984), pp. 381–392.

42. S. C. Jain, "Environmental Scanning in U.S. Corporations," *Long Range Planning* (April 1984), p. 119.

43. C. Wallis, "The Child-Care Dilemma," *Time* (June 22, 1987), pp. 54–60.

44. M. Levin-Epstein, ed., *Older Americans in the Work-force: Challenges and Solutions* (Rockville, Md.: Bureau of National Affairs, 1987) as reported by M. Memmott, "Companies Face Aging Work Force," *USA Today* (July 9, 1987), p. 5B.

Work Force 2000 (Indianapolis: The Hudson Institute, 1987) as reported by A. R. Karr, "Efficiency of Economy's Service Sector Must Be Buttressed, Study for U.S. Says," *Wall Street Journal* (July 3, 1987), p. 13.

45. J. Naisbitt, *Megatrends* (New York: Warner Books, 1982).

46. M. E. Porter, *Competitive Strategy* (New York: Free Press, 1980), p. 3.

47. This summary of the forces driving competitive strategy is taken from M. E. Porter, *Competitive Strategy* (New York: Free Press, 1980), pp. 7–29.

48. Porter, p. 23.

49. R. E. Freeman, *Strategic Management: A Stakeholder Approach* (Boston: Pitman Publishing, 1984), pp. 140–142.

50. R. E. Miles and C. C. Snow, *Organizational Strategy, Structure, and Process* (New York: McGraw-Hill Book Co., 1978).

51. R. T. Pascale, "Perspective on Strategy: The Real Story Behind Honda's Success," *California Management Review* (Spring 1981), p. 70.

52. B. Rosenbloom and R. V. Tripuraneni, "Strategic Planning Catches On In U.S. Retailers," *Long Range Planning* (August 1985), p. 59.

53. D. C. Smith and J. E. Prescott, "Demystifying Competitive Analysis," *Planning Review* (September/October 1987), p. 13. For more in-depth information on the gathering of competitor intelligence, refer to the entire September/October 1987 issue of *Planning Review.*

54. Snyder, p. 16.

55. C. Cox, "Planning in a Changing Environment: The Search for External Data," in *Handbook of Business Strategy, 1985/86 Yearbook,* edited by W. D. Guth (Boston: Warren, Gorham, and Lamont, 1985), p. 5.2.

56. J. L. Roberts, "As Information Swells, Firms Open Libraries," *Wall Street Journal* (September 25, 1983), p. 25.

57. J. Drinkhall, "Hitachi Ltd. Pleads Guilty in IBM Case," *Wall Street Journal* (February 9, 1983), p. 4.

58. G. L. Miles, "Information Thieves Are Now Corporate Enemy No. 1," *Business Week* (May 5, 1986), pp. 120–125.

59. S. P. Schnaars, "How to Develop and Use Scenarios," *Long Range Planning* (February 1987), p. 106.

60. J. Merwin, "A Billion in Blunders," *Forbes* (December 1, 1986), p. 104.

61. H. E. Klein and R. E. Linneman, "Environmental Assessment: An International Study of Corporate Practices," *Journal of Business Strategy* (Summer 1984), p. 72.

62. S. Makridakis and S. C. Wheelwright, "Introduction to Management Forecasting," *The Handbook of Forecasting* (New York: Wiley and Sons, 1982), p. 8.

63. Makridakis and Wheelwright, p. 6.

64. Klein and Linneman, p. 72.

65. Klein and Linneman, p. 73.

66. M. E. Porter, *Competitive Advantage* (New York: The Free Press, 1985), p. 447.

67. This process of scenario development is adapted from M. E. Porter, *Competitive Advantage* (New York: The Free Press, 1985), pp. 448–470.

68. For further information on scenario writing, cross-impact analysis, and the Delphi Technique, refer to *Microenvironmental Analysis for Strategic Management* by L. Fahey and V. K. Narayanan (St. Paul: West Publishing Co., 1986), pp. 213–219.

For information on trend-impact analysis, see W. R. Huss and E. J. Honton, "Scenario Planning—What Style Should You Use?" *Long Range Planning* (August 1987), pp. 23–24.

69. M. Magnet, "How Top Managers Make a Company's Toughest Decisions," *Fortune* (March 18, 1985), p. 55.

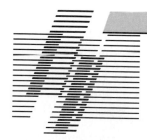

INTEGRATIVE CASE

CSX CORPORATION'S EXTERNAL ENVIRONMENT

During the 1970s, U.S. railroads had faced a bleak future. Starved for capital, the industry deferred maintenance and other badly needed capital improvements so it could meet the financial requirements of its day-to-day operations. The decrease in

SOURCE: J. D. Hunger, B. Ferrin, H. Felix-Gamez, and T. Goetzman, "CSX Corporation," *Cases in Strategic Management and Business Policy* by T. L. Wheelen and J. D. Hunger (Reading, Mass.: Addison-Wesley, 1987), pp. 91–123.

traffic levels and revenue over a three-decade period reflected a shifting industrial base, a changing marketplace, a maturing of competing transportation modes, and a regulatory system that made it almost impossible for the industry to adjust to changing market demands. Between 1947 and 1979, intercity freight tonnage doubled, but railroad tonnage increased only 1%. Barge tonnage in contrast increased 250%, while truck tonnage was up 300%. By the mid-1970s, about one fifth of the industry was facing annual losses and even bankruptcy. Nationalization of the railroads took its first step with the formation of the government-owned Consolidated Rail Corporation (Conrail) in 1976. Formed from the bankrupt Penn Central and five other ailing Northeastern railroads, Conrail was an attempt to keep rail service operating for businesses that were dependent on rail transportation in New York, New Jersey, and New England.

GOVERNMENT DEREGULATION CHANGES INDUSTRY

On October 14, 1980, President Carter signed into law the Staggers Rail Act, allowing the railroad industry to enjoy the first period of real regulatory freedom for many years. This act was the most significant change in federal policy toward this industry since the Interstate Commerce Act of 1887. The Staggers Act overturned many principles derived from the 1887 act and the long subsequent period of regulation.

The goals of the Staggers Act were (1) to assist the industry in its rehabilitation under private ownership, (2) to reform federal regulatory policy so that an efficient, economical, and stable system could be achieved, and (3) to provide the necessary regulation to balance the needs of carriers, shippers, and the public. Under Staggers, rail carriers no longer were obliged to provide unprofitable services. They were then allowed to set rates and services that could generate a profit. However, the Interstate Commerce Commission (ICC) still preserved the power to prevent monopolistic practices. Another important result of the Staggers Act had been the facilitation of rail mergers by speeding the decision process used by the ICC to review applications.

After the merger that formed CSX, the Norfolk and Western Railroad merged with the Southern Railway Company, to form Norfolk Southern Corporation. This combination was almost inevitable, because the Chessie System had been the traditional competitor of the N&W in the North, while Seaboard and Southern had been long-standing rivals in the South. In 1985 three rail systems dominated the eastern United States: *CSX, Norfolk Southern,* and *Conrail.* See Table 4.6 for a comparison of the three systems.

COMPETITIVE RIVALRY INCREASES

Since deregulation occurred, railroad rivalry was like "chess-type playing where you make a move and somebody else makes a countermove and you have to figure out what your next move is," said James A. Hagen, Conrail's Senior Vice-President for Marketing and Sales. This was definitely a new era for railroads. Learning to live in the deregulated environment became a must for everyone in the industry. Competition demanded that mentalities that had been constrained by excessive regulation and were more accustomed to cooperating with competitors than competing with them, be reshaped into outlooks that could generate the fresh ideas required by the newly invigorated market competition, resulting from deregulation.

TABLE 4.6

A Comparison of the Three Major Eastern Railroads

	12/31/84			12/31/83			12/31/82		
	Norfolk Southern	CSX	Conrail	Norfolk Southern	CSX	Conrail	Norfolk Southern	CSX	Conrail
Rail Operating Revenues[1]	3,524.6	5,058.0	3,379.4	3,148.1	4,554.0	3,076.4	3,359.0	4,554.0	3,616.6
Rail Operating Income[1]	734.0	657.0	466.0	543.7	446.0	288.2	659.3	365.0	48.6
Total Net Income[1]	482.2	465.0	500.2	356.5	272.0	313.0	461.8	414.0	174.2

	AS OF 12/31/84		
	Norfolk Southern	CSX	Conrail
Route Miles	18,252	26,000	15,400
Rail Employees	37,998	53,031	39,044

SOURCES: *Moody's Transportation Manual 1985;* CSX Corporation, *1984 Annual Report;* and *Standard Corporate Descriptions* (Standard & Poor's Corporation), October 1985.

NOTE: [1]In millions of dollars.

PRESSURES FOR RE-REGULATION

In March 1983, the National Industrial Traffic League (NITL), a shipper's trade and lobbying group, complained that what it called a growing "balkanization" of the nation's rail network could lead to regional monopolies. On October 22, 1984, both houses of Congress promised to look into shipper's complaints about alleged rate abuses resulting from rail deregulation. The specific issue was the criteria used by the ICC in its deciding whether a rate was excessively high and therefore subject to administrative action. Also at issue were the rate-making guidelines that the ICC recommended for the determining of maximum rates. A good deal of controversy had been generated by the application of these guidelines to coal shipments. "During the early part of 1985, we anticipate that Congress will closely examine the implementation of the Staggers Act, and take any legislative action that must be taken to assure the careful balance (between the interest of shippers and rail carriers) struck in the act," said a letter circulated in Congress and signed by sixteen senators.

Further, there appeared to be some resistance, by shippers, to the idea of a multimodal transportation conglomerate. Commonly held notions about the best relationship between supplier and customer dictated that a firm not let itself get too dependent on any one supplier. (This attitude was one of the major reasons that many coal-fired utility plants had been located along rivers as well as beside railway tracks. With this location the utility had the leverage of threatening to take its traffic elsewhere if rate negotiations with a railroad did not progress satisfactorily.) Many shippers thus were reluctant to become too dependent on railroads, even with promises of lower costs.

IMPACT OF THE PROPOSED SALE OF CONRAIL

Even though the corporation closed 1984 in a strong financial and physical position, a few strategic issues existed in early 1985 that could strongly affect the future of CSX. One of these was the future of Conrail, the largest customer of CSX. Although the U.S. Department of Transportation had decided to sell its 85% stake in Conrail to Norfolk Southern for $1.2 billion, the deal might not be approved by Congress. Both Watkins (Chairman of CSX) and Paul Funkhouser (President) agreed that a merger between Norfolk Southern and the big Northeastern railroad company Consolidated Rail Corporation (Conrail), could have serious consequences for CSX:

> A Norfolk Southern/Conrail combination would raise serious questions as to the ability of other carriers, including major portions of Chessie, to continue serving areas where so much market control is lodged in one rail system. Abandonment of large parts of Chessie's plant, therefore, would have to be seriously considered. The result could be withdrawal from several thousand miles of service, which would worsen, rather than improve, the competitive service picture.

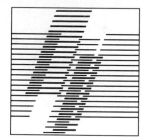

APPENDIX 4.A

HOW COMPETITIVE FORCES SHAPE STRATEGY*

MICHAEL E. PORTER

The nature and degree of competition in an industry hinge on five forces: the threat of new entrants, the bargaining power of customers, the bargaining power of suppliers, the threat of substitute products or services (where applicable), and the jockeying among current contestants. To establish a strategic agenda for dealing with these contending currents and to grow despite them, a company must understand how they work in its industry and how they affect the company in its particular situation. The author details how these forces operate and suggests ways of adjusting to them and, where possible, of taking advantage of them.

The essence of strategy formulation is coping with competition. Yet it is easy to view competition too narrowly and too pessimistically. While one sometimes hears executives complaining to the contrary, intense competition in an industry is neither coincidence nor bad luck.

Moreover, in the fight for market share, competition is not manifested only in the other players. Rather, competition in an industry is rooted in its underlying economics, and competitive forces exist that go well beyond the established combatants in a particular industry. Customers, suppliers, potential entrants, and substitute products are all competitors that may be more or less prominent or active depending on the industry.

The state of competition in an industry depends on five basic forces, which are diagrammed in Figure 4.A.1. The collective strength of these forces determines the ultimate profit potential of an industry. It ranges from *intense* in industries like tires, metal cans, and steel,

where no company earns spectacular returns on investment, to *mild* in industries like oil field services and equipment, soft drinks, and toiletries, where there is room for quite high returns.

In the economists' "perfectly competitive" industry, jockeying for position is unbridled and entry to the industry very easy. This kind of industry structure, of course, offers the worst prospect for long-run profitability. The weaker the forces collectively, however, the greater the opportunity for superior performance.

Whatever their collective strength, the corporate strategist's goal is to find a position in the industry where his or her company can best defend itself against these forces or can influence them in its favor. The collective strength of the forces may be painfully apparent to all the antagonists; but to cope with them, the strategist must delve below the surface and analyze the sources of each. For example, what makes the industry vulnerable to entry? What determines the bargaining power of suppliers?

Knowledge of these underlying sources of competitive pressure provides the groundwork for a strategic agenda of action. They highlight the critical strengths and weaknesses of the company, animate the positioning of the company in its industry, clarify the areas where strategic changes may yield the greatest payoff, and highlight the places where industry trends promise to hold the greatest significance as either opportunities or threats. Understanding these sources also proves to be of help in considering areas for diversification.

CONTENDING FORCES

The strongest competitive force or forces determine the profitability of an industry and so are of greatest importance in strategy formulation. For example, even a company with a strong position in an industry unthreatened by potential entrants will earn low returns

FIGURE 4.A.1
Forces Governing Competition in an Industry.

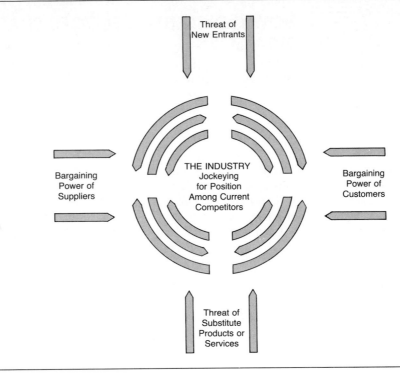

---

if it faces a superior or a lower-cost substitute product—as the leading manufacturers of vacuum tubes and coffee percolators have learned to their sorrow. In such a situation, coping with the substitute product becomes the number one strategic priority.

Different forces take on prominence, of course, in shaping competition in each industry. In the ocean-going tanker industry the key force is probably the buyers (the major oil companies), while in tires it is powerful OEM buyers coupled with tough competitors. In the steel industry the key forces are foreign competitors and substitute materials.

Every industry has an underlying structure, or a set of fundamental economic and technical characteristics, that gives rise to these competitive forces. The strategist, wanting to position his company to cope best with its industry environment or to influence that environment in the company's favor, must learn what makes the environment tick.

This view of competition pertains equally to industries dealing in services and to those selling products. To avoid monotony in this article, I refer to both products and services as "products." The same general principles apply to all types of business.

A few characteristics are critical to the strength of each competitive force. I shall discuss them in this section.

Threat of Entry

New entrants to an industry bring new capacity, the desire to gain market share, and often substantial resources. Companies diversifying through acquisition into the industry from other markets often leverage their resources to cause a shake-up, as Philip Morris did with Miller beer.

The seriousness of the threat of entry depends on the barriers present and on the reaction from existing competitors that the entrant can expect. If barriers to entry are high and a newcomer can expect sharp retaliation from the entrenched competitors, obviously he will not pose a serious threat of entering.

There are six major sources of barriers to entry:

1. **Economics of scale**—These economies deter entry by forcing the aspirant either to come in on large scale or to accept a cost disadvantage. Scale economies in production, research, marketing, and service are probably the key barriers to entry in the mainframe computer industry, as Xerox and GE sadly discovered. Economies of scale can also act as hurdles in distribution, utilization of the sales force, financing, and nearly any other part of a business.

2. **Product differentiation**—Brand identification creates a barrier by forcing entrants to spend heavily to overcome customer loyalty. Advertising, customer service, being first in the industry, and product differences are among the factors fostering brand identification. It is perhaps the most important entry barrier in soft drinks, over-the-counter drugs, cosmetics, investment banking, and public accounting. To create high fences around their businesses, brewers couple brand identification with economies of scale in production, distribution, and marketing.

3. **Capital requirements**—The need to invest large financial resources in order to compete creates a barrier to entry, particularly if the capital is required for unrecoverable expenditures in up-front advertising or R&D. Capital is necessary not only for fixed facilities but also for customer credit, inventories, and absorbing start-up losses. While major corporations have the financial resources to invade almost any industry, the high capital requirements in certain fields, such as computer manufacturing and mineral extraction, limit the pool of likely entrants.

4. **Cost disadvantages independent of size**—Entrenched companies may have cost advantages not available to potential rivals, no matter what their size and attainable economies of scale. These advantages can stem from the effects of the learning curve (and of its first cousin, the experience curve), proprietary technology, access to the best raw materials sources, assets purchased at preinflation prices, government subsidies, or favorable locations. Sometimes cost advantages are legally enforceable, as they are through patents. (For an analysis of the much-discussed experience curve as a barrier to entry, see the boxed insert.)

5. **Access to distribution channels**—The new boy on the block must, of course, secure distribution of his product or service. A new food product, for example, must displace others from the supermarket shelf via price breaks, promotions, intense selling efforts, or some other means. The more limited the wholesale or retail channels are and the more that existing competitors have these tied up, obviously the tougher that entry into the industry will be. Sometimes this barrier is so high that, to surmount it, a new contestant must create its own distribution channels, as Timex did in the watch industry in the 1950s.

6. **Government policy**—The government can limit or even foreclose entry to industries with such controls as license requirements and limits on access to raw materials. Regulated industries like trucking, liquor retailing, and freight forwarding are noticeable examples; more subtle government restrictions operate in fields like ski-area development and coal mining. The government also can play a major indirect role by affecting entry barriers through controls such as air and water pollution standards and safety regulations.

The potential rival's expectations about the reaction of existing competitors also will influence its decision on whether to enter. The company is likely to have second thoughts if incumbents have previously lashed out at new entrants or if:

- The incumbents possess substantial resources to fight back, including excess cash and unused borrowing power, productive capacity, or clout with distribution channels and customers.
- The incumbents seem likely to cut prices because of a desire to keep market shares or because of industrywide excess capacity.
- Industry growth is slow, affecting its ability to absorb the new arrival and probably causing the financial performance of all the parties involved to decline.

Changing Conditions. From a strategic standpoint there are two important additional points to note about the threat of entry.

First, it changes, of course, as these conditions change. The expiration of Polaroid's basic patents on instant photography, for instance, greatly reduced its absolute cost entry barrier built by proprietary technology. It is not surprising that Kodak plunged into the market. Product differentiation in printing has all but disappeared. Conversely, in the auto industry economies of scale increased enormously with post-World War II automation and vertical integration—virtually stopping successful new entry.

Second, strategic decisions involving a large segment of an industry can have a major impact on the conditions determining the threat of entry. For example, the actions of many U.S. wine producers in the 1960s to step up product introductions, raise advertising levels, and expand distribution nationally surely strengthened the entry roadblocks by raising economies of scale and making access to distribution channels more difficult. Similarly, decisions by members of the recreational vehicle industry to vertically integrate in order to lower costs have greatly increased the economies of scale and raised the capital cost barriers.

Powerful Suppliers and Buyers

Suppliers can exert bargaining power on participants in an industry by raising prices or reducing the quality of purchased goods and services. Powerful suppliers can thereby squeeze profitability out of an industry unable to recover cost increases in its own prices. By raising their prices, soft drink concentrate producers have contributed to the erosion of profitability of bottling companies because the bottlers, facing intense competition from powdered mixes, fruit drinks, and other beverages, have limited freedom to raise *their* prices accordingly. Customers likewise can force down prices, demand higher quality or more service, and play competitors off against each other—all at the expense of industry profits.

The power of each important supplier or buyer group depends on a number of characteristics of its market situation and on the relative importance of its sales or purchases to the industry compared with its overall business.

A *supplier* group is powerful if:

- It is dominated by a few companies and is more concentrated than the industry it sells to.
- Its product is unique or at least differentiated, or if it has built up switching costs. Switching costs are

---

THE EXPERIENCE CURVE AS AN ENTRY BARRIER

In recent years, the experience curve has become widely discussed as a key element of industry structure. According to this concept, unit costs in many manufacturing industries (some dogmatic adherents say in *all* manufacturing industries) as well as in some service industries decline with "experience," or a particular company's cumulative volume of production. (The experience curve, which encompasses many factors, is a broader concept than the better-known learning curve, which refers to the efficiency achieved over a period of time by workers through much repetition.)

The causes of the decline in unit costs are a combination of elements, including economies of scale, the learning curve for labor, and capital-labor substitution. The cost decline creates a barrier to entry because new competitors with no "experience" face higher costs than established ones, particularly the producer with the largest market share, and have difficulty catching up with the entrenched competitors.

Adherents of the experience curve concept stress the importance of achieving market leadership to maximize this barrier to entry, and they recommend aggressive action to achieve it, such as price cutting in anticipation of falling costs in order to build volume. For the combatant that cannot achieve a healthy market share, the prescription is usually, "Get out."

Is the experience curve an entry barrier on which strategies should be built? The answer is: not in every industry. In fact, in some industries, building a strategy on the experience curve can be potentially disastrous. That costs decline with experience in some industries is not news to corporate executives. The significance of the experience curve for strategy depends on what factors are causing the decline.

If costs are falling because a growing company can reap economies of scale through more efficient, automated facilities and vertical integration, then the cumulative volume of production is unimportant to its relative cost position. Here the lowest-cost producer is the one with the largest, most efficient facilities.

A new entrant may well be more efficient than the more experienced competitors; if it has built the newest plant, it will face no disadvantage in having to catch up. The strategic prescription, "You must have the fixed costs buyers face in changing suppliers. They arise because, among other things, a buyer's product specifications tie it to particular suppliers, it has invested heavily in specialized ancillary equipment or in learning how to operate a supplier's equipment (as in computer software), or its production lines are connected to the supplier's manufacturing facilities (as in some manufacture of beverage containers).

• It is not obliged to contend with other products for sale to the industry. For instance, the competition between the steel companies and the aluminum companies to sell to the can industry checks the power of each supplier.

• It poses a credible threat of integrating forward into the industry's business. This provides a check against the industry's ability to improve the terms on which it purchases.

• The industry is not an important customer of the supplier group. If the industry *is* an important customer, suppliers' fortunes will be closely tied to the industry, and they will want to protect the industry through reasonable pricing and assistance in activities like R&D and lobbying.

A *buyer* group is powerful if:

• It is concentrated or purchases in large volumes. Large-volume buyers are particularly potent forces if heavy fixed costs characterize the industry—as they do in metal containers, corn refining, and bulk chemicals, for example—which raise the stakes to keep capacity filled.

• The products it purchases from the industry are standard or undifferentiated. The buyers, sure that they can always find alternative suppliers, may play one company against another, as they do in aluminum extrusion.

• The products it purchases from the industry form a component of its product and represent a significant fraction of its cost. The buyers are likely to shop for a favorable price and purchase selectively. Where the product sold by the industry in question is a small fraction of buyers' costs, buyers are usually much less price sensitive.

• It earns low profits, which create great incentive to lower its purchasing costs. Highly profitable buyers, however, are generally less price sensitive (that is,

---

largest, most efficient plant," is a lot different from "You must produce the greatest cumulative output of the item to get your costs down."

Whether a drop in costs with cumulative (not absolute) volume erects an entry barrier also depends on the sources of the decline. If costs go down because of technical advances known generally in the industry or because of the development of improved equipment that can be copied or purchased from equipment suppliers, the experience curve is no entry barrier at all—in fact, new or less experienced competitors may actually enjoy a cost *advantage* over the leaders. Free of the legacy of heavy past investments, the newcomer or less experienced competitor can purchase or copy the newest and lowest-cost equipment and technology.

If, however, experience can be kept proprietary, the leaders will maintain a cost advantage. But new entrants may require less experience to reduce their costs than the leaders needed. All this suggests that the experience curve can be a shaky entry barrier on which to build a strategy.

While space does not permit a complete treatment here, I want to mention a few other crucial elements in determining the appropriateness of a strategy built on the entry barrier provided by the experience curve:

• The height of the barrier depends on how important costs are to competition compared with other areas like marketing, selling, and innovation.

• The barrier can be nullified by product or process innovations leading to a substantially new technology and thereby creating an entirely new experience curve.* New entrants can leapfrog the industry leaders and alight on the new experience curve, to which those leaders may be poorly positioned to jump.

• If more than one strong company is building its strategy on the experience curve, the consequences can be nearly fatal. By the time only one rival is left pursuing such a strategy, industry growth may have stopped and the prospects of reaping the spoils of victory long since evaporated.

---

*For an example drawn from the history of the automobile industry, see William J. Abernathy and Kenneth Wayne, "The Limits of the Learning Curve," *Harvard Business Review,* September-October 1974, p. 109.

of course, if the item does not represent a large fraction of their costs).

- The industry's product is unimportant to the quality of the buyers' products or services. Where the quality of the buyers' products is very much affected by the industry's product, buyers are generally less price sensitive. Industries in which this situation [occurs] include oil field equipment, where a malfunction can lead to large losses, and enclosures for electronic medical and test instruments, where the quality of the enclosure can influence the user's impression about the quality of the equipment inside.

- The industry's product does not save the buyer money. Where the industry's product or service can pay for itself many times over, the buyer is rarely price sensitive; rather, he is interested in quality. This is true in services like investment banking and public accounting, where errors in judgment can be costly and embarrassing, and in business like the logging of oil wells, where an accurate survey can save thousands of dollars in drilling costs.

- The buyers pose a credible threat of integrating backward to make the industry's product. The Big Three auto producers and major buyers of cars have often used the threat of self-manufacture as a bargaining lever. But sometimes an industry engenders a threat to buyers that its members may integrate forward.

Most of these sources of buyer power can be attributed to consumers as a group as well as to industrial and commercial buyers; only a modification of the frame of reference is necessary. Consumers tend to be more price sensitive if they are purchasing products that are undifferentiated, expensive relative to their incomes, and of a sort where quality is not particularly important.

The buying power of retailers is determined by the same rules, with one important addition. Retailers can gain significant bargaining power over manufacturers when they can influence consumers' purchasing decisions, as they do in audio components, jewelry, appliances, sporting goods, and other goods.

Strategic Action. A company's choice of suppliers to buy from or buyer groups to sell to should be viewed as a crucial strategic decision. A company can improve its strategic posture by finding suppliers or buyers who possess the least power to influence it adversely.

Most common is the situation of a company being able to choose whom it will sell to—in other words,

buyer selection. Rarely do all the buyer groups a company sells to enjoy equal power. Even if a company sells to a single industry, segments usually exist within that industry that exercise less power (and that are therefore less price sensitive) than others. For example, the replacement market for most products is less price sensitive than the overall market.

As a rule, a company can sell to powerful buyers and still come away with above-average profitability only if it is a low-cost producer in its industry or if its product enjoys some unusual, if not unique, features. In supplying large customers with electric motors, Emerson Electric earns high returns because its low cost position permits the company to meet or undercut competitors' prices.

If the company lacks a low cost position or a unique product, selling to everyone is self-defeating because the more sales it achieves, the more vulnerable it becomes. The company may have to muster the courage to turn away business and sell only to less potent customers.

Buyer selection has been a key to the success of National Can and Crown Cork & Seal. They focus on the segments of the can industry where they can create product differentiation, minimize the threat of backward integration, and otherwise mitigate the awesome power of their customers. Of course, some industries do not enjoy the luxury of selecting "good" buyers.

As the factors creating supplier and buyer power change with time or as a result of a company's strategic decisions, naturally the power of these groups rises or declines. In the ready-to-wear clothing industry, as the buyers (department stores and clothing stores) have become more concentrated and control has passed to large chains, the industry has come under increasing pressure and suffered falling margins. The industry has been unable to differentiate its product or engender switching costs that lock in its buyers to neutralize these trends.

Substitute Products

By placing a ceiling on prices it can charge, substitute products, or services limit the potential of an industry. Unless it can upgrade the quality of the product or differentiate it somehow (as via marketing), the industry will suffer in earnings and possibly in growth.

Manifestly, the more attractive the price-performance tradeoff offered by substitute products, the firmer the lid placed on the industry's profit potential. Sugar producers confronted with the large-scale commercialization of high-fructose corn syrup, a sugar substitute, are learning this lesson today.

Substitutes not only limit profits in normal times; they also reduce the bonanza an industry can reap in boom times. In 1978 the producers of fiberglass insulation enjoyed unprecedented demand as a result of high energy costs and severe winter weather. But the industry's ability to raise prices was tempered by the plethora of insulation substitutes, including cellulose, rock wool, and styrofoam. These substitutes are bound to become an even stronger force once the current round of plant additions by fiberglass insulation producers has boosted capacity enough to meet demand (and then some).

Substitute products that deserve the most attention strategically are those that (a) are subject to trends improving their price-performance tradeoff with the industry's product, or (b) are produced by industries earning high profits. Substitutes often come rapidly into play if some development increases competition in their industries and causes price reduction or performance improvement.

Jockeying for Position

Rivalry among existing competitors takes the familiar form of jockeying for position—using tactics like price competition, product introduction, and advertising slugfests. Intense rivalry is related to the presence of a number of factors:

- Competitors are numerous or are roughly equal in size and power. In many U.S. industries in recent years foreign contenders, of course, have become part of the competitive picture.

- Industry growth is slow, precipitating fights for market share that involve expansion-minded members.

- The product or service lacks differentiation or switching costs, which lock in buyers and protect one combatant from raids on its customers by another.

- Fixed costs are high or the product is perishable, creating strong temptation to cut prices. Many basic materials businesses, like paper and aluminum, suffer from this problem when demand slackens.

- Capacity is normally augmented in large increments. Such additions, as in the chlorine and vinyl chloride businesses, disrupt the industry's supply-demand balance and often lead to periods of overcapacity and price cutting.

- Exit barriers are high. Exit barriers, like very specialized assets or management's loyalty to a particular business, keep companies competing even though they may be earning low or even negative returns on investment. Excess capacity remains functioning, and the profitability of the healthy competitors suffers as the sick ones hang on [1]. If the entire industry suffers from overcapacity, it may seek government help—particularly if foreign competition is present.

- The rivals are diverse in strategies, origins, and "personalities." They have different ideas about how to compete and continually run head-on into each other in the process.

As an industry matures, its growth rate changes, resulting in declining profits and (often) a shakeout. In the booming recreational vehicle industry of the early 1970s, nearly every producer did well; but slow growth since then has eliminated high returns, except for the strongest members, not to mention many of the weaker companies. The same profit story has been played out in industry after industry—snowmobiles, aerosol packaging, and sports equipment are just a few examples.

An acquisition can introduce a very different personality to an industry, as has been the case with Black & Decker's takeover of McCullough, the producer of chain saws. Technological innovation can boost the level of fixed costs in the production process, as it did in the shift from batch to continuous-line photo finishing in the 1960s.

While a company must live with many of these factors—because they are built into industry economics—it may have some latitude for improving matters through strategic shifts. For example, it may try to raise buyers' switching costs or increase product differentiation. A focus on selling efforts in the fastest-growing segments of the industry or on market areas with the lowest fixed costs can reduce the impact of industry rivalry. If it is feasible, a company can try to avoid confrontation with competitors having high exit barriers and can thus sidestep involvement in bitter price cutting.

FORMULATION OF STRATEGY

Once the corporate strategist has assessed the forces affecting competition in his industry and their underlying causes, he can identify his company's strengths and weaknesses. The crucial strengths and weaknesses from a strategic standpoint are the company's posture vis-à-vis the underlying causes of each force. Where does it stand against substitutes? Against the sources of entry barriers?

Then the strategist can devise a plan of action that may include (1) positioning the company so that its capabilities provide the best defense against the competitive force; and/or (2) influencing the balance of the forces through strategic moves, thereby improving the company's position; and/or (3) anticipating shifts in the factors underlying the forces and responding to them, with the hope of exploiting change by choosing a strategy appropriate for the new competitive balance before opponents recognize it. I shall consider each strategic approach in turn.

Positioning the Company

The first approach takes the structure of the industry as given and matches the company's strengths and weaknesses to it. Strategy can be viewed as building defenses against the competitive forces or as finding positions in the industry where the forces are weakest.

Knowledge of the company's capabilities and of the causes of the competitive forces will highlight the areas where the company should confront competition and where avoid it. If the company is a low-cost producer, it may choose to confront powerful buyers while it takes care to sell them only products not vulnerable to competition from substitutes.

The success of Dr Pepper in the soft drink industry illustrates the coupling of realistic knowledge of corporate strengths with sound industry analysis to yield a superior strategy. Coca-Cola and Pepsi-Cola dominate Dr Pepper's industry, where many small concentrate producers compete for a piece of the action. Dr Pepper chose a strategy of avoiding the largest-selling drink segment, maintaining a narrow flavor line, forgoing the development of a captive bottler network, and marketing heavily. The company positioned itself so as to be least vulnerable to its competitive forces while it exploited its small size.

In the $11.5 billion soft drink industry, barriers to entry in the form of brand identification, large-scale marketing, and access to a bottler network are enormous. Rather than accept the formidable costs and scale economies in having its own bottler network—that is, following the lead of the Big Two and of Seven-Up—Dr Pepper took advantage of the different flavor of its drink to "piggyback" on Coke and Pepsi bottlers who wanted a full line to sell to customers. Dr Pepper

coped with the power of these buyers through extraordinary service and other efforts to distinguish its treatment of them from that of Coke and Pepsi.

Many small companies in the soft drink business offer cola drinks that thrust them into head-to-head competition against the majors. Dr Pepper, however, maximized product differentiation by maintaining a narrow line of beverages built around an unusual flavor.

Finally, Dr Pepper met Coke and Pepsi with an advertising onslaught emphasizing the alleged uniqueness of its single flavor. This campaign built strong brand identification and great customer loyalty. Helping its efforts was the fact that Dr Pepper's formula involved lower raw materials cost, which gave the company an absolute cost advantage over its major competitors.

There are no economies of scale in soft drink concentrate production, so Dr Pepper could prosper despite its small share of the business (6%). Thus Dr Pepper confronted competition in marketing but avoided it in product line and in distribution. This artful positioning combined with good implementation has led to an enviable record in earnings and in the stock market.

Influencing the Balance

When dealing with the forces that drive industry competition, a company can devise a strategy that takes the offensive. This posture is designed to do more than merely cope with the forces themselves; it is meant to alter their causes.

Innovations in marketing can raise brand identification or otherwise differentiate the product. Capital investments in large-scale facilities or vertical integration affect entry barriers. The balance of forces is partly a result of external factors and partly in the company's control.

Exploiting Industry Change

Industry evolution is important strategically because evolution, of course, brings with it changes in the sources of competition I have identified. In the familiar product life-cycle pattern, for example, growth rates change, product differentiation is said to decline as the business becomes more mature, and the companies tend to integrate vertically.

These trends are not so important in themselves;

what is critical is whether they affect the sources of competition. Consider vertical integration. In the maturing minicomputer industry, extensive vertical integration, both in manufacturing and in software development, is taking place. This very significant trend is greatly raising economies of scale as well as the amount of capital necessary to compete in the industry. This in turn is raising barriers to entry and may drive some smaller competitors out of the industry once growth levels off.

Obviously, the trends carrying the highest priority from a strategic standpoint are those that affect the most important sources of competition in the industry and those that elevate new causes to the forefront. In contract aerosol packaging, for example, the trend toward less product differentiation is now dominant. It has increased buyers' power, lowered the barriers to entry, and intensified competition.

The framework for analyzing competition that I have described can also be used to predict the eventual profitability of an industry. In long-range planning the task is to examine each competitive force, forecast the magnitude of each underlying cause, and then construct a composite picture of the likely profit potential of the industry.

The outcome of such an exercise may differ a great deal from the existing industry structure. Today, for example, the solar heating business is populated by dozens and perhaps hundreds of companies, none with a major market position. Entry is easy, and competitors are battling to establish solar heating as a superior substitute for conventional methods.

The potential of this industry will depend largely on the shape of future barriers to entry, the improvement of the industry's position relative to substitutes, the ultimate intensity of competition, and the power captured by buyers and suppliers. These characteristics will in turn be influenced by such factors as the establishment of brand identities, significant economies of scale or experience curves in equipment manufacture wrought by technological change, the ultimate capital costs to compete, and the extent of overhead in production facilities.

The framework for analyzing industry competition has direct benefits in setting diversification strategy. It provides a road map for answering the extremely difficult question inherent in diversification decisions: "What is the potential of this business?" Combining the framework with judgment in its application, a com-

pany may be able to spot an industry with a good future before this good future is reflected in the prices of acquisition candidates.

MULTIFACETED RIVALRY

Corporate managers have directed a great deal of attention to defining their businesses as a crucial step in strategy formulation. Theodore Levitt, in his classic 1960 article in HBR, argued strongly for avoiding the myopia of narrow, product-oriented industry definition [2]. Numerous other authorities have also stressed the need to look beyond product function in defining a business, beyond national boundaries to potential international competition, and beyond the ranks of one's competitors today to those that may become competitors tomorrow. As a result of these urgings, the proper definition of a company's industry or industries has become an endlessly debated subject.

One motive behind this debate is the desire to exploit new markets. Another, perhaps more important motive is the fear of overlooking latent sources of competition that someday may threaten the industry. Many managers concentrate so single-mindedly on their direct antagonists in the fight for market share that they fail to realize that they are also competing with other customers and their suppliers for bargaining power. Meanwhile, they also neglect to keep a wary eye out for new entrants to the contest or fail to recognize the subtle threat of substitute products.

The key to growth—even survival—is to stake out a position that is less vulnerable to attack from head-to-head opponents, whether established or new, and less vulnerable to erosion from the direction of buyers, suppliers, and substitute goods. Establishing such a position can take many forms—solidifying relationships with favorable customers, differentiating the product either substantively or psychologically through marketing, integrating forward or backward, establishing technological leadership.

REFERENCES

1. For a complete discussion of exit barriers and their implications for strategy, see my article, "Please Note Location of Nearest Exit." *California Management Review,* Winter 1976, p. 21.

2. Theodore Levitt: "Marketing Myopia," reprinted as a *Harvard Business Review Classic,* September-October 1975, p. 26.

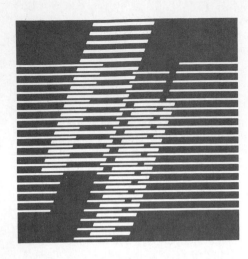

CHAPTER 5

THE INTERNAL ENVIRONMENT

STRATEGIC MANAGEMENT MODEL

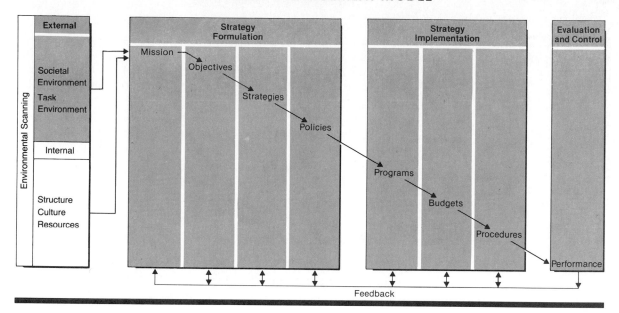

Managers cannot succeed in strategic planning and decision-making at the corporate level without an in-depth understanding of the strategic factors within the corporation. These factors are the internal *strengths* and *weaknesses* that act to either constrain or support a strategy. Part of a firm's internal environment, these factors are not within the short-run control of strategic managers. Instead they form the context within which work is accomplished. Strategic factors in a corporation's internal environment are (1) **structure,** (2) **culture,** and (3) **resources**.

5.1

STRUCTURE

The structure of a corporation is often defined in terms of communication, authority, and work flow. It is the corporation's pattern of relationships, its "anatomy." It is a formal arrangement of roles and relationships of people, so that the work is directed toward meeting the goals and accomplishing the mission of the corporation. Sometimes it is referred to as the chain of command and is often graphically described in an organization chart.[1]

Although there is an almost infinite variety of structural forms, certain types are predominant in modern complex organizations. These are simple, functional, divisional, matrix, and conglomerate structures.[2] Figure 5.1 illustrates some of these structures.

Simple Structure

Firms having a simple structure are usually small in size and undifferentiated laterally—that is, there are no functional or product categories. A firm with a simple structure is likely to be managed by an owner-manager who either does all the work or oversees a group of unspecialized people who do whatever needs to be done to provide a single product or service. A simple structure is appropriate when an organization is new and small and the owner-manager can personally grasp all the intricacies of the business. It becomes increasingly inappropriate as the organization grows, unless the owner-manager is able to find other competent people to whom he/she can delegate some responsibilities.

Functional Structure

In a functional structure, work is divided into subunits on the basis of such functions as manufacturing, finance, and sales. Functional structure enables a firm to take advantage of specialists and to deal with complex production or service-delivery problems more efficiently than it could if everyone performed an undifferentiated task. The functional structure is appropriate as long as top management is willing to invest a lot of energy in coordinating the many activities and as long as the company operates mostly in one industry. The long, specialized, vertical channels of communication and authority typical in large functionally structured companies tend to make the firm slow to respond to environmental changes that require coordination across departments, but are very successful when adaptability is not required and predictability is important.

Divisional Structure

When a corporation is organized on the basis of divisions, an extra management layer—division chiefs—is added between top management and

FIGURE 5.1
Basic Structures.

I. SIMPLE STRUCTURE

II. FUNCTIONAL STRUCTURE

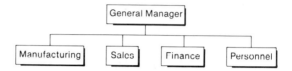

III. DIVISIONAL STRUCTURE*

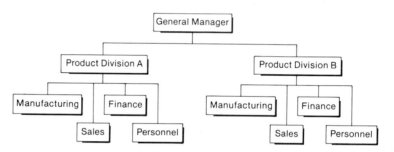

*Conglomerate structure is a variant of the division structure.

IV. MATRIX STRUCTURE

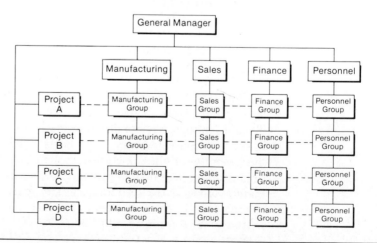

functional managers. The standard functions are then designed around products, clients, or territories. A recent innovation in this area is the use of **strategic business units** (SBUs), in which organizational groups composed of discrete, independent *product-market* segments are identified and given primary responsibility and authority for management of their functional areas. For example, instead of food preparation appliances being housed in three different divisions—such as large appliances, small appliances, and cookware—those divisions can be merged into a single SBU serving the housewares market.

An SBU may be of any size or level, but it must have (1) a unique mission, (2) identifiable competitors, (3) an external market focus, and (4) control of its business functions.[3] Once a large corporation is organized on a divisional basis around strategic business units, there still may be too many SBUs for top management to effectively manage. In this case, an additional management layer—*group executives*—is added between top management and the division or SBU chiefs. The group executive is thus responsible for the management of a number of similar SBUs, such as housewares, building materials, and auto accessories. Approximately 70% of the Fortune 500 corporations are combining divisions or SBUs around group executives.[4] (For more information on SBUs, refer to Chapter 8.)

The divisional structure is appropriate for a firm with many products serving many different markets. Organized so that they operate fairly independently of one another, the divisions can deal with different industries having varying degrees of change and complexity. This structure thus provides the company the flexibility it needs to operate in many industries. It can be inefficient, however, if there is much duplication of equipment and support staff. Furthermore, one division can be operating at overcapacity while another division underutilizes much of its facilities and staff.

Matrix Structure

In matrix structures, functional and divisional areas are combined *simultaneously* at the same level of the corporation. Employees have two superiors, a project manager and a functional manager. The "home" department—that is, engineering, manufacturing, or sales—is usually functional and is reasonably permanent. People from these functional units are assigned on a temporary basis to one or more project units. The project units act like divisions in that they are differentiated on a product-market basis. Pioneered in the aerospace industry, the matrix structure was developed to combine the stability of the functional structure with the flexibility of a project organization. The matrix structure is very useful when the external environment (especially the technological and market aspects) is very complex and changeable. It does, however, produce conflicts revolving around duties, authority, and resource allocation.

Conglomerate Structure

A variant of a divisional structure organized by product, the conglomerate structure is typically an assemblage of separate firms, having different products in different markets but operating together under one corporate umbrella. The divisions (subsidiaries) are independent of each other but share a dependence on central headquarters for financial resources and corporate planning. Its chief advantages to the corporation lie in the limitation of liability, a possible reduction in taxes, and, for the various divisions, the appearance of autonomy. For example, in response to a 1987 rule from the Financial Accounting Standards Board (FASB) requiring greater consolidation of financial statements, Tenneco created a holding company that would permit it to keep separate the heavy debt of its pipeline business from that of its other businesses.[5]

In addition, risks are spread over many different segments of the marketplace. The disadvantages of conglomerate structure derive from its heavy legalistic and financial orientation. In order to keep the legal advantages, the corporation cannot easily combine subsidiaries in attempts to generate operating or marketing synergy. And, the investment orientation at the corporate level can easily prevent top management from understanding divisional (subsidiary) problems in any sense other than financial. There is also a strong temptation for top management to choose a growth by acquisition strategy.[6] Furthermore, the ability to sell off a troubled division can lead to a short-run strategic orientation concerned only with the year-end bottom line.

An understanding of how a particular corporation is structured is very useful in the formulation of a strategy. If the structure is compatible with a proposed change in strategy, it is a corporate strength. If, however, the structure is not compatible with either the present or proposed strategy, it is a definite weakness, and will act to keep the strategy from being implemented properly. Intel Corporation, for example, has had some problems because its successful growth strategy had become incompatible with its centralized decision-making structure. The company had grown too big and its markets too turbulent for the CEO, Andy Grove, to control it so closely. Opportunities were in danger of being missed because of managers' dependence upon Grove for guidance.[7] For this reason, among others, the corporation's particular structure can predispose its strategic managers toward the selection of one strategy over another.[8] For example, research has revealed that diversified corporations using a divisional structure were more likely to move into international activities than were centralized companies using a functional structure.[9]

5.2

CULTURE

A corporation's culture is the collection of beliefs, expectations, and values shared by the corporation's members and transmitted from one generation of employees to another. These create norms (rules of conduct) that define acceptable behavior of people from top management to the operative employee. Myths and rituals, often unrecorded, that emerge over time will emphasize certain norms or values and explain why a certain aspect of the culture is important. Like the retelling of the vision and perseverance of the founder(s) of the corporation, the myth is often tied closely to the corporate mission.

Corporate culture shapes the behavior of people in the corporation. Analysts Schwartz and Davis point this out: "Apparently, the well-run corporations of the world have distinctive cultures that are somehow responsible for their ability to create, implement, and maintain their world leadership positions."[10] Because these cultures have a powerful influence on the behavior of managers, they can strongly affect a corporation's ability to shift its strategic direction.

For example, Exxon Corporation decided in the early 1970s to diversify away from its dependence on the declining petroleum business into the "office of the future." By buying firms from creative entrepreneurs, Exxon acquired three new word processing and printing technologies (named QWIP, QYX, and Vydec) to form Exxon Office Systems. As part of the bargain, the entrepreneurs who had developed these new products were also hired. Unfortunately, the entrepreneurs, who thrived in a helter-skelter world of exciting ideas and quick, risky decisions, were placed under the authority of Exxon's senior executives, people who lived by corporate policy and procedures manuals and made decisions only after many group meetings. One by one, the creative but undisciplined "kids" left the company with its meetings and paperwork and started something new somewhere else. Exxon replaced them with professional managers hired from other office-equipment companies like IBM, Xerox, and Burroughs. Accustomed to large staffs and generous support, the new managers staffed these small business units as if they were the large firms they had just left. Instead of emphasizing research and innovation, they focused on advertising and promotion. The result was an estimated loss of around $2 billion and the eventual sale of Exxon Office Systems to Olivetti and Lanier in 1985. One analyst summarized the basic problem:

> Obviously, Exxon never thought to analyze the subtle nuances of what it takes to run a collection of small technology-driven businesses because it simply wasn't a part of their culture . . . . [Management] never seemed to learn that the lethargic machinery and process technique that works so well in the oil business, simply wouldn't work in the fast-paced office equipment industry.[11]

Peters and Waterman, in their best-selling book *In Search of Excellence*, argue persuasively that the dominance and coherence of culture is an essential ingredient of the excellent companies they studied.

The top performers create a broad, shared culture, a coherent framework within which charged-up people search for appropriate adaptations. Their ability to extract extraordinary contributions from very large numbers of people turns on the ability to create a sense of highly valued purpose. Such purpose invariably emanates from love of product, providing top-quality services, and honoring innovation and contribution from all.[12]

Peters and Waterman also state that poorer performing companies tend to have cultures that focus on internal politics instead of the customer and on "the numbers" instead of the product or the people who make it.

A study of thirty-four corporations by Denison supports the conclusions of Peters and Waterman. Denison found that companies with participative cultures (i.e., strong employee involvement in corporate decision making) not only have better performance records than those without such a culture, but that the performance difference widens over time. Data collected by Hay Associates in hundreds of companies from 1970 to 1985 also revealed that culture bears a significant relationship to corporate performance. The evidence thus suggests a possible cause and effect relationship between culture and performance.[13]

Corporate culture fulfills several important functions in an organization:

- First, culture conveys a sense of identity for employees;
- Second, culture helps generate employees' commitment to something greater than themselves;
- Third, culture adds to the stability of the organization as a social system;
- Fourth, culture serves as a frame of reference for employees to use to make sense out of organizational activities and to use as a guide for appropriate behavior.[14]

Corporate culture generally reflects the mission of firms. It gives a corporation a sense of *identity:* "This is who we are. This is what we do. This is what we stand for." The culture includes the dominant orientation of the company.[15] Some companies are *market-oriented.* Like IBM and John Deere they define themselves in terms of their customers and their customers' needs. For example, one of the secrets given for the success of Deere and Company during a period of agricultural recession is its rural roots. Unlike International Harvester, which had its headquarters in downtown Chicago, Deere has its headquarters in East Moline, Illinois, in the heart of an agricultural region responsible for two of the nation's major crops, corn and soybeans. Deere has "geographical awareness, because most of its executives live on a farm or near one . . . ."[16]

Other companies may be *materials-* or *product-oriented.* They define themselves in terms of the material they work on, the product they make, or the service they provide. They are first and foremost oil companies, steel companies, railroads, banks, or hospitals. This means that the people working for the company tend to identify themselves in the same way. They don't just work for a company; they *are* truckers, railroaders, bankers. This heavy emphasis on materials or product can partially explain why some industries, such as automobiles and steel, have their own distinct culture that reflects and is reflected in the individual cultures of the member companies.[17] This sharing of a common set of beliefs, values, and assumptions makes it easier for people to move among companies within the same industry than to move to companies in other industries with a different culture. For example, when he left Ford Motor Company, Lee Iacocca stated that he had no interest in pursuing possible offers from International Paper, Lockheed, or Tandy Corporation. Said Iacocca, ". . . cars were in my blood."[18]

Other companies are *technology-oriented*. These companies define themselves in terms of the technology they are organized to exploit. Eastman Kodak, for example, ignored the development of xerography and almost missed out on the change to electronic photography because of its strong commitment to the chemical film technology pioneered by George Eastman.[19] Similarly, high-tech firms in Silicon Valley think of themselves primarily as technological entrepreneurs.

The managers' understanding of a corporation's (or division's) culture is thus imperative if the firm is to be managed strategically. As suggested in Chapter 4's discussion of environmental scanning, an organization's culture can produce a **strategic myopia,** in which strategic managers fail to perceive the significance of changing external conditions because they are partially blinded by strongly held common beliefs. In this instance, a strongly held corporate culture can become a major deterrent to success at a time when the corporation most needs to change its strategic direction.[20] An additional problem with a strong culture is that a change in mission, objectives, strategies, or policies is not likely to be successful if it is in opposition to the accepted culture of the corporation. As was true for structure at a time of change, if the culture is compatible with the change, that culture is an internal strength. But if the corporate culture is not compatible with the change, it is, under circumstances of a changing environment, a serious weakness. This does not mean that a manager should *never* consider a strategy that runs counter to the established culture. However, if such a strategy is to be seriously considered, top management must be prepared to attempt to change the culture as well, a task that will take much time, effort, and persistence.

5.3

RESOURCES

William Newman, an authority in strategic management, points out that a practical way to develop a master strategy of the corporation is to "pick particular roles or niches that are appropriate in view of competition and the company's resources."[21] The company's resources are typically considered in terms of financial, physical, and human resources, as well as organizational systems and technological capabilities. Because these resources have functional significance, we can discuss them under the commonly accepted functional headings of Marketing, Finance, Research and Development, Operations, Human Resources, and Information Systems. These resources, among others, should be audited so that internal strengths and weaknesses can be ascertained.

Corporate-level strategy formulators must be aware of the many contributions each functional area can make to divisional and corporate performance. Functional resources include not only the people in each area but also that area's ability to formulate and implement under corporate guidance the necessary functional objectives, strategies, and policies. Thus the resources include both the knowledge of analytical concepts and procedural techniques common to each area and the ability of the people in each area to utilize them effectively. These are some of the most valuable and well-known concepts and techniques: market segmentation, product life-cycle, capital budgeting, financial leverage, technological competence, operating leverage, experience-curve analysis, job analysis, job design, and decision-support systems. There are many others, of course, but these are the basic ones. If used properly, these resources can improve overall strategic management.

Marketing

The major tasks of the marketing manager from a corporation's point of view is to regulate the level, timing, and character of demand, in a way that will help the corporation achieve its objectives.[22] The marketing manager is the corporation's primary link to the customer and the competition. The manager must therefore be especially concerned with the market position and marketing mix of the firm.

Market position deals with the question, "Who are our customers?" It refers to the selection of specific areas for marketing concentration, and can be expressed in terms of market, product, and geographical locations. Through market research, corporations are able to practice **market segmentation** with various products or services so that management can discover what niches to seek, which new types of products to develop, and how to ensure that a company's many products do not directly compete with one another.[23] For example, Procter and Gamble Company, which markets several shampoos, positioned Prell Concentrate shampoo as a practical, convenience-oriented product, in contrast to Liquid Prell's orientation as the more luxury, beauty-oriented product and Head and Shoulders' orientation as the dandruff-protection shampoo.

The **marketing mix** refers to the particular combination of key variables under the corporation's control, that can be used to affect demand and to gain competitive advantage. These variables are *product, place, promotion,* and *price*. Within each of these four variables are several subvariables, listed in Table 5.1, which should be analyzed in terms of their effects upon divisional and corporate performance.

TABLE 5.1
Marketing Mix Variables

PRODUCT	PLACE	PROMOTION	PRICE
Quality	Channels	Advertising	List price
Features	Coverage	Personal selling	Discounts
Options	Locations	Sales promotion	Allowances
Style	Inventory	Publicity	Payment periods
Brand name	Transport		Credit terms
Packaging			
Sizes			
Services			
Warranties			
Returns			

SOURCE: Philip Kotler, *Marketing Management: Analysis, Planning, and Control,* 4th ed. (Englewood Cliffs, N.J.: Prentice-Hall, 1980), p. 89. Copyright © 1980. Reprinted by permission of Prentice-Hall, Inc.

One of the most useful concepts in marketing insofar as strategic management is concerned is that of the **product life cycle.** As depicted in Figure 5.2, the product life-cycle is a graph showing time plotted against the dollar sales of a product as it moves from introduction through growth and maturity to decline. This concept enables a marketing manager to examine the marketing mix of a particular product or group of products in terms of its position in its life cycle. Although marketing people agree that different products will have differently shaped life cycles, research concludes that a consideration of the product life cycle is an important factor in strategy formulation.[24]

Finance

The job of the financial manager is the management of funds. The manager must ascertain the best *sources* of funds, *uses* of funds, and *control* of funds. Cash must be raised from internal or external financial sources and allocated for different uses. The flow of funds in the operations of the corporation must be monitored. Benefits, in the form of returns, repayments, or products and services, must be given to the sources of outside financing. All these tasks must be handled in a way that complements and supports overall corporate strategy.

From a strategic point of view, the financial area should be analyzed to see how well it deals with funds. The mix of externally generated short-term and long-term funds in relation to the amount and timing of internally generated funds should be appropriate to the corporate objectives, strategies,

FIGURE 5.2
The Product Life-Cycle

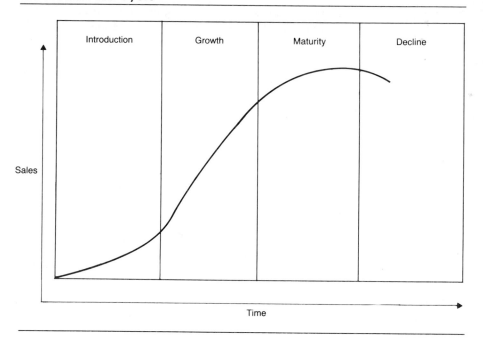

*The right end of the Growth stage is often called Competitive Turbulence because of price and distribution competition that shakes out the weaker competitors. For further information see C. R. Wasson, *Dynamic Competitive Strategy and Product Life Cycles,* 3rd ed., (Austin, Tex.: Austin Press, 1978).

and policies. The concept of **financial leverage** (the ratio of total debt to total assets) is very useful in descriptions of the use of debt to increase the earnings available to common stockholders.[25] When the corporation finances its activities by sales of bonds or notes instead of through stock, the earnings per share are boosted: the interest paid on the debt reduces taxable income, but there are fewer stockholders to share the profits. The debt, however, does raise the firm's break-even point above what it would have if the firm had financed from internally generated funds only. High leverage may therefore be perceived as a corporate strength in times of prosperity and ever-increasing sales, or as a weakness in times of a recession and dropping sales. This is because leverage acts to magnify the effect on earnings *per share* of an increase or decrease in dollar sales.

The knowledge and use of **capital budgeting** techniques is an important financial resource. A good finance department will be able to analyze and rank possible investments in such fixed assets as land, buildings, and equipment, in terms of the additional outlays and additional receipts that will result. Then it can rank investment proposals on the basis of some accepted criteria or "hurdle rate" (for example, years to pay back investment, rate of return, time to break-even point, etc.) and make its decisions. To select acquisition candidates and to analyze the amount of risk present in a corporation's portfolio of business units, financial analysts should also be able to utilize the Capital Asset Pricing Model (CAPM) and the Arbitrage Pricing Model (APM).[26]

Break-even analysis is an analytical technique used by approximately 80% of corporations in their study of the relations among fixed costs, variable costs, and profits.[27] It is a device used for determining the point at which sales will just cover total costs. When used in conjunction with some form of discounted cash flow analysis, like net present value or internal rate of return, it can provide useful information to strategic decision makers. Figure 5.3 shows a basic break-even chart for a hypothetical company. The chart is drawn on a unit basis; the volume produced is shown on the horizontal axis and costs and revenues are measured on the vertical axis. Fixed costs are $80,000, as represented by the horizontal line; variable costs are $2.40 per unit. Total costs rise by $2.40, the amount of the variable costs, for each additional unit produced past $80,000, and the product is sold at $4.00 per unit. The total-revenue line is a straight line increasing directly with production. As is usual, the slope of the total revenue line is steeper than that of the total cost line because, for every unit sold, the firm receives $4.00 of revenue for every $2.40 paid out for labor and material. Up to the break-even point (the intersection of the total revenue and total cost lines), the firm suffers losses. After that point, the firm earns profits at an increasing amount as volume increases. In this instance, the break-even point for the

FIGURE 5.3
Break-even Chart.

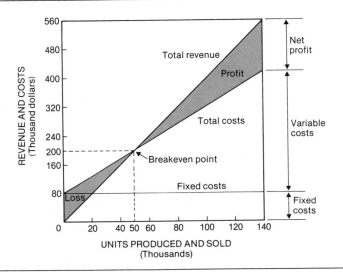

firm is at a sales and cost level of $200,000 and a production level of 50,000 units.

The financial manager must be very knowledgeable of these and other more sophisticated analytical techniques if management is to successfully implement functional strategies, such as internal financing or leveraged buyouts (discussed in Chapter 7).

Research and Development

The R&D manager is responsible for suggesting and implementing a corporation's technological strategy in light of its corporate objectives and policies. The manager's job therefore involves (1) choosing among alternative new technologies to use within the corporation, (2) developing methods of embodying the new technology in new products and processes, and (3) deploying resources so that the new technology can be successfully implemented.[28]

The term *research and development* is used to describe a wide range of activities. In some corporations R&D is conducted by scientists in well-equipped expensive laboratories where the focus is on theoretical problem areas. In other firms, R&D is heavily oriented toward marketing and is concerned with product or product-packaging improvements. In still other firms, R&D takes on an engineering orientation concentrating on quality control, the manufacturing of design specifications, and the development of improved production equipment. Most corporations will have a mix of basic, applied, and engineering R&D. The balance of these types of research is known as the **R&D mix** and should be appropriate to the corporate strategy.

A corporation's R&D unit should be evaluated for **technological competence** in both the development and use of innovative technology. Not only should the corporation make a consistent research effort (as measured by reasonably constant corporate expenditures that result in usable innovations), it should also be proficient in managing research personnel and integrating their innovations into its day-to-day operations. If a company is not proficient in **technology transfer**, the process of taking a new technology from the laboratory to the marketplace, it will not gain much advantage from new technological advances. Both American Telephone and Telegraph (AT&T) and Xerox Corporation have been criticized for their inability to take the research, ideas, and innovations bubbling up from their sophisticated R&D facilities (AT&T's Bell Labs and Xerox's Palo Alto Research Center) and packaging them in improved products and services.

Corporations operating in technology-based industries must be willing to make substantial investments in R&D. For example, the computer and pharmaceutical industries spend an average of 8.3% and 7.8% respectively of their sales dollars for R&D. As shown in Table 5.2 other industries, such as steel and tobacco, spend less than 1%. General Electric spends a large amount of money on R&D. Michael Carpenter, Vice-President of Corporate

TABLE 5.2
R&D Industry Expenditures—1986

INDUSTRY	SALES (Millions of Dollars)	PROFITS (Millions of Dollars)	R&D EXPENSES (Millions of Dollars)	Percent of Sales	Percent of Pretax Profits	Dollars per Employee
Aerospace	79,124	1,680	3,584	4.5	116.7	4,616
Appliances	7,605	(5)	128	1.7	75.1	1,372
Automotive:						
Cars, trucks	201,809	7,577	7,402	3.7	74.0	5,076
Parts, equipment	14,459	334	341	2.4	52.8	2,119
Building materials	13,723	574	223	1.6	20.4	2,073
Chemicals	89,797	4,247	3,662	4.1	48.6	6,093
Conglomerates	52,114	(844)	1,354	2.6	140.9	2,187
Containers	1,192	65	19	1.6	15.7	1,879
Drugs	60,549	6,312	4,721	7.8	48.4	8,172
Electrical	57,211	3,759	1,864	3.3	33.4	2,984
Electronics	59,311	1,622	2,586	4.4	93.8	3,237
Food & beverage	71,748	3,311	611	0.9	10.5	780
Fuel	258,158	9,807	1,958	0.8	10.2	3,329
Informational processing:						
Computers	94,138	6,488	7,857	8.3	69.4	8,905
Office equipment	5,147	286	249	4.8	49.9	3,895
Peripherals	23,021	895	1,615	7.0	108.0	6,356
Software, services	6,086	482	468	7.7	55.8	6,528
Instruments	16,417	476	1,092	6.7	124.7	5,304
Leisure time	24,810	756	1,467	5.9	108.7	5,026
Machinery:						
Farm, construction	23,096	57	693	3.0	1,352	3,276
Machine tools, industrial, mining	14,983	213	487	3.3	121	2,788
Metals & mining	11,267	428	204	1.8	34.9	2,269

Miscellaneous manufacturing	61,055	3,115	1,693	2.8	30.5	2,305
Oil service & supply	21,257	(4,246)	699	3.3	NEG	2,939
Paper & paper products	29,517	1,440	349	1.2	14.7	1,561
Personal & home care products	30,664	1,431	794	2.6	32.6	3,793
Semiconductors	10,760	(327)	1,310	12.2	NEG	7,318
Steel	21,978	(2,069)	113	0.5	NEG	851
Telecommunications	54,502	1,664	2,762	5.1	103.4	5,300
Textiles, apparel	8,836	171	68	0.8	20.4	626
Tires, rubber	20,924	309	550	2.6	78.3	2,272
Tobacco	5,773	469	22	0.4	2.6	267
All-Industry Composite	1,451,300	50,500	50,900	3.5	55.5	4,201

SOURCE: Adapted from "R&D Scoreboard," *Business Week* (June 22, 1987), pp. 141–160.

Business Development and Planning at GE, points out that much of the company's growth has developed internally out of its R&D efforts. He states: "We spend half as much money each year on R&D as all the money going into the venture capital industry. . . . As a result GE has always been at the leading edge of technology."[29] A good rule of thumb for R&D spending is that a corporation should spend at a "normal" rate for that particular industry. According to PIMS data (to be discussed in Chapter 6), those companies that spend 1% of sales more or 1% of sales less than the average have lower ROIs.[30] Simply spending money on R&D or new projects does not mean, however, that the money will produce useful results. Between 1950 and 1979, the United States steel industry spent 20% more on plant maintenance and upgrading for each ton of production capacity added or replaced than did the Japanese steel industry. Nevertheless, U.S. steelmakers failed to recognize and adopt two "breakthroughs" in steel-making—the basic oxygen furnace and continuous casting. Their hesitancy to adopt new technology caused them to lose the world steel market.[31]

In addition to money, another important consideration in the effective management of research and development is the time factor. It is generally accepted that the time needed for meaningful profits to result from the inception of a specific R&D program is typically seven to eleven years.[32] If a corporation is unwilling to invest the large amounts of money and time for its own program of research and development, it might be able to purchase or lease the equipment, techniques, or patents necessary to stay abreast of the competition. To gain some manufacturing advantage over General Motors, Ford Motor Company, for instance, invested $20 million during 1985 in American Robot Corporation. Ford and American Robot planned to fully automate Ford's new electronic components plant near Toronto before GM would be able to complete a comparable facility. Ford's Chairman Donald E. Petersen reported that similar investments might follow: "If the best way to get technology is through acquisitions, we have an open-door policy."[33]

Those corporations that do purchase an innovative technology must, nevertheless, have the technological competence to make good use of it. Unfortunately, some managers who introduce the latest technology into their company's processes do not adequately assess the competence of their organization to handle it. For example, a survey conducted in Great Britain found that 44% of all companies that started to use robots met with initial failure, and that 22% of these firms abandoned the use of robots altogether, mainly because of inadequate technological knowledge and skills.[34] Similar problems with the introduction of robotization and computer-aided manufacturing have been noted at General Motors' new assembly plant in Hamtramck, Michigan, and at Ford's recently remodeled St. Louis assembly plant. "They're now discovering that if you don't have good management, you'll end up with a rotten automated plant," concluded David Cole, Director of the University of Michigan's Office for the Study of Automotive Transportation.[35]

The R&D manager must determine when to abandon present technology and when to develop or adopt new technology. After several years of studying progress and patterns in various technologies, Richard Foster of McKinsey and Company states that the displacement of one technology by another (**Technological Discontinuity**) is a frequent and strategically important phenomenon. For each technology within a given field or industry, the plotting of product performance against research effort/expenditures on a graph results in an S-shaped curve. Foster describes the process depicted in Figure 5.4.

> Early in the development of the technology a knowledge base is being built and progress requires a relatively large amount of effort. Later, progress comes more easily. And then, as the limits of that technology are approached, progress becomes slow and expensive. *That* is when R&D dollars should be allocated to technology with more potential. That is also—not so incidentally—when a competitor who has bet on a new technology can sweep away your business or topple an entire industry.[36]

The presence of such a *technological discontinuity* in the world's steel industry during the 1960s can explain why the large capital expenditures by U.S. steel companies failed to keep them competitive with the Japanese firms adopting the new technologies. As Foster points out: "History has

FIGURE 5.4
Technological Discontinuity.

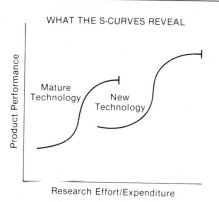

WHAT THE S-CURVES REVEAL

Product Performance

Mature Technology

New Technology

Research Effort/Expenditure

In the corporate planning process, it is generally assumed that incremental progress in technology will occur. But past developments in a given technology cannot be extrapolated into the future, because every technology has its limits. The key to competitiveness is to determine when to shift resources to a technology with more potential.

Source: P. Pascarella, "Are You Investing in the Wrong Technology?" *Industry Week* (July 25, 1983), p. 38. Copyright © 1983 by Penton/IPC. All rights reserved. Reprinted by permission.

shown that as one technology nears the end of its S-curve, competitive leadership in a market generally changes hands."[37] This phenomenon continues to occur in the semiconductor industry with each new wave of microchip technology. Each time, the more established firms, which have much invested in the old technology, cannot risk cannibalizing themselves in a bet on future technology, and are subsequently left behind.[38] Even though numerous companies in various industries have invested substantially in the energy and resources needed for their conversion to leading-edge technologies, there have been relatively few successes.[39]

Ansoff recommends that strategic managers deal with technology substitution by (1) continually searching for sources from which new technologies are likely, (2) as the technology surfaces, making a timely commitment to either acquire the new technology or to prepare to leave the market, and (3) reallocating resources from improvements in the older process-oriented technology to investments in the newer, typically product-oriented, technology as the new technology approaches commercial realization. One way of assessing the need for technology conversion is by calculating a **Deterioration of Cost (DOC) Index,** which compares the average unit cost of the currently installed technology to that of the expected average unit cost of state-of-the-art (SOTA) technology. As proposed by Swamidass, the index is calculated as follows:

$$\text{DOC Index} = \frac{\text{Average unit cost for installed technology}}{\text{Average unit cost for SOTA technology}} \times 100\%$$

When the currently installed technology has a higher unit cost than does the state-of-the-art technology, the DOC Index would have a value greater than 100%. For example, when installed technology is inferior to SOTA technology, the DOC Index might be 135%, meaning that when the currently installed technology is used, the average unit cost is 35% more than the likely average unit cost attainable with the new technology. To reflect how quickly new technologies are gaining advantage over current ones, DOC Indexes could be calculated over time. Top management might agree on a specific DOC figure, such as 150%, to serve as the *modernization point* for conversion to the new technology. The index figure could be based on investment criteria, such as break even, pay back, or rate of return.[40]

Operations (Manufacturing/Service)

If the corporation is in business to transform tangible raw materials, like iron ore or petroleum, into usable products, like automobiles, machine parts, or plastic raincoats, the transformation process can be called *manufacturing*. If, however, the corporation is in the business of using people's skills and knowledge, such as those of doctors, lawyers, or loan officers, to provide services via hospitals, legal clinics, or banks, the work involved can be called *service*. These functions can be found in any corporation producing and providing either a tangible product or an intangible service. Many of the key concepts and techniques popularly used in manufacturing can therefore be applied to service businesses.[41]

The primary task of the manufacturing or service manager is to develop and operate a system that will produce the required number of products or services, with a certain quality, at a given cost, within an allotted time. However, manufacturing plants vary significantly depending on the type of product made. In very general terms, manufacturing can be intermittent or continuous. In **intermittent systems** (job shops), the item normally goes through a sequential process, but the work and sequence of the process vary. At each location, the tasks determine the details of processing and the time required for them. In contrast, **continuous systems** are those laid out as lines on which products can be continuously assembled or processed. An example is an automobile assembly line.

The type of manufacturing system used by a corporation determines divisional or corporate strategy. It makes no sense, for example, to plan to increase sales by saturating the market with low-priced products if the corporation's manufacturing process was designed as an intermittent "job shop" system that produces one-time-only products to a customer's specifications. Conversely, a plan to produce a number of specialty products might not be economically feasible if the manufacturing process was designed to be a mass-producing, continuous system using low-skilled labor or special purpose robots.

Continuous systems are popular because they allow a corporation to take advantage of manufacturing **operating leverage.** According to Weston and Copeland, operating leverage is the impact of a given change in sales volume on net operating income.[42] For example, a highly labor-intensive firm has little automated machinery and thus a small amount of fixed costs. It has a fairly low break-even point, but its variable cost line has a relatively steep slope. Because most of the costs associated with the product are variable (many employees earn piece rate wages), its variable costs are higher than those of automated firms. Its advantage over other firms is that it can operate at low levels and still be profitable. Once its sales reach break-even, however, the huge variable costs as a percentage of total costs keep the profit per unit at a relatively low level. Its low operating leverage thus prevents the firm from gathering the huge profits possible from a high volume of sales. In terms of strategy, this firm should look for a niche in the marketplace for which it can produce and sell a reasonably small quantity of goods.

In contrast, a capital-intensive firm has a lot of money in fixed investments, such as automated processes and highly sophisticated machinery. Its labor force, relatively small but highly skilled, earns salaries rather than piece-rate wages. Consequently, this firm has a high amount of fixed costs. It also has a relatively high break-even point, but its variable cost line rises slowly. Its advantage is that once it reaches break-even, its profits rise faster than do those of less automated firms. In terms of strategy, this firm needs to find a high-demand niche in the marketplace where it can produce and sell a large quantity of goods. Its high operating leverage makes it an extremely profitable and competitive firm once it reaches its high break-even point. Changes in the level of sales have a magnified (leveraged) impact on profits. In times of recession, however, this type of firm is likely to suffer huge losses. During an economic downturn, the firm with less automation and thus less leverage is more likely to survive comfortably, because a drop in sales affects primarily variable costs. It is often easier to lay off labor than to sell off specialized plants and machines.

The operations of a service business can also be continuous or intermittent. Continuous operations describe fairly similar services provided to the *same* clientele over a period of time (such as treatment of patients in a long-term-care hospital), whereas intermittent operations describe somewhat variable services provided to *different* clientele over a period of time (such as once-a-year auditing or income tax counseling by a CPA firm). To use operating leverage, service firms that use continuous operations might be able to substitute diagnostic machinery or videotape machines for highly paid professional personnel. Those using batch or intermittent operations might be able to substitute lower-paid support personnel for some of the more routine services performed by highly paid professionals.

A conceptual framework that many large corporations have used successfully is the **experience curve** (originally called learning curve). The concept as it applies to manufacturing is that unit production costs decline by some fixed percentage (commonly 20%–30%) each time the total accumulated volume of production in units doubles. The actual percentage varies by industry and is based upon many variables: the amount of time it takes a person to learn a new task; scale economies; product and process improvements; lower raw materials costs; and other variables. For example, in an industry where an 85% experience curve can be expected, a corporation might expect a 15% reduction in costs for every doubling of volume. The total costs per unit (adjusted for inflation) can be expected to drop from $100 when the total production is 10 units, to $85 ($100 × 85%) when production increases to 20 units, and to $72.25 ($85 × 85%) when it reaches 40 units.[43] Achieving these results often means making investments in R&D and fixed assets; higher operating leverage and less flexibility thus result. Nevertheless, the manufacturing strategy is one of building capacity ahead of demand, in order to achieve the lower unit costs that develop from the experience curve. On the basis of some future point on the experience curve, price the product or service very low, so as to preempt competition and increase market demand. The resulting high number of units sold and high market share should result in high profits, based on the low unit costs.[44] This idea of management's using the anticipated experience curve to price low, in order to gain high market share and thus high profits underlies the Boston Consulting Group's portfolio matrix (discussed in Chapter 6).

The experience curve is commonly used in management's estimating the production costs of (1) a product never before made with the present techniques and processes or (2) current products produced by newly introduced techniques or processes. The concept was first applied in the airframe industry and can be applied in the service industry as well. While many firms have used experience curves extensively, an unquestioning acceptance of the industry norm (such as 80% for the airframe industry or 70% for integrated circuits) is very risky. The experience curve of the industry as a whole might not hold true for a particular company for a variety of reasons.[45]

Recently, the use of large mass-production facilities to take advantage of experience-curve economies has been criticized. The use of CAD/CAM (computer-assisted design and computer-assisted manufacturing) and robot technology means that learning times are shorter and products can be economically manufactured in small, customized batches. Emphasizing *economies of scope* over *economies of scale,* a number of firms have introduced "flexible manufacturing." The new flexible factories permit a low-volume output of custom-tailored products to produce a profit.[46] It is thus possible to have the cost advantages of continuous systems with the customer-oriented advantages of intermittent systems. For example, Deere's new tractor assembly plant in Waterloo, Iowa, can produce more than 5,000 variations of its tractors to suit its customers' needs.[47]

In conclusion, the operations manager in charge of either manufacturing or services must be very knowledgeable of forecasting, scheduling, purchasing, quality assurance, process design, job design, work measurement, just-in-time production systems, and maintenance and reliability, among other things, in order to develop an appropriate operations functional strategy.[48]

Human Resources

The primary task of the manager of human resources is to improve the match between individuals and jobs. The quality of this match influences job performance, employee satisfaction, and employee turnover.[49] Consequently, human resource management (HRM) is concerned with the selection and training of new employees, appraisal of employee performance, the assessment of employees' promotion potential, and recruitment and personnel planning for the future. HRM is also highly involved in wage and salary administration, labor negotiations, job design, and employee morale.

A good HRM department should be competent in the use of attitude surveys and other feedback devices to assess employees' satisfaction with their jobs and with the corporation as a whole. HRM managers should also be knowledgeable in job analysis and competent in its use. **Job analysis** is a means of obtaining job-description information about what needs to be accomplished by each job in terms of quality and quantity. Up-to-date job descriptions are essential not only for proper employee selection, appraisal, training, and development; wage and salary administration; and labor negotiations, but also for summarizing the corporate-wide human resources in terms of employee-skill categories. Just as a corporation must know the number, type, and quality of its manufacturing facilities, it also must know the kinds of people it employs and the skills they possess. This knowledge is essential for the formulation and implementation of corporate strategy. The best strategies are meaningless if employees do not have the skills to carry them out or if jobs cannot be designed to accommodate the available workers. Honeywell, Inc., for example, uses *talent surveys* to ensure that it has the right mix of talents for implementation of its planned strategies.[50]

A good human resource manager should be able to work closely with the unions if the corporation is unionized. A recent development is the increasing desire by union leaders to work jointly with management in the formulation and implementation of strategic changes. For example, when General Electric announced its intention to close it Charleston, South Carolina, steam-turbine generator plant in 1985, the United Electrical Workers proposed to management eleven alternative products the plant could produce. To save jobs, other unions are making the same argument. The United Food and Commercial Workers Union and the Great Atlantic and Pacific Tea Company (A&P) management jointly developed a strategic plan in 1981 to reverse four years of financial losses. Employees in Philadelphia accepted a 25% pay cut in exchange for more input into store decision making and a cash bonus system equal to 1% of the store's sales—contingent upon their reducing labor costs from 15% to 10%. (The industry average was 12%). Stores were renamed Super Fresh to reflect the company's increased concern for both its customers and employees. By 1986, employees were much happier, costs had dropped to 11% of stores' sales, market shares had doubled, and management had expanded the program along the U.S. East Coast and into its stores in other states.[51] Jerome M. Rosow, President of the Work in America Institute, states that the involvement of union leaders in business decision making is a "major breakthrough which has great potential for improving the competitive edge of those companies."[52]

Human resource departments have found that, to reduce employee dissatisfaction and unionization efforts (or conversely, to improve employee satisfaction and existing union relations), they must consider the quality of work life (QWL) in the design of jobs. Partially a reaction to the traditionally heavy emphasis upon technical and economic factors in job design, QWL emphasizes the human dimension of work.

In general, **quality of work life** is "the degree to which members of a work organization are able to satisfy important personal needs through their experiences in the organization."[53] The knowledgeable human resource manager should therefore be able to improve the corporation's quality of work life by (1) introducing participative problem-solving, (2) restructuring work, (3) introducing innovative reward systems, and (4) improving the work environment.[54] These improvements will lead to hopefully a more participative corporate culture and thus higher performance.

Corporations such as General Motors, AT&T, Ford, Westinghouse, Xerox, Honeywell, Bethlehem Steel, and Procter and Gamble are just a few of the growing number of companies actively involved in improving QWL through job and plant redesigning. About 1,500 companies were using one version of the QWL programs, the quality circle, by the mid-1980s.[55]

The quality of work life becomes especially important in today's world of global communication and transportation systems. Advances in technology are copied almost immediately by competitors around the world. People, however, are not as willing to move to other companies in other countries. It is therefore argued that the only long-term resource advantage remaining to a corporation lies in the area of human resources. Paul Hagusa, President of the American subsidiary of Sharp Corporation of Japan, makes this point very clearly.

> Once there was a time when the Americans had very efficient machines and equipment, and Japan did not. At that time—regardless of the workers—those with the most modern machines had the competitive advantage. But now, one country soon has the same machinery as another. So, what makes the difference today is the quality of the people.[56]

Information Systems

The primary task of the manager of information systems (IS) is to design and manage the information flow of the corporation in ways that improve productivity and decision making. Information must be collected, stored, and synthesized in such a manner that it will answer important operating and strategic questions. This function is growing in importance for three reasons: (1) Corporations are growing in size and complexity. Managers must increasingly rely on second-hand, written information. (2) As corporations become more dispersed and decentralized, control techniques must become more sophisticated, so that managers are operating according to agreed plans. (3) The widespread application and falling costs of the computer make it an ideal aid to information processing.

Information systems can fulfill four major purposes.

- *Provide a basis for the analysis of early warning signals that can originate both externally and internally.* Any information system has a database. Like a library, the system collects, categorizes, and files the data so that the system can be used by other departments in the corporation.

- *Automate routine clerical operations.* Payroll, inventory reports, and other records can be generated automatically from the database and thus the need for fileclerks is reduced.

- *Assist managers in making routine (programmed) decisions.* Scheduling orders, assigning orders to machines, and reordering supplies are routine tasks that can be automated through a detailed analysis of the company's work flow.

- *Provide the information necessary for management to make strategic (non-programmed) decisions.* Increasingly, personal computers coupled with sophisticated software are being used to analyze large amounts of information and to calculate likely payoffs from alternate strategies. In order to fulfill this purpose, decision-support systems are needed that allow easy interaction by the user with the computer.[57]

In assessing the corporation's strengths and weaknesses, one should note the level of development of the firm's information system. There are at least four distinct stages of development.[58] These are depicted in Table 5.3. Stage one, **initiation,** generally involves accounting applications. The information-systems personnel are computer technicians who work to reduce clerical costs. Stage two, **growth,** emerges as applications spread beyond accounting into production and marketing. People now use the system to process information like budgets and sales forecasts. Stage three, **moratorium,** is a consolidation phase and calls for a stop to new applications. The spread of information systems is matched by increasing frustration in attempting to use it and by concern over the large costs of operating the system. Unfortunately, many corporations appear to be caught in this stage, with information systems managers being concerned more with computer technology than with its application.[59] Stage four, **integration,** stresses the acceptance of information systems as a major activity that must be integrated into the total corporation. Decision-support systems to aid managers at all levels of the corporation are now developed. A stage-four system is a significant internal strength for a corporation.

The requirements of a well-designed information system include the following:[60]

1. The system must focus managers' attention on the critical success factors in their jobs.
2. The system must present information that is accurate and of high quality.
3. The system must provide the necessary information when it is needed to those who most need it.
4. The system must process raw data so that it can be presented in a manner useful to the manager.

A corporation's information system can be a strength in all three elements of strategic management: formulation, implementation, and evaluation and control. For example, it can not only aid in environmental scanning and in controlling a corporation's many activities, it can also be used as a strategic weapon in the gaining of competitive advantage.[61] For example, American Hospital Supply (AHS), a leading manufacturer and distributor of a broad line of products for doctors, laboratories, and hospitals, has developed an order entry-distribution system that directly links the majority of its customers to AHS computers. The system has been successful because it simplifies ordering processes for customers, reduces costs for both AHS and

TABLE 5.3
Stages of Development of Information Systems

	STAGE ONE INITIATION	STAGE TWO GROWTH	STAGE THREE MORATORIUM	STAGE FOUR INTEGRATION
Application Focus	Accounting and cost reduction	Expansion of applications in many functional areas	Halt on new applications; emphasis on control	Integrating existing systems into the organization; decision support systems
Example Applications	Accounts payable, accounts receivable, payroll, billing	*Stage one plus:* cash flow, budgeting, forecasting, personnel inventory, sales, inventory control	*Stage two plus:* purchasing control, production scheduling	*Stage three plus:* simulation models, financial planning models, on-line personnel query system
MIS Staffing	Primarily computer experts and other skilled professionals	User-oriented system analysts and programmers	Entry of functional managers into MIS unit	Balance of technical and management specialists
Location of MIS in Structure	Embedded in accounting department	Growth in size of staff, still in accounting area	Separate MIS unit reporting to head financial officer	Same as stage three, or decentralization into divisions
What Top Management Wants from MIS	Speed computations with a reduction in clerical staff	Broader applications into operational areas	Concern over MIS costs and usefulness	Acceptance as a major organizational function, involved in planning and control
User Attitudes	Uncertainty; hands-off approach; anxiety over applications	Somewhat enthusiastic; minimum involvement in system design	Frustration and dissatisfaction over developed systems; concern over costs of developing and operating systems	Acceptance of MIS in their work; involvement in system design, implementation, and operation

SOURCE: Reprinted by permission of the *Harvard Business Review*. An exhibit from "Controlling the Costs of Data Services," by Richard L. Nolan (July/August 1977). Copyright © 1977 by the President and Fellows of Harvard College; all rights reserved.

the customer, and allows AHS to provide pricing incentives to the customer. As a result, customer loyalty is high and AHS's share of the market has become large. Other examples are the automated reservations systems American Airlines and United Airlines made available to travel agents. Because the reservations systems featured either American or United most prominently in the listings, other airlines complained that American and United had an unfair advantage in attracting customers.

Information Systems is quickly becoming a corporation's strategic resource. It can be used to monitor environmental changes, counter competitive threats, and assist in the implementation of strategy.[62]

SUMMARY AND CONCLUSION

Before strategies can be developed, top management needs to assess its internal corporate environment for strengths and weaknesses. Management must have an in-depth understanding of the internal strategic factors, such as the corporation's structure, culture, and resources.

A corporation's *structure* is its anatomy. It is often described graphically with an organizational chart. Corporate structures range from the simple structure of an owner-manager-operated business, to the complex series of structures of a large conglomerate. If compatible with present and potential strategies, a corporation's structure is a great internal strength. Otherwise, it can be a serious weakness that will either prevent a good strategy from being implemented properly or reduce the number of strategic alternatives available to a firm.

A corporation's *culture* is the collection of beliefs, expectations, and values shared by its members. A culture produces norms that shape the behavior of employees. Top management must be aware of this culture and include it in its assessment of strategic factors. Those strategies that run counter to an established corporate culture are likely to be doomed by the poor motivation of the workforce. If a culture is thus antagonistic to a strategy change, the implementation plan will also have to include plans to change the culture.

A corporation's *resources* include not only such generally recognized assets as people, money, and facilities, but also those analytical concepts and procedural techniques known and in use within the functional areas. Because most top managers view their corporations in terms of functional activities, it is simplest to assess resource strengths and weaknesses by functional area. Each area should be audited in terms of financial, physical, and human resources, as well as its organization and technological competencies and capabilities. Just as the knowledge of key functional concepts and techniques is a corporate strength, its absence is a weakness.

DISCUSSION QUESTIONS

1. In what ways can a corporation's structure act as an internal strength or weakness to those formulating corporate strategies?

2. Why should top management be aware of a corporation's culture?

3. What kind of internal factors help determine whether a firm should emphasize the production and sales of a large number of low-priced products, or a small number of high-priced products?

4. What is the difference between operating and financial leverage? What are their implications to strategic planning?

5. Why is technological competence important in strategy formulation?

6. How can management's knowledge of technological discontinuity help to improve a corporation's efficiency?

7. What are the pros and cons of management's using the experience curve to determine strategy?

8. Why should information systems be included in the analysis of a corporation's strengths and weaknesses?

9. What are some of the most important strengths and weaknesses in the internal environment of CSX Corporation as described in the Integrative Case at the end of this chapter. Which of these should have a major impact on strategy formulation at the time of the case and in the future?

NOTES

1. R. L. Daft, *Organization Theory and Design* (St. Paul: West Publishing Co., 1986), pp. 211–212.

2. R. H. Miles, *Macro Organizational Behavior* (Santa Monica, Calif.: Goodyear Publishing, 1980), pp. 28–34.

3. M. Leontiades, "A Diagnostic Framework for Planning," *Strategic Management Journal* (January-March 1983), p. 14.

4. J. M. Stengrevics, "Managing the Group Executive's Job," *Organization Dynamics* (Winter 1984), p. 21.

5. L. Berton, "FASB Issues Rule Making Firms Combine Data of All Their Majority-Owned Firms," *Wall Street Journal* (November 2, 1987), p. 10.

6. D. K. Hurst, "Why Strategic Management Is Bankrupt," *Organizational Dynamics* (Autumn 1986), p. 9.

7. J. W. Wilson, "Can Andy Grove Practice What He Preaches?" *Business Week* (March 16, 1987), pp. 68–69.

8. J. W. Fredrickson, "The Strategic Decision Process and Organizational Structure," *Academy of Management Review* (April 1986), pp. 280–297.

D. Miller, "Configurations of Strategy and Structure: Towards a Synthesis," *Strategic Management Journal* (May-June 1986), pp. 233–249.

9. L. E. Fouraker and J. M. Stopford, "Organization Structure and the Multinational Strategy," *Administrative Science Quarterly* (June 1968), pp. 47–64.

10. H. Schwartz and S. M. Davis, "Matching Corporate Culture and Business Strategy," *Organizational Dynamics* (Summer 1981), p. 30.

11. R. M. Donnelly, "Exxon's 'Office of the Future' Fiasco," *Planning Review* (July/August, 1987), pp. 13 and 14.

12. T. J. Peters and R. H. Waterman, Jr., *In Search of Excellence* (New York: Harper & Row, 1982), pp. 293–294.

13. D. R. Denison, "Bringing Corporate Culture to the Bottom Line," *Organizational Dynamics* (Autumn 1984), pp. 5–22.

G. G. Gordon, "The Relationship of Corporate Culture to Industry Sector and Corporate Performance," in *Gaining Control of the Corporate Culture*, edited by R. H. Kilmann, M. J. Saxton, R. Serpa, and Associates (San Francisco: Jossey-Bass, 1985), p. 103.

14. L. Smircich, "Concepts of Culture and Organizational Analysis," *Administrative Science Quarterly* (September 1983), pp. 345–346.

15. S. C. Wheelwright, "Manufacturing Strategy: Defining the Missing Link," *Strategic Management Journal* (January-March 1984), p. 79.

16. D. Muhm, "John Deere's Company: 145 Years of Farming History," *Des Moines Register* (November 11, 1984), p. 2F.

17. I. I. Mitroff and S. Mohrman, "Correcting Tunnel Vision," *Journal of Business Strategy* (Winter 1987), pp. 49–59.

18. L. Iacocca, *Iacocca: An Autobiography* (Toronto: Bantam Books, 1984), p. 141.

19. T. Moore, "Embattled Kodak Enters the Electronic Era," *Fortune* (August 22, 1983), pp. 120–130.

20. J. Lorsch, "Strategic Myopia: Culture as an Invisible Barrier to Change," in *Gaining Control of the Corporate Culture*, edited by R. H. Kilmann, M. J. Saxton, R. Serpa and Associates (San Francisco: Jossey-Bass, 1985), pp. 84–102.

H. I. Ansoff and T. E. Baker, "Is Corporate Culture the Ultimate Answer?" in *Advances in Strategic Management, Volume 4*, edited by R. Lamb and P. Shrivastava (Greenwich, Conn.: Jai Press, 1986), p. 84.

21. W. H. Newman, "Shaping the Master Strategy of Your Firm," *California Management Review*, vol. 9, no. 3 (1967), p. 77.

22. P. Kotler, *Marketing Management*, 4th ed. (Englewood Cliffs, N.J.: Prentice-Hall, 1980), p. 22.

23. K. J. Roberts, "How to Define Your Market Segment," *Long Range Planning* (August 1986), pp. 53–58.

24. C. A. Anderson and C. P. Zeithaml, "Stage of the Product Life Cycle, Business Strategy, and Business Performance," *Academy of Management Journal* (March 1984), p. 22.

25. C. M. Sandberg, W. G. Lewellen, and K. L. Stanley, "Financial Strategy: Planning and Managing the Corporate Leverage Position," *Strategic Management Journal* (January-February 1987), pp. 15–24.

26. For further information on capital budgeting, discounted cash flow, CAPM, and APM Techniques, see J. F. Weston and T. E. Copeland, *Managerial Finance, 8th Edition* (Chicago: Dryden Press, 1986), pp. 99–138 and 427–478.

27. T. E. Conine, Jr., "The Potential Overreliance On Break-Even Analysis," *Journal of Business Strategy* (Fall, 1986), pp. 84–86.

28. M. A. Maidique and P. Patch, "Corporate Strategy and Technological Policy" (Boston: Intercollegiate Case Clearing House, no. 9-769-033, 1978, rev. March 1980), p. 3.

29. R. J. Allio, "G.E. = Giant Entrepreneur?" *Planning Review* (January 1985), p. 21.

30. M. J. Chussil, "How Much to Spend on R&D?" *The PIMS Letter of Business Strategy, No. 13* (Cambridge, Mass.: The Strategic Planning Institute, 1978), p. 5.

31. T. F. O'Boyle, "Steel's Management Has Itself to Blame," *Wall Street Journal* (May 17, 1983), p. 32.

32. E. F. Finkin, "Developing and Managing New Products," *Journal of Business Strategy* (Spring 1983), p. 45.

33. R. Brandt, M. Rothman, and A. Gabor, "Will Ford Beat GM in the Robot Race?" *Business Week* (May 27, 1985), p. 44.

34. "The Impact of Industrial Robotics on the World of Work," *International Labour Review,* Vol. 125, No. 1, 1986. Summarized in "The Risks of Robotization," *The Futurist* (May-June 1987), p. 56.

35. R. Mitchell, "Detroit Stumbles On Its Way to the Future," *Business Week* (June 16, 1986), p. 103.

36. P. Pascarella, "Are You Investing in the Wrong Technology?" *Industry Week* (July 25, 1983), p. 37.

37. Pascarella, p. 38.

38. M. S. Malone, "America's New Wave Chip Firms," *Wall Street Journal* (May 27, 1987), p. 30.

39. W. P. Sommers, J. Nemec, Jr., and J. M. Harris, "Repositioning With Technology: Making It Work," *Journal of Business Strategy* (Winter 1987), p. 16.

40. H. I. Ansoff, "Strategic Management of Technology," *Journal of Business Strategy* (Winter 1987), p. 35.
P. M. Swamidass, "Planning for Manufacturing Technology," *Long Range Planning* (October 1987), pp. 125–133.
For further information on technological discontinuity, the technology life cycle, and product versus process technology, see M. Tushman and D. Nadler, "Organizing For Innovation," *California Management Review* (Spring 1987), pp. 74–92 and F. Betz, *Managing Technology* (Englewood Cliffs, N.J.: Prentice-Hall, 1987).

41. L. J. Krajewski and L. P. Ritzman, *Operations Management* (Reading, Mass.: Addison-Wesley, 1987), p. 10.

42. Weston and Copeland, p. 220.

43. A. C. Hax and N. S. Majuf, "Competitive Cost Dynamics: The Experience Curve," in A. C. Hax (ed.), *Readings on Strategic Management* (Cambridge, Mass.: Ballinger Publishing Co., 1984), pp. 49–60.

44. B. D. Henderson, *Henderson on Corporate Strategy* (Cambridge, Mass.: Abt Books, 1979), p. 11.

45. G. Hall and S. Howell, "The Experience Curve from the Economist's Perspective," *Strategic Management Journal* (July-September, 1985), pp. 197–212.
R. Luchs, "Successful Businesses Compete on Quality—Not Costs," *Long Range Planning* (February 1986), pp. 16–17.

46. J. Meredith, "The Strategic Advantages of New Manufacturing Technologies for Small Firms," *Strategic Management Journal* (May-June 1987), pp. 249–258.
J. D. Goldhar and M. Jelinek, "Plan for Economies of Scope," *Harvard Business Review* (November-December 1983), pp. 141–148.

47. J. Holusa, "Deere & Co. Leads the Way in 'Flexible' Manufacturing," *Des Moines Register* (January 29, 1984), p. 10F.

48. R. B. Chase and E. L. Prentis, "Operations Management: A Field Rediscovered," *Journal of Management* (Summer 1987), pp. 351–366.

49. H. G. Heneman, D. P. Schwab, J. A. Fossum, and L. D. Dyer, *Personnel/Human Resource Management* (Homewood, Ill.: Richard D. Irwin, Inc., 1986), p. 7.

50. N. Tichy, "Conversation with Edson W. Spencer and Foster A. Boyle," *Organization Dynamics* (Spring 1983), p. 30.

51. C. S. Eklund, "How A&P Fattens Profits By Sharing Them," *Business Week* (December 22, 1986), p. 44.

52. J. Hoerr, "Now Unions Are Helping to Run the Business," *Business Week* (December 24, 1984), p. 69.
"A Bold Tactic to Hold On to Jobs," *Business Week* (October 29, 1984), pp. 70–72.

53. J. L. Suttle, "Improving Life at Work—Problems and Perspectives," *Improving Life at Work: Behavioral Science Approaches to Organizational Change,* eds. J. R. Hackman and J. L. Suttle (Santa Monica, Calif.: Goodyear Publishing, 1976), p. 4.

54. D. A. Nadler and E. E. Lawler III, "Quality of Work Life: Perspectives and Directions," *Organization Dynamics* (Winter 1983), p. 27.

55. C. Camman and G. E. Ledford, Jr., "Productivity Management Through Quality of Work Life Programs," in *Strategic Human Resource Management,* edited by C. J. Fombrun, N. M. Tichy, and M. A. Devanna (New York: John Wiley & Sons, 1984), p. 361.

56. L. E. Calonius, "In a Plant in Memphis, Japanese Firm Shows How to Attain Quality," *Wall Street Journal* (April 29, 1983), p. 14.

57. R. G. Murdick, *MIS: Concepts and Designs* (Englewood Cliffs, N.J.: Prentice-Hall, 1980), p. 253.

58. R. L. Nolan, "Controlling the Costs of Data Services," *Harvard Business Review* (July-August 1977), p. 117.

59. J. E. Izzo, *The Embattled Fortress* (San Francisco: Jossey-Bass, 1987).

60. R. H. Gregory and R. L. Van Horn, "Value and Cost of Information," in J. D. Cougar and R. W. Knapp (eds.), *Systems Analysis Techniques* (New York: Wiley, 1974), pp. 473–489.

61. R. I. Benjamin, J. F. Rockart, M. S. S. Morton, and J. Wyman, "Information Technology: A Strategic Opportunity," *Sloan Management Review* (Spring 1984), p. 5.

62. J. M. Ward, "Integrating Information Systems Into Business Strategies," *Long Range Planning* (June 1987), pp. 19–29.

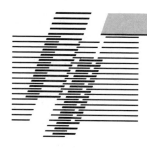

INTEGRATIVE CASE

CSX CORPORATION'S INTERNAL ENVIRONMENT

In early 1985, CSX was composed of two major business segments—*transportation* and *natural resources*. Each segment was composed of two or three business groups. Each business group was in turn made up of CSX subsidiaries, firms owned directly by CSX, or firms controlled by CSX through subsidiaries. Figure 5.5 shows the arrangement of CSX subsidiaries into business segments, business groups, and subsidiaries.

ORGANIZATIONAL STRUCTURE

In the transportation segment were three business groups. The first was the *Rail Transportation Group*, which was composed of the Chessie System Railroad, Seaboard System Railroad, and the Richmond, Fredericksburg and Potomac Railroad (R,F&P), which primarily moved general commodity merchandise and provided the most direct interchange between the Chessie and Seaboard. Chessie Motor Express, a trucking unit, was jointly owned by Chessie and Seaboard and provided coordinated pickup and delivery of intermodal shipments. Motor Express was one of CSX's fastest growing business units. The second business group in the transportation segment was *American Commercial Lines, Inc.*, the barge line acquired as a subsidiary of Texas Gas Resources. The third group was *Other Transportation*, which consisted of four units: CSX Beckett Aviation, a firm that provided aircraft maintenance services and managed the world's largest fleet of executive aircraft; CSX Communications, which represented CSX's participation in a joint venture with Southern New England Telephone; Cybernetics and Systems, a data-processing firm that was a subsidiary of Seaboard and provided MIS services to CSX and outside customers; and Fruit Growers Express, a manufacturer of specialized rail equipment that was owned jointly by Chessie, Seaboard, Conrail, Norfolk Southern, and Denver & Rio Grande Railway, although it was controlled by CSX. In January 1985, however, CSX entered into a letter of intent to sell its aviation subsidiary.

The natural resources segment contained two business groups. The *Energy Group* consisted of four units: Texas Gas Transmission, a natural gas pipeline acquired as part of the Texas Gas Resources (TXG) acquisition in 1983; Texas Gas Exploration, the oil and gas exploration firm also acquired as part of Texas Gas Resources; CSX

SOURCE: J. D. Hunger, B. Ferrin, H. Felix-Gamez, and T. Goetzman, "CSX Corporation," *Cases In Strategic Management and Business Policy* by T. L. Wheelen and J. D. Hunger (Reading, Mass.: Addison-Wesley, 1987), pp. 91–123.

FIGURE 5.5
Major Business Segments and Groups of CSX Corporation in
Early 1985

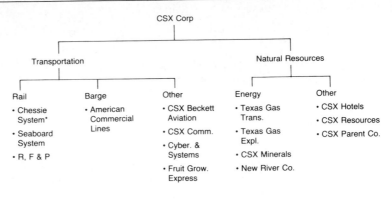

Chessie Motor Express: Trucking unit jointly owned by Chessie and Seaboard.

Minerals, which provided unified management of all CSX coal land development and thereby controlled the rights to 583,000 acres of coal land; and the New River Company, which operated four coal mines on CSX land near New River, West Virginia. The second business group in the natural resources segment was the *Other Natural Resources Group*. This business group consisted of three units: CSX Parent Company (CSX's Corporate Headquarters); CSX Hotels, which represented CSX's investment in the Greenbrier Resort Hotel and its interests in other hotel operations; and CSX Resources, which was established to provide centralized management of all real estate, oil, gas, and timber properties controlled by CSX. CSX Resources had an interest in 330 oil and gas wells and managed 350,000 acres of forest land.

UNIT PERFORMANCE

The transportation segment, with around 69% of CSX's total operating revenue and the same percentage of operating income, dominated the corporation. Rail operations alone accounted for 64% of CSX's operating revenue as well as its operating income. Seaboard was the largest of the three rail units and thus tended to contribute the largest toward the group's operating income. Although coal traffic typically accounted for around 35% of CSX rail units' total revenue, it accounted for around half of Chessie's revenue and around one quarter of Seaboard's revenue. Automobiles and chemicals were next in importance for the Chessie System, as contrasted with paper, phosphates, and fertilizers, for Seaboard. American Commercial Lines' actual annual operating revenue went from $295 million in 1982 to $237 million in 1983, and to $270 million in 1984. Its operating income followed a similar trend, going down from $41 million in 1982 to $22 million in 1983 and up to $32 million in 1984. CSX management indicated that the cause of the overall decline in revenue and income was a result of decreasing rates in the barge transportation industry, and that these decreases were due to equipment oversupply. A record high of 32.3 million tons were transported by American Commercial in 1984 (10% above 1983 and 4% above 1982).

Within the natural resources segment, the energy group accounted for 93% of the segment's operating revenue but only 67% of the segment's operating income. This situation seemed to be a result of low oil and gas prices, caused by depressed world energy demand and the abundance of crude oil and natural gas supplies during the mid-1980s. Insofar as CSX was concerned, the drop in oil and gas prices more than offset any gains in volume sold or transmitted during 1984. Refer to Tables 5.4 and 5.5 for detailed financial information on CSX's transportation and natural resources segments.

INTERNAL PROBLEMS

In early 1985, CSX top management was faced with a problem of strategic significance: *How should the corporation best manage its newly acquired businesses?* The stated mission of CSX was to become a multimodal, one-stop transportation conglomerate. This mission has been pursued throughout the development of the firm. In furthering its attempts to accomplish this mission, CSX continued to use a strategy that it had used successfully in the past. By trying to repeat the process by which Chessie and Seaboard were brought together, CSX management hoped to fully coordinate the operations of ACL with its rail network, without fully integrating the barge line.

However, CSX management faced some difficulties this time around. Barge lines have traditionally been fierce competitors of railroads. Extending CSX's philosophy of teamwork and cooperation was difficult because the railroad personnel and the barge operators were more used to fighting than functioning smoothly in a coordinated fashion. This situation was in direct contrast to the Chessie-Seaboard merger, in which the two partners had no history of competition and no overlap of lines. In addition, the barge industry was substantially different from the railroad industry. As a result, the process of communication that CSX relied so heavily on in its coordination efforts could be more difficult to establish in this acquisition than it had been in the Chessie-Seaboard merger, in which both parties were railroaders and could speak the same language.

The integration of the rest of Texas Gas Resources was also a problem for CSX's top management. Before the merger, more than 90% of CSX revenue had been derived from rail transportation. With the acquisition of TXG the corporation had become a major force in the gas pipeline business. (In 1982, $2.1 billion out of a total of $2.6 billion in TXG revenues came from its pipeline business.) Robert L. Hintz, Senior Vice-President of Finance for CSX, commented that the gas transmission business had been considered a good fit because most of its revenue came in the winter months when railroads go through a seasonally lean period. Nevertheless, the addition of barge and pipeline businesses had created a serious organizational problem for a firm structured around the concept of separate but equal partnership of subsidiaries.

In their March 1985 letter to the stockholders, Watkins and Funkhouser acknowledged their concern about CSX's organization structure.

> Over the past four years, we have operated two corporately separate, but operationally coordinated, rail units. At the same time, we acquired Texas Gas, resulting in CSX having three essentially autonomous operating units.

TABLE 5.4

Financial Information, Transportation Segment of CSX

(In Millions of Dollars)

	1984				1983[1]				1982			
	Total	Rail	Barge	Other	Total	Rail	Barge	Other	Total	Rail	Barge	Other
Transportation operating revenue	$5,427	$5,058	$270	$99	$4,749	$4,554	$104	$91	$4,644	$4,554	$—	$90
Costs and other operating expenses												
Labor and fringe benefits	2,535	2,457	65	13	2,399	2,352	28	19	2,265	2,232	—	33
Materials, supplies, and other	889	728	112	49	715	633	42	40	839	813	—	26
Fuel	455	407	36	12	407	378	14	15	460	446	—	14
Equipment rent	550	538	10	2	500	493	4	3	417	415	—	2
Depreciation	297	271	15	11	269	252	6	11	294	283	—	11
Total	4,726	4,401	238	87	4,290	4,108	94	88	4,275	4,189	—	86
Transportation operating income	$ 701	$ 657	$ 32	$12	$ 459	$ 446	$ 10	$ 3	$ 369	$ 365	$—	$ 4

CAPITAL EXPENDITURES

	1984	1983	1982
Transportation			
Rail	$748	$427	$511
Barge	7	4	—
Other	8	11	12
Total	$763	$442	$523

IDENTIFIABLE ASSETS

	1984	1983	1982
Transportation			
Rail	$9,073	$8,624	$8,631
Barge	366	378	—
Other	213	174	197
Total	$9,652	$9,176	$8,828

LONG-TERM DEBT AND MINORITY INTEREST

	1984	1983	1982
Rail	$1,984	$2,064	$2,099
Barge	64	111	—
Other	47	52	54
Total	$2,095	$2,227	$2,153

SOURCE: CSX Corporation, *1984 Annual Report*, pp. 32–33.

[1]American Commercial Lines added August 1983.

TABLE 5.5
Financial Information, Natural Resources Segment of CSX
(In Millions of Dollars)

	1984			1983[1]			1982		
	Total	Energy	Other	Total	Energy	Other	Total	Energy	Other
Natural resource									
Operating revenue	$2,507	$2,329	$178	$1,142	$989	$153	$265	$55	$210
Costs and other operating expenses									
Gas purchased	1,589	1,589	—	689	689	—	—	—	—
Labor and fringe benefits	116	84	32	62	35	27	72	11	61
Materials, supplies, and other	267	232	35	119	79	40	68	20	48
NGL production payments	85	85	—	40	40	—	—	—	—
Depreciation	133	127	6	55	52	3	17	9	8
Total	2,190	2,117	73	965	895	70	157	40	117
Natural resource operating income	$ 317	$ 212	$105	$ 177	$ 94	$ 83	$108	$15	$ 93

IDENTIFIABLE ASSETS			
	1984	1983	1982
Natural resource			
Energy	$1,764	$1,715	$151
Other	220	113	220
Total	$1,984	$1,828	$371

CAPITAL EXPENDITURES			
	1984	1983	1982
Natural resource			
Energy	$235	$82	$28
Other	11	6	10
Total	$246	$88	$38

LONG-TERM DEBT AND MINORITY INTEREST			
	1984	1983	1982
	$525	$561	$ 9
	12	12	20
	$537	$573	$29

SOURCE: CSX Corporation, *1984 Annual Report*, pp. 38–39.

[1]Texas Gas Resources Corporation added August 1983.

Early after the 1980 merger from which CSX was formed, and since mid-1983 in the case of Texas Gas, this organizational autonomy was critical to our success, as it assisted establishment of responsibility, promoted constructive competition between the units and dramatically eased the personnel distress usually associated with the mergers and major acquisitions.

In light of the accelerating dynamics of the transportation and energy marketplaces and the competitive demands of today's international economy, however, we are examining our overall corporate structure to determine the optimal organization for operating in this ever-changing environment.

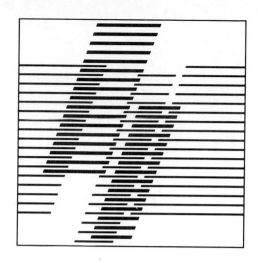

PART THREE

STRATEGY FORMULATION

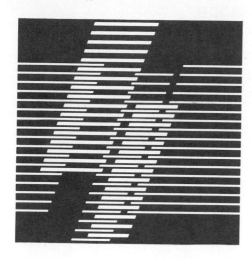

CHAPTER 6

STRATEGY FORMULATION: SITUATION ANALYSIS

STRATEGIC MANAGEMENT MODEL

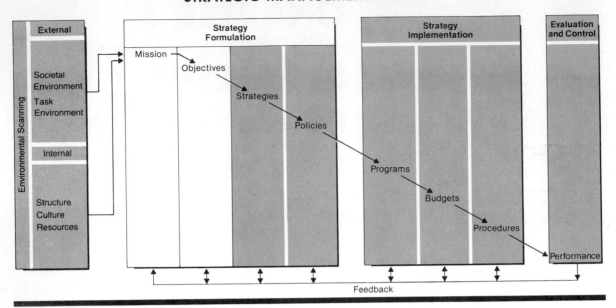

Strategy formulation is often referred to as strategic planning or long-range planning. Regardless of the term used, the process is primarily analytical, not action-oriented. The basic Strategic Management Model, shown first in Chapter 1, reflects the distinction between strategy formulation and strategy implementation. As shown in the model, the formulation process is concerned with developing a corporation's *mission, objectives, strategy,* and *policies.* In order to do this, corporate strategy makers must scan both the *external* and *internal environments* for needed information on strategic factors.

The Strategic Management Model does not show how the formulation process occurs. It merely describes the key *input variables* (internal and external environments) and the key *output factors* (mission, objectives, strategies, and policies). To supplement the Strategic Management Model, Chapters 6 and 7 therefore provide a more detailed discussion of the key activities in the process.

In Chapter 2, a strategic decision-making process was introduced as a graphic representation of the strategic audit. It is also included in this chapter as Fig. 6.1.

The first six steps commonly found in strategy formulation are a series of interrelated activities:

1. **Evaluation of a corporation's current performance results** in terms of (a) return on investment, profitability, etc., and (b) the current mission, objectives, strategies, and policies.

FIGURE 6.1
Strategic Decision-Making Process

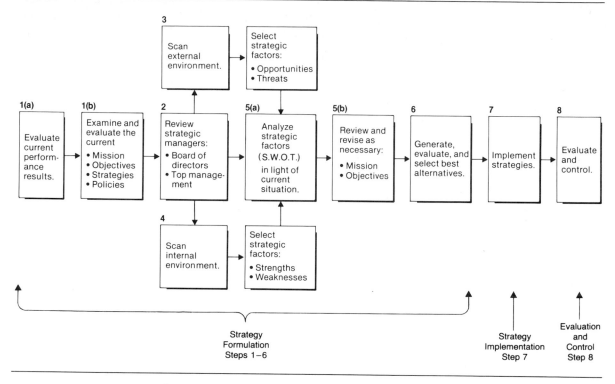

2. **Examination and evaluation of the corporation's strategic managers—** board of directors and top management.

3. **A scan of the external environment,** to locate strategic factors that pose opportunities and threats.

4. **A scan of the internal corporate environment,** to determine strategic factors that are strengths and weaknesses.

5. **Analysis of the strategic factors** from steps 3 and 4 to (a) pinpoint problem areas and (b) review and revise the corporate mission and objectives as necessary.

6. **Generation, evaluation, and selection of the best alternative strategy** in light of the analysis conducted in step 5.

Situation analysis is the first part of the strategy formulation process. Beginning with an evaluation of current performance and ending with the review and possible revision of mission and objectives, the process includes steps one through five. These steps are discussed in this chapter. Step six, the generation, evaluation, and selection of the best alternative strategy, is discussed in Chapter 7.

6.1

EVALUATION OF CURRENT RESULTS

After much research, Henry Mintzberg found that strategy formulation is typically not a regular, continuous process: "It is most often an irregular, discontinuous process, proceeding in fits and starts. There are periods of stability in strategy development, but also there are periods of flux, of groping, of piecemeal change, and of global change."[1] This view of strategy formulation as an irregular process can be explained by most people's tendency to continue on a particular course of action until something goes wrong. In a business corporation, the stimulus for a strategy review lies, in most instances, in current performance results.

Performance results are generally periodic measurements of the developments that have occurred during a given time period. At the corporate level, for example, the board and top management would be most concerned with overall measurements such as return on investment (ROI), profits after taxes, and earnings per share. To see whether a trend exists, management would compare the measurements for the current year to similar measurements from previous years. At the business or divisional level, the manager might be concerned with the return on the division's assets or its net contribution to corporate profits. At the functional level, various managers would be concerned with total sales and market share, plant efficiency, or number of new patents, depending upon their functional area.

Current performance results are compared with current objectives (desired results). If the results are equal to or greater than current objectives, most strategic managers are likely to assume that current strategies and policies are appropriate, as is. In this instance, only incremental changes to present objectives and strategy are likely to be recommended. The strategy formulation process might thus end rather abruptly with a summary statement suggesting that the corporation continue doing what it's already doing— only do it a little better next year. This is basically what occurred at Air Canada between 1955 and 1976. During this time the airline operated in a relatively stable and protected market. The very success of the company worked against any planning for change. The same mission and strategies went unchanged, for the most part, for twenty-one years. Mintzberg, Brunet, and Waters point out in their analysis of Air Canada: ". . . the system was clearly focused on operations, not strategy—the object was to program what was, not to create what hadn't been."[2]

Research does indicate that Air Canada is not an isolated example. Most organizations tend to follow a strategic orientation for around fifteen to twenty years before they make a significant change in direction.[3] After this rather long period of fine-tuning an existing strategy, some sort of **triggering event** is needed to motivate management to seriously reassess the corporation's situation. As shown in Illustrative Example 6.1, one act that is likely to serve as a triggering event is the emergence of a new chief executive officer. By asking a series of embarrassing questions, the new CEO cuts

ILLUSTRATIVE EXAMPLE 6.1

The New CEO: A Triggering Event at Alfred Dunhill PLC

When Anthony Greener became Managing Director of the family-owned British firm of Alfred Dunhill in 1975, he looked at the company's performance record and started to worry. Known widely for its pipes, lighters, and tobacco, nearly half of the company's revenues came from selling cigarette lighters to the Japanese. "We were very vulnerable," Greener stated. "What if the Japanese had suddenly stopped buying lighters?" After a complete reassessment of the firm, Greener used the tweedy, masculine image of Dunhill's English roots to build a world-wide men's fashion business. Following a strategy of growth by acquisition,

Greener plans to keep expanding until Dunhill becomes a premier marketer of luxury goods. By the mid-1980s, the company appeared to be well on its way to fulfilling its new mission. Annual revenues increased to 117 million pounds in 1984 from 20 million pounds in 1975. "This company is about marketing prestige, brand-name goods," stated Greener, emphasizing the change in mission.

SOURCE: "Breaking Dunhill's Dependence On Cigarette Lighters," *Business Week* (August 5, 1985), p. 68.

through the veil of complacency and forces people to question the very reason for the corporation's existence—a very frightening situation for most long-term employees.

Another triggering event is the **performance gap**—when the results of corporate performance do not meet expectations. A typical performance gap is when sales decline and profits fall off from previous years, or else sales and profits stagnate while those of competitors are rising. If top management chooses to confront the problem (and this is not always the case), the formulation process begins in earnest. People at all levels are urged by the board and top management to question present objectives, strategies, and policies. Even the mission may be questioned. Are we aiming too high? Do our strategies make sense? Environmental scanning of both internal and external variables begins. What went wrong? Why? Questions such as these prompt top management to review the corporation's mission, objectives, strategies and policies. As discussed in Illustrative Example 6.2, Eastman Kodak used a deteriorating situation to stimulate a strategy review.

Evaluation of Mission

A well-conceived mission statement defines the fundamental, unique purpose that sets a business apart from other firms of its type and identifies the scope of the business's operations in terms of products offered and markets served.[4] The breadth or narrowness of the corporate mission has an important effect upon corporate performance. The definition of the mission determines the broad limits of a company's growth. For example, amusement

ILLUSTRATIVE EXAMPLE 6.2
The Performance Gap: A Triggering Event at Eastman Kodak Company

Founded in 1880 by George Eastman, Kodak had been an American success story for many years. Unfortunately, its very success lulled management into complacency. Known as the staid, slumbering giant of Rochester, New York, the company had turned down early opportunities to move into xerography, instant photography, and electronic photography. As long as the amateur photography market remained strong, Kodak continued to earn annual profits in the billions of dollars. Unfortunately, the market changed in the early 1980s, but Kodak continued to emphasize its conservative tradition and slow, bureaucratic decision processes. In 1984, one year after earnings plunged by 51%, Chairman Colby H. Chandler commissioned a sweeping review of the company. He wanted to learn why Kodak had let competitors dominate markets like instant photography, 35-mm cameras, and video recorders—natural extensions of Kodak's photography business. The strategic assessment told Chandler that just as the silver-based film technology of George Eastman was being replaced by electronics, Kodak needed more than just a tune-up of its traditional business. "It's essential that we take more risks," contended Chandler. "We didn't need to take risks in the past."

To counter its chief competitor, the Japanese Fuji Photo Film Company, Kodak embarked on a series of acquisitions and restructured the company into seventeen small, autonomous business units. Top management realized that it could no longer afford to be just a photography company. They began investigating the drug industry among other things, as a possible outgrowth of Kodak's expertise in plastics and chemicals. Although the company had no drug products to sell as of mid–1987, management hoped to discover or acquire some soon. Said Leo J. Thomas, head of Kodak's effort in drugs and health care technology: "We need to broaden our base of business to where growth potential will carry us into the next century." Subsequently, Kodak acquired Sterling Drug, Inc. with its successful Lysol and Bayer Aspirin products.

SOURCES: B. Buell and R. Aikman, "Kodak Is Trying to Break Out of Its Shell," *Business Week* (June 10, 1985), pp. 92–95.
L. Helm, "Why Kodak Is Starting to Click Again," *Business Week* (February 23, 1987), pp. 134–138.
L. Helm and S. Benway, "Has Kodak Set Itself Up For a Fall?" *Business Week* (February 22, 1988), pp. 134–138.

parks traditionally defined themselves as in-place carnivals. After floundering in the 1950s, many such businesses went bankrupt. The success of Disneyland in the 1960s caused many parks such as Cedar Point, Inc. in Sandusky, Ohio to redefine themselves as "theme" parks with entertainment "packages" of shows, rides, and nationally known performers. With the aging of the American population, that mission is being further broadened to include a wider spectrum of entertainment, including golf courses and vacation resorts.

Surveys of large North American corporations reveal that approximately 60%–75% of them have formal, written statements of mission. A high percentage of the rest have an unwritten, informal mission.[5] The written mission statements of these corporations tend to contain the following eight components:

- Target customers/markets.
- Principal products/services.

- Geographic domain.
- Core technologies used.
- Commitment to survival, growth, and profitability.
- Key parts of the company's philosophy.
- Company's self-concept.
- Company's desired public image.[6]

The concept of a corporate mission implies that throughout a corporation's many activities there should be a **common thread** or unifying theme and that those corporations with such a common thread are better able to direct and administer their many activities.[7] In acquiring new firms or in developing new products, such a corporation looks for "strategic fit"; that is, the likelihood that new activities will mesh with present ones in such a way that the corporation's overall effectiveness and efficiency will be increased. A common thread may be common distribution channels or similar customers, warehousing economies or the mutual use of R&D, better use of managerial talent or any of a number of possible synergistic effects. For example, Ralston Purina recently acquired Union Carbide's battery business, including the Eveready and Energizer brands. Ralston's CEO, William Stiritz, argued that Ralston Purina would earn better profit margins on batteries than did Union Carbide because of Ralston's expertise in developing and marketing branded consumer products.[8]

Evaluation of Objectives

As pointed out in Chapter 4, each stakeholder in a corporation's task environment will have its own way of measuring the corporation's performance. Stockholders may want dividends and price appreciation, whereas unions want good wages, stability of employment, and opportunities for advancement. Customers, distributors, creditors, suppliers, local communities, and other governments, to name only a few, also have their own criteria by which they judge the corporation. By specifying and prioritizing objectives for the corporation to achieve, top management can recognize and deal with the needs of various corporate stakeholders. Some of the possible objectives a corporation might pursue are the following:

- Profitability (net profits)
- Efficiency (low costs, etc.)
- Growth (increase in total assets, sales, etc.)
- Shareholder wealth (dividends plus stock price appreciation)
- Utilization of resources (ROE or ROI)
- Contributions to customers (quality/price)
- Contributions to employees (employment security, wages)
- Contributions to society (taxes paid, participation in charities)

- Market leadership (market share, reputation)
- Technological leadership (innovations, creativity)
- Survival (avoiding bankruptcy)
- Personal needs of top management (using the firm for personal purposes, such as providing jobs for relatives)

The top management of most large, publicly-traded U.S. corporations like to announce their long-term objectives for the company—partially because that sets measurable goals to work toward and partially because they hope to impress stockholders and financial analysts. Under the direction of Chairman John F. Welch, Jr., for example, General Electric identified its primary objective of making GE worth more than any other U.S. company. In 1986, Chairman Lee Iacocca announced Chrysler's intention to boost its share of U.S. auto sales from its current 11% to 15% by the early 1990s. Admitting that market share drives profits in the auto industry, Iacocca stated, "It's a pretty big niche and we can make a lot of money doing that."[9]

It is likely, however, that many small, closely-held corporations have no formal objectives; rather they have vague, verbal ones that are typically not ranked by priority. It is even more likely that such a corporation's specified, written objectives are not the *real* (personal and probably unpublishable) objectives of top management.[10]

Evaluation of Strategies and Policies

Just as a number of firms have no formal objectives, many CEOs have unstated, incremental, or intuitive strategies that have never been articulated or analyzed. If pressured, these executives might state that they are following a certain strategy. This stated or "explicit" strategy is one with which few could quarrel, such as the development and acquisition of new product lines. Further investigation, however, might reveal the existence of a very different "implicit" strategy. For example, the prestige of a banker in one community is strictly a function of the bank's asset size. Top management, therefore, tends to choose strategies that will increase total bank assets rather than profits. An extremely profitable small bank in the eyes of the community is still just another unimportant small bank.

Often the only way to spot the implicit strategies of a corporation is to look not at what top management says, but at what it does. Implicit strategies can be derived from corporation policies, programs approved (and disapproved), and authorized budgets. Programs and divisions favored by budget increases and staffed by managers who are considered to be on the fast promotion track reveal where the corporation is putting its money and its energy.[11]

It is, nevertheless, not always necessary for strategic planning to be a formal process for it to be effective. Small corporations, for example, may plan informally and irregularly.[12] The president and a handful of top managers might get together casually, to resolve strategic issues and plan their next steps. As discussed in Chapter 12, they need no formal, elaborate planning system because the number of key executives is small enough that they can meet relatively often to discuss the company's future.

In large, multidivisional corporations, however, the planning of strategy can become quite complex. A study of strategic decisions made in thirty large organizations in England revealed that the average amount of time elapsed from the beginning of situation assessment to final decision agreement was a little over twelve months.[13] Because of the relatively large number of people affected by a strategic decision in such a firm, a formalized system is needed to ensure that a hierarchy of objectives and strategy exists. Otherwise, top management becomes isolated from developments in the divisions and lower-level managers lose sight of the corporate mission.

6.2

EVALUATION OF STRATEGIC MANAGERS

As discussed in Chapter 3, the interaction of a corporation's board with its top management is likely to reflect one of four basic styles of strategic management: chaos, entrepreneurial, marionette, and partnership. Firms like Adolph Coors Company, Winnebago, and Tandy Corporation have for years been so dominated by their founders that their boards probably operated passively as an instrument of the founder. Once the founder has died and an outsider is brought in to head the firm, however, the board may take an active role in representing the interests of the family. In such an instance, the new CEO might be quite constrained by the board in terms of strategic options.

The strategic management style of such a corporation can thus change abruptly from entrepreneurial (in which the founder dominates the board) to marionette management (in which the board, made up of the founder's family and friends, dominates top management and makes the significant decisions).

When the board is only moderately involved in strategic management, the CEO often has a free hand to set the direction of the corporation. Then the success or failure of a corporation's strategy must be evaluated in light of the CEO's managerial style.

For example, William Ylvisaker, former-Chairman and CEO of Gould Inc., had a reputation of being "mercurial" and "cavalier" with his people. Credited with reshaping the stodgy battery maker into a high-tech electronics concern, "the unpredictable Mr. Ylvisaker bought and sold properties like someone playing Monopoly."[14] In contrast, John Welch, Chairman of General Electric, carefully orchestrated the corporation's most wrenching change in its 109-year history. When Welch took charge of GE, he sketched three circles containing the fifteen businesses in which he thought GE should be involved. Apart from a few support operations, the rest were marked for sale. He proposed that for a business segment to be contributing to GE's primary objective, it must be either first or second in its market segment.[15] Welch's dynamic personality has radically altered GE's orientation toward strategic management.

Henry Mintzberg has pointed out that a corporation's objectives and strategies are strongly affected by top management's view of the world.[16] This view determines the approach or "mode" to be used in strategy formulation. He names three basic modes: entrepreneurial, adaptive, and planning. Characteristics of each mode are listed in Table 6.1.

- **Entrepreneurial mode.** Strategy is made by one powerful individual. The focus is on opportunities. Problems are secondary. Strategy is guided by the founder's own vision of direction and is exemplified by large, bold decisions. The dominant goal is growth of the corporation.

  As mentioned earlier, Gould Inc. under William Ylvisaker and General Electric under John Welch are examples of corporations being run in the entrepreneurial mode. Surprisingly, both are old, established firms with extremely dynamic and creative CEOs who have striven to change the character of their respective firms so that they will match their vision of the future.

- **Adaptive mode.** Sometimes referred to as "muddling through," this strategy-formulation mode is characterized by reactive solutions to existing problems, rather than a proactive search for new opportunities. Much bargaining goes on concerning priorities of objectives. Strategy is fragmented and is developed to move the corporation forward in incremental steps.

  This mode is typical of most universities, many large hospitals, a large number of governmental agencies, and a surprising number of large corporations. Western Union, for example, has for years successfully plodded along earning a small but predictable annual profit from businesses that largely were outgrowths of the telegraph. Only recently, when it tried to change modes and become more aggressive, did it fall on hard times.

- **Planning mode.** Analysts assume major responsibilities for strategy formulation. Strategic planning includes both the proactive search for new opportunities and the reactive solution of existing problems. Systematic comprehensive analysis is used for the development of strategies that integrate the corporation's decision-making processes.

  Sears, Roebuck and Company, in its strategic move into financial services, exemplified this mode. Rather than simply working to improve their then-stagnant merchandising group, top management chose to capitalize on the firm's successes in insurance and real estate, and to take advantage of unique opportunities emerging in the financial services industry.

In the *entrepreneurial* mode, top management believes that the environment is a force to be used and controlled. In the *adaptive* mode, it assumes the environment is too complex to be completely comprehended. In the

TABLE 6.1

Characteristics and Conditions of the Three Modes

CHARACTERISTIC	ENTREPRENEURIAL MODE	ADAPTIVE MODE	PLANNING MODE
Motive for decisions	Proactive	Reactive	Proactive and reactive
Goals of organization	Growth	Indeterminate	Efficiency and growth
Evaluation of proposals	Judgmental	Judgmental	Analytical
Choices made by	Entrepreneur	Bargaining	Management
Decision horizon	Long-term	Short-term	Long-term
Preferred environment	Uncertainty	Certainty	Risk
Decision linkages	Loosely coupled	Disjointed	Integrated
Flexibility of mode	Flexible	Adaptive	Constrained
Size of moves	Bold decisions	Incremental steps	Global strategies
Vision of direction	General	None	Specific

CONDITION FOR USE			
Source of power	Entrepreneur	Divided	Management
Objectives of organization	Operational	Nonoperational	Operational
Organizational environment	Yielding	Complex, dynamic	Predictable, stable
Status of organization	Young, small, or strong leadership	Established	Large

SOURCE: H. Mintzberg, "Strategy Making in Three Modes." Copyright © 1973 by the Regents of the University of California. Reprinted/Condensed from the *California Management Review*, Vol. No. 2, p. 49. By permission of The Regents.

planning mode, it works on the assumption that systematic scanning and analysis of the environment can provide the knowledge it needs to influence the environment to the corporation's advantage. The use of a specific planning mode reflects top management's perception of the corporation's environment. If we categorize a corporation's top management according to these three planning modes, we can better understand how and why key decisions are made. Then if we look at these decisions in light of the corporation's mission, objectives, strategies, and policies, we can then determine whether the dominant planning mode is appropriate.

In some instances, a corporation might follow an approach called **logical incrementalism,** which is a synthesis of the planning, adaptive, and to a lesser extent, the entrepreneurial modes of strategy formulation. As described by Quinn, top management might have a reasonably clear idea of the corporation's mission and objectives, but, in its development of strategies, chooses to use "an interactive process in which the organization probes the future, experiments and learns from a series of a partial (incremental) commitments rather than through global formulations of total strategies."[17] This approach appears to be useful when it is important to build consensus and develop needed resources before the entire corporation is committed to a new direction.

6.3

SCANNING THE EXTERNAL ENVIRONMENT

At the point in the strategy formulation process in which the external environment is scanned, strategic managers must examine both the societal and task environments for those strategic factors that are likely to strongly influence their corporation's success—factors that are, in other words, opportunities and threats. Long-run developments in the economic, technological, political-legal, and sociocultural aspects of the societal environment tend to affect strongly a corporation's activities: they assert immediate pressures on the corporation's task environment. Such societal issues as consumerism, governmental regulations, environmental pollution, energy cost and availability, inflation-fed wage demands, and heavy foreign competition tend to emerge from stakeholders in the firm's task environment. As indicated earlier in Chapter 4, the task environment of a particular company is often referred to as its industry. Therefore, an examination of the *task environment* may be called **industry analysis.**

As discussed in Chapter 4, strategic managers should evaluate environmental issues in terms of the probability of their occurrence and their probable impact on the corporation. In this manner, the possible societal issues listed in Table 4.4 can be placed on an issues priority matrix as shown in Fig. 4.2. Special emphasis can then be placed on the monitoring of these high-priority issues as strategic factors. Each of the six forces from the task environment depicted in Fig. 4.4, such as the threat of substitute products and services, also can be evaluated in this same manner and marked for special attention. Top management should then request its divisions and functional areas to report to it any significant developments in any of the high- or even medium-priority issues.

Strategic Groups

In the analysis of the various industries (task environments) in which a large multiproduct corporation competes, it can be very useful to categorize competitors within each industry into strategic groups. According to Hatten and Hatten, a **strategic group** is a set of business units or firms that "pursue similar strategies with similar resources."[18] Because a corporation's structure and culture tend to reflect the kinds of strategies it follows (to be discussed further in Chapter 8), companies or business units belonging to a particular strategic group within the same industry tend to be strong rivals and tend to be more similar to each other than to competitors in other strategic groups. For example, although Chevrolet and Rolls Royce are a part of the same automobile industry, they have different missions, objectives, and strategies, and thus belong to different strategic groups. They generally have very little in common and pay little attention to each other when planning competitive actions. Ford and Plymouth, however, have a great deal in common with Chevrolet, in terms of their similar strategy of producing a high volume of low-priced automobiles targeted for sale to the average person. Consequently, they are strong rivals and are organized and operated in a similar fashion.

Mobility Barriers

A corporation or business unit within a particular strategic group makes strategic decisions that competitors outside the group cannot easily imitate without substantial costs and a significant amount of time. These obstacles to casual imitation of a firm's strategy form what are called **mobility barriers** against entry into a particular strategic group.[19] These barriers are of great importance to a strategic manager because their presence in an industry can reduce the likelihood of potential competitors (See "Threat of New Entrants" in Fig. 4.4) in a particular market segment. Mobility barriers protect a particular strategic group from entry not only by competitors from other strategic groups within the industry, but also by companies currently outside the industry who wish to enter it.

The huge vertically integrated manufacturing and distribution facilities of General Motors, Chrysler, and Ford acted as a mobility barrier for many years in the United States. It prevented American Motors from successfully moving outside its niche in small cars and utility vehicles. The heavy costs involved in competing at even a small level in the U.S. acted as an entry (mobility) barrier to most foreign-based auto companies, until Volkswagen found a lucrative niche in the 1960s—that the Japanese soon followed and

TABLE 6.2
Examples of Mobility Barriers and Ways to Avoid or Overcome Them

EXAMPLES OF MOBILITY BARRIERS IN SOME INDUSTRIES

- High fixed asset requirement (steel industry)
- Heavy advertising expenses (beer industry)
- Scarce raw materials (petroleum industry)
- Difficult government requirements (electric utilities)
- Credit sales required (appliance industry)
- Ability to handle trade-ins (retail auto industry)
- Products protected by patents, trademarks, and trade secrets (drug industry)
- Control of key distribution channels (network television)
- Very low competitive prices (consumer electronics industry)

WAYS IN WHICH MOBILITY BARRIERS CAN BE AVOIDED OR OVERCOME

- Find an open niche (Neutrogena's mild soap)
- Find a substitute product (personal computers replace typewriters)
- Develop a technological improvement (P&G's low-fat cooking oil)
- Differentiate product through marketing mix (Zenith's sales of computers to colleges)
- Locate spot where competitors are weak (Toyota's emphasis on low-cost quality)
- Create process improvements (Deere's flexible manufacturing)

expanded. Some of the possible mobility barriers and ways in which they can be avoided or overcome are presented in Table 6.2.

6.4

SCANNING THE INTERNAL ENVIRONMENT

Before top management can properly address the issue of what possible strategies are appropriate for the corporation's future, it must assess its own internal situation—the environment within the firm itself. Strategic decisions should not be made until top management understands the strengths and weaknesses in divisional and functional areas.

In this instance management audits can be very useful as a diagnostic aid. As mentioned in Chapter 5, the key internal variables to be considered are the corporation's structure, culture, and resources. An example of a corporation (AT&T) in which a basic weakness in a functional area seriously hurt the implementation of a reasonable strategy is given in Illustrative Example 6.3.

PIMS Research

A current research effort to help pinpoint relevant strategic factors for business corporations is being made by the Strategic Planning Institute. Its

ILLUSTRATIVE EXAMPLE 6.3

Internal Weakness Negatively Affects Implementation of Strategic Decision at AT&T

In 1984, American Telephone and Telegraph (AT&T) bought 25% of Ing. C. Olivetti and Company, an Italian office-equipment company. AT&T wanted to become a full-blown information processing company and needed a strong presence in computers to complement its virtual domination of telephone networking. It agreed to sell Olivetti's M-24 personal computer in the United States as the AT&T 6300. The M-24 was basically another IBM "clone" with the then-standard MS-DOS operating system. Its price and features made it very competitive against the IBM personal computer in 1985, but it lost its temporary advantage in 1986 as other MS-DOS clones, such as Compaq, began offering more for the money. Sales of the AT&T 6300 dropped significantly from 1985 to 1986. Concerned with AT&T's apparent inability to market its computers, Olivetti arranged for Xerox Corporation to also sell the M-24 personal computer in North America, in competition with AT&T's 6300.

In 1986, AT&T posted an operating loss of $800 million on its computer business. An internal memo to Chairman James E. Olson of AT&T called for "priority" action to reverse the losses for "the successful execution of our strategy."

Former AT&T executives suggested that one reason the company was unable to make its computer business

a success as of 1987 was its lack of a sales force dedicated solely to sales of computers. The current sales force did not report directly to the manager in charge of computers and was expected to sell communications equipment and long-distance telephone service, in addition to computers, to its business accounts. AT&T's lack of marketing expertise was also reflected in its one-year delay in meeting the industry-wide price cuts prevalent in 1986.

Even though the company in November 1986 hired Vittorio Cassoni from Olivetti to run its new Data Systems Division, computer sales continued to drop in 1987. Cassoni demanded a complete review of the computer-development projects. He argued that development money be concentrated on systems that would give AT&T computers distinct competitive advantages so that they would not be simply me-too products. In commenting on AT&T's apparent weaknesses in marketing, one analyst reported, "Corporate management by now realizes that they can't go out and sell computers by just saying 'We're AT&T.' "

SOURCES: J. J. Keller, G. Lewis, M. Maremont, and W. C. Symonds, "AT&T May Be Ready to Cut Its Losses In Computers," *Business Week* (July 6, 1987), p. 30; and J. Guyon, "AT&T to Unveil Desktop Computer and Minicomputer," *Wall Street Journal* (September 2, 1987), p. 6.

PIMS Program (Profit Impact of Market Strategy) is composed of various analyses of a data bank containing about 100 items of information on the strategic experiences of nearly 3,000 strategic business units throughout North America and Europe, for periods ranging from two to twelve years. The research conducted with the data has been aimed at discovering the empirical "principles" that determine which strategy, under which conditions, produces what results, in terms of return on investment and cash flows regardless of the specific product or services. To date, PIMS research has identified nine major strategic factors that account for around 80% of the variation in profitability across the businesses in the database.[20] In working with these factors, the Strategic Planning Institute has prepared profiles of high ROI companies as contrasted with low ROI companies. They found that the companies with high rates of return had the following characteristics:

- Low investment intensity (the amount of fixed capital and working capital required to produce a dollar of sales)
- High market share
- High relative product quality
- High capacity utilization
- High operating effectiveness (the ratio of actual to expected employee productivity)
- Low direct costs per unit, relative to competition[21]

These and other PIMS research findings are quite controversial. For example, PIMS research has reported consistently that a large market share should lead to greater profitability.[22] The reason appears to be that high market share results in low unit costs because of economies of scale. To gain share through low price, a company could therefore take advantage of the experience curve (discussed in Chapter 5). Unfortunately, a number of studies have found that high market share does not always lead to profitability. Firms selling products of high quality relative to the competition have been found to be very profitable even though they do not have large market share.[23] PIMS researchers respond, however, that the single most important factor affecting a business unit's performance relative to its competitors' is the quality of its products or services. They also state that market leaders tend to have products of higher quality relative to those of its competitors and market followers.[24]

From a practitioner's point of view, the most important criticism of PIMS research is that the "significant predictors of performance (investment intensity, market share, relative product quality, capacity utilization, etc.) generally have tended to be variables outside of management's control, at least in the short run."[25] As a result of these and other limitations, one can conclude that we are still quite a distance away from discovering "universal strategic laws." Nevertheless, the PIMS program is useful in helping strategic managers identify some key internal strategic factors, such as investment intensity, market share, product quality, capacity utilization, operating effectiveness, and direct costs per unit. In the assessment of a corporation's relative strengths and weaknesses, these factors can be measured and compared to those of other firms in the same industry.

Strategic Field Analysis

Strategic field analysis, as proposed by Lorange, Morton, and Ghoshal, is a way of examining the nature and extent of the synergies that do or do not exist between the internal components of a corporation.[26] First, one analyzes a company's **value-added chain** in terms of the various functional steps involved in the production of a product or service. Porter, who popularized the "value-chain" concept, identifies five **primary activities** that usually occur in any business corporation: (1) inbound logistics of raw materials, (2) operations, (3) outbound logistics of the finished goods, (4) marketing and sales, and (5) customer service—and four **support activities:** (1) the procurement process, (2) technology development, (3) human resource management, and (4) the infrastructure of planning, accounting, finance, legal, government affairs, and quality management.[27] Porter recommends that one should examine the "linkages" among the value activities. In seeking ways for a corporation to gain competitive advantage in the market place, the same function can be done in different ways with different results. For example, quality inspection of 100% of output instead of the usual 10% would increase production costs, but that increase might be more than offset by the savings obtained from the reduction in the number of repairmen needed to fix defective products and the increase in the amount of salespeople's time devoted to selling instead of exchanging already-sold, but defective, products.

The second step in strategic field analysis is to examine the potential synergies between the company's products, markets, or businesses. Not only does each value element, such as advertising or manufacturing, have an inherent **economy of scale** in which activities are conducted at their lowest possible cost per unit of output, but the value elements can also have **economies of scope** across elements. Such economies of scope come as the value chains of two separate products or services share activities. For example, the cost of joint production of two products can be less than the cost of separate production. This sharing of value-chain activities can take place across functions, products, or markets. In an example provided earlier in this chapter, Ralston Purina bought Union Carbide's battery business because it could apply its expertise in the marketing of its current products to the value chains of the Eveready and Energizer brands.

6.5

ANALYSIS OF STRATEGIC FACTORS

The analysis of the strategic factors in the strategic decision-making process calls for an integration and evaluation of data collected earlier from the scanning of the internal and external environments. External strategic factors are those opportunities and threats found in the present and future task and societal environments. Internal strategic factors are those important strengths and weaknesses within the corporation's divisional and functional areas. Step 5(a) in Fig. 6.1 requires that top management attempt to find a strategic fit between external opportunities and internal strengths. This can result in the identification of a corporation's **distinctive competence**—the company's unique position with regard to its competition and the company's use of its resources. For example, the emphasis by Urschel Laboratories in building high-quality, low-cost food processing machines has provided it a "distinctive competence" in manufacturing that enabled it to dominate the industry. This concept of distinctive competence is also exemplified by a statement from Sears, Roebuck and Company's 1986 annual report, concerning its diversification into financial services:

> Our diversification simply creates new channels and opens up new opportunities. . . . By design, Sears has carefully chosen those areas where our unique strengths give us an advantage over the competition.

S.W.O.T. Analysis

S.W.O.T. is a term used to stand for a summary listing of a corporation's key internal *Strengths* and *Weaknesses* and its external *Opportunities* and *Threats*. These are the strategic factors to be analyzed in step 5(a) of Fig. 6.1. They should include not only those external factors that are most likely to occur and to have a serious impact on the company, but also those internal factors that are most likely to affect the implementation of present and future strategic decisions. For the case of Illustrative Example 6.3, which discusses AT&T's entry into the computer business, a S.W.O.T. analysis should have reflected the great *opportunities* for profits emerging in the 1980s from personal-computers and for the integration of telecommunications with computer technology. It would also have shown the serious *threats* directed not only from IBM, but also from market-oriented, aggressive companies like Compaq. The S.W.O.T. analysis should also have listed AT&T's impressive strengths in research and development, human resources, and customer service. Nevertheless, an objective assessment of weaknesses should have highlighted AT&T's lack of experience in marketing products outside of telephone-related equipment and raised a "red flag" for management to seriously consider before it chose to sell Olivetti computers through its existing marketing channels. Because AT&T failed to note the seriousness of its marketing weaknesses, it was forced to hire an experienced computer executive from Olivetti to redirect AT&T's computer development and to possibly establish a separate sales force.

Finding a Niche

William Newman suggests that a corporation should seek to obtain a "propitious niche" in its strategy formulation process.[28] This niche is a corporation's specific competitive role. It should be so well-suited to the firm's internal and external environment that other corporations are not likely to challenge or dislodge it. The corporation thus has a *distinctive competence* that enables it to take advantage of specific environmental opportunities.

The finding of such a niche is not always easy. A firm's management must always be looking for **strategic windows,** that is, market opportunities.[29] As shown in the case of Electronic Technology Corporation, presented in Illustrative Example 6.4., the first one through the strategic window can occupy a propitious niche and discourage competition (if the firm has the

ILLUSTRATIVE EXAMPLE 6.4

High-Tech Electronic Technology Corporation and *Low-Tech* Zayre's Discount Stores Find Propitious Niches

SILICON VALLEY IN CEDAR RAPIDS?

Just one year after its founding, Electronic Technology Corporation (ETC), is succeeding beyond its founder's fondest dreams. The firm manufactures semi-custom integrated circuits and sells to customers throughout the Midwest. Founder Scott Clark brought the idea to Iowa from the famed "Silicon Valley" of northern California where such companies are more common than hamburger stands. "When we began, our plan was to have a typical production order of $35,000," says Clark. "Within six months, we revised it to $90,000. And by September, orders were averaging $240,000. In fiscal year 1985, orders will average $400,000. . . . We can't grow fast enough to keep up." A significant reason for its success is its location in Cedar Rapids. Because an estimated 90% of the industry is located in Silicon Valley, about 5% on the East Coast, and the remainder scattered throughout the United States, ETC leads the way in the upper Midwest. "We're between Chicago, Minneapolis, Milwaukee, St. Louis, and Kansas City. We're accessible and we're interested in our customers," states Clark. ETC offers its customers *service* and *security*. Clark says that it's not unusual for Silicon Valley engineers to stay with a company only a matter of months. When a company receives a big contract, it can hire the necessary design engineers from one of its competitors. "These guys jump from one job to another and think nothing of it. But what they do when they jump is take the secrets of the last company they did a contract for. They can offer it to a contractor's competitor. And that doesn't happen here. Our engineers come here planning to stay. They like the security of the job and they like being out of the rat race in California. We can guarantee our customers the security they must have," comments Clark. ETC's plans to expand over the next five years conjure up dreams of a Silicon Valley in the Midwest—located in Iowa. "I really believe it will

happen," predicts Clark. "The business is here and our only real competitors are in California."

ZAYRE'S FINDS SUCCESS IN INNER CITIES

In the late 1970s, Zayre Corporation was suffering from low earnings because of the "rummage sale" nature of its discount stores. Zayre responded by renovating its stores and improving its merchandise presentation and inventory. Unlike other discounters, who were leaving the inner city in droves, Zayre decided to stay. The chain made a "significant commitment to become very good at something that [other retailers] were running away from," says President Malcolm L. Sherman. Inner-city Chicago stores were the first to be upgraded. By 1984, approximately 20% of Zayre's 276 stores were in or near black and Hispanic neighborhoods in Chicago, Pittsburgh, Atlanta, Indianapolis, and other cities. They are generally the chain's profit leaders. Zayre has few competitors in the inner city. The inventory of the inner-city stores is tailored to the specific needs and tastes of area residents. The emphasis is on apparel. The inner-city stores stock more apparel than do suburban stores because inner-city residents "have fewer places to shop" and tend to have larger families, states Mr. Sherman. Its hiring and advertising practices also reflect the ethnic mix. Apparently, Zayre's concern for its inner-city customers is reciprocated by the people in the Zayre locations. When riots shook Miami's Liberty City in March, 1984, some residents of the area intervened to protect the store from troublemakers. "We had no damage," said Charles Howze, the inner-city store's manager.

SOURCES: J. Carlson, "Silicon Valley Comes to Iowa—and Sprouts," *Des Moines Register* (January 27, 1985), p. 6X. J. L. Roberts, "Zayre's Strategy of Ethnic Merchandising Proves To Be Successful in Inner-City Stores," *Wall Street Journal* (September 25, 1984), p. 37.

required internal strengths. Zayre's decision to improve and emphasize its inner-city discount stores at a time when competitors were leaving inner-city locations in droves enabled it to build a niche successfully where none had previously existed.

A recent study of high-performing, mid-sized growth companies found these successful corporations to have four characteristics in common:

- They innovate as a way of life.
- They compete on value, not price.
- They achieve leadership in *niche markets*.
- They build on their strengths by competing in *related niches*.[30]

In summary, research reveals that corporate performance is strongly influenced by how well a company positions itself within an industry.[31] The finding of a specific niche in which a corporation's strengths fit well with environmental opportunities is thus a desired outcome of situation analysis and a valuable means for a corporation to gain competitive advantage.

Portfolio Analysis

The business portfolio is the most recommended aid to the integration and evaluation of environmental data. Research suggests that roughly 75% of the U.S. Fortune 500 companies and many smaller companies with multiple product lines or services practice some form of portfolio analysis in their strategy formulations.[32] There is probably a similar rate of usage by companies located in other industrialized nations.

All corporations, except the simplest and smallest, are involved in more than one business. Even if a corporation sells only one product, it might benefit from handling separately a number of distinct product-market segments. Procter & Gamble, for example, managed Prell Liquid and Prell Concentrate as two separate brands of shampoo for a number of years because of their appeal to two separate and distinct market segments.

Portfolio analysis recommends that each product, strategic business unit (SBU), or division be considered separately for purposes of strategy formulation.

There are a number of matrixes available to reflect the variables under consideration in a portfolio. SBUs or products can be compared on the basis of their growth rate in sales, relative competitive position, stage of product/market evolution, market share, and industry attractiveness.

Four-Cell, BCG Growth-Share Matrix _____

The simplest matrix is the *growth-share matrix* developed by the Boston Consulting Group, as depicted in Fig. 6.2. Each of the corporation's SBUs or products is plotted on the matrix according to both the growth rate of the industry in which it competes and its relative market share. A product's or SBU's relative competitive position is defined as its market share in the industry divided by that of the largest other competitor. The business growth rate is the percentage of market growth—that is, the percentage by which sales of a particular product or SBU classification of products have increased.

The line separating areas of high and low relative competitive position is set at 1.5 times. A product or SBU must have relative strengths of this magnitude to ensure that it will have the dominant position needed to be a star or cash cow. On the other hand, a product or SBU having a relative competitive position of 1 times or less has dog status.[33] Each product or SBU is represented in Fig. 6.2 by a circle. The area of the circle represents the relative significance of each SBU or product to the corporation in terms of assets used or sales generated.

The growth-share matrix has a lot in common with the product life-cycle. New products are typically introduced in a fast growing industry. These initially are termed **question mark** products. If one of these products is to gain enough market share to become a market leader and thus a **star,** money must be taken from more mature **cash cow** products and spent on a *question mark. Stars* are typically at the peak of their product life-cycle and are usually able to generate cash enough for maintenance of their high share of the market. Once their market growth rate slows, *stars* become *cash cows.* These products typically bring in far more money than is needed for maintenance of their market share. As these products move along the decline stage of their life cycle, they are "milked" for cash to be invested in new *question mark* products. Those products unable to obtain a dominant market

FIGURE 6.2
The BCG Portfolio Matrix

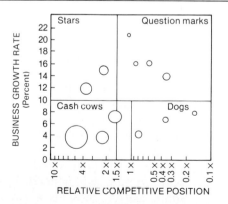

Source: B. Hedley, "Strategy and the Business Portfolio," *Long Range Planning* (February 1977), p. 12. Reprinted by permission.

share by the time the industry growth rate inevitably slows become **dogs,** which are either sold off or managed carefully for the small amount of cash they can generate.

Once the current positions of a corporation's products or SBUs have been plotted on a matrix, a projection can be made of its future position, if there are to be no changes in strategy. Present and projected matrixes can thus be used to assist in the identification of major strategic issues facing the corporation.

Research into the growth-share matrix generally supports its assumptions and recommendations except for the advice that dogs should be promptly harvested or liquidated.[34] A product with a low share in a declining industry can be very profitable if the product has a niche in which market demand remains stable and predictable.[35] If enough of the competition leaves the industry, a product's market share can increase by default until the dog becomes the market leader and thus a cash cow. All in all, the BCG growth-share matrix is a very popular technique. It is quantifiable and easy to use. The barnyard analogies of cash cows and dogs have become trendy buzz-words in management circles.

The growth-share matrix has been criticized for a number of reasons nevertheless:

- The use of highs and lows to make just four categories is too simplistic.
- The link between market share and profitability is not necessarily strong. Low-share businesses can be profitable, too (and vice versa).
- The highest-growth-rate markets are not always the best.
- It considers the product or SBU only in relation to one competitor— the market leader. It misses small competitors with fast-growing market shares.
- Growth rate is only one aspect of industry attractiveness.
- Market share is only one aspect of overall competitive position.[36]

Nine-Cell GE Business Screen

A more complicated matrix is that developed by General Electric with the assistance of the McKinsey and Company consulting firm. As depicted in Fig. 6.3, it includes nine cells based on long-term industry attractiveness and business strength/competitive position. Interestingly, this nine-cell matrix is almost identical to the *Directional Policy Matrix* developed by Shell Oil and used extensively by European firms. Both use the same factors and both use nine cells. The GE Business Screen, in contrast to the BCG growth-share matrix, includes much more data in its two key factors than just business growth rate and comparable market share. For example, at GE, industry attractiveness includes market growth rate, industry profitability, size, and pricing practices, among other possible opportunities and threats.

FIGURE 6.3
General Electric's Business Screen

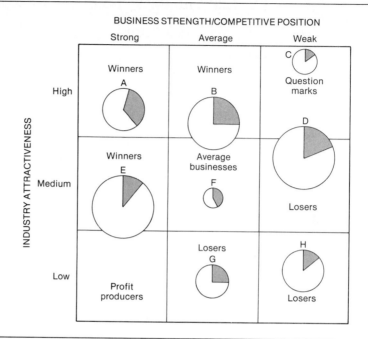

Source: Adapted from *Strategic Management in GE,* Corporate Planning and Development, General Electric Corporation. Used by permission of General Electric Company.

Business strength or competitive position includes market share as well as technological position, profitability, and size, among other possible strengths and weaknesses.[37]

The individual products or SBUs are identified by a letter and plotted as circles on the GE Screen. The area of each circle is in proportion to the size of the industry in terms of sales. The pie slices within the circles depict the market share of each product or SBU.

The following four steps are recommended for the plotting of products or SBUs on the GE Business Screen.[38]

1. **Assess industry attractiveness.**

   a) Select general criteria by which the industry will be rated. These criteria should be key aspects of the industry, such as its potential for sales growth and likely profitability. Table 6.3 lists fifteen criteria for one specific industry.

   b) Weight each criterion according to management's perception of the criterion's importance to the achievement of corporate objectives. For example, because the key criterion of the corporation in Table 6.3 is profitability, it receives the highest weight, 0.20.

TABLE 6.3
An Example of an Industry Attractiveness Assessment Matrix

ATTRACTIVENESS CRITERIA	WEIGHT*	RATING**	WEIGHTED SCORE
Size	0.15	4	0.60
Growth	0.12	3	0.36
Pricing	0.05	3	0.15
Market diversity	0.05	2	0.10
Competitive structure	0.05	3	0.15
Industry profitability	0.20	3	0.60
Technical role	0.05	4	0.20
Inflation vulnerability	0.05	2	0.10
Cyclicality	0.05	2	0.10
Customer financials	0.10	5	0.50
Energy impact	0.08	4	0.32
Social	GO	4	—
Environmental	GO	4	—
Legal	GO	4	—
Human	0.05	4	0.20
	1.00		3.38

SOURCE: Reprinted by permission from *Strategy Formulation: Analytical Concepts* by C. W. Hofer and D. Schendel. Copyright © 1978 by West Publishing Company. All rights reserved.

*Some criteria may be of a GO/NO GO type. For example, many *Fortune 500* firms probably would decide not to invest in industries that are viewed negatively by our society, such as gambling, even if it were both legal and very profitable to do so.

**1 *(very unattractive)* through 5 *(highly attractive).*

c) Rate the industry on each of these criteria from 1 (very unattractive) to 5 (very attractive). For example, if an industry is facing a long-term decline in profitability, this criterion should be rated 2 or less.

d) To get a weighted score, multiply the weight for each criterion by its rating. When these scores are added, the weighted attractiveness score for the industry as a whole is provided for a particular SBU. (3.38 is the weighted industry attractiveness score for the SBU considered in Table 6.3.)

2. **Assess business strength/competitive position.**

a) Identify the SBU's key factors for success in the industry. Table 6.4 lists seventeen such factors for a specific industry.

b) Weight each success factor (market share, for instance) in terms of its relative importance to profitability or some other measure of success within the industry. For example, because market share was believed to have a relatively small impact on most firms in the

TABLE 6.4

An Example of a Business Strength/Competitive Position Assessment Matrix for an SBU

KEY SUCCESS FACTORS	WEIGHT	RATING**	WEIGHTED SCORE
Market share	0.10	5	.50
SBU growth rate	X*	3	—
Breadth of product line	.05	4	.20
Sales distribution effectiveness	.20	4	.80
Proprietary and key account advantages	X	3	—
Price competitiveness	X	4	—
Advertising and promotion effectiveness	.05	4	.20
Facilities location and newness	.05	5	.25
Capacity and productivity	X	3	—
Experience curve effects	.15	4	.60
Raw materials cost	.05	4	.20
Value added	X	4	—
Relative product quality	.15	4	.60
R&D advantages/position	.05	4	.20
Cash throw-off	.10	5	.50
Caliber of personnel	X	4	—
General image	.05	5	.25
	1.00		4.30

SOURCE: Reprinted by permission from *Strategy Formulation: Analytical Concepts* by C. W. Hofer and D. Schendel. Copyright © 1978 by West Publishing Company. All rights reserved.

*For any particular industry, there will be some factors that, while important in general, will have little or no effect on the relative competitive position of firms within that industry. It is usually better to drop such factors from the analysis than to assign them very low weights.

**1 *(very weak competitive position)* through 5 *(very strong competitive position)*.

industry of Table 6.4, this success factor was given a weight of only 0.10.

c) Rate the SBU on each of the factors from 1 (very weak competitive position) to 5 (very strong competitive position). For example, as the products of the SBU of Table 6.4 have a very high market share, market share received a rating of 5.

d) To get a weighted score, multiply the weight of each factor by its rating. When these scores are added, the sum provides a weighted business strength/competitive position score for the SBU as a whole.

(4.30 is the weighted business strength/competitive position score for the SBU considered in Table 6.4.)

3. **Plot each SBU's current position.**
   Once industry attractiveness and business strength/competitive position are calculated for each SBU, the actual position of all the corporation's SBUs should be plotted on a matrix like the one illustrated in Fig. 6.3. The areas of the circles should be proportional to the sizes of the various industries involved (in terms of sales); the company's current market share in each industry should be depicted as a pie-shaped wedge; and the circles should be centered on the coordinates of the SBU's industry attractiveness and business strength/competitive position scores.

   To develop a range of scores for the *industry attractiveness* axis of the matrix, look back at Table 6.3. A highly attractive industry should have mostly 5s in the rating column. An industry of medium attractiveness should have mostly 3s in the rating column. An industry of low attractiveness should have mostly 1s in the rating column. Because the weights of the criteria used for each industry must sum to 1.00 regardless of the number of criteria used, the attractiveness axis of the GE Business Screen matrix should range from 1.00 (low attractiveness) to 5.00 (high attractiveness), with 3.00 as the midpoint. The SBU evaluated in Table 6.3 with an industry attractiveness score of 3.38 is thus classified as "medium" on this factor.

   Similarly, the range of scores for the *business strength/competitive position* axis of the GE Business Screen matrix should also range from 1.00 (weak) to 5.00 (strong), with 3.00 as the midpoint (average). This can be more clearly understood with another look at Table 6.4. Because the criteria weights must sum to 1.00 regardless of the number of criteria used for each SBU, an SBU with a very strong competitive position might have all 5s in the rating column and thus a total weighted score of 5.00. The SBU evaluated in Table 6.4 with a business strength/competitive position score of 4.30 is thus classified as "strong" on this factor.

   The resulting matrix shows the corporation's current portfolio situation. This situation is then contrasted with an ideal portfolio. Figure 6.4 depicts what Hofer and Schendel consider to be such a portfolio. It is considered ideal because it includes primarily winners, and contains enough winners and profit producers to finance the growth of developing (or potential) winners. In reality, however, even a successful firm would probably have a few question marks and perhaps a small loser.

4. **Plot the firm's future portfolio.**
   An assessment of the current situation is complete only when the present portfolio is projected into the future. Assuming that the present corporate and SBU strategies continue unchanged, top management should assess the probable impact that likely changes to the corporation's task and societal environments will have, on both future industry attractiveness and SBU competitive position. They should ask themselves whether future matrixes show an improving or deteriorating portfolio position. Is there a **performance gap** between projected and desired portfolios?

FIGURE 6.4
An Ideal Multi-Industry Corporate Portfolio

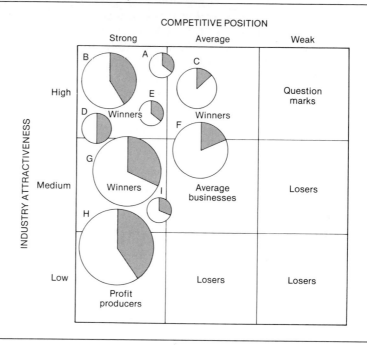

NOTE: It is impossible to identify the orientation (i.e. growth, profit, or balance) of an ideal portfolio based solely on the information contained in the GE Business Screen, because the screen does not reflect all the information needed to do so. For instance, SBUs B, C, F, G, and H could be developing winners in very large markets or established winners in smaller markets. Likewise, SBUs A, D, E, and I could represent either developing potential winners in large markets or established winners in small markets. In the majority of instances, however, the pattern of SBU sizes and positions depicted in this figure would correspond to a balanced ideal portfolio.

If the answer is yes, this gap should serve as a stimulus for them to seriously review the corporation's current mission, objectives, strategies, and policies.

Overall, the nine-cell GE Business Screen is an improvement over the Boston Consulting Group growth-share matrix. The GE Screen considers many more variables and does not lead to such simplistic conclusions. Nevertheless, it can get quite complicated and cumbersome. The calculations used in Tables 6.3 and 6.4 give the appearance of objectivity but are in reality subjective judgments that may vary from one person to another. Another shortcoming of this portfolio matrix is that it cannot effectively depict the positions of new products or SBUs in developing industries.

Fifteen-Cell Product/Market Evolution Matrix

Developed by Hofer and based on the product life-cycle, this matrix depicts the developing types of products or SBUs that cannot be easily shown on the GE Business Screen. Products or SBUs are plotted in terms of their competitive positions and their stages of product/market evolution.[39] As on the GE Business Screen, the circles represent the sizes of the industries involved and the pie wedges represent the market shares of the firm's SBUs or products. Present and future matrixes can be developed to identify strategic issues. In response to Fig. 6.5, for example, one could ask why product or SBU B does not have a greater share of the market, given its strong competitive position.

Advantages and Limitations of Portfolio Analysis

Portfolio analysis is commonly used in strategy formulation because it offers certain **advantages:**

- It encourages top management to evaluate each of the corporation's businesses individually and to set objectives and allocate resources for each.
- It stimulates the use of externally oriented data to supplement management's judgment.
- It raises the issue of cash flow availability for use in expansion and growth.
- Its graphic depiction facilitates communication.

Portfolio analysis does, however, have some very real **limitations** that have caused some companies to reduce their use of the matrixes:

- It is not easy to define product/market segments.
- It suggests the use of standard strategies that can miss opportunities or be impractical.
- It provides an illusion of scientific rigor when in reality positions are based on subjective judgments.
- Its value-laden terms like cash cow and dog can lead to self-fulfilling prophecies.[40]

6.6

REVIEW OF MISSION AND OBJECTIVES

A reexamination of a corporation's current mission and objectives must be done before alternative strategies can be generated and evaluated. The seriousness of this step is emphasized by Tregoe and Zimmerman.

> When making a decision, there is an almost universal tendency to concentrate on the alternatives—the action possibilities—rather than on the objectives we want to achieve. This tendency is widespread because it is much easier to deal

FIGURE 6.5
Product/Market Evolution Portfolio Matrix

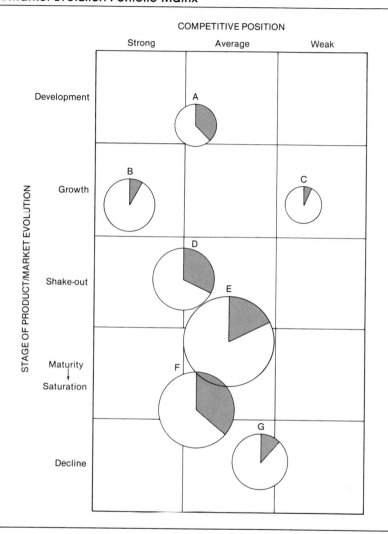

Source: C. W. Hofer and D. Schendel, *Strategy Formulation: Analytical Concepts* (St. Paul, Minn.: West Publishing Co., 1978), p. 34. From C. W. Hofer, "Conceptual Constructs for Formulating Corporate and Business Strategies" (Dover, Mass: Case Publishing), no. BP-0041, p. 3. Copyright © 1977 by Charles W. Hofer. Reprinted by permission.

with alternative courses of action that exist right here and now than to really think about what we want to accomplish in the future. Projecting a set of values forward is hard work. The end result is that we make choices that set our objectives for us, rather than having our choices incorporate clear objectives.[41]

Problems in corporate performance can derive from an inappropriate statement of mission, which may be too narrow or too broad. If the mission does not provide a common thread for a corporation's businesses, managers may be unclear about where the corporation is heading. Objectives and strategies might be in conflict with each other. Divisions might be competing against one another, rather than against outside competition—to the detriment of the corporation as a whole. According to Lorange, "Rapid changes in the environment suggest that the definition of businesses should be reviewed frequently, so that the relevance of the business definitions can be maintained.[42]

An example of a revision of a corporation's mission statement is that by American Telephone and Telegraph (AT&T). The revised mission was published in AT&T's 1980 annual report to the stockholders and had important implications for future corporate strategy:

> No longer do we perceive that our business will be limited to telephony or, for that matter, telecommunications. Ours is the business of information handling, the knowledge business. And the market that we seek is global.

A corporation's objectives can also be inappropriately stated. They can either focus too much on short-term operational goals or be so general that they provide little real guidance. Consequently, objectives should be constantly reviewed so that their usefulness is ensured.

SUMMARY AND CONCLUSION

This chapter describes the key activities involved in the process of strategy formulation. According to the strategic decision-making process introduced in Chapter 2, formulation is described as being composed of six distinct steps. Situation analysis incorporates five steps, beginning with the evaluation of current performance results and ending with the review and revision of mission and objectives. Step six—the generation, evaluation, and selection of the best alternative strategy—is discussed in the next chapter.

Step 1—the evaluation of current performance results and the review of the corporation's mission, objectives, strategies, and policies—deals with the initial stimulus that starts the formulation process. *Step 2*, the review of strategic managers, includes an evaluation of the competencies, level of involvement, and performance of the corporation's top management and board of directors. *Step 3*, scanning the external environment, focuses on the collection of information, the selection of strategic factors, and the forecasting of future events likely to affect the corporation's strategic decisions. An industry analysis includes a consideration of strategic groups and of mobility barriers. *Step 4*, scanning the internal environment, deals with the assessment of internal strengths and weaknesses in terms of structure, culture, and resources. PIMS research and strategic field analysis are valuable aids in the ascertaining of a company's strengths and weaknesses versus those of comparable firms in the company's industry. *Step 5(a)*, analysis of strategic factors in light of the current situation, proposes S.W.O.T. analysis and portfolio analysis as techniques to locate a business' propitious niche in light of its distinctive competence. Matrixes developed by the Boston Consulting Group,

General Electric, and Hofer are described as three ways by which business strengths and weaknesses can be compared to its environmental opportunities and threats. *Step 5(b)*, review and revision of the mission and objectives, completes the situation analysis: it forces a strategic manager to reexamine corporate purpose and objectives before initiating alternative strategies.

DISCUSSION QUESTIONS

1. Does strategy formulation need to be a regular, continuous process? Explain.

2. Is it necessary that a corporation have a "common thread" running through its many activities in order to be successful? Why or why not?

3. How can a knowledge of mobility barriers contribute to an understanding of competitive behavior within an industry?

4. What is likely to happen to an SBU that loses its propitious niche?

5. What value has portfolio analysis in the consideration of strategic factors?

6. Compare and contrast S.W.O.T. analysis with portfolio analysis.

7. Is the GE Business Screen just a more complicated version of the Boston Consulting Group growth/share matrix? Why or why not?

8. Is portfolio analysis used to formulate strategy at the corporate, divisional, or functional level of the corporation?

9. What are the key strategic factors facing CSX Corporation at the time of the case and in the future as described in the Integrative Case at the end of this chapter?

NOTES

1. H. Mintzberg, "Planning on the Left Side and Managing on the Right," *Harvard Business Review* (July-August 1976), p. 56.

2. H. Mintzberg, J. P. Brunet, and J. A. Waters, "Does Planning Impede Strategic Thinking? Tracking the Strategies of Air Canada from 1937 to 1976," in *Advances in Strategic Management, Vol. 4,* edited by R. Lamb and P. Shrivastava (Greenwich, Conn.: Jai Press, 1986), p. 29.

3. D. Miller and P. H. Friesen, "Momentum and Revolution in Organizational Adaptation," *Academy of Management Journal* (December 1980), pp. 600–601.
H. Mintzberg and A. McHugh, "Strategy Formulation In An Adhocracy," *Administrative Science Quarterly* (June 1985), p. 190.

4. J. A. Pearce and F. David, "Corporate Mission Statements: The Bottom Line," *Academy of Management Executive* (May 1987), p. 109.

5. Pearce and David, p. 113.
L. L. Byars and T. C. Neil, "Organizational Philosophy and Mission Statements," *Planning Review* (July-August 1987), p. 35.

6. Pearce and David, pp. 109–115.

7. H. I. Ansoff, *Corporate Strategy* (New York: McGraw-Hill, 1965), pp. 104–108.

8. K. Dreyfack, "What Purina Really Wanted From Carbide," *Business Week* (April 21, 1986), p. 33.

9. J. R. Norman, "General Electric Is Stalking Big Game Again," *Business Week* (March 16, 1987), p. 113.
M. G. Guiles, "Chrysler Is Aiming to Boost Its Share of the U.S. Market," *Wall Street Journal* (September 25, 1986), p. 26.

10. M. D. Richards, *Setting Strategic Goals and Objectives,* 2nd ed. (St. Paul: West Publishing Co., 1986), pp. 30–32.

11. K. R. Andrews, *The Concept of Corporate Strategy,* 2nd ed. (Homewood, Ill.: Irwin, 1987), p. 18.

12. R. B. Robinson, Jr., and J. A. Pearce, III, "Research Thrusts in Small Firm Strategic Planning," *Academy of Management Review* (January 1984), pp. 128–137.

13. D. J. Hickson, R. J. Butler, D. Cray, G. R. Mallory, and D. C. Wilson, *Top Decisions: Strategic Decision-Making in Organizations* (San Francisco: Jossey-Bass, 1986), pp. 100–101.

14. J. Bussey, "Gould Reshapes Itself into High-Tech Outfit Amid Much Turmoil," *Wall Street Journal* (October 3, 1985), p. 1.

15. M. A. Harris, Z. Schiller, R. Mitchell, and C. Power, "Can Jack Welch Reinvent GE?" *Business Week* (June 30, 1986), pp. 62–67.

16. H. Mintzberg, "Strategy-Making in Three Modes," *California Management Review* (Winter 1973), pp. 44–53.

17. J. B. Quinn, *Strategies For Change: Logical Incrementalism* (Homewood, Ill.: Irwin, 1980), p. 58.

18. K. J. Hatten and M. L. Hatten, "Strategic Groups, Asymmetrical Mobility Barriers, and Contestability," *Strategic Management Journal* (July-August 1987), p. 329.

19. J. McGee and J. Thomas, "Strategic Groups: Theory, Research, and Taxonomy," *Strategic Management Journal* (March-April 1986), pp. 141–160. Mobility barrier is used here as a more general form of *entry barrier*—a term usually referring only to entry into an industry. See M. E. Porter, *Competitive Strategy* (New York: Free Press, 1980), pp. 132–135.

20. S. Schoeffler, "Nine Basic Findings On Business Strategy," *The PIMS Letter On Business Strategy*, No. 1 (Cambridge, Mass.: The Strategic Planning Institute, 1984), pp. 3–5.

21. G. Badler, "Strategizing for a Spectrum of Possibilities," *Planning Review* (July 1984), pp. 28–31.

22. R. D. Buzzell and B. T. Gale, *The PIMS Principles* (New York: The Free Press, 1987), pp. 8–10.

23. C. Y. Woo, "Market-Share Leadership—Not Always So Good," *Harvard Business Review* (January-February 1984), pp. 50–54.

J. K. Newton, "Market Share—Key to Higher Profitability?" *Long Range Planning* (February 1983), pp. 37–41.

D. Bourantas and Y. Mandes, "Does Market Share Lead to Profitability?" *Long Range Planning* (October 1987), pp. 102–108.

24. Buzzell and Gale, pp. 7 and 183.

25. V. Ramanujan and N. Venkatraman, "An Inventory and Critique of Strategy Research using the PIMS Database," *Academy of Management Review* (January 1984), p. 147.

26. P. Lorange, M. F. S. Morton, and S. Ghoshal, *Strategic Control* (St. Paul: West Publishing Co., 1986), pp. 104–107.

27. M. E. Porter, *Competitive Advantage* (New York: The Free Press, 1985), pp. 33–61.

28. W. H. Newman, "Shaping the Master Strategy of Your Firm," *California Management Review*, vol. 9, no. 3 (1967), pp. 77–88.

29. D. F. Abell, "Strategic Windows," *Journal of Marketing* (July 1978), pp. 21–26, as reported by K. R. Harrigan, "Entry Barriers in Mature Manufacturing Industries" in R. Lamb (ed.), *Advances in Strategic Management,* Vol. 2 (Greenwich, Conn.: Jai Press, 1983), pp. 67–97.

30. D. K. Clifford and R. E. Cavanagh, "The Winning Performance of Midsized Growth Companies," *Planning Review* (November 1984), pp. 18–23, 35.

31. L. Fahey and H. K. Christensen, "Evaluating the Research on Strategy Content," *Journal of Management* (Summer 1986), p. 180.

32. R. G. Hamermesh, "Making Planning Effective," *Harvard Business Review* (July-August 1986), p. 115.

33. B. Hedley, "Strategy and the Business Portfolio," *Long Range Planning* (February 1977), p. 9.

34. D. C. Hambrick, I. C. MacMillan, and D. L. Day, "Strategic Attributes and Performance in the BCG Matrix—A PIMS-Based Analysis of Industrial Product Businesses," *Academy of Management Journal* (September 1982), pp. 510–531.

35. C. Y. Woo and A. C. Cooper, "The Surprising Case for Low Market Share," *Harvard Business Review* (November-December 1982), pp. 106–113.

36. P. McNamee, "Competitive Analysis Using Matrix Displays," *Long Range Planning* (June 1984), pp. 98–114.

R. E. Walker, "Portfolio Analysis in Practice," *Long Range Planning* (June 1984), pp. 63–71.

D. A. Aaker and G. S. Day, "The Perils of High-growth Markets," *Strategic Management Journal* (September-October 1986), pp. 409–421.

37. R. G. Hamermesh, *Making Strategy Work* (New York: Wiley & Sons, 1986), p. 14.

For a more complete list of characteristics, see P. McNamee, pp. 102–103.

38. C. W. Hofer and D. Schendel, *Strategy Formulation: Analytical Concepts* (St. Paul: West Publishing Co., 1978), pp. 72–87.

39. Similar to the Hofer model, but using twenty instead of fifteen cells is the Arthur D. Little (ADL) strategic planning matrix. For details see M. B. Coate, "Pitfalls in Portfolio Planning," *Long Range Planning* (June 1983), pp. 47–56.

40. F. W. Gluck, "A Fresh Look at Strategic Management," *Journal of Business Strategy* (Fall 1985), pp. 4–19.

41. B. B. Tregoe and J. W. Zimmerman, "The New Strategic Manager," *Business* (May-June 1981), p. 19.

42. P. Lorange, *Implementation of Strategic Planning* (Englewood Cliffs, N.J.: Prentice-Hall, 1982, p. 211.

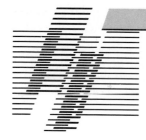

CSX CORPORATION'S STRATEGIC FACTORS

Three rail systems dominated the eastern United States in 1985: CSX, Norfolk Southern, and Conrail. West of the Mississippi also lay three major systems: Union Pacific, Santa Fe Southern Pacific Corporation (pending approval of the merger by the ICC), and the Burlington Northern Railroad. There appeared to be no one reason why railroads in the United States had developed into separate east-west domains generally separated by the Mississippi River. In some instances the personalities of the owner-managers kept railroads separate. According to Dr. Michael Crum at Iowa State University, an expert on rail transportation, rail traffic has traditionally been an interregional instead of transcontinental phenomenon. The emphasis has been on the gaining of access to individual markets, such as St. Louis or New York City, rather than the crossing of the country. Rail lines connected coastal population centers with the interior sources of commodities and products. What little traffic stretched from east to west coasts had typically been handled through standard interline agreements, allowing one railroad to transport for a fee the railcars of another railroad. Thus boxcars of the Seaboard Line (among many other railroads) could be seen traveling through California and Western Canada via agreements with Santa Fe, Canadian Pacific, and others. This phenomenon had made the management of such information a major task of any modern North American railroad. According to Dr. Crum, the interlining of rail traffic has created additional costs and some decrease in the quality of rail service in terms of time in transit. Negotiations for the division of revenues were often very complex. As a consequence, interlining, with its paperwork and delays, has been viewed by rail management as a necessary evil due to the historical fragmentation of rail system ownership.

KEY COMPETITORS

Although the Norfolk Southern and CSX rail systems had several characteristics in common, such as a high dependence upon coal as a revenue-producing commodity (coal composed around 32%–36% of CSX's total annual commodity revenues and approximately 36%–40% of Norfolk Southern's total annual commodity revenues), Norfolk Southern (NS) was a more efficient rail operation. NS has been characterized by analysts as a very lean operation in terms of costs and expenses, whereas both the Chessie and Seaboard systems have been criticized for having too many employees and higher salaries. CSX resulted from the merger of two railroads with high unit-labor costs, while NS represented a combination of two rail systems with historically low labor costs. Hays T. Watkins, Chairman of CSX, was well aware of the danger that NS, serving the same markets as CSX, could use its labor-cost advantage to undercut the rates of CSX. Mr. Watkins stated in 1981, "I don't think the CSX labor cost ratio will ever be as low as the Norfolk & Western and Southern despite

SOURCE: J. D. Hunger, B. Ferrin, H. Felix-Gamez, T. Goetzman, "CSX Corporation," in *Cases in Strategic Management and Business Policy* by T. L. Wheelen and J. D. Hunger (Reading, Mass.: Addison-Wesley, 1987), pp. 91–123.

anything we can do, due to geography, the locations of the mines, and the location of the facilities." He added,

> We have not found any practical way to run a good service railroad on the Chessie side and equal the N&W's figures. On the bottom line, I am not sure we can beat them. I'm not even sure we can match them, but we can't match AT&T or a lot of other companies. What we do is take what we have and do the best we can.

CSX management has worked hard, however, to reduce its rail employment from 75,336 employees in 1980 to 53,031 at year-end 1984.

Another significant difference between NS and CSX was that, after the respective mergers, NS had carried the consolidation of operations much farther than did CSX. While CSX operated its two rail systems as separate units, NS had combined most staff activities as well as the sales offices of its component railroads in every location. For example, all the functions commonly included in a traffic department—including sales, marketing, pricing, and industrial development—were directed by a chief marketing officer for the entire NS system.

Robert Claytor, NS Chairman, raised the possibility on October 23, 1984, that NS might also buy a barge line. NS already owned about 18% of Piedmont Aviation, a fast-growing regional airline. NS's acquisition plans did not stop there. The firm had expressed serious intentions of buying a major trucking operation and had entered an agreement for the purchase of North American Van Lines from Pepsico for over $300 million.

The third major railroad in the eastern United States was the government-owned Consolidated Rail Corporation (Conrail). Conrail operated a 15,400-mile track network that was basically oriented in a straight east-west line. Although analysts believed in 1976, when Conrail was formed, that it would take something of a minor miracle to make the system profitable, the miracle occurred thanks to significant government investment and easing of regulatory restrictions (e.g., branch line abandonments). Conrail's significant advantage over both CSX and Norfolk Southern was that it alone of the three major eastern systems had track north of Philadelphia and east of Rochester into the populous New York-New Jersey-New England area.

In early February 1985, Transportation Secretary Dole announced her decision to sell the government's 85% share of Conrail to Norfolk Southern. (The remaining 15% was owned by Conrail employees.) This decision took CSX top management by surprise. They had assumed that the bid by Norfolk Southern would never get past the Justice Department's anti-trust review.

RIVALRY INCREASES UNDER DEREGULATION

Deregulation had led to the industry-wide implementation of rate-cutting tactics designed to increase market share. The battle was taking place all over the country, but in the East the leading practitioner had been Conrail. On April 3, 1981, Conrail cut its rates 22% on import-export containers moving between Chicago and New York, Philadelphia, and Baltimore. "CSX Corporation, which controls 80% of the container traffic between Chicago and Baltimore, responded with a 25% reduction," reported Robert D. Long, analyst at First Boston Corporation.

In addition to the practice of cutting rates on desirable traffic, the railroads had employed several other tactics intended to increase market share and enhance profits.

Some companies had increased rates for services like short hauls in joint moves of cars; these companies argued that when the revenues were shared with the line offering the long-haul service, those carriers stuck with a very short-haul part of the movement were not justly compensated. Since the passage of the Staggers Act, railroads were allowed to charge joint rates that generated at least 110% of variable, or direct costs, or the cancel those routes.

Another tactic adopted by rail carriers was the canceling of joint routes with other railroads when they could provide service over the entire movement themselves. Railroads also substantially increased charges for switching services, in order to prevent competitors from entering certain of their markets. (The switching service was a mutual agreement that enabled one railroad to pick up or deliver a shipment for another carrier that did not have direct access to the shipper or receiver. The switching carrier received a per-car fee for its move, which was generally less than twenty miles.)

CONSIDERATION OF STRATEGIC FACTORS

Hays Watkins pondered the many variables still facing the industry and CSX in particular. CSX had come a long way in five short years. Leading the way in marketing innovations, the company's rail units had captured the rail industry's top marketing award twice in the last three years. At the same time, CSX had moved aggressively to broaden its transportation and natural resources horizons, improve rates of return, and accomplish its number one goal—increased shareholder wealth. The stated mission of CSX, to become a multimodal, one-stop transportation system, seemed to be within reach. The corporation's objectives for the near future would be directed toward increasing the returns on the assets, capital, and equity employed in its businesses. Given the company's internal strengths and weaknesses, and the various opportunities and threats within the transportation industry, how should CSX assess its position and plan for the future?

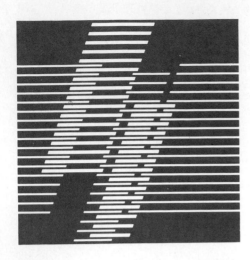

CHAPTER 7

STRATEGY FORMULATION: STRATEGIC ALTERNATIVES

STRATEGIC MANAGEMENT MODEL

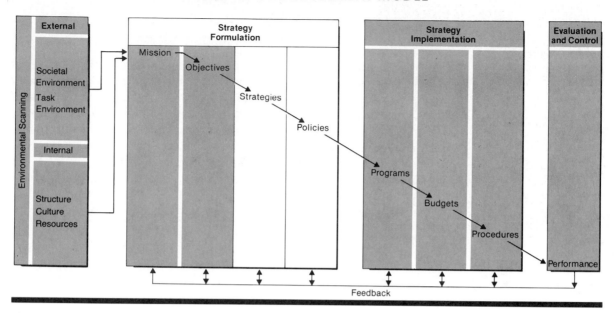

A key part of strategy formulation is the development of alternative courses of action that specify means by which the corporate mission and objectives are to be accomplished. As explained in Chapter 6 and depicted in Fig. 6.1, the generation, evaluation, and selection of the best strategic alternative is the sixth step of the strategic decision-making process. Once the best strategy is selected, appropriate policies must be established to define the ground rules for implementation. This chapter, therefore, will (a) explain the many alternative strategies available at the corporate, divisional, and functional levels of the corporation; (b) suggest criteria for use in the evaluation of these strategies; (c) explain how an optimal strategy is selected; and (d) suggest how strategy is translated into policies.

7.1

ALTERNATIVE STRATEGIES

As described in Chapter 1, the typical large, multidivisional business corporation operating in a number of different industries has three levels of strategy: corporate, business, and functional (see Fig. 1.1). **Corporate-level strategy** specifies the firm's portfolio of businesses, that is, the industries within which it will operate. **Business-level strategy** specifies how the company or its units will compete within each industry or industry segment. **Functional-level strategy** specifies how the company or its units will maximize resource productivity, so that it can develop the distinctive competence necessary for successful competition within each industry.[1] Even the smallest company operating in only one industry with one product line must, at one time or another, consider the questions embedded within each level of strategy:

> *Corporate:* Should we expand, cut back, or continue our operations with no change? If we want to grow and expand, should we do so through internal development or through external acquisitions, mergers, or joint ventures? Should we concentrate our activities within our current industry or should we diversify into other industries?

> *Business:* Should we compete on the basis of low cost or should we differentiate our products/services on some basis other than cost, such as quality or prestige? Should we compete head-to-head with our major competitors for the biggest but most sought-after share of the market, or should we focus on a niche in which we can satisfy a less sought-after but also profitable segment of the market?

> *Functional:* Depending on the corporate- and business-level strategies we're following, how should we carry out our functional activities so that we maximize productivity and develop a distinctive competence? For example, if we plan to concentrate our activities in one industry (concentration corporate-level growth strategy) and compete as the low cost producer (overall low cost business-level competitive strategy), should we, to keep costs down, use a follower rather than a leader R&D strategy? To finance our manufacturing facility, should we go into debt or sell stock? To generate market demand cheaply, should we emphasize promotion over advertising? Should we build a highly automated plant close to our markets, or a labor-intensive plant in a foreign country where labor is cheap?

Following is a discussion of the most popular strategies within each of the three levels. Regardless of which strategies are selected for a particular company or business unit, the corporate, business, and functional strategies must be internally consistent (that is, fit together in a mutually supportive manner that forms an integrated hierarchy of strategy).

Corporate Strategies

Corporate-level strategy looks at the entire firm and specifies the firm's overall approach to the achievement of its mission and objectives. It is composed of three grand strategies: **stability, growth,** and **retrenchment.** Each of these grand strategies is composed of appropriate sub-strategies.

Assume for the purposes of this section that the corporation either operates *only* in one industry, like Caterpillar in heavy construction equipment, or *primarily* in one industry, like Anheuser-Busch, which derives around 80% of its sales and over 90% of its profits from brewing beer and related products. For this type of company, strategic managers need to decide the overall direction of the firm through its corporate-level strategy. Management can do so by analyzing (1) the attractiveness of the industry in which the company primarily operates, and (2) the business strength/competitive position of the company within this primary industry. This analysis was discussed earlier in Chapter 6, under S.W.O.T. and portfolio analysis, and was depicted in Fig. 6.3. The nine-cell, GE business screen matrix, depicted in Figure 7.1, can plot the alternative corporate strategies that could fit the company's situation. This matrix suggests which corporate strategy from twelve possible strategies will be most appropriate for a firm's overall situation within its primary industry.

Stability Strategies

The *stability* family of strategies is appropriate for a successful corporation operating in an industry of medium attractiveness. The task environment

FIGURE 7.1
Corporate Strategies of a Company Operating Primarily in One Industry

BUSINESS STRENGTH/COMPETITIVE POSITION

INDUSTRY ATTRACTIVENESS		Strong	Average	Weak
	High	Growth: Concentration– Vertical	Growth: Concentration– Horizontal	Retrenchment: Turnaround
	Medium	Stability: Pause or Proceed with Caution	Stability: No Change or Profit Strategy	Retrenchment: Captive Company
	Low	Growth: Diversification– Concentric	Growth: Diversification– Conglomerate	Retrenchment: Divestment or Liquidation

Source: Thomas L. Wheelen and J. David Hunger, "Corporate Strategies of a Company Operating Primarily in One Industry." Copyright © 1988 by Wheelen and Hunger Associates. Reprinted by permission.

may be reasonably predictable, with little change expected. The industry probably faces a moderate growth situation, so there is little current incentive for heavy investment in the business or diversification out of the industry. Epitomized by a steady-as-she-goes philosophy, these strategies involve no major changes. In order to build upon and improve its competitive advantage, a corporation concentrates its resources on its present businesses. It retains the same mission and similar objectives; it simply increases its level of achievement by approximately the same percentage each year. Its main strategic decisions concern improving the performance of functional areas, because its business-level competitive strategies continue to be successful. A stability strategy can also be used if the task environment is likely to change radically at any moment and top management wants to see what happens before they change the course of the company. Some stability strategies are as follows:

NO-CHANGE STRATEGY In this strategy, a corporation continues on its course and adjusts only for inflation in its objectives. Rarely articulated as a definite strategy, the success of a no-change strategy depends on a lack of change in a corporation's internal or external environments. This strategy might evolve from a lack of interest in or need to engage in hard strategic analysis. After all, if everything is going along fine, why change anything?

PROFIT STRATEGY The profit strategy involves the sacrifice of future growth for present profits. The result is often short-term success coupled to long-term stagnation. By reducing expenditures for R&D, maintenance, or advertising, short-term profits increase and are reflected in the stockholders' dividends. For example, many U.S. airlines were accused during the 1980s of reducing their maintenance budgets and of cutting back on their purchases of new planes so that they could stay profitable during a period of aggressive price competition. A corporation having a number of "cash cow" divisions or product lines can "milk" these of cash for dividends instead of investing the cash in new products or services. Obviously, the profit strategy is useful only to help a company get through a temporary difficulty. Unfortunately, the profit strategy is seductive and if continued long enough will lead to bankruptcy.

PAUSE STRATEGY After a period of prolonged fast growth, a corporation might become inefficient or unmanageable. The addition of new divisions through acquisition or internal development can stretch management and resources thin. A pause strategy involves reducing the levels of a corporation's objectives so that it is able to consolidate its resources. The strategy is generally considered temporary—a way to get a corporate house in order. For example, after making a series of acquisitions and internally developing new machines to put the company at the cutting edge of robotics and computer-controlled parts-making systems, Cincinnati Milicron decided in 1988 to emphasize reorganizing to improve its efficiency and to reduce its recent losses.[2]

PROCEED-WITH-CAUTION STRATEGY This strategy results from a specific decision to proceed slowly because of important factors developing in the external environment. Top management might believe that a growth strategy is no longer feasible, because of, for instance, a sudden scarcity of needed raw materials, new governmental regulations, or a poor economic climate. The top management of CSX, for example, was very hesitant in 1985 to take any major steps in the railroad industry until Conrail's future was definitely decided by the U.S. government.

Growth Strategies

Growth strategies are extremely popular because most executives tend to equate growth with success. Research by Glueck of 358 executives over a 45-year period revealed growth to be the most frequently used corporate strategy—it was used six times more often than stability and seven times more often than retrenchment.[3] Those corporations that are in dynamic environments *must* grow in order to survive. Continuing growth means increasing sales and a chance to take advantage of the experience curve to reduce the per unit cost of products sold and thereby increase profits. This cost reduction becomes extremely important if a corporation's industry is growing quickly and competitors are engaging in price wars in attempts to increase their shares of the market. Those firms that have not reached "critical mass" (that is, gained the necessary economy of large-scale production) will face large losses unless they can find and fill a small, but profitable, niche where higher prices can be offset by special product or service features.

Growth is a very seductive strategy for two key reasons:

• A growing firm can cover up mistakes and inefficiencies more easily than can a stable one. A growing flow of revenue into a highly leveraged corporation can create a large amount of "organization slack"[4] (unused resources) that can be used to quickly resolve problems and conflicts between departments and divisions. There is also a big cushion for a turnaround in case a strategic error is made. Larger firms also have more clout and are more likely to receive support in case of impending bankruptcy, as was the situation with Chrysler Corporation in 1979.

• There are more opportunities for advancement, promotion, and interesting jobs in a growing firm. Growth, per se, is exciting and ego-enhancing for CEOs. A growing corporation tends to be seen as a "winner" or "on the move" by the marketplace and by potential investors. Large firms are also more difficult to acquire than are smaller ones—thus an executive's job is more secure.[5]

There are two basic growth strategies at the corporate level: *concentration* in one industry and *diversification* into other industries. If, as depicted in Figure 7.1, the current industry is highly attractive in terms of growth rate and other criteria, concentration of resources on that one industry makes sense as a strategy for growth. If, however, the current industry has low attractiveness, it makes sense for a corporation to diversify out of that industry if management wishes to pursue growth. As shown in Table 7.1, each growth strategy has its own set of sub-strategies, such as horizontal and vertical growth under concentration, and concentric and conglomerate growth under diversification. Each of these corporate growth strategies can be conducted through *internal* development or through *external* acquisitions, mergers, or joint ventures. First, we examine some concentration and diversification strategies. Later, we consider internal versus external growth.

CONCENTRATION A corporation may choose to grow by the concentration of all or most of its resources in one industry; it emphasizes a single product or product line, single market, or single technology. Corporations such as McDonald's (fast food), Caterpillar (construction equipment), and Apple Computer (personal computers) that concentrate their efforts on a single product line are able to stay ahead of competitors who dilute their effort in many industries. Gerber, for example, failed miserably when it tried to diversify out of baby foods into adult foods, mail-order insurance, furniture, and day-care centers. A concentration strategy allows the corporation to put

TABLE 7.1
Major Corporate Growth Strategies

GROWTH STRATEGY	INTERNAL	EXTERNAL
I. Concentration (One-industry strategy)		
A. Horizontal	Coors move into Eastern U.S.	Chrysler's purchase of American Motors, Lamborghini, and part of Maserati
B. Vertical		
1. Backward	Ford's River Rouge steel mill	Turner Broadcasting's purchase of MGM/United Artists
2. Forward	Goodyear's & Firestone's retail tire stores	Boeing's purchase of part of Allegis (United Airlines)
II. Diversification (Multi-industry strategy)		
A. Concentric	Anheuser-Busch's Eagle Snacks	Reynold's purchase of Nabisco
B. Conglomerate	CSX's use of its land for resorts, hotels, office buildings	Xerox's purchase of Crum & Forster insurance

SOURCE: Thomas L. Wheelen and J. David Hunger, "Major Corporate Growth Strategies."
Copyright © 1988 by Wheelen and Hunger Associates. Reprinted by permission.

more time, energy, and resources into the development of innovative product/service concepts so that it can better compete in an attractive industry. Two concentration strategies are horizontal and vertical growth. An example of an effective use of the concentration strategy is shown in Illustrative Example 7.1.

Horizontal Growth Strategy The horizontal growth strategy is an appropriate strategy for a company with an average competitive position wishing to increase its presence in an attractive industry. To enlarge its operations, the company spreads into other segments of its current market or into other geographic areas. The objectives are generally to increase the sales and profits of the firm's current business, through larger economies of scale in production and marketing, as well as to reduce current and/or potential competition for customers and supplies. As shown in Table 7.1, a company can grow horizontally through internal or external means. External horizontal growth, usually called **horizontal integration,** is defined as the acquisition by one corporation of another corporation or business unit in the same industry. Chrysler's purchase of American Motors, U.S. Air's merger with Piedmont Airlines, and Tonka's acquisition of Kenner Parker Toys are examples of external horizontal growth. In these instances, because the acquiring firm is buying a current competitor, the transaction can be liable to antitrust suits and/or government intervention to prevent the formation of a monopoly. The acquisition of a major competitor will also cost a lot of money and will probably force the acquiring firm into debt. A strong dislike of such debt is one reason why the Adolph Coors Company chose to expand into the eastern United States through internal means instead of through the acquisition of an eastern brewer.

Vertical Growth Strategy This strategy, often called **vertical integration,** is the strategy of a corporation that enters one or more businesses that provide goods or services necessary to the manufacture and distribution of its own products but that were previously purchased from other companies. These can range from the obtaining of raw materials to the merchandising of the product. **Backward vertical growth** (also called *backward integration*) is the corporation's entry into the business of supplying some of its present raw materials. Henry Ford I internally achieved this growth when he built his own steel mill at River Rouge to supply Ford's assembly lines. **Forward vertical growth** (also called *forward integration*) is the corporation's entry into the business of distributing its products: it enters marketing channels closer to the ultimate consumer. The internal form of this growth is common in the tire industry, where manufacturers, such as Firestone and Goodyear, build and manage their own retail outlets. Examples of vertical growth through external means are Turner Broadcasting's purchase of the MGM/United Artists film studios, by which TBC gained access to 2,200 films to be shown on its cable television channels (this is backward integration); and

ILLUSTRATIVE EXAMPLE 7.1

Concentration Strategy at Shell Oil

During the 1970s, oil companies throughout the world were awash in profits. Overwhelmed by cash inflows, they spent millions on acquisitions outside the oil industry and on expensive overhead. By the mid-1980s, these acquisitions, such as Exxon's purchase of Reliance Electric, Mobil's purchase of Montgomery Ward, and Standard Oil's purchase of Kennecott Copper, had turned to losses that measured in the hundreds of millions. By 1986, most of these acquisitions had been sold at a loss and the oil companies were laying off people and paring down their huge overhead costs.

Shell Oil Company was different. When John F. Bookout assumed the position of Chief Executive Officer in 1976 at Shell, the U.S. subsidiary of the Royal Dutch/Shell Group, the corporation ranked seventh in the industry in net profits. Nine years later Shell had moved to fourth place with net profits of $1.65 billion. "The first thing I was confronted with by our board was, 'Should Shell Oil diversify?'," recalled Bookout. After spending a year and a half weighing opportunities both inside and outside the oil business, Bookout decided against diversification. "It had to be almost egotistical to think that Shell could pay a premium to take over a company we knew nothing about and cause it to perform 2 to 2½ times better than it had been, which would have been necessary to get the return on investment we needed," stated Bookout. "We decided we have abundant opportunity in our mainline businesses, and that's where we should stay."

Because of its conclusion that the oil business was an attractive industry on which to concentrate, Shell chose to streamline its operations in the late 1970s, to increase its oil reserves, and to become a low-cost, efficient company. "You have to decide what game you're going to play," said Bookout. "Are you going to play the game that scatters you all over? That means you're playing other people's technology, or their ideas, aren't you?"

As were most large oil companies, Shell was fully vertically integrated from the oil well to the service station. Shell's emphasis on oil-production technology had led to an expertise in enhanced oil recovery and to its becoming an effective and highly efficient oil finder. Developing these skills enabled it to actually increase its oil and gas reserves internally at a time when overall U.S. oil reserves shrank 11%. Bookout in 1986 proudly pointed to the results of his concentration strategy: "In 1976 we had 3.2 billion barrels of reserves. Since then we've used 3.1 billion barrels, and our reserves now stand at 3.9 billion."

SOURCE: T. Mack, "It's Time to Take Risks," *Forbes* (October 6, 1986), pp. 125–133.

Boeing Company's acquisition of around 16% of the stock of Allegis Corporation, the parent of United Airlines, in order to keep a valued customer for its airlines (forward integration).

The vertical growth strategy is quite common in the oil, basic metals, automobile, and forest products industries. As pointed out in Table 7.2, some of its advantages are the lowering of costs and the improvement of coordination and control. It is a good way for a strong firm to increase its competitive advantage in an attractive industry. Although backward integration is usually more profitable than forward integration,[6] it can reduce a corporation's strategic flexibility: by creating an encumbrance of expensive assets that might be hard to sell, it can thus create an exit barrier to the corporation's leaving that particular industry.[7]

A study by Harrigan reveals at least four types of vertical integration

TABLE 7.2

Some Advantages and Disadvantages of Vertical Integration (Vertical Growth Strategy)

ADVANTAGES	DISADVANTAGES
Internal Benefits	*Internal Costs*
Integration economies reduce costs by eliminating steps, reducing duplicate overhead, and cutting costs (technology dependent)	Need for overhead to coordinate vertical integration increased costs
Improved coordination of activities reduces inventorying and other costs	Burden of excess capacity from unevenly balanced minimum efficient scale plants (technology dependent)
Avoid time-consuming tasks, such as price shopping, communicating design details, or negotiating contracts	Poorly organized vertically integrated firms do not enjoy synergies that compensate for higher costs
Competitive Benefits	*Competitive Dangers*
Avoid foreclosure to inputs, services, or markets	Obsolete processes may be perpetuated
Improved marketing or technological intelligence	Creates mobility (or exit) barriers
Opportunity to create product differentiation (increased value added)	Links firm to sick adjacent businesses
Superior control of firm's economic environment (market power)	Lose access to information from suppliers or distributors
Create credibility for new products	Synergies created through vertical integration may be overrated
Synergies could be created by coordinating vertical activities skillfully	Managers integrated before thinking through the most appropriate way to do so

SOURCE: K. R. Harrigan, "Formulating Vertical Integration Strategies," *Academy of Management Review* (October 1984), p. 639. Copyright © 1984 by the Academy of Management. Reprinted by permission.

ranging from **full integration** to **long-term contracts.**[8] For example, if a corporation does not want to have the disadvantages of full vertical integration, it may choose either **taper** or **quasi-integration** strategies. With taper integration, a firm produces part of its own requirements and buys the rest from outside suppliers. In the case of quasi-integration, a company gets most of its requirements from an outside supplier that is under its partial control. For example, by purchasing 20% of the common stock of Intel Corporation, IBM guaranteed its access to 16-bit microprocessors for its personal computers.

DIVERSIFICATION This is the corporate growth strategy in which *different* products or divisions are added to the corporation. These new products may be developed internally or purchased externally, and may be related (concentric) or unrelated (conglomerate) to the corporation's current product line. So that the corporation can reduce its dependence on an industry with low attractiveness, a diversification strategy allows it to move into other industries with greater opportunities. The A. T. Cross Co., for example, decided that further growth in the heavily saturated pen market would be very difficult. It already had more than 50% of the U. S. market share in expensive pens. Rather than diluting its prestige name by attempting to sell inexpensive pens, it chose to diversify into the premium gift business and acquired the Mark Cross, Inc., leather goods stores. As corporations become larger there is a natural tendency for them to diversify into other industries. In the United States, for example, fewer than 15% of the Fortune 500 companies remain largely in a single business.[9] The trend is similar for corporations throughout the world. In the United Kingdom, for example, the percentage of companies that had heavily diversified out of their original business increased from 25% in 1950, to 65% of the total by 1980.[10]

As shown in Table 7.1, there are two types of diversification—concentric and conglomerate.

Concentric Diversification *Concentric diversification* is the addition to a corporation of **related** products or divisions. The corporation's lines of business still possess some "common thread" that serves to relate them in some manner. The point of commonality may be similar technology, customer usage, distribution, managerial skills, or product similarity. Examples of concentric diversification were the internally developed addition of "Eagle Snacks" to Anheuser-Busch's successful line of beers and the external purchase of Nabisco Brands by R. J. Reynolds Industries. In both instances, the new products were complementary to the company's other products and combining the new with the old was likely to provide some product-market synergy that would hopefully increase sales and/or reduce the costs of current products as well as new ones. Concentric diversification is thus most appropriate for companies wishing to take advantage of their competitive position strengths as they diversify out of an unattractive industry.

Conglomerate Diversification *Conglomerate diversification,* in contrast to concentric diversification, is the addition to the firm of **unrelated** products or divisions. Rather than keeping a common thread throughout their corporation, top managers who adopt this strategy are primarily concerned with a return on investment criterion: Will it increase the corporation's level of profitability? The addition may, however, be justified in terms of strategic fit. A cash-rich corporation with few opportunities for growth in its industry might, for example, move into another industry where opportunities are great, but cash hard to find. An example of this strategy was the purchase of Vydec Corporation, a maker of word processors, by Exxon Corporation, the oil company. Another instance of conglomerate diversification might be the purchase by a corporation with a seasonal and, therefore, uneven, cash flow of a firm in an unrelated industry with complementing seasonal sales that will level out the cash flow. The purchase of a natural gas transmission business (Texas Gas Resources) by CSX Corporation was considered by CSX management to be a good fit because most of its revenue came in the winter months when railroads go through a seasonally lean period. Conglomerate diversification is thus most appropriate for companies with only average competitive position strengths as they diversify out of an unattractive industry.

Concentric vs. Conglomerate Diversification Beginning with a classic study by Rumelt, a number of researchers have argued that conglomerate (unrelated) diversification into other industries is less profitable than is concentric (related) diversification.[11] Peters and Waterman support this proposition in their book *In Search of Excellence.*

> Our principal finding is clear and simple. Organizations that do branch out (whether by acquisition or internal diversification) but stick very close to their knitting outperform the others. The most successful of all are those diversified around a single skill—the coating and bonding technology at 3M, for example.
>
> The second group, in descending order, comprises those companies that branch out into related fields—the leap from electric power generation turbines to jet engines (another turbine) from GE, for example.
>
> Least successful, as a general rule, are those companies that diversify into a wide variety of fields. Acquisitions, especially among this group, tend to wither on the vine.[12]

Supporting this argument are the recent spinoffs by conglomerate corporations of formerly acquired units. In the past few years ITT, RCA, Gulf & Western, Beatrice Foods, Quaker Oats, General Electric, Exxon, and R. J. Reynolds have sold off major nonrelated holdings.

Nevertheless, studies reported by *Fortune* magazine and by the management consulting firm of Booz, Allen & Hamilton, Inc., found that conglomerate diversifiers not only performed as well as concentric diversifiers, but that over certain periods of time conglomerates actually outperformed industry peers.[13]

It is most probable that concentric and conglomerate diversification are equally valuable strategies for corporate growth, but are successful in different situations.[14] Figure 7.1 suggests that a corporation with a strong competitive position in a particular industry will do better if it diversifies concentrically into a related industry where it can most easily apply its distinctive competence. Corporations with only average competitive positions should thus do better by diversifying into unrelated industries. Leontiades, a well-known scholar in the area, argues that conglomerate acquisitions do not at first appear to be as successful as concentric because the conglomerate acquisition causes an initial reduction in efficiency. (This conclusion, of course, assumes diversification through external means). He states:

> Until a company learns to manage and integrate its acquisitions, it is dependent on autonomous units operating profitably enough to overcome the lack of administrative coordination. This leaves the company vulnerable to unexpected downturns in the new businesses which it cannot directly control nor totally avoid. Over time, the level of administrative control tends to rise. If this aspect of diversification is mastered, and an optimum "family" of businesses emerges, then the fruits of the labor of diversification can be enjoyed.[15]

This argument thus suggests that the real issue may not be concentric vs. conglomerate diversification, but concerns the level of difficulty of managing an acquisition. If the firms are managed with a similar **dominant logic,** they can be integrated quickly and profitably.[16] This concept is exemplified by the comments of F. Ross Johnson, Chief Executive of Nabisco Brands, upon the company's pending acquisition by R. J. Reynolds Industries:

> We studied each other's track records and hit a common road. How we manage our businesses is practically identical. What we believe in—divesting the bad businesses, tight control of the balance sheet, understanding cash flow—is pretty much the same.[17]

EXTERNAL VERSUS INTERNAL GROWTH STRATEGIES Corporations can follow the growth strategies of either concentration or diversification through the internal development of new products and services, or through external acquisitions, mergers, and joint ventures. A study of forty-two large U.S. business firms that had engaged in diversification over a five-year period revealed that 45% diversified through internal means, 19% diversified through external means, and 36% diversified through both internal and external methods. It is interesting that the economic performances of the companies in the three categories were very similar. There appears to be no significant sales or profits advantage to either external or internal growth.[18]

Some of the more common examples of external growth strategies are mergers, acquisitions, and joint ventures.

Mergers A *merger* is a transaction involving two or more corporations in which stock is exchanged, but from which only one corporation survives. Mergers are usually between firms of somewhat similar size and are usually "friendly." The resulting firm is likely to have a name derived from its composite firms. One example is the merging of Allied Corporation and Signal Companies to form Allied Signal.

Acquisitions An *acquisition* is the purchase of a corporation that is completely absorbed as an operating subsidiary or division of the acquiring corporation. Examples are the acquisition by Procter and Gamble of Richardson-Vicks and the purchase of the Chicago Cubs baseball team by the Tribune Company (parent company of the *Chicago Tribune* newspaper and WGN television superstation). Acquisitions are usually between firms of different sizes and can be either "friendly" or "hostile." A friendly acquisition usually begins with the acquiring corporation discussing its desires with the other firm's top management. The top management of the firm to be acquired agrees to work for the acquisition, in return for fair consideration after acquisition. Friendly acquisitions are thus very similar to mergers. Hostile acquisitions, in contrast, are often called "takeovers." The acquiring firm ignores the other firm's top management or board of directors and simply begins buying up the other firm's stock until it owns a controlling interest. The takeover target, in response, begins defensive maneuvers, such as buying up its own stock, calling in the Justice Department to initiate an anti-trust suit in order to stop the acquisition, or looking for a friendly merger partner (as Gulf Oil did with Standard Oil of California when Texas oilman T. Boone Pickens mounted a takeover effort to buy Gulf's stock).

Slang terms are very popular in mergers and acquisitions. For example, a "pigeon" (highly vulnerable target) or "sleeping beauty" (more desirable than a pigeon) might take a "cyanide pill" (taking on a huge long-term debt on the condition that the debt falls due immediately upon the firm's acquisition) so that it can avoid being "raped" (forcible hostile takeover sometimes accompanied by looting of the target's profitability) by a "shark" (extremely predatory takeover artist) using "hired guns" (lawyers, merger and acquisition specialists, and certain investment bankers).[19] To avoid takeover threats, a number of corporations have chosen to stagger the elections of board members (as discussed in Chapter 3), to prohibit two-tier tender offers (the offering of a higher price to stockholders who sell their shares first), to prohibit "green-mail" (the buying back of a company's stock from a "shark" at a premium price), and to require an 80% shareholder vote for approval of a takeover. The ultimate countermeasure appears to be the *poison pill*, a procedure granting present shareholders the right to acquire at a substantial discount a large equity stake in an acquiring company whose offer does not have the support of the acquired company's board of directors.

Joint Ventures A *joint venture* is the strategy of forming a temporary partnership or consortium for the purpose of gaining synergy. Joint ventures occur because the corporations involved do not wish to or cannot legally merge permanently. Joint ventures provide a way to temporarily fit the different strengths of partners together so that an outcome of value to both is achieved.[20] For example, IBM and Sears have formed a joint venture called Trintex to develop and market *videotex*—the sending and receiving of words and pictures to at-home video screens; through this service people can order merchandise, do banking, and carry out other functions. A major innovation in this joint-venture plan is the sending of data to personal computers instead of to special-purpose video-screen terminals. Named "Prodigy," this service costs subscribers $9.95 a month. Sears can use the venture to market its merchandise catalogue and financial services products electronically. Joint ventures are extremely popular in international undertakings because of financial and political-legal constraints. They are also a convenient way for a privately owned and a publicly owned (state-owned) corporation to work together. Joint ventures are discussed further in Chapter 10.[21]

Retrenchment Strategies

Retrenchment strategies are relatively unpopular because retrenchment seems to imply failure—that something has gone wrong with previous strategies.

With these strategies there *is* a great deal of pressure to improve performance. As are the coaches of losing football teams, the CEO is typically under pressure to do something quickly or be fired.

TURNAROUND STRATEGY The turnaround strategy emphasizes the improvement of operational efficiency. It is appropriate when a corporation is in a highly attractive industry and when the corporation's problems are pervasive, but not yet critical. Analogous to going on a diet, a turnaround strategy includes two initial phases. The first phase is **contraction,** the initial effort to reduce size and costs. It typically involves a general cutback in personnel and all noncritical expenditures. Hiring stops, and across-the-board reductions in R&D, advertising, training, supplies, and services are usual. The second phase is **consolidation,** the development of a program to stabilize the now-leaner corporation. An in-depth audit is conducted in order to identify areas in which long-run improvements can be made in corporate efficiency. To streamline the corporation, plans are developed to reduce unnecessary overhead and to make functional activities "cost-effective." Financial expenditures in all areas must be justified on the basis of their contribution to profits. This is a crucial time for the corporation. If the consolidation phase is not conducted in a positive manner, many of the best people will leave the organization. If, however, all employees are encouraged to get involved in productivity improvements, the corporation is likely to emerge from this strategic retrenchment period a much stronger and better organized company.

If the corporation successfully emerges from these two phases of contraction and consolidation, it is then able to enter a third phase, **rebuilding.** At this point, an attempt is made to once again expand the business.[22] For an example of an effective use of the turnaround strategy, see Illustrative Example 7.2.

DIVESTMENT STRATEGY Divestment is appropriate when corporate problems can be traced to the poor performance of an SBU or product line, or when a division or SBU is a "misfit," unable to synchronize itself with the rest of the corporation. Divestment is especially appropriate when a weak SBU is in an industry of low attractiveness (see Figure 7.1). Because over 50% of acquisitions fail to achieve their objectives, it is not surprising that divestment is a popular strategy of corporations that had earlier chosen to grow through external means.[23]

Still another situation appropriate for divestment is that of a division's needing more resources to be competitive than a corporation is willing to provide. Some corporations elect divestment instead of the more painful turnaround strategy. With divestment, top management is able to do one of two things: (1) select a scapegoat to be blamed for all of the corporation's problems, or (2) generate a lot of cash in the sale, which can be used to reduce debt and buy time. The second reason might explain why Pan American chose to sell the most profitable parts of its corporation, the Pan

ILLUSTRATIVE EXAMPLE 7.2

Turnaround Strategy at Toro Company

Top management at Toro Company was astonished when a 1974 marketing survey showed that the brand name of the little lawn-mower manufacturer ranked second only to Hershey chocolate in consumer recognition. Rushing to transform Toro, they broadened both its product lines and distribution system. By 1979 the company had 33,000 new chain-store outlets to sell a stream of new products, such as lightweight snow-throwers and chain saws. Sales of $358 million with earnings of $17.4 million both tripled 1974 levels. "The idea is to make the Toro name an umbrella under which we can market just about anything," said Chairman David T. McLaughlin.

Seeds for disaster had been planted. The pressure to increase sales led to a slide in product quality. New products were rushed to market in the late 1970s and early 1980s before the usual time-consuming development and testing phases were completed. The distribution of mowers and snow-throwers through mass merchandisers like K-Mart and J. C. Penney infuriated Toro's traditional dealer network. Not only were the dealers forced to compete with their own products being sold at lower prices by discounters; they were being stuck with servicing the products the discounters sold! Some dealers refused to service machines they did not sell and actually told prospective customers not to buy a Toro.

The crisis arrived when the two snowless winters of 1979–80 and 1980–81 plunged the company into ten straight quarters of losses. In early 1981, as sales fell from $400 million to $247 million annually, McLaughlin resigned as chairman. Before leaving, he fired 125 managers including Toro's president, John Cantu. The dismissals were probably long overdue. One manager admitted that the firm's staff was that of a billion-dollar company—far too large for a small company like Toro.

Executive Vice-President Kendrick Melrose was named president. The fight for survival began. Dividends were suspended. Melrose acted to cut the work force in half, to 1,800 people; cut sales and administrative costs by 23%; consolidated production to five plants from eight; and suspended production of snow-throwers until sales caught up with inventories, two years later. More importantly, Melrose worked to salvage the dealer network, by stopping sales to discounters of equipment that required servicing. He also improved Toro's inventory-support program, giving independent dealers and distributors more protection from losses when their inventories exceeded a "normal year's" level.

"The toughest decision was to terminate half the employment force," admitted President Melrose. "The second toughest was to go to the half that remained and tell them that not only do we have fewer resources, but we still need greater productivity, and that they're going to have to make some financial sacrifices." That meant no incentive compensation for executives for at least four years, salary freezes and mandatory furlough days for office employees, and wage freezes or reductions for hourly workers. Stringent controls were set in place to keep management aware of inventory levels. "Now we can go through a year with little snow and still be fairly solid," says Mr. Melrose. Embarrassed by Toro's poor-quality image, the new president re-dedicated the company to quality and appointed a vice-president for product excellence.

By 1985, the Minneapolis firm was a much slimmer, more carefully managed, and apparently healthier company. Fiscal 1984 earnings were $8.3 million on sales of $280 million, compared with a modest profit in 1983. Sales have not returned to pre-disaster levels and probably will not for some time. Nevertheless, the dividend has been restored and top management is cautiously optimistic. To keep costs down, some manufacturing is done outside the U.S. Parts are being produced in South Korea, Taiwan, Japan, and Singapore. An assembly plant has opened near Winnepeg, Manitoba. Fabrication joint ventures are under way in New Zealand and Venezuela.

As a result of its successes, Toro management has switched from what it called "a defensive, survival mode" to "a more opportunistic direction." Mr. Melrose put two executive vice-presidents in charge of

(Continued)

ILLUSTRATIVE EXAMPLE 7.2 (Continued)

day-to-day operations so that he could focus on new ventures. According to Melrose, the company is "emphasizing businesses that deliver high margins and don't have a lot of vulnerability on the downside," such as turf irrigation and commercial lawn care equipment. "Long-range planning is something new at Toro," he says. "In the past we didn't spend much time thinking about the future. We thought only about how we're going to get out of the mess."

SOURCE: R. Gibson, "Toro Breaks Out of Its Slump after Taking Drastic Measures," *Wall Street Journal* (January 23, 1985), p. 7. "Toro: Coming to Life after Warm Weather Wilted Its Big Plans," *Business Week* (October 10, 1983), p. 118.

Am Building in New York and Intercontinental Hotels, while keeping its money-losing airline.[24]

CAPTIVE COMPANY STRATEGY Rarely discussed as a separate strategy, the captive strategy is similar to divestment; but instead of selling off divisions or product lines, the corporation reduces the scope of some of its functional activities and becomes "captive" to another firm. In this manner, it reduces expenses and achieves some security through its relationship with the stronger firm. An agreement is reached with a key customer that in return for a large number of long-run purchases, the captive company will guarantee delivery at a favorable price. At least 75% of its product is sold to a single purchaser, so the captive company can reduce its marketing expenditures and develop long-run production schedules that reduce costs. If supplies ever become a problem for the captive company, it can call on its key customer to help put pressure on a reluctant supplier.

This is a popular strategy in the moderately attractive U.S. auto parts and electronic parts industries for small firms with weak competitive positions. Until the mid-1980s, GM, Ford, and Chrysler each bought from thousands of companies; they preferred to maintain competition between suppliers and backups in case a key parts maker failed. In their quest for higher quality, however, the auto companies have chosen instead to rely on only those companies that could guarantee high quality, low costs, and just-in-time delivery. In order to survive, auto parts firms had to become captive companies. For example, in order to become the sole supplier of a part to GM, Simpson Industries, an engine parts manufacturer in Birmingham, Michigan, agreed to having its facilities and books inspected and its employees interviewed by a special team from General Motors. In return, nearly 80% of Simpson Industries' production was sold to GM through long-term contracts.[25]

LIQUIDATION STRATEGY A strategy of last resort, used when other retrenchment strategies have failed, an early liquidation can serve stockholders' interests better than an inevitable bankruptcy. To the extent that top management identifies with the corporation, liquidation is perceived as an admission of failure. Pride and reputation are liquidated as well as jobs and financial assets. Nevertheless, this can be the most appropriate strategy for a corporation with a weak competitive position in an unattractive industry.

From their research of companies in difficulty, Nystrom and Starbuck conclude that top management very often does not perceive that crises are developing. When top managers do eventually notice trouble, they are prone to attribute the problems to temporary environmental disturbances and tend to follow profit strategies of postponing investments, reducing maintenance, halting training, liquidating assets, denying credit to customers, and raising prices. They adopt a weathering-the-storm attitude. "A major activity becomes changing the accounting procedures in order to conceal the symptoms."[27] Even when things are going terribly wrong, there is a strong temptation for top management to avoid liquidation in the hope of a miracle. It is for this reason that a corporation needs a strong board of directors who, to safeguard stockholders' interests, can tell top management when to quit.

Evaluation of Corporate Strategies

Before they select a particular corporate strategy, top management must critically analyze the pros and cons of each feasible alternative in light of the corporation's situation. The tendency to select the most obvious strategy can sometimes lead to serious trouble in the long run. The orientation of most top management toward growth strategies has resulted in a strong preference for acquisitions and mergers. In fact, a survey of 236 chief executive officers of the largest 1,000 U.S. industrial firms found that CEOs prefer diversification and acquisition over new product planning and development as a growth strategy.[28] A similar survey of chief financial officers found that the major motive for acquisition of another firm was to generate fast growth.[29] Given these attitudes of strategic managers, it is not surprising that more mergers were announced in the first six months of 1988 than in *all* of 1985. The dollar value of the acquisitions for only half a year exceeded that for *all* of 1984.[30] Growth through external means shows no signs of slacking in the 1990s.

Business (SBU) Strategies

Sometimes referred to as division strategy, business strategy focuses on improving the competitive position of a corporation's products or services within the specific industry or market segment that the division serves. It is a strategy that a division develops to complement the overall corporate strategy.

Porter's Competitive Strategies

Porter, an authority on business level strategies, proposes three generic strategies for outperforming other corporations in a particular industry: overall cost leadership, differentiation, and focus.[31]

1. **Overall cost leadership.** This strategy requires "aggressive construction of efficient-scale facilities, vigorous pursuit of cost reductions from experience, tight cost and overhead control, avoidance of marginal customer accounts, and cost minimization in areas like R&D, service, sales force, advertising, and so on."[32] Having a low-cost position gives an SBU a defense against rivals. Its lower costs allow it to continue to earn profits during times of heavy competition.

   Backward vertical integration (a corporate-level strategy that can also be used at the divisional level) is one route to an overall low-cost position. For example, Humana, Inc., the hospital operator, has moved into the health-insurance field as the low-cost competitor. It is able to underprice Blue Cross, Blue Shield because it controls the source of 60% of all medical bills, the hospital. "The one feature of our product that is clearly understood by employers is that because we own and operate hospitals, we can control costs," states William Werroven, Chief Operating Officer of Humana's group health division.[33]

2. **Differentiation.** This strategy involves the creation of a product or service that is perceived throughout its industry as being unique. This uniqueness can be accomplished through design or brand image, technology, features, dealer network, or customer service. Differentiation is a viable strategy for the earning of above-average returns in a specific business, because the resulting brand loyalty lowers customers' sensitivity to price.

   Examples of the successful use of a differentiation strategy are Walt Disney Productions, Maytag appliances, Mercedes-Benz automobiles, and WordPerfect Corporation. Started in 1980 in Orem, Utah, WordPerfect Corporation chose to compete against Wordstar for the MS-DOS, IBM-compatible word-processing market. To differentiate its WordPerfect software from the competition, it became the only company to offer customers a toll-free help line. At first, the company spent very little on advertising, and sales grew largely through word of mouth. By 1987, WordPerfect had gathered a 30% market share of word-processing programs, a share greater than any of its competitors had.[34]

3. **Focus.** Similar to the corporate strategy of concentration, this business strategy focuses on a particular buyer group, product line segment, or geographic market. This strategy is valued because of a belief that an SBU that focuses its efforts is better able to serve its narrow strategic target more effectively or efficiently than can its competition. Focus does, however, necessitate that a trade-off between profitability and overall market share be made.

   The focus strategy has two variants: *cost focus* and *differentiation focus*. In using cost focus, the company seeks a cost advantage in its target segment; in using differentiation focus, a company seeks differentiation in its target segment. "The target segments must either have buyers with unusual needs or else the production and delivery system that best serves the target must differ from that of the other industry segments."[35] A good example of cost focus is Hammermill Paper's move into low-volume, high-quality specialty papers. By focusing on the quality niche of the market, Hammermill is able to compete against larger companies that need high-volume production runs to reach break-even. Johnson Products, in contrast, has successfully used a differentiation focus by manufacturing and selling hair care and cosmetic products to black consumers. This strategy was most successful when the large cosmetics companies ignored the product preferences of the black community.

Porter argues that, to be successful, a business unit must achieve one of these three "generic" business strategies. Otherwise, the business unit is **stuck in the middle** of the competitive marketplace with no competitive advantage and is doomed to below-average performance.[36] Although research generally supports Porter's contention, there is some evidence that businesses with *both* a low cost and a high differentiation position can be very successful.[37] Before selecting one of these strategies for a particular corporate business or SBU, management should assess its feasibility in terms of divisional strengths and weaknesses. Porter lists some of the commonly required skills and resources, as well as organizational requirements, in Table 7.3.

Functional Strategies

The principal focus of functional strategy is to maximize corporate and divisional resource productivity. Within the constraints of corporate and divisional strategies, functional strategies are developed to pull together the various activities and competencies of each function so that performance improves. For example, a manufacturing department would be very concerned with developing a strategy to reduce costs and to improve the quality of its output. Marketing, in comparison, typically would be concerned with developing strategies to increase sales.

Some typical marketing functional strategies are

- capturing a larger share of an existing market through market saturation and market penetration,
- developing new products for existing markets,
- developing new markets for existing products, and
- developing new products for new markets.[38]

The first and third strategies support a corporate concentration strategy, whereas the second and fourth support a diversification corporate strategy.

TABLE 7.3
Requirements for Generic Competitive Strategies

GENERIC STRATEGY	COMMONLY REQUIRED SKILLS AND RESOURCES	COMMON ORGANIZATIONAL REQUIREMENTS
Overall cost leadership	Sustained capital investment and access to capital	Tight cost control
	Process engineering skills	Frequent, detailed control reports
	Intense supervision of labor	Structured organization and responsibilities
	Products designed for ease in manufacture	Incentives based on meeting strict quantitative targets
	Low-cost distribution system	
Differentiation	Strong marketing abilities	Strong coordination among functions in R&D, product development, and marketing
	Product engineering	
	Creative flair	
	Strong capability in basic research	Subjective measurement and incentives instead of quantitative measures
	Corporate reputation for quality or technological leadership	Amenities to attract highly skilled labor, scientists, or creative people
	Long tradition in the industry or unique combination of skills drawn from other businesses	
	Strong cooperation from channels	
Focus	Combination of the above policies directed at the particular strategic target	Combination of the above policies directed at the particular strategic target

SOURCE: Adapted/reprinted with permission of The Free Press, a Division of Macmillan, Inc. from *Competitive Strategy: Techniques for Analyzing Industries and Competitors* by Michael E. Porter, pp. 40–41. Copyright © 1980 by The Free Press.

Some of the many possible functional strategies are listed in the decision tree depicted in Fig. 7.2. These are some of the many functional strategy decisions that need to be made if corporate and divisional strategies are to be implemented properly by functional managers. For example, once top management decides to acquire another publicly held corporation, it must decide how it will obtain the funds necessary for the purchase. A very popular financial strategy is the **leveraged buyout.** In a leveraged buyout, a company is acquired in a transaction financed largely by debt. Ultimately, the debt is paid with money generated by the acquired company's operations or by sales of its assets. This is what happened when Westray Transportation, Inc., an affiliate of Westray Corporation, purchased Atlas Van Lines. Under the leveraged buyout plan, Atlas stockholders received $18.35 for each share of stock outstanding and the company was taken private by Westray. The money was funded by Merrill Lynch Interfunding, Inc. and Acquisition Funding Corporation. Westray then paid the debt from the operations of its new subsidiary, Atlas Van Lines.[39]

FIGURE 7.2
Functional Strategy Decision Tree

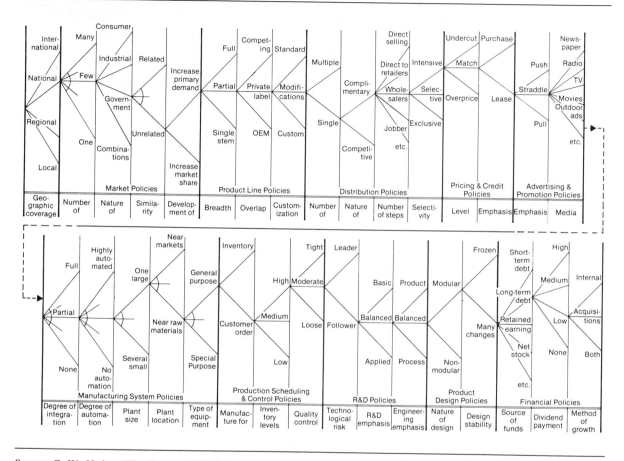

Source: C. W. Hofer, "The Uses and Limitations of Statistical Division Theory" (Boston: Intercollegiate Case Clearing House), no. 9-171-653, 1971, p. 34. Copyright © 1971 by C. W. Hofer. Reprinted by permission.

A functional area that has received a great deal of attention recently in terms of strategy is technology (R&D). Those corporations that are dependent on technology for their success are becoming increasingly concerned with the development of R&D strategies that complement business level strategies.[40] As shown in Fig. 7.2, one of the R&D choices is to either be a **leader** or a **follower.** Porter suggests that making the decision to become a technological leader or follower can be a way of achieving either overall low cost or differentiation.[41] This choice is described in more detail in Table 7.4. An effective use of the follower R&D functional strategy to achieve a low-cost competitive advantage is presented in Illustrative Example 7.3.

TABLE 7.4
Technological Leadership and Competitive Advantage

	TECHNOLOGICAL LEADERSHIP	TECHNOLOGICAL FOLLOWERSHIP
Cost Advantage	Pioneer the lowest-cost product design	Lower the cost of the product or value activities by learning from the leader's experience
	Be the first firm down the learning curve	
	Create low-cost ways of performing value activities	Avoid R&D costs through imitation
Differentiation	Pioneer a unique product that increases buyer value	Adapt the product or delivery system more closely to buyer needs by learning from the leader's experience
	Innovate in other activities to increase buyer value	

SOURCE: Reprinted with permission of The Free Press, a Division of Macmillan, Inc. from *Competitive Advantage: Creating and Sustaining Superior Performance* by Michael E. Porter, p. 181. Copyright © 1985 by Michael E. Porter.

Other functional strategies, such as the location and scale of manufacturing facilities, distribution channels, and the choice of push (promotion) versus pull (advertising) marketing emphasis can only be mentioned briefly in this book. For a detailed discussion of functional strategies, refer to advanced texts in each of the functional areas.

Strategies to be Avoided

There are a number of strategies, used at various levels, that are very dangerous. They might be considered by managers who have made a poor analysis or lack creativity.

Follow the leader. Imitating the strategy of a leading competitor might seem a good idea, but it ignores a firm's particular strengths and weaknesses. The decision by Standard Oil of Ohio to follow Exxon and Mobil Oil into conglomerate diversification resulted in disaster for the company's top management.

Hit another home run. If a corporation is successful because it pioneered an extremely successful product, it has a tendency to search for another superproduct that will ensure growth and prosperity. Like betting on "long shots" at the horse races, the probability of finding a second winner is slight. Polaroid spent a lot of money developing an "instant" movie camera, but the public ignored it.

Arms race. Entering into a spirited battle with another firm for an increase in market share might increase sales revenue, but that increase will probably be more than offset by increases in advertising, promotion, R&D, and manufacturing costs. Since the deregulation of airlines, price wars and rate "specials" have contributed to the low profit margins or bankruptcy of many major airlines.

Do everything. When faced with a number of interesting opportunities, management might tend to take all of them. At first, a corporation

ILLUSTRATIVE EXAMPLE 7.3

Dean Foods Uses a Follower R&D Functional Strategy to Achieve Low-Cost Competitive Advantage

As big food companies battle to build powerful national brand names, Dean Foods Company keeps a low profile by emphasizing a line of copycat private label brands it sells to supermarket chains who want good products at low prices. These increasingly powerful and sophisticated supermarket chains wish to offer their own private label products and to take more control over shelf space and marketing. Dean Foods, located outside Chicago in Franklin Park, Illinois, satisfies the supermarket demands by quickly imitating brand name products and offering them at low cost. "We're able to have the customer come to us and say, 'If you can produce X, Y, and Z product for the same quality and service, but at a lower price and without that expensive label on it, you can have the business,' "

says Howard Dean, President of the company. As a result, Dean's product offerings are typically developed on a shoestring budget with advertising costs far below the industry's average. The emphasis is on rigid cost control and exceptional customer service. Profit in 1986 was $41.1 million on sales of $1.43 billion. The company ranked second to some of the nation's most familiar brand names in the sales of certain foods: Borden's dairy products, Campbell Soups, Vlassic pickles, Carnation's Coffee-mate nondairy creamer, and Kraft's Cracker Barrel aged cheddar cheese.

SOURCE: T. Due, "Dean Foods Thrives On Regional, Off-Brand Products," *Wall Street Journal* (September 17, 1987), p. 6.

might have enough resources to develop each opportunity into a project, but the well soon runs dry as the many projects demand large infusions of time, money, and energy. Convinced that its brand name would serve as an effective umbrella for a whole series of new products, Toro Company quickly ran out of money and time (see Illustrative Example 7.2).

Losing hand. A corporation might have invested so much in a particular strategy that top management is unwilling to accept the fact that the strategy is not successful. Believing that it has "too much invested to quit," the corporation continues to throw good money after bad. Pan American chose to sell its Pan Am Building and Intercontinental Hotels, the most profitable parts of the corporation, to keep its money-losing airline flying. With operating losses of more than $1.4 billion between 1980 and 1987; plus a negative net worth of $68.3 million, $914 million in long-term debt, and $550 million in unfunded pension liability; and one of the industry's oldest jet fleets, Pan American agreed to pay $1.1 billion to Airbus Industries for twenty-eight new jet planes![42]

7.2
SELECTION OF THE BEST STRATEGY

Once potential strategic alternatives have been identified and evaluated in terms of their pros and cons, one must be selected for implementation. By this point, it is likely that a number of alternatives will have emerged as feasible. How is the decision made that determines the "best" strategy?

Choosing among a set of acceptable alternative strategies is often not easy. Each alternative is likely to have its proponents as well as critics. Steiner and Miner suggest using the twenty questions listed below before one strategy is selected over another. Perhaps the most important criterion is the ability of the proposed strategy to deal with the specific *strategic factors* developed earlier in the S.W.O.T. analysis. If the alternative doesn't take advantage of environmental opportunities and corporate strengths, and lead away from environmental threats and corporate weaknesses, it will probably fail. Another important consideration in the selection of a strategy is the ability of each alternative to satisfy agreed-upon objectives with the least use of resources and with the fewest number of negative side effects. It is therefore important to develop a tentative implementation plan so that the difficulties management is likely to face are addressed. Is the alternative worth the probable short-term as well as long-term costs?

A number of techniques to aid strategic planners in estimating the likely effects of strategic changes are available. One of these was derived from the research project on the profit impact of market strategies (PIMS), which was discussed in Chapter 6. From the analysis of data from a large number of business corporations, key factors were identified in regression equations to explain large variations in ROI, profitability, and cash flow. As part of PIMS, reports for a participating corporation's business units show how its expected level of ROI is influenced by each factor. A second report shows how ROI can be expected to change, both in the short and long runs, if particular changes are made in its strategy.[43]

One of the best ways to assess the likely economic impact of each alternative on the future of the corporation is through the construction of

---

TWENTY QUESTIONS FOR USE IN EVALUATION OF STRATEGIES

1. Does the strategy conform with the basic mission and purpose of the corporation? If not, a new competitive arena with which management is not familiar might be entered.

2. Is the strategy consistent with the corporation's external environment?

3. Is the strategy consistent with the internal strengths, objectives, policies, resources, and personal values of managers and employees? A strategy might not be completely in tune with all of these, but major dissonance should be avoided.

4. Does the strategy reflect the acceptance of minimum potential risk, balancing it against the maximum potential profit consistent with the corporation's resources and prospects?

5. Does the strategy fit a niche in the corporation's market not now filled by others? Is this niche likely to remain open long enough for the corporation to return capital investment plus the required level of profit? (Niches have a habit of filling up fast.)

6. Does the strategy conflict with other corporate strategies?

7. Is the strategy divided into substrategies that interrelate properly?

8. Has the strategy been tested with appropriate criteria (such as consistency with past, present, and prospective trends) and by the appropriate analytical tools (such as risk analysis, discounted cash flows, and so on)?

9. Has the strategy been tested by developing feasible implementation plans?

10. Does the strategy really fit the life cycles of the corporation's products?

detailed scenarios. Once these scenarios are adjusted for management's attitude toward risk, pressures from the external and internal environments, and the personal needs and desires of key managers, they are invaluable aids to management's selecting the alternative with the best chance of achieving corporate objectives.

Scenario Construction

Using pro forma balance sheets and income statements, management can construct detailed *scenarios* to forecast the likely effect of each alternative strategy and its various programs on division and corporate return on investment. These scenarios are simply extensions of the industry scenarios discussed in Chapter 4. If, for example, industry scenarios suggest the probable emergence of a strong market demand for certain products, a series of alternative strategy scenarios can be developed. The alternative of acquiring another company having these products can be compared with the alternative of developing the products internally. Using three sets of estimated sales figures (optimistic, pessimistic, and most likely) for the new products over the next five years, the two alternatives can be evaluated in terms of their effect on future company performance as reflected in its probable future financial statements. Pro forma balance sheets and income statements can be generated with spreadsheet software, such as Lotus 1-2-3, on a personal computer.

To construct a scenario, **first** use the industry scenarios discussed earlier in Chapter 4 and develop a set of assumptions about the task environment.

---

11. Is the timing of the strategy correct?

12. Does the strategy pit the product against a powerful competitor? If so, reevaluate carefully.

13. Does the strategy leave the corporation vulnerable to the power of one major customer? If so, reconsider carefully.

14. Does the strategy involve the production of a new product for a new market? If so, reconsider carefully.

15. Is the corporation rushing a revolutionary product to market? If so, reconsider carefully.

16. Does the strategy imitate that of a competitor? If so, reconsider carefully.

17. Is it likely that the corporation can get to the market first with the new product or service? (If so, this is a great advantage. The second firm to market has much less chance of high returns on investment than the first.)

18. Has a really honest and accurate appraisal been made of the competition? Is the competition under- or overestimated?

19. Is the corporation trying to sell abroad something it cannot sell in the United States? (This is not usually a successful strategy.)

20. Is the market share likely to be sufficient to assure a required return on investment? (Market share and return on investment generally are closely related but differ from product to product and market to market.) Has this relationship of market and product been calculated?

SOURCE: Adapted with permission of Macmillan Publishing Company from *Management Policy and Strategy* by George A. Steiner and John B. Miner, pp. 219–221. Copyright © 1977 by Macmillan Publishing Company.

Optimistic, pessimistic, and most likely assumptions should be listed for key economic factors such as the GNP, CPI, and prime interest rate, as well as for other key external strategic factors, such as governmental regulation and industry trends. These same underlying assumptions should be listed for each of the alternative scenarios to be developed.

Second, for each strategic alternative, develop a set of optimistic, pessimistic, and most likely assumptions about the impact of key variables on the company's future financial statements. Forecast three sets of sales and cost-of-goods-sold figures for at least five years into the future. Look at historical data from past financial statements and make adjustments based on the environmental assumptions listed in step one. Do the same for other figures that can vary significantly. For the rest, assume that they will continue in their historical relationship to sales or some other key determining factor. Plug in expected inventory levels, accounts receivable, accounts payable, R&D expenses, advertising and promotion expenses, capital expenditures, and debt payments (assuming that debt is used to finance the strategy), among others. Consider not only historical trends, but also programs that might be needed for the implementation of each alternative strategy (such as building a new manufacturing facility or expanding the sales force).

Third, construct detailed pro forma financial statements for *each* of the strategic alternatives. Using a spreadsheet program on a personal computer, list the *actual* figures from this year's financial statements in the left column. To the right of this column, list the *optimistic* figures for year one, year two, year three, year four, and year five. Go through this same process with the same strategic alternative, but now list the *pessimistic* figures for the next five years. Do the same with the *most likely* figures. Once this is done, develop a similar set of optimistic (O), pessimistic (P), and most likely (ML) pro forma statements for the second strategic alternative. This process will generate six different pro forma scenarios reflecting three different situations (O, P, & ML) for two strategic alternatives. Next, calculate financial ratios and common-size income statements, and balance sheets to accompany the pro formas. To determine the feasibility of the scenarios, compare assumptions underlying the scenarios with these financial statements and ratios. For example, if cost of goods sold drops from 70% to 50% of total sales revenue in the pro forma income statements, this drop should result from a change in the production process or a shift to cheaper raw materials or labor costs, rather than from a failure to keep the cost of goods sold in its usual percentage relationship to sales revenue when the predicted statement was developed.

The result of this detailed scenario construction should be anticipated net profits, cash flow, and net working capital for each of three versions of the two alternatives for five years into the future. Once this is done, the strategist might wish to go further into the future if the strategy is expected to have a major impact on the company's financial statements beyond five years. The result of this work should provide sufficient information upon which forecasts of the likely feasibility and probable profitability of each of the strategic alternatives could be based.

Obviously, these scenarios can quickly become very complicated, especially if three sets of acquisition prices as well as development costs are calculated. Nevertheless, this sort of detailed "what if" analysis is needed for realistic comparisons of the projected outcome of each reasonable alternative strategy and its attendant programs, budgets, and procedures.

Regardless of the quantifiable pros and cons of each alternative, the actual decision will probably be influenced by a number of subjective factors that are difficult to quantify. Some of these factors are management's attitude toward risk, pressures from the external environment, influences from the corporate culture, and the personal needs and desires of key managers.

Management's Attitude Toward Risk

The attractiveness of a particular strategic alternative is partially a function of the amount of risk it entails. The risk is composed not only of the *probability* that the strategy will be effective, but also of the amount of *assets* the corporation must allocate to that strategy, and the length of *time* the assets will be unavailable for other uses. To quantify this risk, a number of people suggest the use of the *Capital Asset Pricing Model* (CAPM). CAPM is a financial method for linking the risk involved in a particular alternative with expected returns on a company's equity.[44] Another technique is the *Arbitrage Pricing Model* (APM), which screens acquisition candidates.[45] Everett proposes a simpler approach for the assessment of the probability of success or failure for a particular strategic alternative; his approach uses a Lotus 1-2-3 spreadsheet.[46]

The greater the amount of assets involved and the longer they are tied up, the more likely top management is to demand a high probability of success. This might be one reason why innovations seem to occur more often in small firms than in large, established corporations.[47] The small firm managed by an entrepreneur is willing to accept greater risk than would a large firm of diversified ownership. It is one thing to take a chance if you are the primary stockholder. It is something else if throngs of widows and orphans depend on your corporation's monthly dividend checks for living expenses.

Pressures from the External Environment

The attractiveness of a strategic alternative will be affected by its perceived compatibility with the key stakeholders in a corporation's task environment. These stakeholders are typically concerned with certain aspects of a corporation's activities. Creditors want to be paid on time. Unions exert pressure for comparable wages and employment security. Governments and interest groups demand social responsibility. Stockholders want dividends. All of these pressures must be considered in the selection of the best alternative. Hicks B. Waldron, Chairman of Avon Products, argues that corporations have duties beyond the maximizing of value for shareholders:

> We have a number of suppliers, institutions, customers, communities. None of them have the democratic freedom as shareholders do to buy or sell their shares. They have much deeper and much more important stakes in our company than our shareholders.[48]

Questions management should raise in their attempting to assess the importance to the corporation of stakeholder concerns are the following:

1. Which stakeholders are most crucial for corporate success?
2. How much of what they want are they likely to get, under this alternative?
3. What are they *likely* to do if they don't get what they want?
4. What is the probability that they will do it?

By ranking the key stakeholders in a corporation's task environment and asking these questions, strategy makers should be better able to choose strategic alternatives that minimize external pressures and maximize the probability of gaining stakeholder support.[49] In addition, top management can propose a political strategy to influence its key stakeholders. Some of the most commonly used political strategies are constituency building, political action committee contributions, advocacy advertising, lobbying, and coalition building.[50]

Pressures from the Corporate Culture

As pointed out in Chapter 5, the norms and values shared by the members of a corporation do affect the attractiveness of certain alternatives. If a strategy is incompatible with the corporate culture, the likelihood of its success will be very low. Footdragging and even sabotage will result, as employees fight to resist a radical change in corporate philosophy.

Precedents from the past tend to restrict the kinds of objectives and strategies that can be seriously considered. The "aura" of the founders of a corporation can linger long past their lifetime because their values have been imprinted on the corporation's members. According to Cyert and March,

> Organizations have memories in the form of precedents, and individuals in the coalition are strongly motivated to accept the precedents as binding. Whether precedents are formalized in the shape of an official standard operating procedure or are less formally stored, they remove from conscious consideration many agreements, decisions, and commitments that might well be subject to renegotiation in an organization without a memory.[51]

In considering a strategic alternative, the strategy makers must assess its compatibility with the corporate culture. If there is little fit, management must decide if it should (1) take a chance on ignoring the culture, (2) manage

ILLUSTRATIVE EXAMPLE 7.4

Changing the Culture at Procter & Gamble

In choosing to emphasize overall low cost as the key competitive strategy for each of its product lines, Procter & Gamble under President Smale is attempting a turnaround strategy of large proportions. By firing people to boost overall management performance, Smale risks undermining the employee loyalty that has been one of the company's greatest strengths. Apparently some board members are unsettled by what they see as a conflict between P&G's time-honored dedication to quality, high-performance products and its new emphasis on controlling costs. Similarly, the drive to move quickly and to take more risks with new products goes counter to the firm's traditional cautious style. Nevertheless, P&G must do something. Because its detergent and consumer paper goods markets are maturing, the company has been unable to attain its cherished goal of doubling its unit volume every ten years. The reason given is that consumers are increasingly responsive to price. The question remains, nonetheless: Will Smale be successful in changing P&G's corporate culture to implement a change from its traditional quality differentiation strategy to one of overall low cost?

SOURCE: "Why Procter & Gamble Is Playing It Even Tougher," *Business Week* (July 18, 1984), pp. 176–186.

---

around the culture and change the implementation plan, (3) try to change the culture to fit the strategy, or (4) change the strategy to fit the culture.[52] If the culture will be strongly opposed to a strategy, it is foolhardy to ignore the culture. Further, a decision to proceed with a particular strategy without a commitment to changing the culture or managing around the culture (both very tricky and time consuming) is dangerous. Nevertheless, restricting a corporation to only those strategies that are completely compatible with its culture might eliminate from consideration the most profitable alternatives. For an example of an attempt to change a corporate culture in order to implement a change in strategy, see Illustrative Example 7.4.

Needs and Desires of Key Managers

Even the most attractive alternative might not be selected if it is contrary to the needs and desires of important top managers. A person's ego may be tied to a particular proposal to the extent that all other alternatives are strongly lobbied against. Key executives in operating divisions, for example, might be able to influence other people in top management in favor of a particular alternative so that objections to it are ignored.

Such a situation was described by John DeLorean when he was at Pontiac Division of General Motors in 1959. At that time, General Motors was developing a new rear-engined auto called Corvair. Ed Cole, the General Manager of Chevrolet Division, was very attracted to the idea of building the first modern, rear-engine American automobile. A number of engineers, however, were worried about the safety of the car and made vigorous attempts to either change the "unsafe" suspension system or keep the Corvair out of production. "One top corporate engineer told me that he showed his test results to Cole but by then he said, 'Cole's mind was made up.' "[53] By this time, there had developed quite a bit of documented evidence that the car should not be built as designed. However, according to DeLorean,

> . . . Cole was a strong product voice and a top salesman in company affairs. In addition, the car, as he proposed it, would cost less to build than the same car with a conventional rear suspension. Management not only went along with Cole, it also told the dissenters in effect to "stop these objections. Get on the team, or you can find someplace else to work." The ill-fated Corvair was launched in the fall of 1959.
>
> The results were disastrous. I don't think any one car before or since produced as gruesome a record on the highway as the Corvair. It was designed and promoted to appeal to the spirit and flair of young people. It was sold in part as a sports car. Young Corvair owners, therefore, were trying to bend their cars around curves at high speeds and were killing themselves in alarming numbers.[54]

In only a few years, General Motors was inundated by lawsuits over the Corvair. Ralph Nader soon published a book primarily about the Corvair called *Unsafe at Any Speed,* launching his career as a consumer advocate.

7.3
DEVELOPMENT OF POLICIES

The selection of the best strategic alternative is not the end of strategy formulation. Policies to define the ground rules for implementation must now be established. As defined earlier, policies are broad guidelines for the making of decisions. Flowing from the selected strategy, they provide guidance for decision making throughout the organization. Corporate policies are broad guidelines for divisions to follow in compliance with corporate strategy. These policies are interpreted and implemented through each division's own objectives and strategies. Divisions may then develop their own policies that will be guidelines for their functional areas to follow. At General Electric, for example, Chairman Welch insists that GE be Number One or Number Two wherever it competes. This policy gives clear guidance to managers throughout the organization.[55]

Another example of a corporate-level policy is that developed by Ford Motor Company. Concerned with the historic lack of cooperation between Ford U.S. and Ford of Europe, Ford's top management developed a company-wide policy requiring any new car design to be easily adaptable to any market in the world. Previous to this policy, Ford of Europe developed cars strictly for its own market, while engineers in the United States separately designed their own products. The new policy was a natural result of Ford's emphasis on manufacturing efficiency and global integration as a corporation. One result of this new policy was the program to produce the European Sierra and its U.S. counterpart the Merkur. The cost to convert the European Sierra to meet all U.S. safety and emission standards was about one-fourth of what the conversion of previous European models would have cost. The Taurus and Sable models were also engineered for easy conversion to overseas markets.[56]

Some policies will be expressions of a corporation's **critical success factors** (CSF). Critical success factors are those elements of a company that determine its strategic success or failure. They vary from company to company. IBM, for example, sees customer service as its critical success factor. McDonald's CSF is quality, cleanliness, and value. Hewlett-Packard is concerned with new product development.[57] As guidelines for decision making, policies can therefore be based on a corporation's critical success factors. At Lazarus Department Store in Columbus, Ohio, for example, customer service is a critical success factor. Store policies state that the customer is *always* right. Even if a department manager believes that a customer bought a particular shirt from a competitor, the manager is bound by policy to accept the shirt and to give back money to the customer. Lazarus's top management believes that even though a few people might take advantage of the store in the short run, the store will make up for it in the long run with good will and increased market share.

Chaparral Steel, a successful company following a low-cost business strategy with its mini-mills, followed five basic policies to ensure its successful growth through the 1980s:

- Design for maximum labor productivity.
- Design for efficient use of capital.
- Continue to upgrade existing processes.
- Maintain a work environment that nourishes people, innovation, and accomplishment.
- Give priority to the needs of customers and to the threat of foreign producers.[58]

Policies tend to be rather long lived and can even outlast the particular strategy that caused their creation. Interestingly, these general policies, such as "The customer is always right" or "Research and development should get first priority on all budget requests," can become, in time, part of a corporation's culture. Such policies can make the implementation of specific strategies easier. They can also restrict top management's strategic options in the future. It is for this reason that a change in strategy should be followed quickly by a change in policies. Managing policy is one way to manage the corporate culture.

SUMMARY AND CONCLUSION

This chapter has focused on the last stage of the strategy formulation process: generating, evaluating, and selecting the best strategic alternative.

It also has discussed the development of policies for implementing strategies.

There are three main kinds of strategies: corporate, business (divisional), and functional. Corporate strategies fall into three main families: *stability, growth,* and *retrenchment.* Epitomized by a steady-as-she-goes philosophy, *stability* strategies are (1) no change, (2) profit, (3) pause, and (4) proceed with caution. The very popular *growth* strategies are (1) concentration, with its sub-strategies of horizontal and vertical growth, and (2) diversification—concentric and conglomerate. Any of these growth strategies can be achieved through internal development or through external acquisition. *Retrenchment* strategies are generally unpopular because they imply failure. They include (1) turnaround, (2) divestment, (3) captive company, and (4) liquidation.

Business or divisional strategies focus on improving the competitive position of a corporation's products or services within a particular industry or market segment. Porter suggests three generic competitive strategies: *overall cost leadership, differentiation,* and *focus.* Functional strategies act to maximize corporate and divisional resource productivity, so that a distinctive competence within an industry will develop. Within any corporation, these three levels of strategy must fit together in a mutually supporting manner so that they form an integrated hierarchy of strategy.

The selection of the best strategic alternative from projected scenarios will probably be affected by a number of factors. Among them are management's attitude toward risk, pressures from the external environment, influences from the corporate culture, and the personal needs and desires of key managers.

As broad guidelines for divisions to follow, corporate policies assure the divisions' compliance with corporate strategy. Divisions may then generate their own internal policies to be followed by their functional areas. These policies define the ground rules for strategy implementation and serve to align corporate activities in the new strategic direction.

DISCUSSION QUESTIONS

1. Is the profit strategy really a stability strategy? Why or why not?

2. Why is growth the most frequently used corporate-level strategy?

3. How does horizontal growth (horizontal integration) differ from concentric diversification?

4. What are the tradeoffs between an internal and an external growth strategy?

5. How is Chapter 11 bankruptcy being used in the United States by major corporations? Is it a strategy?

6. Is it possible for a business unit to follow an overall cost-leadership strategy and a differentiation-through-high-quality-strategy simultaneously? Why or why not?

7. Suggest some methods by which a corporation's culture can be changed.

8. As described in the Integrative Case at the end of this chapter, should CSX in 1986 have continued to grow through external acquisitions or should it have changed its growth strategy to one of internal development?

9. If acquisitions continued to make sense for CSX, as described in the Integrative Case, in what industries should CSX's top management have been looking for attractive acquisition candidates in 1986—railroads, pipelines, trucking, barge lines, ocean freight, airlines, or in some other areas not related to transportation, such as financial services? Give the pros and cons for each industry in terms of their relationship to CSX's mission and growth strategy.

10. From the Integrative Case, what were the pros and cons to CSX of the Sea-Land acquisition?

NOTES

1. M. A. Hitt and R. Duane Ireland, "Corporate Distinctive Competence, Strategy, Industry and Performance," *Strategic Management Journal* (July-September 1985), p. 273.

2. R. E. Winter, "Cincinnati Milacron Starts Third Revamp," *Wall Street Journal* (April 28, 1988), p. 4.

3. W. F. Glueck, *Business Policy and Strategic Management,* 3rd ed. (New York: McGraw-Hill, 1980), p. 290. Glueck uses the term *stable growth* instead of *stability.*

4. R. M. Cyert and J. G. March, *A Behavioral Theory of the Firm* (Englewood Cliffs, N.J.: Prentice-Hall, 1963).

5. D. R. Dalton and I. F. Kesner, "Organizational Growth: Big Is Beautiful," *Journal of Business Strategy* (Summer 1985), pp. 38–48.

6. J. Vesey, "Vertical Integration: Its Effects on Business Performance," *Managerial Planning* (May-June 1978), pp. 11–15.

7. K. R. Harrigan, "Exit Barriers and Vertical Integration," *Academy of Management Journal* (September, 1985), pp. 686–697.

8. K. R. Harrigan, *Strategies for Vertical Integration* (Lexington, Mass.: D. C. Heath-Lexington Books, 1983), pp. 16–21.

9. M. Leontiades, *Managing the Unmanageable* (Reading, Mass.: Addison-Wesley, 1986), p. 4.

10. J. Constable, "Diversification as a Factor in U.K. Industrial Strategy," *Long Range Planning* (February 1986), p. 53.

11. R. P. Rumelt, *Strategy, Structure, and Economic Performance* (Cambridge, Mass.: Harvard University Press, 1974).

K. Palepu, "Diversification Strategy, Profit Performance, and the Entropy Measure," *Strategic Management Journal* (July-September 1985), pp. 239–255.

P. Varadarajan and V. Ramanujan, "Diversification and Performance: A Reexamination Using a New Two-Dimensional Conceptualization of Diversity in Firms," *Academy of Management Journal* (June 1987), pp. 380–393.

H. Singh and C. A. Montgomery, "Corporate Acquisition Strategies and Economic Performance," *Strategic Management Journal* (July-August 1987), pp. 377–386.

12. T. J. Peters and R. H. Waterman, Jr., *In Search of Excellence* (New York: Harper & Row, 1982), pp. 293–294.

13. R. Little, "Conglomerates Are Doing Better Than You Think," *Fortune* (May 28, 1984), p. 60.

M. J. Dolan, "In Defense of Conglomerates," *Business Week* (July 29, 1985), p. 5.

14. G. Johnson and H. Thomas, "The Industry Context of Strategy, Structure, and Performance: The U. K. Brewing Industry," *Strategic Management Journal* (July-August 1987), pp. 343–361.

15. M. Leontiades, pp. 62–63.

16. C. K. Prahalad and R. A. Bettis, "The Dominant Logic: A New Linkage Between Diversity and Performance," *Strategic Management Journal* (November-December 1986), pp. 485–501.

17. S. Scredon and A. Dunkin, "Why Nabisco and Reynolds Were Made For Each Other," *Business Week* (June 17, 1985), p. 34.

18. B. T. Lamont and C. A. Anderson, "Mode of Corporate Diversification and Economic Performance," *Academy of Management Journal* (December 1985), pp. 926–936.

19. P. M. Hirsch, "Ambushes, Shootouts, and Knights of the Roundtable: The Language of Corporate Takeovers" (Paper presented to the 40th Meeting of the Academy of Management, Detroit, Mich., August 1980).

20. K. R. Harrigan, "Joint Ventures: Linking For a Leap Forward," *Planning Review* (July 1986), pp. 10–14.

21. For a good summary of guidelines for the formation and management of joint ventures, see P. P. Pekar, "Joint Venture: A New Information System Is Born," *Planning Review* (July 1986), pp. 15–19.

22. D. C. Hambrick, "Turnaround Strategies," in W. D. Guth (ed.), *Handbook of Business Strategy* (Boston: Warren, Gorham & Lamont, 1985), pp. 10.1–10.32.

23. C. J. Clarke and F. Gall, "Planned Divestment—A Five-step Approach," *Long Range Planning* (February 1987), p. 18.

24. For more information on reasons for the divestment of units, see W. R. Fannin, S. Markell, and C. B. Gilmore, "A New Strategic View of Divestitures," in *Handbook of Business Strategy, 1985/86 Yearbook,* edited by W. D. Guth (Boston: Warren, Gorham & Lamont, 1985), pp. 10.1–10.8.

25. J. B. Treece, "U. S. Parts Makers Just Won't Say 'Uncle'," *Business Week* (August 10, 1987), pp. 76–77.

26. R. L. Sutton and A. L. Callahan, "The Stigma of Bankruptcy: Spoiled Organizational Image and Its Management," *Academy of Management Journal* (September 1987) pp. 405–436.

27. P. C. Nystrom and W. H. Starbuck, "To Avoid Organizational Crises, Unlearn," *Organizational Dynamics* (Spring 1984), p. 55.

28. R. Hise and S. McDonald, "CEOs' Views On Strategy: A Survey," *Journal of Business Strategy* (Winter 1984), pp. 81 and 86.

29. H. K. Baker, T. O. Miller, and B. J. Ramsperger, "An Inside Look at Corporate Mergers and Acquisitions," *MSU Business Topics* (Winter 1981), p. 51.

30. B. Burrough, "Takeover Boom Is Expected to Continue Through 1988 After a Strong First Half," *Wall Street Journal* (July 5, 1988), p. 5.

31. M. E. Porter, *Competitive Strategy* (New York: Free Press, 1980), pp. 36–46.

32. Porter, 1980, p. 35.

33. J. B. Hull, "Hospital Chains Battle Health Insurers, But Will Quality Care Lose in the War?" *Wall Street Journal* (February 5, 1985), p. 35.

34. W. M. Bulkeley, "Upstart WordPerfect Corporation Finds Niche," *Wall Street Journal* (April 7, 1987), p. 6.

35. M. E. Porter, *Competitive Advantage* (New York: Free Press, 1985), p. 15.

36. Porter, 1985, p. 16.

37. G. G. Dess and P. S. Davis, "Porter's Generic Strategies as Determinants of Strategic Group Membership and Organizational Performance," *Academy of Management Journal* (September 1984), p. 484.

R. E. White, "Generic Business Strategies, Organizational Context and Performance: An Empirical Approach," *Strategic Management Journal* (May-June 1986), pp. 217–231.

38. F. E. Webster, Jr., "Marketing Strategy in a Slow Growth Economy," *California Management Review* (Spring 1986), p. 94.

39. J. Zaslow, "Atlas Van Lines Agrees to Buyout for $71.6 Million," *Wall Street Journal* (June 25, 1984), p. 10.

40. A. S. Lauglaug, "A Framework for the Strategic Management of Future Tyre Technology," *Long Range Planning* (October 1987), pp. 21–41.

N. K. Sethi, B. Movsesian, and K. D. Hickey, "Can Technology Be Managed Strategically?" *Long Range Planning* (August 1985), pp. 89–99.

41. Porter, 1985, p. 181.

42. C. Hawkins, R. Grover, and A. Bernstein, "Will It Be Kerkorian to the Rescue of Pan Am?" *Business Week* (October 19, 1987), pp. 57–58.

43. S. Schoeffler, R. D. Buzzell, and D. F. Heany, "Impact of Strategic Planning on Profit Performance," *Harvard Business Review* (March-April 1974), pp. 144–145.

44. M. Hergert, "Strategic Resource Allocation Using Divisional Hurdle Rates," *Planning Review* (January-February 1987), pp. 28–32.

D. R. Harrington, "Stock Prices, Beta, and Strategic Planning," *Harvard Business Review* (May-June 1983), pp. 157–164.

45. M. Kroll and S. Caples, "Managing Acquisitions of Strategic Business Units with the Aid of the Arbitrage Pricing Model," *Academy of Management Review* (October 1987), pp. 676–685.

46. M. D. Everett, "A Simplified Guide to Capital Investment Risk Analysis," *Planning Review* (July 1986), pp. 32–36.

47. Peters and Waterman, pp. 115–116.

48. B. Nussbaum and J. H. Dobrzynski, "The Battle For Corporate Control," *Business Week* (May 18, 1987), p. 103.

49. E. Weiner and A. Brown, "Stakeholder Analysis for Effective Issues Management," *Planning Review* (May 1986), pp. 27–31.

50. G. D. Keim and C. P. Zeithaml, "Corporate Political Strategy and Legislative Decision Making: A Review and Contingency Approach," *Academy of Management Review* (October 1986), pp. 828–843.

51. R. M. Cyert and J. G. March, "A Behavioral Theory of Organizational Objectives," *Management Classics,* eds. M. T. Matteson and J. M. Ivancevich (Santa Monica, Calif.: Goodyear Publishing, 1977), p. 114.

52. H. Schwartz and S. M. Davis, "Matching Corporate Culture and Business Strategy," *Organizational Dynamics* (Summer 1981), p. 43.

53. J. P. Wright, *On a Clear Day You Can See General Motors* (Grosse Point, Mich.: Wright Enterprises, 1979), p. 54.

54. Wright, p. 55.

55. M. A. Harris, Z. Schiller, R. Mitchell, and C. Power, "Can Jack Welch Reinvent GE?" *Business Week* (June 30, 1986), p. 67.

56. M. Edid and W. J. Hampton, "Now That It's Cruising, Can Ford Keep Its Foot on the Gas?" *Business Week* (February 11, 1985), pp. 48–52.

57. A. L. Mendlow, "Setting Corporate Goals and Measuring Organizational Effectiveness—A Practical Approach," *Long Range Planning* (February 1983), p. 72.

58. R. T. Jaffre, "Chaparral Steel Company: A Winner in a Market Decimated by Imports," *Planning Review* (July 1986), p. 22.

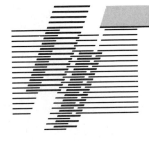

INTEGRATIVE CASE

CSX CORPORATION'S STRATEGIC ALTERNATIVES

In the spring of 1986, CSX Corporation's top management continued to work toward its objective of reaching and exceeding a 15% return on invested capital by 1990. Still following growth strategies aimed at creating America's leading multi-modal transportation system, the corporation's management committee (composed of eleven CSX senior executives and headed by Chairman Hays T. Watkins) pondered alternatives for future growth. The U.S. Senate on February 5, 1986, by a 54–39 vote, had approved the sale of Conrail to CSX's major competitor, Norfolk Southern Corporation. This was no surprise to CSX management, who had supported instead a Morgan Stanley proposal for a public offering of Conrail's stock (in which CSX might secure a minority interest). Nevertheless, the Senate's Conrail bill faced major opposition in the House of Representatives. CSX's management continued to hope for the eventual defeat of the legislation.

CSX closed 1985 in a reasonably strong financial and physical position. Although revenue and operating income were slightly less than they had been in 1984, net earnings increased if one's accounting excluded a special charge for the restructuring of the company's business segments. The issue facing the management committee was planning for future growth given the uncertainty of Conrail's future. In the last couple of years, the company had followed a temporary pause strategy as it worked to digest its recent acquisition of Texas Gas Resources and to make its two rail systems more efficient. How should the corporation continue its growth? Because of its success in forging a multi-modal transportation and natural resource company out of a group of rather diverse acquisitions, top management leaned toward external over internal growth. CSX top management believed that it needed to move quickly, before Norfolk Southern made its next move. Internal growth seemed too slow a method, in the high-stakes chess match being played by U.S. railroads in the 1980s.

CHANGING COMPETITIVE SITUATION

Norfolk Southern had not put all its hopes on the Conrail deal. The ICC had approved in April 1985 Norfolk Southern's acquisition of North American Van Lines—the first purchase of a trucking firm since deregulation. In urging his people to "think like truckers," Robert Claytor, Chief Executive of the Norfolk, Virginia-based railroad, stated that Norfolk Southern wants to "combine the service of trucks with the efficiencies of rail." He went on to say that "the company can begin a new service, when business is usually light, using North American's over-the-road operation. When volume grows, we can then switch the business to rail."[1]

Even after paying $350 million for North American Van Lines, Norfolk Southern had quite a bit left of the $1 billion in cash it had accumulated over the past few years. It had purchased a 19% stock interest in Piedmont Airlines, a 5% interest in Santa Fe Industries, and a 10% interest in Florida's Southeast Banking Corporation.[2] The cash would soon disappear if the Conrail purchase was finally approved by the House. If approval was denied, however, Norfolk Southern would be free to look elsewhere for an investment opportunity. Most in the industry were aware that the five-year agreement restricting Norfolk Southern's ability to increase or sell its stock in Piedmont Airlines would end in January 1987, but, until the Conrail issue was settled, no one would predict what might happen.

SEA-LAND OPPORTUNITY

In April 1986, while CSX's top management was considering possible future directions, a sudden opportunity presented itself. Sea-Land Corporation, one of the pioneer companies in the containerized ocean shipping business, let it be known that it was looking for a "white knight" to help it fight a takeover attempt by Harold Simmons' Contran Corporation. In 1966, Sea-Land became the first U.S. flag carrier to compete in the North Atlantic trade route with containerships and, in 1968, it began commercial service to the Far East. Only a few months after its being incorporated in Delaware in 1969, it was acquired by R. J. Reynolds (now R. J.

Reynolds Industries). In 1984, Reynolds distributed 0.2 shares of Sea-Land common stock in exchange for each share of Reynolds common stock. Sea-Land was once again autonomous.

By 1986, Sea-Land was the largest U.S. containership operation, with a fleet of fifty-eight containerships, averaging seven years of age, serving ports between the continental U.S. and the Far East, Northern Europe, the Mediterranean and the Middle East, Alaska, the Caribbean, and Central America. It had exclusive-use terminals in fifteen ports worldwide, and preferential-use agreements in many others. It operated vessels without federal subsidies and used its own marketing staff. It owned over 100,000 containers. Thanks to deregulation, Sea-Land bought its own double-stack rail cars in 1985 to carry its containers to inland destinations. By stacking two containers on these specially designed rail cars, Sea-Land nearly doubled train capacity and cut rail costs more than 25%. Because the major railroads had no double-stack cars, shipping lines chose to buy their own and contract with rail companies like CSX to haul the cars over the rail company's system.[3]

1985 had been a rather poor year for Sea-Land. Although revenues were 93% of those in 1984, net earnings were only 18% of 1984's because of declining freight rates. (Refer to Tables 7.5 and 7.6 for Sea-Land's financial information.) By April 1986, there appeared to be some firming of rates, but a projected increase in industry capacity of around 14% in 1986 was very likely to stimulate another round of rate cutting. Value Line forecasted that good prospects would develop for the industry by 1990, as additions to the world container fleet slowed and some of the current excess capacity was absorbed. This forecast assumed that a number of the weaker firms would soon leave the business. By cutting personnel costs and other expenses,

TABLE 7.5
Consolidated Statement of Earnings: Sea-Land Corporation
(In Thousands of Dollars)

	YEARS ENDED	
	1985	1984
Revenue	$1,634,183	$1,759,207
Expense		
Operating	1,283,976	1,276,646
Selling, general & administrative	249,618	235,346
Depreciation and amortization	105,409	101,351
Total Expenses	1,639,003	1,613,343
Earnings (loss) from operations	(4,820)	145,864
Interest income	28,969	43,196
Interest expense	(45,085)	(44,251)
Other financial income (expense), net	(1,025)	(12,746)
Earnings (loss) before income taxes	(21,961)	132,063
Provision (benefit) for income taxes	(36,163)	51,560
Net Earnings (loss)	$ 14,202	$ 80,503

TABLE 7.6
Consolidated Statement of Financial Position:
Sea-Land Corporation
(In Thousands of Dollars)

	YEARS ENDED	
	1985	1984
Assets		
Current assets		
Cash and short-term investments	$ 10,330	$ 31,236
Accounts and notes receivable (less allowances of $21,858 and $20,454)	164,185	188,963
Materials and supplies	33,357	34,345
Prepaid expenses	10,348	9,097
Total current assets	218,220	263,641
Property and equipment, at cost	2,146,068	1,862,833
Less depreciation and amortization	916,160	832,645
	1,226,908	1,030,188
Capital construction fund	169,102	326,054
Good will	87,735	87,908
Other assets	263,593	103,511
Total assets	$1,965,558	$1,811,302
Liabilities and Shareholders' Equity		
Current liabilities		
Accounts payable and accrued liabilities	$ 215,491	$ 179,132
Notes payable	—	60,000
Current portion of long-term debt	5,927	6,916
Total current liabilities	221,418	246,048
Long-term debt, less current portion	575,196	416,268
Other liabilities	55,408	46,943
Deferred income taxes	325,732	324,192
Shareholder's Equity		
Common stock, $.10 stated value at 12/29/85 and 12/30/84	2,333	2,319
Paid-in capital	230,359	223,485
Cumulative translation adjustments	(602)	(611)
Retained earnings (deficit)	555,714	552,658
Total shareholders' equity	787,804	777,851
Total liabilities and shareholders' equity	$1,965,558	$1,811,302

Sea-Land was attempting to survive a very rocky year, after posting a first quarter loss in March 1986.[4]

Sea-Land's top management and its board of directors were finding it increasingly difficult to fend off a hostile takeover attempt by Harold Simmons. By April, Simmons' Contran Corporation owned around 39% (approximately 9.2 million shares) of Sea-Land's stock and was in the process of being given three seats on the corporation's board at Sea-Land's annual meeting in May. Sea-Land's management was in a serious bind. Because of the weak state of the oceanic shipping business and the fact that 35% of Sea-Land's capitalization consisted of long-term debt, analysts thought it unlikely that any bank would be willing to finance a leveraged buyout by Sea-Land's executives to avoid Simmons' takeover. The only other feasible option was to seek out a friendly merger with a compatible company.

STRATEGIC DECISION POINT

CSX's top management was well aware of Sea-Land's problems with Simmons and wondered if Sea-Land would be a good candidate for acquisition. In its search for growth opportunities, CSX had been studying opportunities in ocean shipping as well as in other areas. Some quiet discussions with Sea-Land executives revealed that Sea-Land might welcome an offer from CSX. By mid-April, Simmons offered $26 for those Sea-Land shares he didn't already own. The company's stock, which had been trading earlier at $23, was now selling for around $25 per share. The question facing the management committee of CSX was what to do about Sea-Land. Would the possible synergies from such a merger more than offset the overcapacity problem in containerized oceanic shipping? It would probably cost $700 million to $800 million to buy all the 26.6 million fully diluted shares (composed of common stock outstanding, plus existing stock options, and the conversion of subordinated notes) of Sea-Land. Was this a good time for CSX to get involved in an international transportation business or should CSX "stick to its knitting" in the U.S.? Some analysts believed that because ocean-container companies were becoming one of the railroad industry's biggest set of customers, railroads would either compete with each other for the business or capture it permanently through acquisition. CSX's management committee did not have much time to decide. Because of Simmons' interest, Sea-Land seemed to be a now or never opportunity.

NOTES

1. L. Abruzzese, "NS Chairman Urges Rails To Be More 'Truck-Like,' " *Journal of Commerce and Commercial* (October 22, 1986), p. 1A(2).
2. J. Cook, "The $1 Billion Holding Action," *Forbes* (December 19, 1983) p. 67.
3. D. Machalaba, "Shipping Lines Find Competitive Edge In Adding Their Own Rail Operations," *Wall Street Journal* (December 26, 1985), p. 3.
4. "Sea-Land," *Value Line Investment Survey,* Part 3: Ratings and Reports, Edition 2 (April 4, 1986), p. 303.

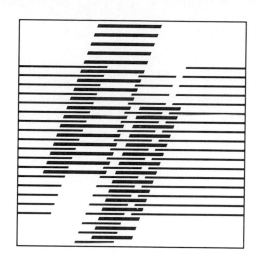

PART FOUR

STRATEGY IMPLEMENTATION AND CONTROL

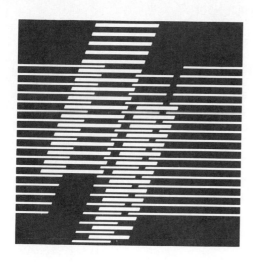

CHAPTER 8

STRATEGY IMPLEMENTATION

STRATEGIC MANAGEMENT MODEL

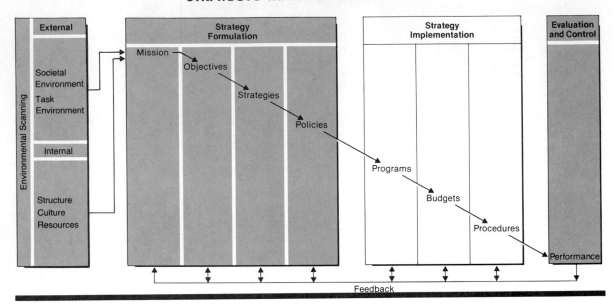

Once a strategy and a set of policies have been formulated, the focus of strategic management shifts to implementation. **Strategy implementation** is the sum total of the activities and choices required for execution of a plan. It is the process by which strategies and policies are put into action, through the development of programs, budgets, and procedures. To begin the implementation process, strategy makers must consider three questions:

Who are the people who will carry out the strategic plan?

What must be done?

How are they going to do what is needed?

These questions and similar ones should have been addressed initially when the pros and cons of strategic alternatives were analyzed. They must also be addressed now before appropriate implementation plans can be made. Unless top management can answer these basic questions in a satisfactory manner, even the best planned strategy is unlikely to have the desired results.

For example, the acquisition of Republic Airlines by Northwest Airlines was a well-conceived, horizontal growth strategy, but it created massive problems when first implemented. Traffic exceeded projections—and overwhelmed Northwest's computer systems. Reservations were lost and passengers were ticketed into the same seats. As ex-Republic workers struggled to learn a new system for baggage transfer, there was a dramatic increase in the number of misplaced bags. Before the merger, 85% of both airlines' flights departed on time. In the first week of the merger, on-time performance plunged to 25%! The U.S. Transportation Department's Consumer

Affairs Division received 4.74 complaints per 100,000 Northwest passengers for the first month of the merged operation—nearly 2½ times the industry average. "We anticipated some problems," said John F. Horn, President of Northwest's parent company, NWA, Inc., "but we had no idea they were going to be the level they were."[1]

Alexander's survey of ninety-three company presidents and divisional managers revealed that the following ten problems were experienced by over half of the group when they attempted to implement a strategic change. These problems are listed in order of frequency of occurrence.

1. More time needed for implementation than originally planned.
2. Unanticipated major problems.
3. Ineffective coordination of activities.
4. Crises that distracted attention away from implementation.
5. Insufficient capabilities of the involved employees.
6. Inadequate training and instruction of lower-level employees.
7. Uncontrollable external environmental factors.
8. Inadequate leadership and direction by departmental managers.
9. Poor definition of key implementation tasks and activities.
10. Inadequate monitoring of activities by the information system.[2]

As shown in Fig. 8.1, poor implementation of an appropriate strategy can result in failure of the strategy. An excellent implementation plan,

FIGURE 8.1

Interaction of Strategy Formulation and Implementation

	STRATEGY FORMULATED	
	Appropriate	Inappropriate
Excellent	*Success* Targets for growth, share, profits are met.	*Rescue or Ruin* Good execution may save a poor strategy or may hasten failure.
Poor	*Trouble* Poor execution hampers good strategy. Management may conclude strategy is inappropriate.	*Failure* Cause of failure hard to diagnose. Poor strategy marked by inability to execute.

(STRATEGY IMPLEMENTED)

Source: Reprinted by permission of the *Harvard Business Review.* An exhibit from "Making Your Marketing Strategy Work" by Thomas V. Bonoma (March/April 1984). Copyright © 1984 by the President and Fellows of Harvard College; all rights reserved.

however, will not only cause the success of an appropriate strategy; it can also rescue an inappropriate strategy. This is why an increasing number of chief executives are turning their attention to the problems of implementation. Now more than ever before, they realize that the successful implementation of a strategy depends on having the right organization structure, resource allocation, compensation program, information system, and corporate culture.[3]

8.1

WHO IMPLEMENTS STRATEGY?

Depending on how the corporation is organized, those who implement corporate strategy might be a different set of people from those who formulate it. In most large, multi-industry corporations, the implementers will be everyone in the organization except top management and the board of directors. Vice-presidents of functional areas and directors of divisions or SBUs will work with their subordinates to put together large-scale implementation plans. From these plans, plant managers, project managers, and unit heads will put together plans for their specific plants, departments, and units. Therefore, every operational manager down to the first-line supervisor will be involved in some way in the implementing of corporate, divisional, and functional strategies.

It is important to note that most of the people in the corporation who are crucial to successful strategy implementation probably had little, if anything, to do with the development of the corporate strategy. Therefore, they might be entirely ignorant of the vast amount of data and work that went into the formulation process. Unless changes in mission, objectives, strategies, and policies and their importance to the corporation are communicated clearly to all operational managers, there can be a lot of resistance and footdragging. When top management formulates a strategy that challenges the corporation's culture, lower-level managers might even sabotage the implementation. These managers might hope to influence top management to abandon its new plans and return to the old ways. For an example of one company's problems with corporate culture see Illustrative Example 8.1.

8.2

WHAT MUST BE DONE?

The managers of divisions and functional areas work with their fellow managers to develop *programs, budgets,* and *procedures* for the implementation of strategy. A **program** is a statement of the activities or steps needed to accomplish a single-use plan, the purpose of which is to make the strategy action-oriented. For example, top management might have chosen forward vertical integration as its best strategy for growth. It purchased existing retail outlets from another firm instead of building its own. To integrate the new

ILLUSTRATIVE EXAMPLE 8.1

Two Cultures Clash at HNG/InterNorth, Inc.

When InterNorth, Inc., acquired Houston Natural Gas Corporation for $2.4 billion in July 1985, industry analysts predicted that it would soon become a dominant firm in the pipeline industry. The combined company had a good position in growing markets in Southern California and Florida and access to cheap, unregulated Texas natural gas. Unfortunately, the two companies had very different cultures, which created serious implementation problems. Forced to deal with constant infighting, top management couldn't even settle on a name for the company. Even though Inter-North had bought Houston Natural Gas, the temporary name of HNG/InterNorth listed Houston first "because it came off the tongue better," reported Kenneth Lay, Chairman of the corporation. With the help of a New York consulting firm, Lay proposed changing the name to Enteron. Once word spread, however, that the word literally meant the alimentary canal, or digestive tract, Lay became the target of much ridicule. "We know which end of the alimentary canal we are," complained one constituent.

When the merger originally took place, Samuel Segnar, Chairman of InterNorth, agreed that Lay, head of HNG, would serve initially as president and then as chairman of the combined company. Segnar was to serve as chairman until Lay took over the position.

Personnel rivalry throughout the two merged companies, however, created some bizarre situations. From the beginning, there was conflict over which company was to be dominant. To placate both sides, management established dual headquarters in Omaha and Houston. The controller was located in Omaha, while the treasurer had his office in Houston. Matters continued to deteriorate. With the early retirement of Segnar in November 1985, Lay assumed the chairman's position. Lay's decisive, hands-on style conflicted with InterNorth's decentralized approach. Nearly a dozen top executives quit. Noticing the instability of the company, Houston Lighting and Power Company, HNG/InterNorth's biggest customer, cancelled its contract. To try to stem the constant infighting, Lay communicated his desire to form one cohesive company. "Throughout the organization there continues to be too much of the we and they, Omaha versus Houston, and InterNorth or HNG winning or losing." Unfortunately, Lay's attempt to cut costs by eliminating around 10% of the combined workforce did not contribute to improved morale.

SOURCE: J. E. Davis, "A Mega-Pipeline With a Massive Identity Crisis," *Business Week* (April 14, 1986), pp. 65–66.

stores into the corporation, various programs—such as the following—would now have to be developed:

1. A re-structuring program to move the stores into the existing marketing chain of command, so that store managers report to regional managers, who report to the merchandising manager, who reports to the vice-president in charge of marketing.

2. An advertising program. ("Jones Surplus is now a part of Ajax Continental. Prices are lower. Selection is better.")

3. A training program for newly hired store managers as well as for those Jones Surplus managers the corporation has chosen to keep.

4. A program to develop reporting procedures that will integrate the stores into the corporation's accounting system.

5. A program to modernize the stores and to prepare them for a "grand opening."

Once these and other programs are developed, the budget process begins. A **budget** is a statement of a corporation's programs in terms of dollars. The detailed cost of each program is listed for planning and control purposes. Planning a budget is the last real check a corporation has on the feasibility of its selected strategy. An ideal strategy might be found to be completely impractical only after specific implementation programs are costed in detail.

Once program, divisional, and corporate budgets are approved, procedures to guide the employees in their day-to-day actions must be developed. Sometimes referred to as Standard Operating Procedures, **procedures** are a system of sequential steps or techniques that describe in detail how a particular task or job is to be done. They typically detail the various activities that must be carried out to complete a corporation's programs. In the case of the corporation that decided to acquire another firm's retail outlets, new operating procedures must be established for, among others, in-store promotions, inventory ordering, stock selection, customer relations, credits and collections, warehouse distribution, pricing, paycheck timing, grievance handling, and raises and promotions. These procedures ensure that the day-to-day store operations will be consistent over time (that is, next week's work activities will be the same as this week's) and consistent among stores (that is, each store will operate in the same manner as the others). To ensure that its policies are carried out to the letter in every one of its fast-food retail outlets, McDonald's, for example, has done an excellent job of developing very detailed procedures (and policing them!).

8.3

HOW IS STRATEGY TO BE IMPLEMENTED?

Up to this point, both strategy formulation and implementation have been discussed in terms of planning. Programs, budgets, and procedures are simply more greatly detailed plans for the eventual implementation of strategy. The total management process includes, however, several additional activities crucial to implementation, such as organizing, staffing, directing, and controlling. Before *plans* can lead to actual performance, top management must ensure that the corporation is appropriately *organized*, programs are adequately *staffed*, and activities are being *directed* toward the achievement of desired objectives. These activities are reviewed briefly in this chapter. Top management must also ensure that there is progress toward the objectives, according to plan; this is a *control* function that will be discussed in Chapter 9.

Organizing

It is very likely that a change in corporate strategy will require some sort of change in the way a corporation is structured and in the kind of skills needed in particular positions. In a classic study of large American corporations, such as DuPont, General Motors, Sears Roebuck, and Standard Oil, Chandler concluded that changes in corporate strategy lead to changes in organization structure. He also concluded that American corporations follow a pattern of development from one kind of structural arrangement to another as they expand. According to him, these structural changes occur because inefficiencies caused by the old structure have, by being pushed too far, become too obviously detrimental to live with: "The thesis deduced from these several propositions is then that structure follows strategy and that the most complex type of structure is the result of the concatenation [linking together] of several basic strategies."[4] Chandler therefore proposed the following as the sequence of what occurs:

1. New strategy is created.
2. New administrative problems emerge.
3. Economic performance declines.
4. New appropriate structure is invented.
5. Profit returns to its previous level.

Structure Follows Strategy

Chandler found that in their early years, corporations such as DuPont tend to have a centralized organizational structure that is well suited to their producing and selling a limited range of products. As they add new product lines, purchase their own sources of supply, and create their own distribution networks, they become too complex for highly centralized structures. In order to remain successful, this type of successful organization needs to shift to a decentralized structure with several semi-autonomous divisions (referred to as the divisional structure in Chapter 5). This type of structure is also called the *M-form* (for multidivisional structure) by the noted economist, O. E. Williamson.[5]

In his book, *My Years with General Motors,* Alfred P. Sloan detailed how General Motors conducted such structural changes in the 1920s.[6] He saw decentralization of structure as centralized policy determination coupled with decentralized operating management. Once a strategy was developed for the total corporation by top management, the individual divisions, such as Chevrolet, Buick, etc., were free to choose how they would implement that strategy. Patterned after DuPont, GM found the decentralized multi-divisional structure to be extremely effective in allowing the maximum amount of freedom for product development. Return on investment was used as a financial control.

Research generally supports Chandler's proposition that structure follows strategy (as well as the reverse proposition from Chapter 5 that structure influences strategy).[7] Galbraith and Kazanjian propose that the early adoption of an appropriate structure can give a company a competitive advantage.[8] In support of this argument, research indicates that when companies that diversify into unrelated products change from a functional structure to a divisional structure, the companies' rates of return increase. Teece, in particular, found reorganization to generally contribute around 1.2 percentage points to a company's ROA.[9] Research also reveals that the fit between a business-level strategy and the amount of autonomy that corporate headquarters allows the business unit have an effect upon business unit performance.[10]

There is some evidence, however, that a change in strategy might not necessarily result in a corresponding change in structure if the corporation has very little competition. If a firm occupies a monopolistic position, with tariffs in its favor or close ties to a government, it can raise prices to cover internal administrative inefficiencies. This is an easier path for these firms to take than going through the pain of corporate reorganization.[11]

Although it is agreed that organizational structure must vary with different environmental conditions, which, in turn, affect an organization's strategy, there is no agreement about an optimal organizational design.[12] What was appropriate for DuPont and General Motors in the 1920s might not be appropriate today. Firms in the same industry do, however, tend to organize themselves in a similar fashion. For example, automobile manufacturers tend to emulate General Motors' decentralized division concept, whereas consumer-goods producers tend to emulate the brand-management concept pioneered by Procter & Gamble Company. The general conclusion seems to be that firms following similar strategies tend to adopt similar structures.[13] Nevertheless, Galbraith and Kazanjian propose more specific guidelines to better match structure to the strategy:

- Single-business and dominant-business corporations (companies operating primarily in one industry) should be organized in a functional structure. (See Fig. 5.1 in Chapter 5.)
- Related, diversified corporations should be organized into a divisional structure.
- Unrelated, diversified corporations should be organized into a conglomerate (or holding company) structure.[14]

Organic and Mechanistic Structure

Research by Burns and Stalker concluded that a "mechanistic" structure, with its emphasis on the centralization of decision-making and bureaucratic rules and procedures, appears to be well suited to organizations operating in a reasonably stable environment. In contrast, however, they found that successful firms operating in a constantly changing environment, such as those in the electronics and aerospace industries, find that a more "organic" structure, with the decentralization of decision making and flexible procedures, is more appropriate.[15] Studies by Lawrence and Lorsch support this conclusion. They found that successful firms in a reasonably stable environment, such as the container industry, coordinate activities primarily through fairly centralized corporate hierarchies, which place some reliance on direct contact by managers as well as on paperwork directives. Successful firms in more dynamic environments, such as the plastics industry, coordinate activities through integrative departments and permanent cross-functional teams as well as through the hierarchical contact and paperwork.[16] These differences in the use of structural integrating devices are detailed in Table 8.1. The container industry is the most stable; foods, intermediate; plastics, the least stable.

Strategic Business Units

A successful method for the structuring of a large and complex business corporation was developed in 1971 by GE. Referred to as *strategic business units* or SBUs, organizational groups composed of discrete, independent product-market segments served by the firm were identified and given primary responsibility and authority for management of their own functional areas. Recognizing that its structure of decentralized operating divisions was not working efficiently (massive sales growth was not being matched by profit growth), GE's top management decided to reorganize. They restruc-

TABLE 8.1

Integrating Mechanisms in Three Different Industries

	PLASTICS	FOOD	CONTAINER
Percent new products in last 20 years	35%	15%	0%
Integrating devices	Rules. Hierarchy. Goal setting. Direct contact. Teams at 3 levels. Integrating departments.	Rules. Hierarchy. Goal setting. Direct contact. Task forces. Integrators.	Rules. Hierarchy. Goal setting. Direct contact.
Percent integrators/ managers	22%	17%	0%

SOURCE: J. Galbraith, *Designing Complex Organizations*. Copyright © 1973 by Addison-Wesley Publishing Co., Inc. Table on page 111. Reprinted by permission.

tured nine groups and forty-eight divisions into forty-three strategic business units, many of which crossed traditional group, divisional, and profit center lines. For example, food-preparation appliances in three separate divisions were merged into a single SBU serving the "housewares" market.[17] The concept thus is to decentralize on the basis of strategic elements rather than on the basis of size or span of control. As mentioned in Chapter 5, an organization by SBUs is simply another version of the divisional structure.

General Electric was so pleased with the results of its experiment in organizational design that it reported " . . . the system helped GE improve its profitability, and return on investment has been rebuilt to a healthier level. In the last recession, General Electric's earnings dropped much less than the overall decline for the industry generally."[18] Following this lead, other firms such as General Foods, Mead Corporation, Eastman Kodak, Campbell Soup, Union Carbide, and Armco Steel, have implemented the strategic business unit concept. In introducing the concept, General Foods organized certain products on the basis of menu segments like breakfast food, beverage, main meal, dessert, and pet foods.

It is interesting that one of the reasons companies convert to SBUs is to reduce the number of units that top management must monitor. GE's top management found it easier to keep track of forty-eight SBUs than the previous 180 departments. Chief executive officers have limited time and a limited ability for their focus on strategic issues in each of the corporation's many units. This might be one reason why a survey of U.S. Fortune 1000 companies found the mean average number of SBUs in a firm to be thirty regardless of company size.[19]

Typically, once a corporation organizes itself around SBUs, it combines similar SBUs together under a group or sector (as mentioned in Chapter 5). In 1985, Eastman Kodak, for example, reorganized into seventeen business units under three operating groups. This type of reorganization on the basis of markets is a way a **horizontal strategy,** based upon competitive considerations that cut across divisional boundaries, is developed. The group or sector executive therefore is responsible for developing and implementing a horizontal strategy to coordinate the various goals and strategies of related business units. This strategy can help a firm compete with **multipoint competitors**—that is, firms that compete with each other not only in one business unit but in a number of related business units.[20] For example, Procter & Gamble, Kimberly-Clark, Scott Paper, and Johnson and Johnson compete with each other in varying combinations of consumer paper products, from disposable diapers to facial tissue. If (purely hypothetically), Johnson and Johnson had just developed a toilet tissue with which they chose to challenge Procter & Gamble's high-share Charmin brand in a particular district, it might charge a low price for its new brand to build sales quickly. Procter & Gamble might not choose to respond to this attack on its share by cutting prices on Charmin. Because of Charmin's high-market share, Procter & Gamble would lose significantly more sale dollars in a price war than would

Johnson and Johnson with Johnson and Johnson's initially low-share brand. To retaliate Procter & Gamble might thus challenge Johnson and Johnson's high-share baby shampoo with Procter & Gamble's own low-share brand of baby shampoo in a different district. Once Johnson and Johnson had perceived this response by Procter & Gamble, it might choose to stop challenging Procter & Gamble's Charmin brand of toilet tissue in one district so that Procter & Gamble would stop challenging Johnson and Johnson's baby shampoo in a different district.

Matrix Structure

As pointed out in Chapter 5, the matrix structure simultaneously combines the stability of the functional structure with the flexibility of the project organization. It is likely to be used within an SBU when the following three conditions exist:

- There is a need for cross-fertilization of ideas across projects or products.
- Resources are scarce.
- There is a need to improve the abilities to process information and to make decisions.[21]

The matrix structure is appealing but must be carefully managed. To the extent that the goals to be achieved are vague and the technology used is poorly understood, there is likely to be a continuous battle for power between project and functional managers.[22]

Organizing for Innovation

Those corporations that emphasize the latest technology as part of their missions, objectives, and strategies are finding that their structure tends to lag behind their technology. Keen suggests that there is a lag time before a new technology can be fully exploited because more change is expected than a system can handle. An infrastructure needs to be built within a corporation to deal with the implications and impact of rapid technological change.[23] Frohman makes a similar argument: "Many aspects of an organization— from technical talent to reward systems, from climate to equipment—affect the payoff a company will receive from its investments in technology."[24]

A large corporation that wishes to encourage innovation and creativity within its firm must choose a type of structure that will give the new business unit an appropriate amount of freedom with headquarters still having some degree of control. This statement is in agreement with the views of authorities in the area that the entrepreneurial project has to be organized separately from the existing, mainstream organization.[25] This separation is needed because the large, successful corporation tends to have a fairly bureaucratic corporate culture emphasizing efficiency, and thus tends to conflict with the type of loose, often free-wheeling culture that is needed to nurture innovation.

Burgelman proposes, as seen in Fig. 8.2, that the use of a particular organizational design should be determined by the **strategic importance** of the new business to the corporation and the **relatedness** of the unit's operations to those of the corporation.[26] The combination of these two factors results in nine organizational designs for corporate entrepreneurship (or *intrapreneurship,* as it is called by Pinchot).[27]

1. *Direct integration.* If the new business has high strategic importance and operational relatedness, it must be a part of the corporation's mainstream. Product "champions"—people who are respected by others in the corporation and who know how to work the system—are needed to manage these projects. When he was with Ford Motor Company, Lee Iacocca, for example, championed the Mustang.

2. *New product business department.* If the new business has high strategic importance and partial operational relatedness, it should be a separate department, organized around an entrepreneurial project in the division where skills and capabilities can be shared.

3. *Special business units.* If the new business has high strategic importance and low operational relatedness, it should be a special new business unit with specific objectives and time horizons. General Motor's new Saturn unit is one example of this approach.

4. *Micro new-ventures department.* If the new business has uncertain strategic importance and high operational relatedness, it is a "peripheral" project, which is likely to emerge in the operating divisions on a continuous basis. Each division thus has its own new ventures department. Xerox Corporation, for example, uses its SBUs to generate and nurture

FIGURE 8.2
Organizational Designs for Corporate Entrepreneurship

OPERATION RELATEDNESS		Very Important	Uncertain	Not Important
Unrelated		3. Special Business Units	6. Independent Business Units	9. Complete Spin-Off
Partly Related		2. New Product Business Department	5. New Venture Division	8. Contracting
Strongly Related		1. Direct Integration	4. Micro New Ventures Department	7. Nurturing and Contracting

STRATEGIC IMPORTANCE

Source: Reprinted from R. A. Burgelman, "Designs for Corporate Entrepreneurship in Established Firms." Copyright © 1984 by the Regents of the University of California. Reprinted/Condensed from the *California Management Review,* Vol. 26, No. 3, p. 161. By permission of The Regents.

new ideas. Small product-synthesis teams within each SBU test the feasibility of new ideas. Those concepts receiving a "go" decision are managed by an SBU product-delivery team, headed by a chief engineer, who take the prototype from development through manufacturing.[28]

5. *New venture division*. When the new business has uncertain strategic importance and is only partly related to present corporate operations, it belongs in a new venture division. It brings together projects that either exist in various parts of the corporation or can be acquired externally; sizable new businesses are built. R. J. Reynolds Industries, for example, established a separate company, R. J. Reynolds Development, to evaluate new business concepts with growth potential. The development company nurtures and develops businesses that might have the potential to become one of RJR's core businesses.[29]

6. *Independent business units*. Uncertain strategic importance coupled with no relationship to present corporate activities can make external arrangements attractive. Procter and Gamble took this approach when it established a separate unit to manage the uncertain, but potentially major business, created by the synthetic fat substitute, olestra, invented by the company. The company claimed that olestra as a food additive was free of calories and cholesterol, and that it had no serious side effects. While awaiting the Food and Drug Administration's approval for marketing the product, the new unit had to decide which uses of olestra it should reserve for its own products and which it should license.[30]

7. *Nurturing and contracting*. When an entrepreneurial proposal might not be important strategically to the corporation but is strongly related to present operations, top management might help the entrepreneurial unit "spin off" from the corporation. This allows a friendly competitor, instead of one of the corporation's major competitors, to capture a small niche. For example, Tektronix, a maker of oscilloscopes, formed a unit to act as an in-house venture capitalist to its own employees; this relationship allowed the corporation to swap the parent company's operational knowledge for equity in the new company. The arrangement is intended to provide Tektronix with a better return on its R&D expenditures and to help it maintain ties with innovative employees who want to run their own companies.[31]

8. *Contracting*. As the required capabilities and skills of the new business are less related to those of the corporation, the parent corporation may spin off the strategically unimportant unit yet keep some relationship through a contractual arrangement with the new firm. The connection is useful in case the new firm eventually develops something of value to the corporation.

9. *Complete spin off*. If both the strategic importance and the operational relatedness of the new business are negligible, the corporation is likely to completely sell off the business to another firm or to the present employees in some form of ESOP (Employee Stock Ownership Plan). Or the corporation can sell off the unit through a leveraged buyout (executives of the unit buy the unit from the parent company with

money from a third source, to be repaid out of the unit's anticipated earnings). This is what happened to Lifeline Technology, originally a part of Allied Corporation. Lifeline, an inventory management system, had been developed in Allied's new ventures unit (cell #5 in Fig. 8.2). After Allied's merger with Signal Companies in 1985, new ventures that didn't fit into the company's existing businesses were refused further funding. Noting that Lifeline lacked any strategic fit with Allied, Stephen Fields, Lifeline's manager, quit Allied and together with six partners from Allied formed Lifeline Technology to market the product.[32]

Organizing for innovation has become especially important for those corporations in "high tech" industries that wish to recapture the entrepreneurial spirit but are really too large to do so. IBM formed "independent business units," each with its own mini-board of directors. One such IBU produced the company's successful personal computer. IBM spared the personal-computer unit many of the company's usual controls and formalized reporting procedures. Because of this freedom, the original PC moved from preliminary planning to introduction in thirteen months, compared to the years of effort needed for the development of most IBM products. Even Levi Strauss and Company, the clothing manufacturer, is encouraging "in-house entrepreneurs" by financing new fashion-apparel businesses.

Rather than attempting such in-house innovation, a number of corporations are investing venture capital in existing small firms. Wang, for example, purchased a minority interest in InteCom, Inc., a maker of telephone switching equipment. General Motors, Procter and Gamble, and six other companies did the same by buying $20 million of equity in a small artificial-intelligence company called Teknowledge. GM hoped that Teknowledge's expert systems-software would help it to design cars and to prepare factory schedules. Increasingly referred to as *strategic partnerships,* these ventures are similar to Burgelman's nurturing and contracting design (cell #7 in Fig. 8.2) and can be viewed as a form of quasi-vertical integration as well.[33] In such arrangements, it often becomes difficult to tell where one firm begins and the other leaves off!

Stages of Corporate Development

A key proposition of Chandler's was that successful corporations tend to follow a pattern of structural development as they grow and expand. Further work by Thain, Scott, and Tuason specifically delineates three distinct structural stages.[34]

Stage I is typified by the entrepreneur, who founds the corporation to promote an idea (product or service). The entrepreneur tends to make all the important decisions personally, and is involved in every detail and phase of the organization. The Stage I corporation has a structure allowing the entrepreneur to directly supervise the activities of every employee (see Fig.

5.1). The corporation in Stage I is thus characterized by little formal structure. Planning is usually short range or "fire-fighting" in nature. The typical managerial functions of planning, organizing, directing, staffing, and controlling are usually performed to a very limited degree, if at all. The greatest strengths of a Stage I corporation are its flexibility and dynamism. The drive of the entrepreneur energizes the corporation in its struggle for growth. Its greatest weakness is its extreme reliance on the entrepreneur to decide general strategies as well as detailed procedures. If the entrepreneur falters, the corporation usually flounders.

Stage I described Polaroid Corporation, whose founder Dr. Edwin Land championed *Polarvision,* a financially disastrous instant-movie system, while ignoring industrial and commercial uses. Growing concern by stockholders over declines in sales and net income resulted in Dr. Land's resignation from his top management position in 1980 and from the board of directors in 1982. In 1983, analysts reported that Polaroid was in the throes of a "mid-life crisis," worrying about its mortality and the loss of Dr. Land's inspiring vision.[35] Polaroid Corporation was, in effect, a Stage II corporation being managed by Dr. Land as if it still were a Stage I corporation.

This is an example of what Greiner calls the *crisis of leadership,* which an organization must solve before it can move into the second stage of growth.[36]

At **Stage II,** the entrepreneur is replaced by a team of managers with functional specializations (see Fig. 5.1). The transition to this state requires a substantial managerial style change for the chief officer of the corporation, especially if the chief officer was the Stage I entrepreneur. Otherwise, having additional staff members yields no benefits to the corporation. At this juncture, the corporate strategy favors protectivism through dominance of the industry, often through vertical or horizontal integration. The great strength of a Stage II corporation lies in its concentration and specialization in one industry. Its great weakness is that all of its eggs are in one basket.

McDonald's, the world's largest food service company, is a Stage II corporation that is concentrating on fast food. Fred Turner, Chairman of the Board, commented in 1984 on the company's specialization in one industry:

> My view is that we can maintain a growth rate in the teens through this decade. And if you believe that, it makes the question of diversification beside the point.[37]

By concentrating on one industry as long as that industry remains attractive, a Stage II company can be very successful. Once a functionally structured firm diversifies into other products in other industries, however, the advantages of the functional structure break down. A crisis of autonomy can develop, in which people managing diversified product lines need more decision-making freedom than top management is willing to delegate to them.

The **Stage III** corporation focuses on managing diverse product lines in numerous industries; it decentralizes decision-making authority. These corporations grow by diversifying their product lines and expanding to cover wider geographical areas. These corporations move to a divisional structure with a central headquarters. Headquarters attempts to coordinate the activities of its operating divisions through performance- and results-oriented control and reporting systems, and by the stressing of corporate planning techniques. The divisions are not tightly controlled, but are held responsible for their own performance results. Therefore, to be effective, the corporation has to have a decentralized decision process. The greatest strength of a Stage III corporation is its almost unlimited resources. Its most significant weakness is that it is usually so large and complex that it tends to become relatively inflexible. General Electric, DuPont, and General Motors are Stage III corporations.

These descriptions of the three stages of corporate development are supported by research.[38] The differences among the stages are specified in more detail by Thain in Table 8.2.

In his study, Chandler noted that the empire builder was rarely the person who created the new structure to fit the new strategy, and that, as a result, the transition from one stage to another is often a painful one. This was true of General Motors Corporation under the management of William Durant, Ford Motor Company under its founder Henry Ford, Polaroid Corporation under Edwin Land, and Apple Computer under its founder Steven Jobs. (See Illustrative Example 8.2.) This difficulty in moving to a new stage is compounded by the founder's tendency to maneuver around the need to delegate by carefully hiring, training, and grooming his/her own team of managers. These managers eventually hold the same beliefs and attitudes as the founder who hired them. In this way a corporation's culture is formed and perpetuated. The team tends to maintain the founder's influence throughout the organization long after the founder is gone.[39] The successors to Ray Kroc, the founder of McDonald's Corporation, promised not to change the fast-food company and to stay true to the founder's vision. This faithfulness gave the hamburger chain a definite strength, but also created a significant roadblock to innovation and change. For example, Mr. Kroc's quick-cooking systems were not geared to the individual service increasingly desired by consumers. More importantly, Kroc's strong emphasis on the continuous expansion of McDonald's hamburger-and-french-fries business kept top management from seriously considering diversification alternatives—even 10 years after Kroc's death! Thain, in Table 8.3, summarizes the internal and external blocks to movement from one stage to another.

Galbraith and Kazanjian propose the existence of a **Stage IV** corporation based on the *matrix* structure. They argue that the matrix is the essential form for diversified multinational corporations.[40] (Refer to Chapter 10 for additional information on multinational corporations.) Others suggest that

TABLE 8.2

Key Factors in Top Management Process in Stage I, II, and III Companies

Function	STAGE I	STAGE II	STAGE III
1. Size-up: Major problems	Survival and growth dealing with short-term operating problems.	Growth, rationalization, and expansion of resources, providing for adequate attention to product problems.	Trusteeship in management and investment and control of large, increasing, and diversified resource. Also, important to diagnose and take action on problems at division level.
2. Objectives	Personal and subjective.	Profits and meeting functionally oriented budgets and performance targets.	ROI, profits, earnings per share.
3. Strategy	Implicit and personal; exploitation of immediate opportunities seen by owner-manager.	Functionally oriented moves restricted to "one product" scope; exploitation of one basic product or service field.	Growth and product diversification; exploitation of general business opportunities.
4. Organization: Major characteristic of structure	One unit, "one-man show."	One-unit, functionally specialized group.	Multiunit general staff office and decentralized operating divisions.
5. (a) Measurement and control	Personal, subjective control based on simple accounting system and daily communication and observation.	Control grows beyond one man; assessment of functional operations necessary; structured control systems evolve.	Complex formal system geared to comparative assessment of performance measures, indicating problems and opportunities and assessing management ability of division managers.
5. (b) Key performance indicators	Personal criteria, relationships with owner, operating efficiency, ability to solve operating problems.	Functional and internal criteria such as sales, performance compared to budget, size of empire, status in group, personal relationships, etc.	More impersonal application of comparisons such as profits, ROI, P/E ratio, sales, market share, productivity, product leadership, personnel development, employee attitudes, public responsibility.

(Continued)

TABLE 8.2 (Continued)

Function	STAGE I	STAGE II	STAGE III
6. Reward-punishment system	Informal, personal, subjective; used to maintain control and divide small pool of resources to provide personal incentives for key performers.	More structured; usually based to a greater extent on agreed policies as opposed to personal opinion and relationships.	Allotment by "due process" of a wide variety of different rewards and punishments on a formal and systematic basis. Company-wide policies usually apply to many different classes of managers and workers with few major exceptions for individual cases.

SOURCE: D. H. Thain, "Stages of Corporate Development," *Business Quarterly* (Winter 1969), p. 37. Copyright © 1969 by *Business Quarterly*. Reprinted by permission.

ILLUSTRATIVE EXAMPLE 8.2

Matching the Manager to the Appropriate Strategy and Stage of Corporate Development

What do Apple Computer, Wang Laboratories, Control Data Corporation, Ashton-Tate, Inc. and Lotus Development Corporation have in common—other than heavy involvement in computers and computer software? Answer: All are successful corporations that have recently made or are in the process of making a transition from an entrepreneur-managed Stage I small business to a professionally managed, Stage II corporation. In the case of **Apple Computer,** Chairman and co-founder Steven P. Jobs resigned from the company in 1985 after several years of management turmoil. After only eight years of existence, the two-man start-up had become a $2 billion company with 5,000 employees. The company grew either because of or in spite of spur-of-the-moment decisions by founders Jobs and Stephen Wozniak and fights by staff over competing projects. John Sculley, Jobs' handpicked successor as Chairman at Apple, restructured the company and introduced rules, strict financial controls, and product-development deadlines to go with his strategy of selling Apple Computers to business people. In selecting Sculley one of its "business people of the year," *Fortune* stated:

> What makes him one of the top business people of the year is his success in harnessing Apple's famous combination of blue-jeaned idealism and arrogance—and turning the company, once widely dismissed as a glorified toymaker, into a highly profitable producer of serious computers for the desktops of corporate America.

In the first two months after taking office as President of **Wang Laboratories, Inc.,** in 1986, Frederick Wang, son of founder An Wang, reorganized the company's marketing operation and began implementing a retrenchment strategy. The company had been faltering for two years while the founder had been unable to delegate operating authority for the running of his creation. Even though Wang Laboratories had excellent products, its lack of marketing skills was crippling its growth. "Wang couldn't sell life jackets on the Titanic," said Vincent Flanders, Associate Editor of *Access 87,* an independent magazine for Wang cus-

tomers, in comments on the company's marketing weakness under its founder.

By the time William C. Norris, the founder and Chief Executive Officer of **Control Data Corporation,** resigned from the company in 1986, there was a rising chorus of critics complaining that Norris had stayed too long. Through the late 1960s and 1970s, Control Data had been the world's leading maker of computer peripherals, like disk drives and other data-storage devices. Increased competition during the 1980s cut into the company's sales and profits—to the point that the company was being forced in 1985 to sell some of its businesses to raise cash. Just before Norris resigned, a banker involved with the debt negotiations stated, "They really need outside people—especially in the financial area. There's a sense that this management isn't prepared for the situation."

By the time Edward M. Esber, Jr., became CEO of **Ashton-Tate, Inc.,** in late 1984, most industry analysts had categorized the company as just another one-product software maker that couldn't evolve beyond its beginnings. Under its founder, George Tate, and his successor, David Cole, the company had made dBASE I, II, and III the world's largest selling database management program. Unfortunately, top management had failed to create a stable, well organized corporation. As the new CEO, Esber replaced Cole's charismatic and entrepreneurial one-man rule with a lower-key participatory approach. He also introduced formalized planning, budgeting, and product development procedures. Meetings about new products, once held at the chairman's whim, now took place every other week. Although turnover slowed in the company's managerial positions, the changes did cause the resignation in 1986 of Wayne Ratliff, the programmer who single-handedly wrote dBASE I, II, and most of III. Ratliff said his "distaste" for the corporate environment had been building for more than a year. "Corporations are more interested in keeping the corporation alive than generating quality products," com-

(Continued)

ILLUSTRATIVE EXAMPLE 8.2 (Continued)

mented Ratliff. "Ultimately, I like to sit back and work—write code. But the corporation is like a corpse you have to drag around." In response to the changes at Ashton-Tate and the departure of Ratliff, industry analyst William Shattuck concluded, "Historically, Wayne was a real critical force in the company, but at this stage of the game, given that you're dealing with a much more mature and larger company, the product-development effort is a more controlled, systematic process."

On July 10, 1986, Mitchell "Mitch" Kapor, founder and Chairman of **Lotus Development Corporation,** resigned unexpectedly and handed the chairman's position to Jim Manzi, a marketing-oriented consultant whom Kapor had hired earlier from McKinsey and Company to help manage the growing corporation. Kapor, widely regarded as a software "guru," had developed Lotus 1-2-3, the highly successful spreadsheet program—a product that accounted for more than 70% of the company's operating profits. Kapor had been turning over management responsibilities to

Manzi for the past year, a trend that was capped by Manzi's assumption of the chief executive office in April 1986. Commenting on his resignation, Kapor stated that he had been rethinking his role at Lotus for several months. He said that leaving a large company "is a natural evolution for founders and entrepreneurs." Five years ago, he added, "we were a small band setting out on a great adventure. Now we have 1,200 employees and two million customers. It's a radically different situation."

SOURCES: B. O'Reilly, "Growing Apple Anew For the Business Market," *Fortune* (January 4, 1988), pp. 36–37. A. Beam, "Strong Medicine From the Son of Doctor Wang," *Business Week* (January 19, 1987), p. 33. R. Gibson, "Control Data Betting Smaller Is Better," *Wall Street Journal* (December 3, 1985), p. 6. S. Ticer, "The Dark Horse Who Has Ashton-Tate Galloping Again," *Business Week* (February 10, 1986), pp. 89–92. G. Spector, "Wayne Ratliff, Writer of dBASE, Quits Ashton-Tate," *PC Week* (March 11, 1986), pp. 176 and 178. W. M. Bulkeley, "Kapor, Founder of Lotus Development, Resigns as Chairman of Software Firm," *Wall Street Journal* (July 11, 1986), p. 2.

the further development of corporations will be based on *networks* instead of hierarchies.[41] In such companies, span of communication using information technology can replace span of control. Instead of building large, but cumbersome vertically integrated companies, a number of firms are cultivating strategic relationships with outside vendors, that will give them the flexibility and adaptability they need for success. In arguing for the emergence of the **network organization,** Drake states:

> Organizations will increasingly be seen as flexible networks, expanding and cutting back in response to need. By using subcontractors, a company gains the freedom to cut off contracts or change vendors if the service level doesn't make the grade. Staff can be added or dropped quickly, increasing the firm's flexibility.[42]

The increasing use of joint ventures and quasi-vertical integration strategies, coupled with the popularity of just-in-time delivery using captive company suppliers, supports the proposal of the network organization as a fourth stage of corporate development.

Organizational Life-Cycle

Another approach to a better understanding of the development of corporations is that of the organizational "life cycle."[43] Instead of considering

TABLE 8.3
Blocks to Development

A) INTERNAL BLOCKS STAGE I TO II	STAGE II TO III
Lack of ambition and drive.	Unwillingness to take the risks involved.
Personal reasons of owner-manager for avoiding change in status quo.	Management resistance to change for a variety of reasons including old age, aversion to risk taking, desire to protect personal empires, etc.
Lack of operating efficiency.	
Lack of quantity and quality of operating personnel.	
Lack of resources such as borrowing power, plant and equipment, salesmen, etc.	Personal reasons among managers for defending the status quo.
	Lack of control system related to appraisal of investment of decentralized operations.
Product problems and weaknesses.	Lack of budgetary control ability.
Lack of planning and organizational ability.	Organizational inflexibility.
	Lack of management vision to see opportunities for expansion.
	Lack of management development, i.e., not enough managers to handle expansion.
	Management turnover and loss of promising young managers.
	Lack of ability to formulate and implement strategy that makes company relevant to changing conditions.
	Refusal to delegate power and authority for diversification.

B) EXTERNAL BLOCKS STAGE I TO II	STAGE II TO III
Unfavorable economic conditions.	Unfavorable economic, political, technological, and social conditions and/or trends.
Lack of market growth.	
Tight money or lack of an underwriter who will assist the company "to go public."	Lack of access to financial or management resources.
Labor shortages in quality and quantity.	Overly conservative accountants, lawyers, investment bankers, etc.
Technological obsolescence of product.	Lack of domestic markets necessary to support large diversified corporation.
	"The conservative mentality," e.g., cultural contentment with the status quo and lack of desire to grow and develop.

SOURCE: D. H. Thain, "Stages of Corporate Development," *Business Quarterly* (Winter 1969), pp. 43–44. Copyright © 1969 by *Business Quarterly*. Reprinted by permission.

stages in terms of structure, this approach places the primary emphasis on the dominant issue facing the corporation. The specific organizational structure, therefore, becomes a secondary concern. These stages are *Birth* (Stage I), *Growth* (Stage II), *Maturity* (Stage III), *Decline* (Stage IV), and *Death* (Stage V). The impact of these stages on corporate strategy and structure is summarized in Table 8.4. Note that the first three stages of the organizational life cycle are basically the same as the three stages of corporate development mentioned previously. The only significant difference is the addition of the decline and death stages to complete the cycle.

Miller and Friesen place a *Revival* phase between Maturity and Decline; this reflects how the corporation's life cycle can be extended by innovations in a manner similar to the extension of a product's life-cycle. Nevertheless, revival is not included here as a separate stage because it can occur anytime during a corporation's maturity stage, when a new growth strategy is implemented, or during its decline stage, when a turnaround strategy is being followed.

The Stage IV firm became widespread in the western world during the 1970s and 1980s as many corporations in basic industries such as steel and automobiles seemed to lose their vitality and competitiveness. Most of the product lines of a Stage IV firm are at the mature or declining phase of their product life-cycle. Sales are stagnant and actually declining if adjusted for inflation. An emphasis on company-wide cost-cutting further erodes future competitiveness. The major objective changes from stability to survival. Retrenchment coupled with pleas for government assistance is the only feasible strategy. Chrysler Corporation was a good example of a Stage IV corporation in the early 1980s.

Unless a corporation is able to resolve the critical issues facing it in Stage IV (as Chrysler was able to do), it is likely to move into Stage V, corporate death. This is what happened in the mid-1980s to AM International (pre-

TABLE 8.4
Organizational Life Cycle

	STAGE I	STAGE II	STAGE III	STAGE IV	STAGE V
Dominant issue	Birth	Growth	Maturity	Decline	Death
Popular strategies	Concentration in a niche	Horizontal and vertical integration	Concentric and conglomerate diversification	Profit strategy followed by retrenchment	Liquidation or bankruptcy
Likely structure	Entrepreneur-dominated	Functional management emphasized	Decentralization into profit or investment centers	Structural surgery	Dismemberment of structure

viously known as the Addressograph-Multigraph Corporation), Baldwin-United, and Osborne Computers, as well as many other firms. The corporation is forced into bankruptcy. As in the cases of Rolls Royce and Penn Central, both of which went bankrupt in the 1970s, a corporation might nevertheless rise like a phoenix from its own ashes and live again. The company may be reorganized or liquidated, depending upon the individual circumstances. In some liquidations, the corporation's name is purchased, and the purchasing corporation places that name on some or all of its products. For example, Wordtronix, a maker of stand-alone word processors, acquired the Remington Rand trademark, even though Remington Rand no longer made typewriters. Top management planned to change the Wordtronix name to Remington Rand to give its machines some name recognition in the marketplace.

It is important to realize that not all corporations will move through these five stages in order. Some corporations, for example, might never move past Stage II. Others, like General Motors, might go directly from Stage I to Stage III. A large number will go from Stage I into Stages IV and V. Ford, for example, was unable to move from Stage I into Stage II as long as Henry Ford, I was in command. Its inability to realign itself no doubt contributed to its movement into Stage IV just before World War II. After the war, Henry Ford, II's turnaround strategy successfully restructured the corporation as a Stage II firm. With the death of Henry Ford, II, and the ascent of Donald Peterson to the chairman's position, Ford Motor Company might be ready to diversify and move into a mature Stage III configuration during the 1990s with more decentralized decision making.

Staffing

The implementation of new strategy and policies often calls for a different utilization of personnel. If growth strategies are to be implemented, new people need to be hired and trained. Experienced people with the necessary skills need to be found for promotion into newly created managerial positions. For example, if a firm has decided to integrate forward by opening its own retail outlets, one key concern is the ability of the corporation to find, hire, and train store managers. If a corporation adopts a retrenchment strategy, however, a large number of people may need to be laid off or fired; and top management, as well as the divisional managers, need to specify criteria used in the making of these personnel decisions. Should employees be fired on the basis of low seniority or on the basis of poor performance? Sometimes corporations find it easier to close an entire division than to choose which individuals to fire.

A change in competitive strategy can also have a significant impact on staffing needs. For example, J. C. Penney decided in 1986 to decentralize its purchasing down to the store level so that store managers would have greater opportunity to buy the merchandise most suited to regional needs.

Although it seemed that this strategy would help Penney to better compete with local stores, top management was concerned with implementation. Instead of a corporate buyer purchasing entire lines of merchandise and forcing all stores to carry them, the buyer now presented the items on Penney's satellite television network, and gave local buyers the opportunity to choose all the lines, some of the lines, or none of the lines. Penney's top management and suppliers feared that some local buyers weren't experienced enough to spot potentially popular fashion trends. The job of the corporate buyer had also become riskier. "Their job is going to be selling merchandise on television," said a Penney official. "You may buy good products but might not be able to sell. If the person showing the merchandise turns you off, you as a buyer in Omaha may not go for the line." Although Penney officials denied that a lack of TV skills would cost corporate buyers their jobs, the company considered using video screen-tests to help select future buyers.[44]

Some authorities have suggested that the type of general manager needed to effectively implement a new divisional, corporate, or SBU strategy depends upon the desired strategic direction of that business unit.[45] Illustrative Example 8.3 tells how this approach was followed by the board of AM International in their selecting the corporation's chief executive officer.

Depending on the situation of a specific division, as determined by the GE Business Screen Matrix (Fig. 6.3), the "best" or most appropriate division manager might need to have a specific mix of skills and experiences. Some of these suggested "types" are depicted in Fig. 8.3.

One research study of business executives found that strategic business units with a "build" strategy as compared to SBUs with a "harvest" strategy tend to be headed by managers with a great willingness to take risks and a high tolerance for ambiguity.[46] Another study also found that managers with a particular mix of behaviors, skills, and personality factors tend to be linked with one type of strategy and those with a different mix, to a different type of strategy. For example, SBUs with a stability strategy tend to be run by a manager with a conservative style, a production or engineering background, and experience with controlling budgets, capital expenditures, inventories, and standardization procedures.[47] In summary, there is growing support for matching executive "types" with the dominant strategic direction of a business unit. Unfortunately, there is little available to help top management or the board select the most appropriate manager when a corporation or SBU does not have a specific strategy formulated for that manager to implement. In this instance, the board of directors has no choice; they must search for a person with a proven capability to exercise initiative and leadership in the industry, and hope that the person selected can lead the board and other managers in formulating and implementing a strategy.[48]

Research into the value of selecting a CEO from outside the company as compared to promoting someone already with the company has mixed conclusions. Some studies report that the top performing companies hire

ILLUSTRATIVE EXAMPLE 8.3

AM International Matches the Manager to the Strategy

The board of directors of AM International followed the theory that the general manager should match the firm's desired strategy, when it both hired and fired Joe B. Freeman as the corporation's chief executive officer. Hired originally when the company filed for Chapter 11 bankruptcy in April 1982, Freeman worked hard to turn the firm around. He concentrated on cutting costs, boosting sales, and soothing both creditors and employees. By January 1984, the corporation was beginning to show a profit—and Joe B. Freeman was fired by the board. Looking back on the experience, Freeman admitted that some of the problem had been with his analytically oriented accounting background:

"The company had reached a new phase. My skills had been successful in bringing it to this phase but the board wanted a person with a different set of skills to lead it. . . . [The board wanted] an orientation toward business strategy and people skills. . . . I chose to devote most of my time to managing the company, to working with the creditors, and didn't spend much time on the image side with shareholders and directors."

SOURCE: R. Johnson, "AM International's Ex-Chief Freeman Tells How His Success Got Him Fired," *Wall Street Journal* (August 27, 1984), p. 21.

their CEOs from within; however, other studies report that the percentage of CEOs hired from outside the corporation is higher for prosperous firms than for firms in decline. Another study reports that the incidence of outsiders becoming CEOs of failing (bankrupt) firms is higher than that of solvent firms.[49] Obviously, more research is needed before any clear conclusion can be reached.

There are a number of ways that a continuous development of people for important managerial positions can be ensured. One approach is to establish a sound **performance appraisal system** to identify good performers with managerial potential. A survey of thirty-four corporate planners and human resource executives from twenty-four large U.S. corporations revealed that approximately 80% made some attempt to identify managers' talents and behavioral tendencies, so that they could find a manager with a likely fit to a given competitive strategy.[50] A number of large organizations are using **assessment centers** to evaluate a person's suitability for a management position. Popularized by AT&T in the mid-1950s, corporations such as Standard Oil of Ohio and GE now use them. Because each is specifically tailored to its corporation, these assessment centers are unique. They use special interviews, management games, in-basket exercises, leaderless group discussions, case analyses, decision-making exercises, and oral presentations to assess the potential of employees for higher-level positions. People's promotions into specific positions are based on their performances in the assessment center. Many assessment centers have proved to be highly predictive of subsequent managerial performance.[51]

FIGURE 8.3
The Types of General Managers Needed to Strategically Manage
Different Types of Businesses

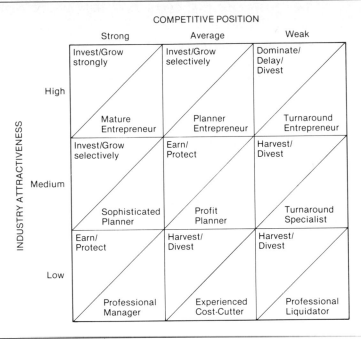

Source: Adapted from C. W. Hofer and M. J. Davoust, *Successful Strategic Management* (Chicago: A. T. Kearney, Inc., 1977), pp. 45 and 82. Used by permission.

The implementation of strategy should be concerned not only with the selection of strategic managers, but also with the selection of the appropriate mix of professional, skilled, and unskilled labor. At IBM, for example, top management decided in 1984 to emphasize software development in its reach for corporate growth objectives. Key divisions were then directed to expand their programming staffs by 20% per year for the next ten years.[52] Research reveals that corporations that pursue related diversification strategies through internal development make greater use of interdivisional transfers of people than do companies that grow through unrelated acquisitions. Apparently, the companies that grow internally attempt to transfer important knowledge and skills throughout the corporation, so that some sort of managerial synergy is achieved.[53]

Directing

To effectively implement a new strategy, top management must delegate appropriate authority and responsibility to the operational managers. People should be motivated to act in desired ways. Further, the actions must be coordinated so that they result in effective performance. Managers should be stimulated to find creative solutions to implementation problems without getting bogged down in conflict. When the proper people have been placed in the proper positions, a corporation needs a system to direct them toward the proper implementation of corporate, business, and functional strategies. Sometimes this is informally accomplished through a strong corporate culture, with well-accepted norms and values regarding teamwork and commitment to the company's objectives and strategies. New employees are "socialized" into the culture through a series of planned training experiences.

If the current culture does not fit with the formulated strategy, however, Shrivastava and Guth propose a five-step process by which the culture can be changed:

1. Identify mismatches between the culture and the strategy content.

2. Identify mismatches between the culture and the strategic decision processes.

3. Unfreeze cultural elements by informing employees of the problems.

4. Change the cultural elements by changing organizational structure, key personnel, training programs, and administrative systems and procedures.

5. Institutionalize the new culture through the constant support of key managers and the reward system.[54]

Activities can also be directed toward accomplishing strategic goals through programs such as Management By Objectives (MBO) and incentive management.

Management By Objectives

Management By Objectives (MBO) is one organization-wide approach to help assure purposeful action toward desired objectives. MBO links organizational objectives and the behavior of individuals. Because it is a system that links plans with performance, it is a powerful implementation technique.

Although there is some disagreement about the purpose of MBO, most authorities agree that this approach involves (1) establishing and communicating organizational objectives, (2) setting individual objectives that help implement organizational ones, and (3) periodically reviewing performance as it relates to the objectives.[55] MBO provides an opportunity for the corporation to connect the objectives of people at each level to those at the next higher level: "If carried out logically and ideally, the goals at each level would be contributing most directly toward overall organizational objectives. . . . MBO provides a potential method of integrating the physical, financial, and human resource plans of the organization to the goals that an individual is expected to achieve."[56] MBO, therefore, acts to tie together corporate, business, and functional objectives as well as the strategies developed to achieve them. This tying together forms a hierarchy of objectives similar to the hierarchy of strategy discussed in Chapter 1. The MBO process is depicted in Fig. 8.4.

Research conclusions on the effectiveness of corporate MBO programs is mixed, but tends to support the belief that MBO should result in higher levels of performance than would be achieved by other approaches that do not include performance goals, relevant feedback, and joint supervisor/subordinate goal setting.[57] Galbraith and Kazanjian point out that the existence of an MBO program at Dow-Corning permits its matrix structure (as discussed in Chapter 5) to function effectively: "Because people work against goals and problems, rather than against each other, they have less need for hierarchy and tie-breaking."[58] At Dow-Corning, the agreed-upon objectives are used to help reach consensus and thus reduce the potential for the conflict inherent in a matrix-style organization.

FIGURE 8.4
The Process of Management by Objectives

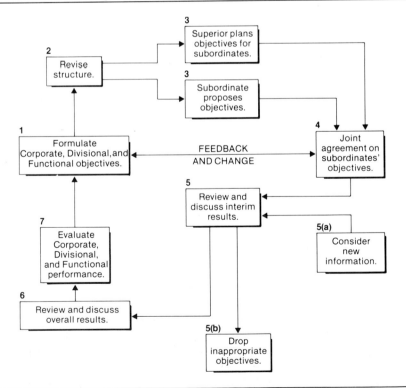

Incentive Management

To ensure that there is a congruence between the needs of the corporation as a whole and the needs of the employees as individuals, managers should develop an incentive system that rewards desired performance. Research confirms the conventional wisdom that when pay is tied to performance, it motivates higher productivity, and strongly affects both absenteeism and work quality.[59] Corporations have, therefore, developed various types of incentives for executives that range from stock options to cash bonuses. All these incentive plans should be linked in some way to corporate and divisional strategy. Ansoff, an authority on strategic management, proposes that one of the key means of changing corporate culture is by changing formal and informal rewards and incentives.[60] Performance appraisal and incentive systems are discussed in more detail under "Evaluation and Control," Chapter 9.

SUMMARY AND CONCLUSION

This chapter explains the implementation of strategy in terms of (1) *who* the operational managers are who must carry out strategic plans, (2) *what* they must do in order to implement strategy, and (3) *how* they should go about their activities. Vice-presidents of functional areas and directors of divisions or SBUs work with their subordinates to put together large-scale implementation plans. These plans include *programs, budgets,* and *procedures* and become more detailed as they move down the corporate "chain of command."

Strategy is implemented by management through planning, organizing, staffing, and directing activities.

Planning results in fairly detailed programs, budgets, and procedures.

Organizing deals with the design of an appropriate structure for the corporation. Research generally supports Chandler's proposal that changes in corporate strategy tend to lead to changes in organizational structure. The growing use of strategic business units, matrix structures, and entrepreneurial units reflects a need for more flexible structures to manage increasingly diversified corporations. Not only should a firm work to make its structure congruent with its strategy, it should also be aware that there is an organizational life-cycle composed of stages of corporate development through which a corporation is likely to move.

Staffing focuses on the finding and developing of appropriate people for key positions. Without capable and committed managers and staff, strategy can never be implemented satisfactorily. To survey and develop candidates, performance appraisal systems and assessment centers are used by a number of large corporations.

Directing deals with organization-wide approaches that direct operational managers and employees to effect the implementation of corporate, business, and functional strategies. One such approach is Management By Objectives (MBO), which links organizational objectives and the behavior of operational managers. Its ability to tie planning with performance makes it a powerful implementation technique. The proper use of incentives, when integrated with a change in corporate culture or with a goal-centered approach such as MBO, is another method by which effort is directed toward the desired results.

DISCUSSION QUESTIONS

1. Japanese corporations typically involve many more organizational levels and people in the development of implementation plans than do U.S. corporations. Is this appropriate? Why or why not?

2. To what extent should top management be involved in strategy implementation?

3. Does structure follow strategy or does strategy follow stucture? Why?

4. What can be done to encourage innovation in large corporations?

5. Should a corporation's selection of a certain type of person to be a general manager of a division depend on the strategic situation of that particular division? Why or why not?

6. Suppose a successful entrepreneur is creating problems for the corporation by continuing a one-person rule long after it is appropriate. If the founder owns a majority of the stock in the company, what could concerned people (employees, other stockholders, board members, other managers, customers, creditors, among others) do about this Stage I entrepreneur mismanaging his/her own Stage II corporation?

7. Do you agree with the way CSX structured itself for 1986, as described in the Integrative Case at the end of this chapter? What are the pros and cons of the 1986 organization structure depicted in Figure 8.5?

8. Even with the 1986 restructuring as described in the Integrative Case, what implementation problems did CSX still have to overcome? What could have been done to resolve them?

NOTES

1. P. Houston, "Northwest's Merger Has Passengers Fuming," *Business Week* (November 24, 1986), p. 64.

2. L. D. Alexander, "Successfully Implementing Strategic Decisions," *Long Range Planning* (June 1985), p. 92.

3. J. R. Galbraith and R. K. Kazanjian, *Strategy Implementation: Structure, Systems, and Process,* 2nd ed. (St. Paul: West Publishing Co., 1986), p. 108.

P. Miesing, "Integrating Planning with Management," *Long Range Planning* (October 1984), pp. 118–124.

4. A. D. Chandler, *Strategy and Structure* (Cambridge, Mass.: MIT Press, 1962), p. 14.

5. O. E. Williamson, "The Multidivisional Structure," in *Markets and Hierarchies* (The Free Press, 1975), as reprinted in *Organizational Economics* by J. B. Barney and W. G. Ouchi (eds.) (San Francisco, Jossey-Bass, 1986), pp. 163–187.

6. A. P. Sloan, Jr., *My Years with General Motors* (Garden City, N.Y.: Doubleday & Company, 1964).

7. D. Miller, "Strategy Making and Structure: Analysis and Implications for Performance," *Academy of Management Journal* (March 1987), pp. 7–32.

Galbraith and Kazanjian, pp. 13–27.

P. Lorange, *Implementation of Strategic Planning* (Englewood Cliffs, N.J.: Prentice-Hall, 1982), p. 109.

L. G. Hrebiniak and W. F. Joyce, *Implementing Strategy* (New York: Macmillan, 1984), pp. 65–92.

8. Galbraith and Kazanjian, p. 45.

9. R. E. Hoskisson, "Multidivisional Structure and Performance: The Contingency of Diversification Strategy," *Academy of Management Journal* (December 1987), pp. 625–644.

R. E. Hoskisson and C. S. Galbraith, "The Effect of Quantum Versus Incremental M-form Reorganization on Performance: A Time-Series Exploration of Intervention Dynamics," *Journal of Management* (Fall-Winter 1985), pp. 55–70.

D. J. Teece, "Internal Organization and Economic Performance: An Empirical Analysis of the Profitability of Principal Firms," *The Journal of Industrial Economics,* Vol. 30 (1981), pp. 173–199.

10. R. E. White, "Generic Business Strategies, Organizational Context and Performance: An Empirical Investigation," *Strategic Management Journal* (May-June 1986), pp. 217–231.

A. K. Gupta, "SBU Strategies, Corporate–SBU Relations, and SBU Effectiveness in Strategy Implementation," *Academy of Management Journal* (September 1987), pp. 477–500.

11. Galbraith and Kazanjian, p. 24.

12. D. R. Dalton, W. D. Todor, M. J. Spendolini, G. J. Fielding, and L. W. Porter, "Organization Structure and Performance: A Critical Review," *Academy of Management Review* (January 1980), pp. 49–64.

13. Hrebiniak and Joyce, p. 70.

14. Galbraith and Kazajian, pp. 67–68.

15. T. Burns and G. M. Stalker, *The Management of Innovation* (London: Tavistock Publications, 1961).

16. P. R. Lawrence and J. W. Lorsch, *Organization and*

Environment (Homewood, Ill.: Richard D. Irwin, Inc., 1967), p. 138.

17. William K. Hall, "SBUs: Hot New Topic in the Management of Diversification," *Business Horizons* (February 1978), p. 19.

18. "Evolving the GE Management System," *General Electric Monogram* (November-December 1977), p. 4.

19. R. G. Hamermesh, *Making Strategy Work* (New York: John Wiley and Sons, 1986), p. 91.

20. M. E. Porter, *Competitive Advantage* (New York: The Free Press, 1985), pp. 395–398 and p. 322.

21. Hrebiniak and Joyce, pp. 85–86.

22. E. W. Larson and D. H. Gobeli, "Matrix Management: Contradictions and Insights," *California Management Review* (Summer 1987), pp. 131–132.

23. P. G. W. Keen, "Communications in the 21st Century: Telecommunications and Business Policy," *Organizational Dynamics* (Autumn 1981), pp. 54–67.

24. A. L. Frohman, "Technology as a Competitive Weapon," *Harvard Business Review* (January-February 1982), p. 97.

25. P. F. Drucker, *Innovation and Entrepreneurship* (New York: Harper & Row, 1985), pp. 161–170.

J. R. Galbraith, "Human Resource Policies for the Innovating Organization," in *Strategic Human Resources Management,* edited by C. J. Fombrun, N. M. Tichy, and M. A. Devanna (New York: John Wiley and Sons, 1984), pp. 319–341.

P. Strebel, "Organizing for Innovation Over an Industry Cycle," *Strategic Management Journal* (March-April 1987), pp. 117–124.

26. R. A. Burgelman, "Designs for Corporate Entrepreneurship," *California Management Review* (Spring 1984), pp. 154–166.

27. G. Pinchot, *Intrapreneuring, or Why You Don't Have to Leave the Corporation to Become an Entrepreneur* (New York: Harper & Row, 1985) as reported by J. S. DeMott, "Here Come the Intrapreneurs," *Time* (February 4, 1985), pp. 36–37.

28. "How Xerox Speeds Up the Birth of New Products," *Business Week* (March 19, 1984), pp. 58–59.

29. J. T. Wilson, "Strategic Planning at R. J. Reynolds Industries," *Journal of Business Strategy* (Fall 1985), p. 26.

30. R. Koenig, "P&G Establishes Division to Manage Fat Substitute Line," *Wall Street Journal* (September 9, 1987), p. 20.

31. C. Dolan, "Tektronix New-Venture Subsidiary Brings Benefits to Parent, Spinoffs," *Wall Street Journal* (September 18, 1984), p. 31.

32. U. Gupta, "The Perils of a Corporate Entrepreneur," *Wall Street Journal* (September 10, 1987), p. 35.

33. N. W. Miller, "Art of 'Strategic Partnerships' Is Refined by California Firm," *Wall Street Journal* (December 6, 1985), p. 25.

34. D. H. Thain "Stages of Corporate Development,"

The Business Quarterly (Winter 1969), pp. 32–45.

B. R. Scott, "Stages of Corporate Development" (Boston: Intercollegiate Case Clearing House, no. 9-371-294, 1971); and "The Industrial State: Old Myths and New Realities," *Harvard Business Review* (March-April 1973).

R. V. Tuason, "Corporate Life Cycle and the Evaluation of Corporate Strategy," *Proceedings, The Academy of Management* (August 1973), pp. 35–40.

35. W. M. Bulkeley, "As Polaroid Matures, Some Lament a Decline in Creative Excitement," *Wall Street Journal* (May 10, 1983), p. 1.

36. L. E. Greiner, "Evolution and Revolution as Organizations Grow," *Harvard Business Review* (July-August 1972), pp. 37–46.

37. M. J. Williams, "McDonald's Refuses to Plateau," *Fortune* (November 12, 1984), p. 40.

38. N. R. Smith and J. B. Miner, "Type of Entrepreneur, Type of Firm, and Managerial Motivation: Implications for Organizational Life Cycle Theory," *Strategic Management Journal* (October-December 1983), pp. 325–340.

F. Hoy, B. C. Vaught, and W. W. Buchanan, "Managing Managers of Firms in Transition from Stage I to Stage II," *Proceedings, Southern Management Association* (November 1982), pp. 152–153.

K. Smith and T. Mitchell, "An Investigation into the Effect of Changes in Stages of Organizational Maturation on a Decision Maker's Decision Priorities," *Proceedings, Southern Management Association* (November 1983), pp. 7–9.

39. K. G. Smith and J. K. Harrison, "In Search of Excellent Leaders," in *Handbook of Business Strategy, 1986/87 Yearbook,* edited by W. D. Guth (Boston: Warren, Gorham & Lamont, 1986), p. 27.8.

40. Galbraith and Kazanjian, pp. 153–154.

41. J. Child, "Information Technology, Organization, and the Response to Strategic Challenges," *California Management Review* (Fall 1987), pp. 33–50.

R. L. Drake, "Innovative Structures for Managing Change," *Planning Review* (November 1986), pp. 18–22.

42. Drake, p. 22.

43. D. Miller and P. H. Friesen, "A Longitudinal Study of the Corporate Life Cycle," *Management Science* (October 1984), pp. 1161–1183.

J. R. Kimberly, R. H. Miles, and Associates, *The Organizational Life Cycle* (San Francisco: Jossey-Bass, 1980).

44. H. Gilman, "J. C. Penney Decentralizes Its Purchasing," *Wall Street Journal* (May 8, 1986), p. 6.

45. T. T. Herbert and H. Deresky, "Should General Managers Match Their Business Strategies?" *Organizational Dynamics* (Winter 1987), pp. 40–51.

R. Chaganti and R. Sambharya, "Strategic Orientation and Characteristics of Upper Management," *Strategic Management Journal* (July-August 1987), pp. 393–401.

M. Leontiades, "Choosing the Right Manager to Fit the Strategy," *Journal of Business Strategy* (Fall 1982), pp. 58–69.

J. G. Wissema, H. W. Van Der Pol, and H. M. Messer, "Strategic Management Archetypes," *Strategic Management*

Journal (January-March 1980), pp. 37–47.

A. D. Szilagyi, Jr. and D. M. Schweiger, "Matching Managers to Strategies: A Review and Suggested Framework," *Academy of Management Review* (October 1984), pp. 626–637.

46. A. K. Gupta and V. Govindarajan, "Business Unit Strategy, Managerial Characteristics, and Business Unit Effectiveness at Strategy Implementation," *Academy of Management Journal* (March 1984), p. 36.

47. Herbert and Deresky, pp. 43–45.

48. W. F. McCanna and T. E. Comte, "The CEO Succession Dilemma: How Boards Function in Turnover at the Top," *Business Horizons* (May-June 1986), pp. 17–22.

49. D. R. Dalton and I. F. Kesner, "Organizational Performance as An Antecedent of Inside/Outside Chief Executive Succession: An Empirical Assessment," *Academy of Management Journal* (December 1985), pp. 749–762.

R. S. Schuler and S. E. Jackson, "Linking Competitive Strategies with Human Resource Management Practices," *Academy of Management Executive* (August 1987), pp. 207–219.

K. H. Chung, R. C. Rogers, M. Lubatkin, and J. E. Owers, "Do Insiders Make Better CEOs Than Outsiders?" *Academy of Management Executive* (November 1987), pp. 323–329.

K. B. Schwartz and K. Menon, "Executive Succession in Failing Firms," *Academy of Management Journal* (September 1985), pp. 680–686.

50. P. Lorange and D. Murphy, "Bringing Human Resources Into Strategic Planning: System Design Characteristics," in *Strategic Human Resource Management*, ed. C. J. Fombrun, N. M. Tichy, and M. A. Devanna (New York:

Wiley and Sons, 1984), pp. 281–283.

51. H. G. Heneman, III, D. P. Schwab, J. A. Fossum, L. D. Dyer, *Personnel/Human Resources Management*, 3rd edition (Homewood, Illinois: Irwin, Inc., 1986), pp. 351–353.

52. M. A. Harris, "IBM: More Worlds to Conquer," *Business Week* (February 18, 1985), p. 85.

53. R. A. Pitts, "Strategies and Structures for Diversification," *Academy of Management Journal* (June 1977), pp. 197–208.

54. P. Shrivastava and W. D. Guth, "The Culture-Strategy Grid," in *Handbook of Business Strategy, 1985/86 Yearbook,* ed. W. D. Guth (Boston: Warren, Gorham, and Lamont, 1985), pp. 2.18–2.19.

55. S. J. Carroll, Jr. and H. L. Tosi, Jr., *Management by Objectives* (New York: Macmillan, 1973), p. 3.

56. M. D. Richards, *Setting Strategic Goals and Objectives,* 2nd ed. (St. Paul: West Publishing Co., 1986), pp. 122–123.

57. E. J. Seyna, "MBO: The Fad That Changed Management," *Long Range Planning* (December 1986), pp. 116–123.

58. Galbraith and Kazanjian, p. 120.

59. E. E. Lawler III, *Pay and Organizational Effectiveness* (New York: McGraw-Hill, 1971).

E. A. Locke, "How to Motivate Employees" (Paper presented at the NATO conference on changes in the nature and quality of working life, Thessaloniki, Greece, August 19–24, 1979.) Cited in E. E. Lawler III, *Pay and Organizational Development* (Reading Mass.: Addison-Wesley, 1981), p. 3.

60. H. I. Ansoff, "Strategic Managment of Technology," *Journal of Business Strategy* (Winter 1987), p. 37.

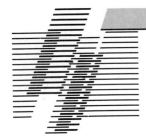

INTEGRATIVE CASE

CSX CORPORATION'S STRATEGY IMPLEMENTATION

In early 1985, CSX Corporation had been composed of a set of independently managed subsidiaries, organized as business groups in transportation and natural resources segments (See Fig. 5.5 in Chapter 5). CSX's top management, however, faced a real problem in the management of these operations so as to gain some synergy. The current organizational chart reflected nothing more than a quick attempt to somehow patch the units together into what was hoped would become one multi-modal transportation (and natural resources) company.

CORPORATE CULTURE

Because CSX Corporation had grown from acquisitions, each of the business units had its own distinctive culture and way of structuring its work activities. American Commercial Barge Lines, for example, had a river-going culture that traditionally looked upon the railroad as an enemy, not as something with which to cooperate and to share revenues. Even railroaders from the Chessie and Seaboard systems—

the two rail lines that originally formed CSX—had difficulty working together. From the very beginnings of CSX in 1980, corporate top management had bent over backwards to assure that the company was a true "partnership of equals." Corporate headquarters had been established in Richmond, Virginia, partly because of its closeness to Washington, D. C., and partially because it was halfway between Cleveland (Chessie's headquarters) and Jacksonville (Seaboard's headquarters). Although some integration of activities had been achieved, by and large the two rail systems continued to function autonomously as independent profit centers. Each maintained its own corporate headquarters staff, marketing, and sales teams. Consequently, CSX rail operations were not so efficient as those of its major competitor, Norfolk Southern.

REORGANIZATION

Finally, in December, 1985, the company adopted a plan for the reorganization and restructuring of CSX's business units. The restructuring resulted in a $954 million pre-tax special charge and reduced net earnings in 1985 by $560 million. The special charge included a provision of $327 million for separation pay liabilities, a $533 million write-down to net realizable value of a number of marginal and unproductive assets, and a provision of $94 million related to reorganization expenses, litigation costs, and other claims. The provision for separation pay liabilities was for a workforce reduction of 6,700 employee positions.

The organizational chart was radically altered. The Chessie and Seaboard rail systems were reorganized into three operating units: Distribution Services (marketing/sales), Equipment (freight-car maintenance and management), and Transportation (maintenance and management of track and locomotives). The Chessie and Seaboard systems were fully integrated. No more attempts were made to keep separate identities. Even the famous "Chessie the cat" logo of the old C&O line was eliminated and replaced by the letters "CSX" on all rail equipment. The R.F.&P. continued to be operated separately as a rail link between the old Chessie and Seaboard systems, for legal reasons and because of its ownership of key real estate in the Richmond and Washington, D. C., areas.

CSX's new corporate structure was now composed of four strategic groups—Transportation, Energy, Properties, and Technology. As shown in Figure 8.5, the three rail operating units, plus R.F.&P. and American Commercial Barge Lines, were placed in the **Transportation Group** of CSX. Sea-Land, acquired by CSX in April 1986, was also placed in that segment, even though the merger application was still being considered by the Interstate Commerce Commission. By year-end 1986, ACL and Sea-Land continued to be managed separately, primarily because of ICC anti-trust concerns. Deciding against a presence in air transportation, CSX sold Beckett Aviation.

The **Energy Group** included Texas Gas Transmission, a 6,000-mile pipeline system, and CSX Oil and Gas, an exploration and production unit (formerly Texas Gas Exploration Corporation). By year-end 1986, nearly all of CSX's coal properties and mineral rights had been sold.

The creation of a **Properties Group** signaled a change in the corporation's strategy for real estate and highlighted its potential for growth. Like other railroads, CSX

FIGURE 8.5
CSX Corporation's New Corporate Structure

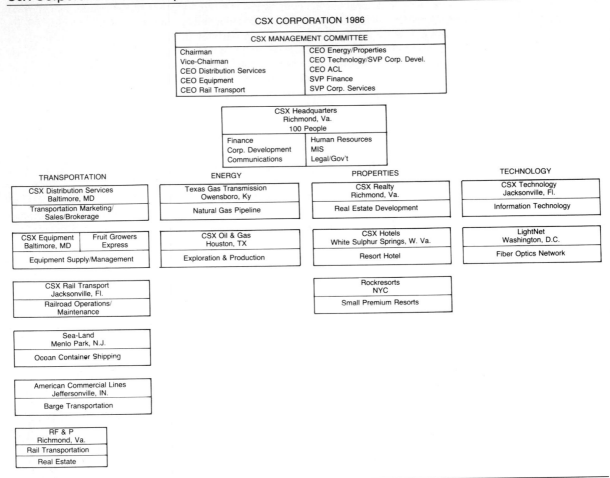

Source: Courtesy of R. Barth Strempek, CSX Corporation.

had historically used real estate as cash in the bank. In the United States, railroads had traditionally either bought or were given (by the government) large areas of undeveloped land on which they placed rails and built transportation depots and maintenance facilities. To finance further expansion, the railroads could then sell unused land. This was the U. S. federal government's approach to encourage nationwide railroad development in the 1800s. CSX's management concluded that although its previous land strategy had provided a good return on its investment for little risk, it offered only a limited opportunity for the company to capitalize on long-term growth prospects in real estate. Consequently, the Properties Group was formed to consolidate a billion-dollar inventory of properties and to examine opportunities in the real estate market. In addition to CSX Realty were CSX Hotels, which owned and operated The Greenbrier resort hotel, and Rockresorts, an April 1986 purchase that owned or managed small premium resorts such as Caneel Bay and Little Dix Bay in the Caribbean, and The Boulders in Arizona. CSX Hotels also had interests in the New Orleans Hilton and the Montgomery, Alabama Sheraton Hotel.

The **Technology Group** included CSX Technology, which combined Chessie Computer Services, Inc. and Cybernetics and Systems, Inc. One of its tasks was to assist other parts of CSX in the development and installation of modern communication and information systems. Examples of its work were an advanced fleet distribution and utilization system developed for CSX Equipment, and a national telemarketing center that provided comprehensive sales coverage to CSX Distribution Services. This telecommunications center enabled CSX sales people to move away from the use of traditional railroad sales techniques to logistics consulting for shippers. These uses of technology were crucial as CSX attempted to better integrate its operations and become a true "one-stop shipper." Also in the Technology Group was Lightnet, a CSX joint venture with Southern New England Telecommunications. It was expected that by the end of 1987 Lightnet would serve more than thirty major U.S. urban markets over its 5,000-mile system, offering customers quality, high-speed data transmission over a cable network.

Impact of Reorganization

Hays T. Watkins, CSX Chairman and Chief Executive Officer, was optimistic about CSX's ability to manage these businesses. In discussing the reorganization, he stated in December 1985 that "the actions will have a very positive effect on future cash flow, earnings, and rates of return."[1] In particular, a $327 million program designed to entice employees to take early retirement, was expected to produce savings of more then $650 million over the next five years. Regarding the Sea-Land acquisition, Watkins predicted a "new era in the transportation industry and a new generation of transportation services." Customers, he said, "want to make one call for the whole haul and we are committed to making that concept a reality around the globe."[2]

Others, however, were not quite so optimistic. Analysts felt that Sea-Land was a risky bet for CSX because it made the corporation even more difficult to manage. Unless CSX could develop the synergy its top management was working toward, lower-cost carriers like Norfolk Southern could threaten CSX's competitive position. The chances were very good that the highly competitive rail-transportation companies in the eastern U.S. would continue to battle for market share for the near future regardless of Conrail's situation. Merging the different cultures of the three rail systems, a barge line, and Sea-Land would certainly be a significant chore. John Snow, who took over as President and Chief Executive Officer of the Transportation Group in 1987, remarked, "My job is to keep peace in the family." Pointing to the American Commerical Lines acquisition, Snow said that the rail-barge combination has helped to change an "atmosphere of suspicion and mistrust" that had undermined efforts to make railroad-to-barge connections. By 1986, the percentage of American Commercial Lines tonnage being transferred to CSX rail lines had increased to 5% from only 2% in 1982.[3]

NOTES

1. D. Machalaba, "CSX Announces Major Restructuring, Will Take $954 Million Pre-Tax Charge," *Wall Street Journal* (December 12, 1985), p. 6.

2. L. McGinley, "CSX's Purchase of Sea-Land Gets Go-Ahead," *Wall Street Journal* (February 12, 1987), p. 4.

3. R. Koenig, "At CSX, Snow Gets His Show on the Road," *Wall Street Journal* (April 8, 1987), p. 36.

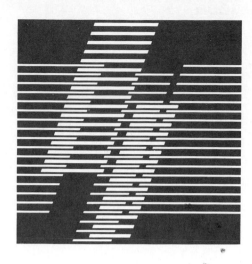

CHAPTER 9

EVALUATION AND CONTROL

STRATEGIC MANAGEMENT MODEL

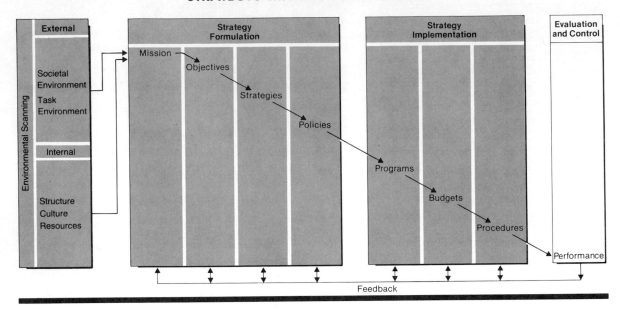

The last part of the strategic management model is the evaluation of performance and the control of work activities. Control follows planning. It ensures that the corporation is achieving what it set out to accomplish. Just as planning involves the setting of objectives along with the strategics and programs necessary to accomplish them, the control process compares performance with desired results and provides the feedback necessary for management to evaluate results and take corrective action, as needed.[1] This process can be viewed as a five-step feedback model, as depicted in Fig. 9.1.

1. **Determine what to measure.** Top managers as well as operational managers need to specify what implementation processes and results will be monitored and evaluated. The processes and results must be capable of being measured in a reasonably objective and consistent manner. The focus should be on the most significant elements in a process—the ones that account for the highest proportion of expense or the greatest number of problems.

2. **Establish standards of performance.** Standards used to measure performance are detailed expressions of strategic objectives. They are *measures* of acceptable performance results. Each standard usually includes a *tolerance range* within which deviations accepted as satisfactory are defined. Standards can be set not only for final output, but also for intermediate stages of production output.

3. **Measure actual performance.** Measurements must be made at predetermined times.

FIGURE 9.1
Evaluation and Control Process

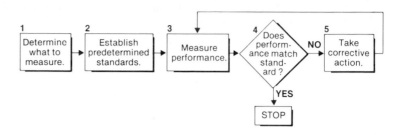

4. **Compare actual performance with the standard.** If actual performance results are within the desired tolerance range, the measurement process stops here.

5. **Take corrective action.** If actual results fall outside the desired tolerance range, action must be taken to correct the deviation. The following must be determined:

   a) Is the deviation only a chance fluctuation?

   b) Are the processes being carried out incorrectly?

   c) Are the processes appropriate to the achievement of the desired standard?

   Action must be taken that will not only correct the deviation, but also prevent its happening again.

The strategic management model shows that evaluation and control information is fed back and assimilated into the entire management process. This information consists of performance data and activity reports (gathered in step 3 of Fig. 9.1). If undesired performance is the result of an inappropriate *use* of the strategic management processes, operational managers must know about it so that they can correct the employee activity. Top management need not be involved. If, however, undesired performance results from the processes themselves, top managers, as well as operational managers, must know about it so that they can develop new implementation programs or procedures.

Lorange, Morton, and Ghoshal, in their book on strategic control, propose three types of control: strategic, tactical, and operational. **Strategic control** deals with the basic strategic direction of the corporation in terms of its relationship with its environment. **Tactical control,** in contrast, deals primarily with the implementation of the strategic plan. **Operational control** deals with near-term corporate activities.[2] Lorange, Morton, and Ghoshal further suggest that just as there is a hierarchy of strategy, there is also a **hierarchy of control,** as depicted in Figure 9.2. At the corporate level, control

FIGURE 9.2
Hierarchy of Control

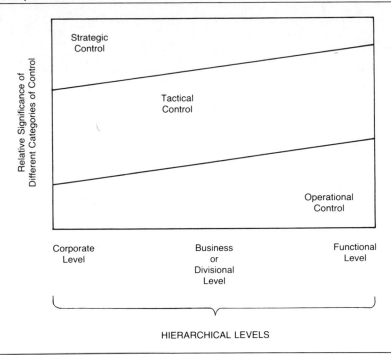

focuses on maintaining a balance among the various activities of the corporation as a whole. Strategic and tactical controls are most important. At the divisional level, control is primarily concerned with the maintenance and improvement of competitive position. Tactical control dominates. At the functional level, the role of control becomes one of developing and enhancing function-based distinctive competencies. Because of the short-term time horizon, operational and tactical controls are most important at this level, with only a modest concern for strategic control.[3]

To help achieve organizational objectives, strategic managers have an obligation to ensure that the entire hierarchy of control is integrated and working properly. As reported by Meredith, according to W. Edwards Deming, the quality-control expert who helped the Japanese build their successful business economy, 85% of the causes of product defects are due to the system within which the worker must perform and only 15% are directly due to the worker.[4] Unfortunately, in the last few decades top management has almost forgotten the importance of strategic control, and when control was called for, they have reverted to more direct tactical and operational control—often becoming crisis management.[5]

9.1

MEASURING PERFORMANCE

Which measures will be used depends on the organizational unit to be measured, as well as on the objectives to be achieved. Some measures, such as return on investment, are very appropriate to evaluating the corporation's or division's ability to achieve a profitability objective. These measures, however, are inadequate for evaluating other objectives that a corporation might want to achieve: social responsibility or employee development, for instance. Different measures are required for different objectives. Even though profitability is the major objective for a corporation, return on investment alone might be insufficient as a control device. ROI, for example, can be computed only *after* profits are totaled for a period. It tells what happened—not what *is* happening or what *will* happen. A firm, therefore, needs to develop measures that predict likely profitability. These are referred to as "steering" or "feed-forward" controls because they measure variables that influence future profitability.

Measures of Corporate Performance

The most commonly used measure of corporate performance (in terms of profits) is return on investment. As discussed in Chapter 2, it is simply the result of dividing net income before taxes by total assets. Although there are a number of advantages to the use of ROI, there are also a number of distinct limitations. Some of these are detailed in Table 9.1.

Other popular measures are earnings per share (EPS) and return on equity (ROE). Earnings per share also has several deficiencies as an evaluation of past and future performance. For one thing, because alternative accounting principles are available, EPS can have several different but equally acceptable values, depending on the principle selected for its computation. Second, because EPS is based on accrual income, the conversion of income to cash can be near term or delayed. Therefore, EPS does not consider the time value of money. Return on equity also has its share of limitations because it is also derived from accounting-based data. Because of these and other limitations, EPS and ROE by themselves are not adequate measures of corporate performance.[6]

Stakeholder Measures

As mentioned in Chapter 4, stakeholders in the corporation's task environment are often very concerned about corporate activities and performance. Each has its own set of criteria to determine how well the corporation is

TABLE 9.1

Advantages and Limitations of ROI as a Measure of Corporate Performance

ADVANTAGES

1. ROI is a single comprehensive figure influenced by everything that happens.

2. It measures how well the division manager uses the property of the company to generate profits. It is also a good way to check on the accuracy of capital investment proposals.

3. It is a common denominator that can be compared with many entities.

4. It provides an incentive to use existing assets efficiently.

5. It provides an incentive to acquire new assets only when doing so would increase the return.

LIMITATIONS

1. ROI is very sensitive to depreciation policy. Depreciation write-off variances between divisions affect ROI performance. Accelerated depreciation techniques reduce ROI, conflicting with capital budgeting discounted cash-flow analysis.

2. ROI is sensitive to book value. Older plants with more depreciated assets have relatively lower investment bases than newer plants (note also the effect of inflation), thus increasing ROI. Note that asset investment may be held down or assets disposed of in order to increase ROI performance.

3. In many firms that use ROI, one division sells to another. As a result, transfer pricing must occur. Expenses incurred affect profit. Since, in theory, the transfer price should be based on the total impact on firm profit, some investment center managers are bound to suffer. Equitable transfer prices are difficult to determine.

4. If one division operates in an industry that has favorable conditions and another division operates in an industry that has unfavorable conditions, the former division will automatically "look" better than the other.

5. The time span of concern here is short range. The performance of division managers should be measured in the long run. This is top management's time-span capacity.

6. The business cycle strongly affects ROI performance, often despite managerial performance.

SOURCE: Table, "Advantages and Limitations of ROI as a Measure of Corporate Performance" from *Organizational Policy and Strategic Management,* Second Edition, copyright © 1983 by The Dryden Press, a division of Holt, Rinehart and Winston, Inc., reprinted by permission of the publisher.

performing. These criteria typically deal with the direct and indirect impact of corporate activities on stakeholder interests. Freeman proposes that top management needs to "keep score" with these stakeholders; it should establish one or more simple measures for each stakeholder category.[7] A few of these measures are listed in Table 9.2.

Value-Added Measures

Assuming that any one measure is bound to have some shortcomings, Hofer recommends the use of three new measures in an evaluation of a corpora-

TABLE 9.2
A Sample Score Card for "Keeping Score with Stakeholders"

STAKEHOLDER CATEGORY	POSSIBLE NEAR-TERM MEASURES	POSSIBLE LONG-TERM MEASURES
Customers	Sales ($ and volume) New customers Number of new customer needs met ("tries")	Growth in sales Turnover of customer base Ability to control price

Suppliers	Cost of raw material
	Delivery time
	Inventory
	Availability of raw material
		Growth rates of
		  Raw material costs
		  Delivery time
		  Inventory
		New ideas from suppliers

Financial Community	EPS Stock price Number of "buy" lists ROE	Ability to convince Wall Street of strategy Growth in ROE
Employees	Number of suggestions Productivity Number of grievances	Number of internal promotions Turnover
Congress	Number of new pieces of legislation that affect the firm Access to key members and staff	Number of new regulations that affect industry Ratio of "cooperative" vs. "competitive" encounters
Consumer Advocate	Number of meetings Number of "hostile" encounters Number of times coalitions formed Number of legal actions	Number of changes in policy due to C.A. Number of C.A. initiated "calls for help"
Environmentalists	Number of meetings Number of hostile encounters Number of times coalitions formed Number of EPA complaints Number of legal actions	Number of changes in policy due to environmentalists Number of environmentalist "calls for help"

SOURCE: R. E. Freeman, *Strategic Management: A Stakeholder Approach* (Boston: Ballinger Publishing Company, 1984), p. 179. Copyright © 1984 by R. E. Freeman. Reprinted by permission.

tion's performance results (see Table 9.3). These measures are based on **value added** and are attempts to measure directly the contribution a corporation makes to society. Value added is the difference between dollar sales and the cost of raw materials and purchased parts. Return on value added (ROVA) is a second measure, one that divides net profits before tax by value added and converts the quotient to a percentage. Preliminary studies

TABLE 9.3
Three New Measures of Corporate Performance

Performance Characteristic	SOME TRADITIONAL MEASURES	PROPOSED NEW MEASURES
Growth	Dollar sales, unit sales, dollar assets	Value added[1]
Efficiency	Gross margin, net profits, net profits/ dollar sales	ROVA[2]
Asset utilization	ROI, return on equity, earnings per share	ROVA/ROI

SOURCE: C. W. Hofer, "ROVA: A New Measure for Assessing Organizational Performance," in R. Lamb, ed., *Advances in Strategic Management*, vol. 2 (Greenwich, Conn.: JAI Press, 1983), p. 50. Copyright © 1983 by C. W. Hofer. Reprinted by permission.

[1]Value added = Dollar sales − Cost of raw materials and purchased parts.

[2]ROVA: Return on Value Added = $\dfrac{\text{Net profits before tax}}{\text{Value added}} \times 100\%$.

by Hofer suggest that ROVA tends to stabilize in the range of 12% to 18% for most industries in the maturity or saturation phases of market evolution. Hofer argues that ROVA might be a better measure of corporate performance across various industries than other measures currently in use.[8]

Unfortunately, the major disadvantage of using value added is that the figures are not readily available. There is no way to calculate value added from traditional financial reports in the United States, for example, because of the allocation and application of direct labor, indirect costs, and overhead that become part of the cost of goods manufactured. Nevertheless, authorities on the subject argue that combining value-added measures with traditional performance measures creates a more complete and realistic picture of a corporation's performance.[9]

Shareholder Value

Because of the belief that accounting-based numbers such as return on investment, return on equity, and earnings per share are not reliable indicators of a corporation's economic value, many corporations are using shareholder value as a better measure of corporate performance and strategic management effectiveness.[10] **Shareholder value** (or shareholder wealth) is defined as the sum of dividends plus stock appreciation. It determines if a corporation is earning a rate of return greater than that demanded by investors in the security market. Rappaport, one of the principal advocates of this measure, explains its use:

> What I have termed the "shareholder value approach" estimates the economic value of any strategy as the expected cash flows discounted by the market discount rate. These cash flows in turn serve as the basis for expected shareholder returns from dividends and stock-price appreciation.[11]

A survey of the senior managers of Fortune 500 companies revealed that 30% of their selections of investment proposals are based on their expected contributions to shareholder wealth. The survey also noted that a number of corporations not now using this approach are starting to experiment with value-based techniques.[12]

Performance Objectives

The objectives that were established earlier in the strategy formulation stage of the strategic management process should certainly be used to measure corporate performance once the strategies have been implemented. Drucker, one of the originators of managing by objectives, proposed eight key areas in which overall corporate objectives should be established and monitored:

1. Market standing
2. Innovation
3. Productivity
4. Use of physical and financial resources
5. Profitability
6. Manager performance and development
7. Worker performance and attitude
8. Public responsibility.[13]

Westinghouse Electric Corporation, for example, established a productivity-improvement objective for the entire corporation. Concerned that the company had slipped from the position of number two in the world in its industry, top management decided in 1979 that the firm had to do a better job with the resources it controlled. Consequently, it developed a series of productivity-improvement programs, such as the introduction of quality circles, improved inventory control, and the global location of its manufacturing facilities. To measure the overall impact of these programs upon the corporation, Westinghouse's top management developed a productivity improvement formula:

$$\frac{\text{Constant dollar value} - \text{Added change}}{\text{Total employee costs}} = \% \text{ P I}$$

Top management established an overall corporate objective for productivity improvement at $6 + \%$ per year. The productivity improvement measure thus became one of the key indicators of corporate performance.[14]

Evaluation of Top Management

Through its strategy, audit, and compensation committees, a board of directors closely evaluates the job performance of the CEO and the top management team. Of course, it is concerned primarily with overall profitability as measured by return on investment, return on equity, earnings per share, and shareholder wealth. The absence of short-run profitability is certainly a factor contributing to the firing of any CEO. The board will also, however, be concerned with other factors.

As shown in Fig. 9.3, the board should evaluate top management not only on quantitative measures, but also on factors relating to its strategic

FIGURE 9.3
Assessing Top Management's Performance

Measure	Excellent	Above Average	Average	Below Average	Poor
Qualitative: Establishing Strategic Direction					
Building Management Team					
Leadership Qualities					
Providing for Succession					
Implementing Strategy					
Employee/Labor Relations					
Technology Leadership					
Board Relations					
Investor Relations					
Community/Gov't Relations					
Quantitative: EPS Over 2–5 years					
Total Return to Shareholders					
Return on Invested Capital					
Return Measure Trends					
Return on Stockholders Equity					
Cash Flow					
Yearly/Quarterly EPS					
Stock Price Performance					
Book Value Performance					
Dividend Payout Ratio					

Source: Suggested by R. Brossy, "What Directors Say About Their Role in Managing Executive Pay," *Directors & Boards* (Summer 1986), pp. 38–40.

management practices. Has the top management team set reasonable long-run as well as short-run objectives? Has it formulated innovative strategies? Has it worked closely with operational managers in the development of realistic implementation plans, schedules, and budgets? Has it developed and used appropriate measures of corporate and divisional performance for feedback and control? Has it provided the board with appropriate feedback on corporate performance in advance of key decision points? These and other questions should be raised by a board of directors as they evaluate the performance of top management.

The specific items that are used by a board to evaluate its top management should be derived from the objectives agreed to earlier by both the board and top management. If better relations with the local community and improved safety practices in work areas were selected as objectives for the year (or for five years), these items should be included in the evaluation. In addition, other factors that tend to lead to profitability might be included, such as market share, product quality, or investment intensity (from the PIMS research discussed in Chapter 6).

Strategic Audits

Used by various consulting firms as a way to measure performance, audits of corporate activities are frequently suggested for use by boards of directors as well as by others in managerial positions. Management audits have been developed to evaluate activities such as corporate social responsibility; functional areas such as the marketing department, divisions such as the international division, as well as to evaluate the corporation itself in a strategic audit (see Chapter 2). The strategic audit is likely to be increasingly used by corporations that have become concerned with closely monitoring those activities that affect overall corporate effectiveness and efficiency. To be effective, the strategic audit should parallel the corporation's strategic management process and/or model.

Measures of Divisional and Functional Unit Performance

Corporations use a variety of techniques to evaluate and control performance in divisions, SBUs, and functional units. If a corporation is composed of SBUs or divisions, it will use many of the same performance measures (ROI, for instance) that it uses to assess overall corporation performance. To the extent that it can isolate specific functional units, such as R&D, the corporation may develop responsibility centers.

Budgets are certainly an important control device. During strategy formulation and implementation, top management approves a series of programs and supporting operating budgets from its business units.[15] During evaluation and control, actual expenses are contrasted with planned expenditures and the degree of variance is assessed. This is typically done on a monthly basis. In addition, top management will probably require *periodic statistical reports* summarizing data on key factors, such as the number of new customer contracts, volume of received orders, and productivity figures, among others.[16]

Evaluating a Division or SBU

At Norton Company, each SBU is evaluated in depth every two years. This evaluation is conducted by the Strategy Guidance Committee, composed of the CEO, the financial vice-president, eight vice-presidents in charge of operations, the controller, assistant controller, vice-president for corporate development, and an assistant vice-president. At the time that the line manager in charge of an SBU comes before the committee with a detailed strategy for each major segment of the unit's operations, the committee is evaluating the unit's performance according to past objectives, and arriving at its strategic position within the corporation and, therefore, its potential.

> The Strategy Guidance Committee looks at a strategic business unit from many viewpoints—return on net assets, return on sales, asset turnover, market share strategy. The committee might test sales growth rate against market growth rate against market share strategy. The committee also looks at competition, relative strengths and weaknesses, and cash generation plotted against market share strategy. It also places the unit on a balloon chart or growth/market share matrix for the entire company, to see how this unit fits in with all the others.[17]

The Strategy Guidance Committee looks at the SBU from all angles and asks a number of penetrating questions. Some of these questions are listed below:

EVALUATION OF A STRATEGIC BUSINESS UNIT AT NORTON COMPANY

- How does this unit contribute to the overall scheme of things?
- Does it help to balance the total?
- Does it increase or decrease the cyclical nature of the company?
- How does it relate to other Norton technologies, processes, or distribution systems?
- How successfully does it compete?
- How is it regarded by its customers and by its competitors?
- Does it hurt or improve the company's image with the investment community?

- What are its mission and mode of operation in terms of build, maintain, or harvest?
- Is its current strategy appropriate?
- Can we win and, if so, how?
- If it has changed its strategy or performance since the last review, why has it changed?
- What does our analysis suggest about the unit's profitability in comparison with similar businesses?

SOURCE: D. R. Melville, "Top Management's Role in Strategic Planning," *The Journal of Business Strategy*, vol. 1, no. 4, (Spring 1981), p. 63. Reprinted by permission from the *Journal of Business Strategy*. Copyright © 1981 by Warren, Gorham & Lamont Inc., Boston. All rights reserved.

Responsibility Centers

Control systems can be established to monitor specific functions, projects, or divisions. One type of control system, budgets typically are used to control the financial indicators of performance. Responsibility centers are used to isolate a unit so that it can be evaluated separately from the rest of the corporation. Each responsibility center therefore has its own budget and is evaluated on its use of budgeted resources. A responsibility center is headed by the manager responsible for the center's performance. The center uses resources (measured in terms of costs) to produce a service or a product (measured in terms of volume or revenues). There are five major types of responsibility centers. The type is determined by the way these resources and services or products are measured by the corporation's control system:[18]

1. **Standard cost centers.** Primarily used in manufacturing facilities, standard (or expected) costs are computed for each operation on the basis of historical data. In evaluation of the center's performance, its total standard costs are multiplied by the units produced; the result is the expected cost of production, which is then compared to the actual cost of production.

2. **Revenue centers.** Production, usually in terms of unit or dollar sales, is measured without consideration of resource costs (e.g., salaries). The center is thus judged in terms of effectiveness rather than efficiency. The effectiveness of a sales region, for example, is determined by the comparison of its actual sales to its projected or previous year's sales. Profits are not considered because sales departments have very limited influence over the cost of the products they sell.

3. **Expense centers.** Resources are measured in dollars without consideration of service or product costs. Thus budgets will have been prepared for "engineered" expenses (those costs that can be calculated) and for "discretionary" expenses (those costs that can only be estimated). Typical expense centers are administrative, service, and research departments. They cost an organization money, but they only indirectly contribute to revenues.

4. **Profit centers.** Performance is measured in terms of the difference between revenues (which measure production) and expenditures (which measure resources). A profit center is typically established whenever an organizational unit has control over both its resources and its products or services. By having such centers, a corporation can be organized into divisions of separate product lines. The manager of each division is given autonomy to the extent that she or he is able to keep profits at a satisfactory (or better) level. Some organizational units that are not usually considered potentially autonomous can, for the purpose of profit-center evaluations, be made so. A manufacturing department, for example, can be converted from a standard cost center (or expense center) into a profit center: it is allowed to charge a **transfer price** for each product it "sells" to the sales department. The difference between the manufacturing cost per unit and the agreed-upon transfer price is the

unit's "profit." Transfer pricing is commonly used in vertically integrated corporations and can work quite well when a price can be easily determined for a designated amount of product. When a price cannot be set easily, however, the relative bargaining power of the centers, rather than strategic considerations, tend to influence the agreed-upon price.[19] Top management has an obligation to make sure that these political considerations do not overwhelm the strategic ones. Otherwise, profit figures for each center will be biased and provide poor information for strategic decisions at the corporate level.

5. **Investment centers.** As with profit centers, an investment center's performance is measured in terms of the difference between its resources and its services or products. Most divisions in large manufacturing corporations use huge assets, such as plants and equipment, to make their products, and evaluating their performance on the basis of profits alone can be misleading because it ignores the size of their assets. For example, two divisions in a corporation make identical profits, but one division owns a $3 million plant, whereas the other owns a $1 million plant. Both make the same profits, but one is obviously more efficient: The smaller plant provides the stockholders with a better return on their investment.

The most widely used measure of investment center performance is ROI (see Table 2.1). Another measure, called residual income, is found by subtracting an interest charge from the net income. This interest charge could be based on the interest the corporation is actually paying to lenders for the assets being used. It could also be based on the amount of income that could have been earned if the assets had been invested somewhere else.

Sloan reports that the concept of rate of return on investments was crucial to General Motors' exercise of its permanent control of the whole corporation in a way consistent with its decentralized organization.[20] Donaldson Brown, who came to GM from DuPont in 1921, defined return on investment as a function of the profit margin and the rate of turnover of invested capital. Multiplying the profit margin by the investment turnover equals the percent of return on investment. To increase the return on investment, management can, therefore, increase the rate of capital turnover in relation to sales (that is, increase volume) or increase profit margins (increase revenue and/or cut costs and expenses).[21]

Investment center performance can also be measured in terms of its contribution to shareholder value. One example is given by the CEO of a large corporation:

We value our businesses by computing the net present value of each unit's equity cash flow, using the appropriate cost of capital. Then we subtract out the market value of assigned debt and arrive at an estimate of the warranted market value of the unit. These techniques allow us to evaluate and rank our units based on their relative contribution to the creation of overall corporate equity value, which is our overall objective.[22]

Most single-business corporations tend to use a combination of cost, expense, and revenue centers. In these corporations, most managers are functional specialists and manage against a budget. Total profitability is integrated at the corporate level. Dominant-product companies, which have diversified into a few small businesses but which still depend upon a single product line for most of their revenue and income, generally use a combination of cost, expense, revenue, plus *profit centers*. Multidivisional corporations, however, will tend to emphasize *investment centers*—although in various units throughout the corporation other types of responsibility centers will also be used.[23]

9.2

STRATEGIC INFORMATION SYSTEMS

Before performance measures can have any impact on strategic management, they must first be communicated to those people responsible for formulating and implementing strategic plans. Strategic information systems can perform this function. They can be computer-based or manual, formal or informal. They serve the information needs of top management.[24] As discussed in Chapter 5, an information system is meant to provide a basis for early warning signals that can originate either externally or internally. These warning signals grow out of the corporation's need to ensure that programs and procedures are being implemented in ways that will achieve corporate and divisional objectives. One of the key reasons given for the bankruptcy of International Harvester was the inability of the corporation's top management to precisely determine its income by major class of similar products. Because of this inability, management kept trying to fix ailing businesses and was unable to respond flexibly to major changes and unexpected events.[25]

As mentioned in Chapter 5, the information system should focus managers' attention on the critical success factors in their jobs. **Critical success factors** are those few things that must go well if a corporation's success is to be ensured. They are typically those 20% of the total factors that determine 80% of the corporation's or business unit's performance. They therefore represent those areas that must be given the special and continuous attention needed for high performance.[26] These critical success factors provide a focal point from which a computer-based information system can be developed. Such an information system will thus pinpoint key areas that require a manager's attention.

The Diversified Products and Services Group of GTE, for example, established in 1984 a formal system, based on critical success factors, to track the implementation of the group's strategic plans. Management referred to this system as their Strategic Tracking System (STS). Charles M. Jones, Vice-President of Administration for GTE Diversified Products relates how it was done:

> We called the things that had to be done well Critical Success Factors (CSFs). The first criteria in defining CSFs was that they had to be very specific and

action oriented. In addition, we developed performance measures for each CSF. Then we set up a monthly STS reporting system, reviewed by the president of Diversified Products. . . .

Each organization developed its own STS reporting process, determining from the various line managers what factors were critical to their particular operation. At the next higher level, these success factors and performance measures were reviewed and the most important were selected as monitors for the monthly report. In theory, and in practice, there's nothing in the STS that general managers don't use to run their businesses, but not everything they use was included.[27]

At the divisional or SBU level of a corporation, the information system should be used to support, reinforce, or enlarge its business-level strategy.[28] An SBU pursuing a strategy of overall cost leadership could use its information system to reduce costs either by the improvement of labor productivity or the utilization of other resources such as inventory or machinery. Another SBU, in contrast, might wish to pursue a differentiation strategy. It could use its information system to add uniqueness to the product or service and contribute to quality, service, or image through the functional areas.[29] American Hospital Supply and both United and American Airlines took this approach to increase their market shares: they offered unique information-systems services to their customers. The choice of the business-level strategy will thus dictate the type of information system that the SBU needs to both implement and control strategic activities. Table 9.4 lists the differences between an information system needed to evaluate and control a low-cost strategy and an information system needed for product differentiation. The information systems will be constructed differently to monitor different activities because the two types of business-level strategies have different critical-success factors.[30]

9.3

PROBLEMS IN MEASURING PERFORMANCE

The measurement of performance is a crucial part of evaluation and control. The lack of quantifiable objectives or performance standards and the inability of the information system to provide timely, valid information are two obvious control problems.[31] Without objective and timely measurements, it would be extremely difficult to make operational, let alone strategic, decisions. Nevertheless, the use of timely, quantifiable standards does not guarantee good performance. The very act of monitoring and measuring performance can cause side-effects that interfere with overall corporate performance. Among the most frequent negative side-effects are a *short-term orientation* and *goal displacement*.

Short-Term Orientation

Hodgetts and Wortman state that in many situations top executives do not analyze *either* the long-term implications of present operations on the strategy they have adopted *or* the operational impact of a strategy on the

TABLE 9.4

Use of Information Systems to Monitor Implementation of Business Strategies

	GENERIC STRATEGIES	
	Low Cost	Product Differentiation
Product Design & Development	Product engineering systems Project control systems	R&D data bases Professional work stations Electronic mail CAD Custom engineering systems Integrated systems for manufacturing
Operations	Process engineering systems Process control systems Labor control systems Inventory management systems Procurement systems Quality monitoring systems	CAM Quality assurance systems Systems for suppliers Quality monitoring systems
Marketing	Streamlined distribution systems Centralized control systems Econometric modeling systems	Sophisticated marketing systems Market data bases Graphic display systems Telemarketing systems Competition analysis systems Modeling systems Service-oriented distribution systems
Sales	Sales control systems Advertising monitoring systems Systems to consolidate sales function Strict incentive/monitoring systems	Differential pricing systems Office/field communications Customer/sales support systems Dealer support systems Customer order entry systems
Administration	Cost control systems Quantitative planning & budgeting systems Office automation for staff reduction	Office automation to integrate functions Environment scanning & nonquantitative planning systems Teleconferencing systems

SOURCE: G. L. Parsons, "Information Technology: A New Competitive Weapon," *Sloan Management Review* (Fall 1983), p. 12. Reprinted by permission of the publisher. Copyright © 1983 by the Sloan Management Review Association. All rights reserved.

corporate mission. They report that long-run evaluations are *not* conducted because executives (1) may not realize their importance, (2) may believe that short-run considerations are more important than long-run considerations, (3) may not be personally evaluated on a long-term basis, or (4) may not have the time to make a long-run analysis.[32] There is no real justification for the first and last "reasons." If executives realize the importance of long-run evaluations, they make the time needed to conduct them. The short-term nature of most incentive and promotion plans, however, provides a rationale for the second and third reasons.

In 1986, according to Sibson and Company, a compensation consulting firm, long-term incentives comprised only 28% of the total annual income of CEOs of large corporations. Although this was an increase from just 15% in 1975, most of the typical chief executive's annual compensation came from salary (46%) and an annual bonus linked to pre-tax profit (26%).[33] A survey of corporate planners and human resource executives from twenty-four U.S. Fortune 500 firms revealed that only about half of the companies attempted to tailor their business-unit managers' incentive systems to the strategic position of the business unit. Fully 90% of the planners and executives that were surveyed reported that their companies were not adequately combining long- and short-term criteria in assessing a business-unit manager's performance.[34]

Table 9.1 indicates that one of the limitations of ROI as a performance measure is its short-term nature. In theory, ROI is not limited to the short run, but in practice it is often difficult to use this measure to realize long-term benefits for the corporation. If the performance of corporate and divisional managers is evaluated primarily on the basis of an annual ROI, the managers tend to focus their effort on those factors that have positive short-term effects. Therefore, division managers often undertake capital investments with early paybacks that will establish a favorable track record for the division. These results are often inconsistent with corporate long-run objectives. Because managers can often manipulate both the numerator (earnings) as well as the denominator (investment), the resulting ROI figure can be meaningless. Advertising, maintenance, and research efforts can be reduced. Mergers can be undertaken that will do more for this year's earnings than for the division's or corporation's future profits. Expensive retooling and plant modernization can be delayed as long as a manager can manipulate figures on production defects and absenteeism. Efforts to compensate for these distortions tend to create a burdensome accounting-control system, which stifles creativity and flexibility, and leads to even more questionable "creative accounting" practices.[35] For example, the manager of Doughtie's Foods' wholesaling operation in Richmond, Virginia, admitted to SEC investigators that he routinely gave false inventory figures to his superiors in order to overstate his division's profits. He admitted that he did it "just to look good." His division had not been doing well and his bosses had been routinely singling him out for criticism at corporate planning meetings.[36]

Goal Displacement

The very monitoring and measuring of performance (if not carefully done) can actually result in a decline in overall corporate performance. A dysfunctional side-effect known as *goal displacement* can occur. This is the confusion of means with ends. Goal displacement occurs when activities originally intended to help managers attain corporate objectives become ends in themselves—or are adapted to meet ends other than those for which they were intended.[37] Two types of goal displacement are *behavior substitution* and *suboptimization.*

Behavior Substitution

Not all activities or aspects of performance can be easily quantified and measured. It can be very difficult to set standards for such desired activities as cooperation or initiative. Therefore, managers tend to focus more of their attention on those behaviors that are measurable than on those that are not.[38] They thus reward those people who do well on these types of measures. Because the managers tend to ignore behaviors that are either unmeasurable or difficult to measure, people receive little to no reward for engaging in these activities. The problem with this phenomenon is that the easy-to-measure activities might have little to no relationship to the desired good performance. Rational people, nevertheless, will tend to work for the rewards the system has to offer. Therefore, employees will tend to substitute behaviors that are recognized and rewarded for those behaviors that are ignored without regard to their contribution to goal accomplishment.[39] A U.S. Navy quip sums up this situation: "What you inspect is what you get." If the evaluation and control system of an auto plant rewards the meeting of quantitative goals while paying only lip-service to qualitative goals, consumers can expect to get a very large number of very poorly built cars!

The most frequently mentioned problem with Management By Objectives (MBO) is that the measurement process partially distorts the realities of the job. Objectives are made for areas in which the measurement of accomplishments is relatively easy, such as ROI, increased sales, or reduced cost. But these might not always be the most important areas. This problem becomes crucial in professional, service, or staff activities in which the making of quantitative measurements is difficult. If, for example, a division manager is achieving all of the quantifiable objectives, but in so doing, alienates the work force, the result could be a long-term drop in the division's performance. If promotions are strictly based on measurable short-term performance results, this manager is very likely to be promoted or transferred before the employees' negative attitudes result in complaints to the personnel office, strikes, or sabotage. The law governing the effect of measurement on behavior seems to be: *Quantifiable measures drive out nonquantifiable measures.*

Suboptimization

The emphasis in large corporations to develop separate responsibility centers can create some problems for the corporation as a whole. To the extent that a division or functional unit views itself as a separate entity, it might refuse to cooperate with other units or divisions in the same corporation if cooperation could in some way negatively affect its performance evaluation. The competition between divisions to achieve a high ROI can result in one division's refusal to share its new technology or work-process improvements. One division's attempt to optimize the accomplishment of its goals can cause other divisions to fall behind and thus negatively affect overall corporate performance. One common example of this type of suboptimization occurs when a marketing department approves an early shipment date to a customer as a means of getting an order and forces the manufacturing department into overtime production for this one order. Production costs are raised, which reduces the manufacturing department's overall efficiency. The end result might be that, although marketing achieves its sales goal, the corporation fails to achieve its expected profitability.

9.4

GUIDELINES FOR PROPER CONTROL

In designing a control system, top management should remember that controls should follow strategy. Unless controls ensure the use of the proper strategy to achieve objectives, there is a strong likelihood that dysfunctional side-effects will completely undermine the implementation of the objectives. The following guidelines are recommended:

1. Control should involve only the minimum amount of information needed to give a reliable picture of events. Too many controls create confusion. Focus on those 20% of the factors that determine 80% of the results.

2. Controls should monitor only meaningful activities and results, regardless of measurement difficulty. If cooperation between divisions is important to corporate performance, some form of qualitative or quantitative measure should be established to monitor cooperation.

3. Controls should be timely so that corrective action can be taken before it is too late. *Steering controls,* controls that monitor or measure the factors influencing performance, should be stressed so that advance notice of problems is given.

4. Long-term as well as short-term controls should be used. If only short-term measures are emphasized, a short-term managerial orientation is likely.

5. Controls should aim at pinpointing exceptions. Only those activities or results that fall outside a predetermined tolerance range should call for action.

6. Emphasize the reward of meeting or exceeding standards rather than punishment for failing to meet standards. Heavy punishment of failure will typically result in goal displacement. Managers will "fudge" reports and lobby for lower standards.

It is surprising that the best-managed companies often have only a few formal objective controls. They focus on measuring the critical success factors—those few things whose success ensures overall success. Other factors are controlled by the social system in the form of the corporate culture. To the extent that the culture complements and reinforces the strategic orientation of the firm, there is less need for an extensive formal control system. In their book, *In Search of Excellence,* Peters and Waterman state that "the stronger the culture and the more it was directed toward the marketplace, the less need was there for policy manuals, organization charts, or detailed procedures and rules. In these companies, people way down the line know what they are supposed to do in most situations because the handful of guiding values is crystal clear."[40]

9.5

STRATEGIC INCENTIVE MANAGEMENT

In an assessment of the strategic planning of large U.S. corporations, Steiner reports that there is a significant overall weakness in corporations' rewarding managers for strategic thinking.[41] His view agrees with the data reported earlier that only around half of the large U.S. corporations link compensation to business unit performance.[42] Traditionally, in the United States the level of compensation for chief executive officers has been a function of CEOs' compensations in comparable firms. Therefore, CEO compensation in the U.S. is related more to the size of the corporation than to the size of its profits. (This is not so much the case in Great Britain, where there is a closer connection between pay and corporate performance).[43] The gap between CEO compensation and corporate performance is most noticeable in those corporations with widely dispersed stock ownership and no dominant stockholder group to demand performance-based pay.[44] This association between firm size and executive compensation, according to Rappaport, can only fuel top management's natural inclination to grow businesses as quickly as possible.[45]

Boards of directors need to take the initiative in the development of long-term controls and corresponding incentive plans. According to Andrews, "The best criterion for appraising the quality of management performance, in the absence of personal failures or unexpected breakdowns, is management's success over time in executing a demanding and approved strategy that is continually tested against opportunity and need."[46]

Executive compensation must be clearly linked to strategic performance—to the management of the corporate portfolio, to the business unit's mission, to short-term financial as well as long-term strategic performance, and to the degree of risk involved in effective and efficient management of a portfolio.[47] One study of over 20,000 managers in fifty-six companies revealed that business units generated higher profits when incentive pay was a larger part of top management's total compensation.[48] A separate study of fifty-eight business units in fifteen different corporations concluded that "the payment of incentive compensation to managers is associated with more profitable businesses of all types."[49]

The following three approaches are tailored to help match measurements and rewards with explicit strategic objectives and timeframes: (1) the *weighted-*

factor method, (2) the *long-term evaluation method,* and (3) the *strategic-funds method.* These approaches can also be combined to best suit a corporation's circumstances.[50]

1. **Weighted-factor method.** The *weighted-factor method* is particularly appropriate for measuring and rewarding the performance of top SBU managers and group-level executives when performance factors and their importance vary from one SBU to another. The measurements used by one corporation might contain the following variations: the performance of high-growth SBUs measured in terms of market share, sales growth, designated future payoff, and progress on several future-oriented strategic projects; the performance of low-growth SBUs, in contrast, measured in terms of ROI and cash generation; and the performance of medium-growth SBUs measured for a combination of these factors. Refer to Table 9.5 for an example of the weighted-factor method applied to three different SBUs.

2. **Long-term evaluation method.** The *long-term evaluation method* compensates managers for achieving objectives set over a multiyear period. An executive is promised some company stock or "performance units" (convertible into dollars) in amounts to be based on long-term perfor-

TABLE 9.5

A Weighted-Factor Approach to Strategic Incentive Management

STRATEGIC BUSINESS UNIT CATEGORY	FACTOR	WEIGHT
High growth	Return on assets	10%
	Cash flow	0%
	Strategic-funds programs	45%
	Market-share increase	45%
		100%
Medium growth	Return on assets	25%
	Cash flow	25%
	Strategic-funds programs	25%
	Market-share increase	25%
		100%
Low growth	Return on assets	50%
	Cash flow	50%
	Strategic-funds programs	0%
	Market-share increase	0%
		100%

SOURCE: Reprinted, by permission of the publisher, from "The Performance Measurement and Reward System: Critical to Strategic Management," by Paul J. Stonich, from *Organization Dynamics,* Winter 1984, p. 51. Copyright © 1984 American Management Association, New York. All rights reserved.

mance. An executive committee, for example, might set a particular objective in terms of growth in earnings per share during a five-year period. The giving of awards would be contingent on the corporation's meeting that objective within the designated time limit. Any executive who leaves the corporation before the objective is met receives nothing. The typical emphasis on stock price makes this approach more applicable to top management than to business unit managers.

3. **Strategic-funds method.** The *strategic-funds method* encourages executives to look at developmental expenses as being different from those expenses required for current operations. The accounting statement for a corporate unit enters strategic funds as a separate entry below the current ROI. It is therefore possible to distinguish between those expense dollars consumed in the generation of current revenues and those invested in the future of the business. Therefore, the manager can be evaluated on both a short- and a long-term basis and has an incentive to invest strategic funds in the future. Refer to Table 9.6 for an example of the strategic-funds method applied to a business unit.

According to Stonich, "An effective way to achieve the desired strategic results through a reward system is to combine the weighted-factor, long-term evaluation, and strategic-funds approaches."[51] To do this, first segregate strategic funds from short-term funds, as is done in the strategic-funds method. Second, develop a weighted-factor chart for each SBU. Third, measure performance on three bases: the pre-tax profit indicated by the strategic-funds approach; the weighted factors; and the long-term evaluation of the SBU's and the corporation's performance. These incentive plans will probably gain increasing acceptance with business corporations in the near future. General Electric and Westinghouse are two firms using a version of these measures.

TABLE 9.6

A Strategic-Funds Approach Applied to an SBU's Profit-and-Loss Statement

Sales	$ 12,300,000
Cost of sales	6,900,000
Gross margin	$ 5,400,000
Operating (general and administrative expense)	−3,700,000
Operating (return on sales)	$ 1,700,000 or 33%
Strategic funds	−1,000,000
Pre-tax profit	$ 700,000 or 13.6%

SOURCE: Reprinted, by permission of the publisher, from "The Performance Measurement and Reward System" by Paul J. Stonich, *Organizational Dynamics*, Winter 1984. Copyright © 1984 American Management Association, New York. All rights reserved.

SUMMARY AND CONCLUSION

The evaluation and control of performance is a five-step process: (1) determine what to measure, (2) establish standards for performance, (3) measure actual performance, (4) compare actual performance with the standard, and (5) take corrective action. Information coming from this process is fed back into the strategic control system so that managers at all levels in the hierarchy of control can monitor and correct performance deviations.

Although the most commonly used measures of corporate performance are the various return ratios, measures based on a value-added or shareholder value approach can be of some use. Most corporations also monitor key performance objectives. If a corporation sets goals other than simple profitability or return on investment, it might wish to follow the example of Westinghouse and establish specific performance objectives, such as productivity improvement, for special attention. A stakeholder "scorecard" can also be of some value in the assessment of the corporation's impact on its environment. The strategic audit is recommended as a method by which activities throughout the corporation can be evaluated.

Divisions, SBUs, and functional units are often broken down into responsibility centers to aid control. Such areas are often categorized as standard cost centers, revenue centers, expense centers, profit centers, and investment centers. Budgets and periodic statistical reports are important control devices used in the monitoring of the implementation of major programs in business units.

A strategic information system is an important part of the evaluation and control process. By focusing on critical success factors, it can provide early warning signals to strategic managers. The system can be tailored to the business-level strategy being implemented in the SBU, so that the success of the strategy is ensured.

The monitoring and measurement of performance can result in dysfunctional side effects that negatively affect overall corporate performance. Among the likely side-effects are a short-term orientation and goal displacement. These problems can be reduced if top management remembers that controls must focus on strategic goals. There should be as few controls as possible, and only meaningful activities and results should be monitored. Controls should be timely to both long-term as well as short-term orientations. They should pinpoint exceptions but should be used more to reward than to punish individuals.

Incentive plans should be based upon long-term as well as short-term considerations. Three suggested approaches are the weighted-factor method, the long-term evaluation method, and the strategic-funds method.

A proper evaluation and control system should act to complete the loop shown in the strategic management model. It should feed back information important not only to the implementation of strategy, but also to the initial formulation of strategy. In terms of the strategic decision-making process depicted in Fig. 6.1, the data coming from evaluation and control are the basis for step 1—evaluating current performance results. Because of this feedback effect, evaluation and control is the beginning as well as the end of the strategic management process.

DISCUSSION QUESTIONS

1. Is Fig. 9.1 a realistic model of the evaluation and control process? Why or why not?

2. Why bother with value-added, shareholder value, or a stakeholder's scorecard? Isn't it simpler to eval-uate a corporation and its SBUs by just using standard measures like ROI or earnings per share?

3. What are the differences between strategic, tactical, and operational controls?

4. What are the pros and cons of using performance objectives to evaluate performance?

5. What is the difference between performance objectives and critical success factors?

6. How much faith can a division or SBU manager place in a *transfer price* as a surrogate for a market price, in measurement of a profit center's performance?

7. Why are goal displacement and short-run orientation likely side-effects of the monitoring of performance? What can a corporation do to avoid them?

8. Is the evaluation and control process appropriate for a corporation that emphasizes creativity? Are control and creativity compatible? Explain.

9. Evaluate the performance of CSX Corporation and that of its key strategic managers as of mid-1987, as described in the Integrative Case at the end of the chapter. Beginning with the formation of CSX in 1980, determine how successfully the corporation's strategic managers have formulated and implemented their strategic plans.

N O T E S

1. L. G. Hrebiniak and W. F. Joyce, *Implementing Strategy* (New York: Macmillan, 1984), p. 195.

2. P. Lorange, M. F. S. Morton, and S. Ghoshal, *Strategic Control* (St. Paul: West Publishing Co., 1986), pp. 11–14.

3. Lorange, Morton, Ghoshal, p. 124.

4. J. R. Meredith, "Strategic Control of Factory Automation," *Long Range Planning* (December 1987), p. 109.

5. Meredith, p. 112.

6. B. C. Reimann and R. Thomas, "Value-Based Portfolio Planning: Improving Shareholder Return," in *Handbook of Business Strategy, 1986/87 Yearbook,* ed. W. D. Guth (Boston: Warren, Gorham and Lamont, 1986), pp. 21.2–21.3.
V. E. Millar, "The Evolution Toward Value-Based Financial Planning," *Information Strategy: The Executive's Journal* (Winter 1985), p. 28.

7. R. E. Freeman, *Strategic Management: A Stakeholder Approach* (Boston: Pitman Publishing Co., 1984), pp. 177–181.

8. C. W. Hofer, "ROVA: A New Measure for Assessing Organizational Performance," in R. Lamb (ed.), *Advances in Strategic Management,* Vol. 2 (Greenwich, Conn.: Jai Press, 1983), pp. 43–55.
C. W. Hofer and D. Schendel, *Strategy Formulation: Analytical Concepts* (St. Paul, Minn.: West Publishing Co., 1978), p. 130.

9. N. E. Swanson and L. A. Digman, "Organizational Performance Measures for Strategic Decisions: A PIMS-Based Investigation," in *Handbook of Business Strategy, 1986/1987 Yearbook,* ed. W. D. Guth (Boston: Warren, Gorham & Lamont, 1986), pp. 17.2–17.4.

10. A. Rappaport, "Corporate Performance Standards and Shareholder Wealth," *Journal of Business Strategy* (Spring 1983), pp. 28–38.

11. A. Rappaport, "Have We Been Measuring Success with the Wrong Ruler?" *Wall Street Journal* (June 25, 1984), p. 22.

12. Millar, pp. 29–30. For more information on shareholder value measures, see A. H. Seed, "Winning Strategies for Shareholder Value Creation," *Journal of Business Strategy* (Fall 1986), pp. 44–51; B. C. Reimann, "Strategy Valuation on Portfolio Planning: Combining Q and VROI Ratios," *Planning Review* (January 1986), pp. 18–32, 42–45; and M. L. Blyth, E. A. Friskey, and A. Rappaport, "Implementing the Shareholder Value Approach," *Journal of Business Strategy* (Winter 1986), pp. 48–58.

13. P. Drucker, *The Practice of Management* (New York: Harper and Brothers, 1954) as reported by M. D. Richards, *Setting Strategic Goals and Objectives* (St. Paul: West Publishing Co., 1986), pp. 16–17.

14. C. C. Borucki and G. D. Childs, "Productivity and Quality Improvement: The Westinghouse Story," in *Strategic Human Resources Management,* ed. C. Fombrun, N. Tichy, and M. A. Devanna (New York: John Wiley and Sons, 1984), pp. 381–401.

15. C. H. Roush, Jr., "Strategic Resource Allocation and Control," in W. D. Guth (ed.), *Handbook of Business Strategy* (Boston: Warren, Gorham, and Lamont, 1985), pp. 20.1–20.25.

16. R. L. Daft and N. B. Macintosh, "The Nature and Use of Formal Control Systems for Management Control and Strategy Implementation," *Journal of Management* (Spring 1984), pp. 43–66.

17. D. R. Melville, "Top Management's Role in Strategic Planning," *Journal of Business Strategy* (Spring 1981), p. 63.

18. This discussion is based on R. N. Anthony, J. Dearden, and R. F. Vancil, *Management Control Systems* (Homewood, Ill.: Richard D. Irwin, Inc., 1972), pp. 200–203.

19. Lorange, Morton, and Ghoshal, p. 69.

20. A. P. Sloan, Jr., *My Years with General Motors* (Garden City, N.Y.: Doubleday, Anchor Books, 1972), p. 159.

21. Sloan, p. 161.

22. Millar, p. 30.

23. J. R. Galbraith and R. K. Kazanjian, *Strategy Implementation: Structure, Systems and Process* (St. Paul: West Publishing Co., 1986), pp. 85–86.

24. J. A. Turner and H. C. Lucas, Jr., "Developing Strategic Information Systems," in W. D. Guth (ed.), *Handbook*

of Business Strategy (Boston: Warren, Gorham and Lamont, 1985), p. 21.2.

25. N. Gross, "Inquest for International Harvester," *Planning Review* (July-August 1987), p. 9.

26. J. Rockart, "Chief Executives Define Their Own Data Needs," *Harvard Business Review* (March-April 1979).

P. V. Jenster, "Using Critical Success Factors in Planning," *Long Range Planning* (August 1987), pp. 102–109.

A. C. Boynton and R. W. Zmud, "An Assessment of Critical Success Factors," *Sloan Management Review* (Summer 1984), p. 17.

27. C. M. Jones, "GTE's Strategic Tracking System," © *Planning Review* (September 1986), p. 28.

28. G. L. Parsons, "Information Technology: A New Competitive Weapon," *Sloan Management Review* (Fall 1983), p. 11.

29. Parsons, p. 11.

30. For other examples of the use of strategic information systems to gain competitive advantage, see J. M. Ward, "Integrating Information Systems Into Business Strategy," *Long Range Planning* (June 1987), pp. 19–29; and B. C. Reimann, "Strategic Management in an Electronic Age: Exploiting the Power of Information Technology," *International Journal of Management* (September 1987), pp. 438–451.

31. Hrebiniak and Joyce, pp. 198–199.

32. R. M. Hodgetts and M. S. Wortman, *Administrative Policy,* 2nd ed. (New York: John Wiley & Sons, 1980), p. 128.

33. L. Reibstein, "Firms Trim Annual Pay Increases and Focus on Long Term: More Employers Link Incentives to Unit Results," *Wall Street Journal* (April 10, 1987), p. 25.

34. P. Lorange and D. Murphy, "Bringing Human Resources Into Strategic Planning: Systems Design Considerations," in *Strategic Human Resources Management,* ed. C. Fombrun, N. M. Tichy, and M. A. Devanna (New York: John Wiley & Sons, 1984), pp. 281–285.

35. J. Dutton and A. Thomas, "Managing Organizational Productivity," *Journal of Business Strategy* (Summer 1982), p. 41.

36. R. L. Hudson, "SEC Charges Fudging of Corporate Figures Is a Growing Practice," *Wall Street Journal* (June 2, 1983), p. 1.

37. H. R. Bobbitt, Jr., R. H. Breinholt, R. H. Doktor, and J. P. McNaul, *Organizational Behavior,* 2nd ed. (Englewood Cliffs, N.J.: Prentice-Hall, 1978), p. 99.

38. J. P. Worthy and R. P. Neuschel, *Emerging Issues in Corporate Governance* (Evanston: Northwestern University Press, 1984), p. 84.

39. S. Kerr, "On the Folly of Rewarding A, While Hoping for B," *Academy of Management Journal* (December 1975), pp. 769–783.

40. T. J. Peters and R. H. Waterman, *In Search of Excellence* (New York: Harper & Row, 1982), pp. 75–76.

41. G. A. Steiner, "Formal Strategic Planning in the United States Today," *Long Range Planning* (June 1983), pp. 12–17.

42. Lorange and Murphy, pp. 283–284.

43. S. P. Sethi and N. Namiki, "Top Management Compensation and Corporate Performance," *Journal of Business Strategy* (Spring 1987), p. 39.

D. Norburn, "GOGOs, YOYOs and DODOs: Company Directors and Industry Performance," *Strategic Management Journal* (March-April 1986), p. 109.

44. L. R. Gomez-Mejia, H. Tosi, and T. Hinkin, "Managerial Control, Performance, and Executive Compensation," *Academy of Management Journal* (March 1987), pp. 51–70.

45. A. Rappaport, "How To Design Value-Contributing Executive Incentives," *Journal of Business Strategy* (Fall 1983), p. 50.

46. K. R. Andrews, "Directors' Responsibility for Corporate Strategy," *Harvard Business Review* (November-December 1980), p. 32.

47. L. J. Brindisi, Jr., "Paying for Strategic Performance: A New Executive Compensation Imperative," in R. B. Lamb (ed.), *Competitive Strategic Management* (Englewood Cliffs, N.J.: Prentice-Hall, 1984), p. 334.

48. H. E. Glass, "The Challenges for Strategic Planning in the Late 1980s and Beyond," in *Handbook of Business Strategy, 1987/1988 Yearbook,* ed. H. Babian and H. E. Glass (Boston: Warren, Gorham, and Lamont, 1987), p. 2.9.

49. A. Giller, "Organizational Characteristics of Successful Business Units," in *Handbook of Business Strategy, 1987/1988 Yearbook,* ed. H. Babian and H. E. Glass (Boston: Warren, Gorham, and Lamont, 1987), p. 8.7.

50. P. J. Stonich, "The Performance Measurement and Reward System: Critical to Strategic Management," *Organizational Dynamics* (Winter 1984), pp. 45–57.

51. Stonich, p. 53.

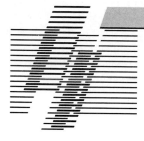

CSX CORPORATION'S EVALUATION OF ITS PERFORMANCE

By mid-1987 a number of environmental issues of significant importance to the rail transportation industry and to CSX Corporation had resolved themselves. Conrail's future was settled at last. Serious opposition in the U.S. House of Representatives to the sale of the U.S. government's 85% of Conrail's stock to Norfolk Southern doomed passage of the Senate's bill. On August 22, 1986, Norfolk Southern's top management, citing tax law changes that made the purchase less attractive, withdrew its bid. After the Conrail Privatization Act of 1986, which restricted other railroads from owning more than 10% of Conrail for a three-year period, was passed, Conrail's stock was sold to the general public in March 1987. Conrail's top management was unwilling, in March 1987, to state publicly if they planned to concentrate on rail operations or diversify into other areas, as CSX and Norfolk Southern had done.[1]

DEVELOPMENTS IN THE RAIL INDUSTRY

In a move to recoup their loss of Conrail, Norfolk Southern's top management made a bid in February 1987 for the 81% of Piedmont Airlines stock that NS didn't already own. Because of Norfolk Southern's sale of its stock (a small minority interest) in Santa Fe Southern Pacific Corporation in 1985, NS appeared to be focusing its future for the time being on multi-modal transportation alternatives in the Eastern United States. Unfortunately for the Roanoke-based company, a bidding war developed around Piedmont, between U.S. Air and TWA. Norfolk Southern dropped out of the bidding and sold much of its stock in Piedmont to U.S. Air for a good profit.

The proposed merger of the Atchison Topeka & Santa Fe Railway with the Southern Pacific railroad was rejected by the Interstate Commerce Commission in a surprise decision in April 1987. Some analysts contended that the insistence by John Schmidt, the Chairman of Santa Fe Southern Pacific Corporation, that the ICC must either approve the entire proposal intact or reject it completely was a primary reason for the ICC's rejection of the merger. Others argued that the decision reflected a movement toward re-regulation in the U.S. This action forced the parent corporation of both railroads to sell at least one of the railroads. In considering the likely sale of either the Santa Fe or the Southern Pacific, analysts wondered if the time was right for an Eastern railroad to create a transcontinental rail system. In response to a question asking if his company might be interested in such an acquisition, Norfolk Southern's new chairman, Arnold McKinnon, told analysts that "we'll look" if one of the Western railroads became available.[2]

Not content to watch other rail companies going multi-modal, Union Pacific Corporation acquired in September 1986 the Overnite Transportation Company. The acquisition of Overnite, the nation's fifth-largest motor carrier of general freight, extended Union Pacific's reach into the Eastern half of the United States. Overnite, headquartered in Richmond, Virginia, had trucking operations in the Northeast, Southeast, and Great Lakes regions. William S. Cook, Chairman and Chief Executive of Union Pacific, explained that the rail company had decided to purchase a trucking firm rather than an Eastern railroad because "the eastern part of the country is more truck oriented." He added that "our studies indicated that it would be a mistake to merge with an Eastern railroad."[3]

CSX'S PERFORMANCE

In reviewing the actions of CSX Corporation over the past few years, Hays T. Watkins, Chairman and Chief Executive Officer of CSX, stated in his letter to the shareholders in the 1986 Annual Report that he was quite pleased with the past performance of the corporation. He was also quite optimistic about CSX's future.

TABLE 9.7

Consolidated Statement of Earnings and Retained Earnings: CSX Corporation

(In Millions of Dollars, Except Per-Share Amounts)

Years Ended December 31,	1986	1985	1984
Operating Revenue			
Transportation	$ 4,803	$ 5,067	$ 5,328
Energy	1,268	1,967	2,303
Other	274	254	269
Total revenues	6,345	7,288	7,900
Operating Expense			
Transportation	4,201	4,404	4,638
Energy	1,131	1,873	2,200
Other	142	130	128
Special charge	—	954	—
Total expenses	5,474	7,361	6,966
Earnings (loss)			
Operating income (loss)	871	(73)	934
Equity in loss of Sea-Land	(2)	—	—
Other income	141	40	33
Interest expense	281	230	242
Earnings (loss) before income taxes	729	(263)	725
Income tax expense (credit)	311	(145)	311
Net earnings (loss)	$ 418	$ (118)	$ 414
Earnings (loss) per share	$ 2.73	$ (.78)	$ 2.80
Retained Earnings			
Balance—January 1	$ 2,741	$ 3,029	$ 2,769
Net earnings (loss)	418	(118)	414
Dividends	(179)	(170)	(154)
Balance—December 31	$ 2,980	$ 2,741	$ 3,029
Per share dividends—common	$ 1.16	$ 1.13	$ 1.04
Common shares outstanding at year-end (thousands)	154,016	152,399	149,566
Average common shares outstanding (thousands)	153,329	151,046	147,608

SOURCE: CSX Corporation, *1986 Annual Report and Form 10-K*, p. 16.

"The programs and plans implemented in the year just past—a transition year as we put our new organization into place—are designed to improve profitability, rates of return and shareholder value through the next decade and beyond." He went on to discuss the operating results of 1986 (see Tables 9.7 to 9.10 for financial results):

TABLE 9.8

Consolidated Statement of Financial Position: CSX Corporation

(In Millions of Dollars)

December 31,	1986	1985	1984
Assets			
Current assets			
Cash and short-term investments	$ 315	$ 187	$ 377
Accounts receivable	1,182	1,299	1,178
Inventories	356	428	458
Other current assets	248	136	124
Total current assets	2,101	2,050	2,137
Investments			
Properties	9,403	9,107	8,987
Investment in Sea-Land	802	—	—
Affiliates and other companies	150	121	137
Other assets	205	198	212
Total investments	10,560	9,426	9,336
Total assets	$12,661	$11,476	$11,473
Liabilities			
Current liabilities			
Accounts payable and other current liabilities	$ 1,511	$ 1,744	$ 1,645
Current maturities of long-term debt	336	208	261
Total current liabilities	1,847	1,952	1,906
Claims and other long-term liabilities	515	598	343
Deferred income taxes	1,903	1,554	1,773
Long-term debt	3,285	2,499	2,302
Redeemable preferred stock and minority interest	238	278	331
Shareholders' Equity			
Common stock, $1 par value	154	152	150
Other capital	1,739	1,702	1,639
Retained earnings	2,980	2,741	3,029
Total common shareholders' equity	4,873	4,595	4,818
Total liabilities and shareholders' equity	$12,661	$11,476	$11,473

SOURCE: CSX Corporation, *1986 Annual Report and Form 10-K*, p. 20.

Earnings for 1986 were $418 million, $2.73 a share, on revenue of $6.3 billion. The 1986 results compare with the $118 million, $.78 per share, net loss reported in 1985. Excluding the special charge announced in the fourth quarter 1985, CSX would have reported earnings of $442 million, $2.92 per share.

Revenue for 1986 ($6,345 million) was down $943 million, 13 percent, from 1985 ($7,288 million). The decline reflects, in part, lower gas transmission revenue due to a change in mix, as substantial sales volumes were replaced by transportation volumes, as well as lower energy prices overall.

In addition, results in 1986 reflect continued weakness in the industrial and agricultural segments of the economy served by rail, increased interest costs associated with the acquisition of Sea-Land, and higher taxes arising from the repeal of investment tax credits retroactive to January 1, 1986.

Transportation results were affected in 1986 by an overall weakness in rail traffic, most notably the decline in the phosphate and fertilizer commodity group, as well as weak export coal loadings. Partially offsetting this were reductions in rail operating expenses, which were cut four percent from 1985 levels, excluding the special charge, as a result of lower fuel costs and aggressive cost controls.

CSX's barge unit, American Commercial Lines, recorded an 89 percent increase, excluding the special charge, in operating income in 1986 over the previous year, led by record coal movements and increases in intermodal tonnages handled jointly and coordinated with the CSX rail units.

Sea-Land had a loss of $2 million on an equity basis for the seven-month period since its acquisition by CSX, but showed improvement in the fourth quarter, reporting earnings of $3 million for the final quarter of 1986.

Energy results were significantly improved by Texas Gas Transmission's record earnings in 1986. CSX Oil & Gas results were impacted unfavorably by lower energy prices.

This was the first reporting year for the company's Technology and Properties groups. The Technology group increased its contribution to income by $17 million as CSX's joint venture in Lightnet, a 5,000-mile fiber optic network, neared completion. In the Properties area, The Greenbrier had a record year and Rockresorts improved its earnings over 1985 and added a new resort, Carambola Beach in the Caribbean, to its list of management properties. Realty earnings were up slightly in 1986, due to stronger fourth quarter results.

Other income increased significantly as a result of two transactions in the fourth quarter of 1986: completion of the sale of nearly all of the company's coal properties and mineral rights and a special, one-time dividend from Trailer Train Company.[4]

NORFOLK SOUTHERN'S PERFORMANCE

Norfolk Southern, in contrast, reported three years of consistently increasing revenues and net profits. Thanks partially to its North American Van Lines acquisition, the corporation's revenues increased from $3.5 billion in 1984 to $4.1 billion in 1986. Its net income increased from $482.2 million in 1984 to $518.7 million in 1986—three years of record net income. In contrast to CSX, NS added to its coal reserves in December 1986 around 225 million tons in West Virginia—reaffirming its commitment to vertically integrated coal mining and transportation. Even with this purchase, NS ended 1986 with cash totaling $724 million and debt comprising less than 15% of capital. In their letter to the stockholders in Norfolk Southern's *1986 Annual Report,* then-Chairman Robert Claytor and Vice-Chairman Arnold Mc-

TABLE 9.9

Business Unit Information: CSX Corporation's Transportation Group
(In Millions of Dollars)

RAIL TRANSPORTATION	1986	1985	1984
Rail revenues			
Merchandise	$2,932	$3,102	$3,195
Coal	1,496	1,570	1,687
Other	149	152	176
Total revenues	4,577	4,824	5,058
Rail expenses			
Labor and fringe	2,246	2,352	2,469
Materials, supplies and other	752	699	736
Fuel	223	368	411
Equipment rent	479	496	504
Depreciation	313	266	280
Special charge	—	844	—
Total expenses	4,013	5,025	4,400
Operating income	$ 564	$ (201)	$ 658
Operating ratio	87.7%	104.1%	87.0%
Property additions	$ 672	$ 903	$ 778
BARGE TRANSPORTATION			
Barge revenues	$226	$243	$270
Barge expenses			
Labor and fringe	48	66	65
Materials, supplies and other	79	88	112
Fuel	26	37	36
Equipment rent	19	13	10
Depreciation	16	19	15
Special charge	—	14	—
Total expenses	188	237	238
Operating income	$ 38	$ 6	$ 32
Property additions	$ 23	$ 30	$ 10
SEA-LAND*			
Revenues	$1,553	$1,634	$1,759
Operating expense	1,601	1,632	1,606
Operating incomc (loss)	$ (48)	$ 2	$ 153

SOURCE: CSX Corporation, *1986 Annual Report and Form 10-K,* pp. 30, 34, and 35.

*This information is presented on a pro forma basis solely for the purpose of comparative analysis. Sea-Land's earnings are currently included in CSX's earnings on an equity basis from the date of acquisition.

TABLE 9.10

Business Unit Information: CSX Corporation's Energy, Properties, and Technology Groups

(In Millions of Dollars)

ENERGY	1986	1985	1984
Energy revenues			
Gas transmission	$1,070	$1,662	$2,002
Oil and gas	215	307	325
Coal*	21	58	55
Intrasegment eliminations	(38)	(60)	(79)
Total revenues	1,268	1,967	2,303
Energy expenses			
Gas transmission	948	1,556	1,898
Oil and gas	217	328	338
Coal*	4	49	43
Special charge coal*	—	96	—
Intrasegment eliminations	(38)	(60)	(79)
Total expenses	1,131	1,969	2,200
Energy operating income (loss)			
Gas transmission	122	106	104
Oil & gas	(2)	(21)	(13)
Coal*	17	(87)	12
Total operating income	$ 137	$ (2)	$ 103
Energy property additions			
Gas transmission	$ 28	$ 35	$ 41
Oil and gas	51	75	126
Coal*	2	1	1
Total property additions	$ 81	$ 111	$ 168
PROPERTIES			
Operating revenues	$250	$202	$210
Operating expenses	91	57	53
Operating income	$159	$145	$157
TECHNOLOGY			
Computer services			
CSX rail services	$ 88	$ 75	$ 63
Public services	16	12	9
Fiber optic right of occupancy sales	8	5	—
Total revenues	112	92	72

(Continued)

TABLE 9.10 (Continued)

TECHNOLOGY	1986	1985	1984
Computer services			
CSX rail services	88	75	63
Public services	13	9	6
Total expenses	101	84	69
Total operating income	11	8	3
Equity in LIGHTNET®	10	(4)	(5)
Total contribution	$ 21	$ 4	$ (2)

SOURCE: CSX Corporation, *1986 Annual Report and Form 10-K,* pp. 36, 38, and 40.

*Substantially all coal properties were disposed of in December 1986.

Kinnon made the following comment about Norfolk Southern's strategic direction:

> Even as Norfolk Southern works to increase the efficiency and profitability of its railroads, it actively seeks attractive opportunities to strengthen its position in the transportation business and enhance its ability to serve customers. The purchase of North American Van Lines, Inc. in 1985 reflects Norfolk Southern's determination to be the nation's premier provider of transportation services. . . .[5]

THE NEW CSX

Taking advantage of its recent acquisition of Sea-Land, however, CSX altered its mission statement and re-defined itself. In one of a series of advertisements appearing in business publications during 1987, CSX described itself as follows:

> If you think we're just a railroad, take another look.
>
> We're a lot more. We're Sea-Land, one of the largest container ship lines on earth, serving 76 ports in 64 countries.
>
> We're also trucks. Barges. Pipelines. Energy resources. Fiber optics. Resorts and property development. And, of course, the railroad. And we're developing new technology to make it all work together.
>
> We're CSX, the first true global transporter. If you've never heard of one before, it's because there's never been one before. This is a company on the move.[6]

NOTES

1. G. Anders and R. Koenig, "Conrail Offering Raises Record of $1.65 Billion," *Wall Street Journal* (March 26, 1987), p. 4.

2. L. McGinley, J. Valente, and D. Machalaba, "ICC Reaffirms Its Rejection of Merger of Santa Fe, Southern Pacific Railroads," *Wall Street Journal* (July 1, 1987), p. 3.

3. D. Machalaba and L. Williams, "Union Pacific To Buy Overnite For $1.2 Billion," *Wall Street Journal* (September 19, 1986), p. 3.

4. H. T. Watkins, "To Our Shareholders," *1986 Annual Report and Form 10-K,* CSX Corporation, p. 3.

5. R. B. Claytor and A. B. McKinnon, "Dear Stockholder," *1986 Annual Report,* Norfolk Southern Corporation, p. 3.

6. Advertisement, *Business Week* (December 18, 1987), p. 33.

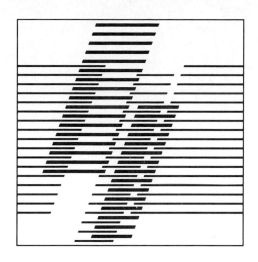

PART FIVE

OTHER STRATEGIC CONCERNS

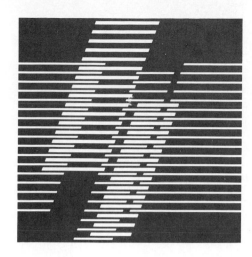

CHAPTER 10

STRATEGIC ISSUES IN MULTINATIONAL CORPORATIONS

STRATEGIC MANAGEMENT MODEL

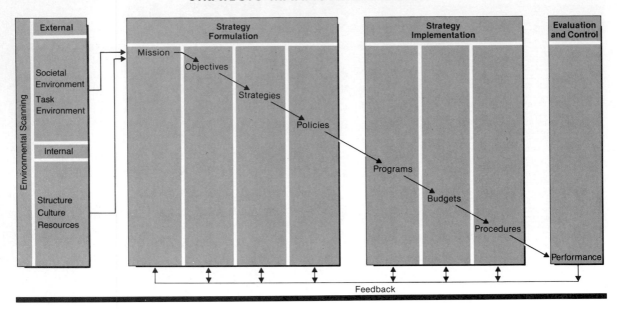

Throughout much of its history, North America has been virtually self-sufficient. During the 1700s and 1800s, the distance between America and Europe encouraged the United States and Canada to develop their own industries. As late as the 1960s, the combined exports and imports of merchandise represented only 7%–8% of the U.S. gross national product—the lowest of any major industrialized nation.[1] A large domestic market, plus a bountiful supply of natural resources and labor, enabled major corporations to grow and become successful while having only a casual interest in "foreign" markets. High tariff laws served to keep the business interests of other countries out of the United States while the infant domestic companies matured.

Since 1960, however, international trade has increased dramatically. In the past quarter-century, the volume of goods traded between all nations has climbed from less than $100 million to around $2 trillion.[2] U.S. exports from 1960 to 1986 increased from $20.6 billion to $217.3 billion—a three-fold increase in constant dollars. At the same time, U.S. imports increased from $16.4 billion to $387.1—a more than five-fold increase in constant dollars.[3] Almost one-fifth of U.S. industrial production is now exported. At least 70% of the goods produced in the U.S. compete with products from other countries.[4]

In the United States alone, there are more than 3,500 multinational corporations (MNCs), 30,000 exporting manufacturers, 25,000 companies with overseas branches and affiliates, and 40,000 firms operating in other countries on an ad-hoc basis. Not only are U.S.-based multinationals increasing their investments in production facilities and companies in other countries, but foreign-based MNCs are also doing the same in the U.S., Canada, and Mexico. In 1983, foreign buyers spent $2.2 billion to buy 116 U.S. companies. In 1987, they spent a record $40.7 billion for 316 companies.[5] The value of U.S. companies and other assets in which Canadians alone hold at least 10% of the equity totals over $100 billion. This total is not surprising: 24% of Canadian corporate assets are owned by foreign investors, many of them U.S. companies or private citizens.[6] International considerations have become crucial to the strategic decisions of any large business corporation.

10.1

THE COMING GLOBAL VILLAGE

In 1965, Marshall McLuhan suggested that advances in communications and transportation technologies were drawing the people of the world closer together. As intercontinental travel times decreased, the world went toward becoming a "global village" of interdependent people.[7] People in all countries were finding themselves affected by huge multinational corporations (MNCs).

In 1984, for example, the Chicago Mercantile Exchange linked with a futures exchange in Singapore in a major step toward global 24-hour financial trading. To increase the number of potential shareholders, an increasing number of corporations are listing their stock at exchanges around the world. R. J. Reynolds Industries, for example, lists its common shares on exchanges in London, Geneva, Zurich, Amsterdam, Dusseldorf, Berlin, Paris, and Brussels. Tokyo is next. Television is rapidly becoming a global phenomenon—linking nations together to watch the Olympics and other high interest events. Ted Turner's Cable Network News was the first truly global television channel, reaching 40% of U.S. homes on cable in 1986 and beaming news to viewers around the world via satellite. CNN's major overseas clients are hotels and government offices in Europe and Japan, but it is also available to homes in Australia and Canada, among other areas.[8] As noted in Illustrative Example 10.1, the modern world is reaching into the most remote locations. We are truly becoming one interdependent global village, with multinational corporations acting as the conduits for the international exchange of information, goods, and services.

Going International

Three basic **reasons** can be listed for business corporations' expanding their operations internationally:

1. To increase their sales and profits, corporations can expand market outlets and exploit growth opportunities. Foreign sales can thus absorb extra capacity and reduce unit costs. They can also spread economic risks over a wider number of markets. For example, realizing that the

The Global Village Comes to Borneo

James Sterba, a staff reporter for the *Wall Street Journal,* journeyed to the island of Borneo to search for "civilization's edge." What he found surprised and impressed him:

> An hour by boat from this tiny river port (of Kapit, Malaysia) and five hours by truck over slick mountain trails gets us to three primitive huts occupied by heavily tattooed Iban natives who cut trees for a logging company. Except for the pack of Dunhills that one of the Ibans offer, the 20th century seems distant.
>
> Until a phone rings. The caller is in a motel room in Anaheim, California. He is the logging company's local manager, and he is phoning via satellites and hilltop relay towers to say that his Disneyland vacation is going great. He dialed the jungle direct. . . .
>
> It is a trifle disconcerting to arrive at a village market six hours by longboat from the coast only to find that Australian apples, Chinese pears, and Sunkist oranges got there first; and to travel another two hours to an Iban longhouse—a motel-like structure on stilts—and find that politicians had popped in by helicopter the day before to festoon the place with party banners; and to watch at a tiny river port, the unloading of boxes that contain frozen chicken wings "Made in the U.S.A."
>
> The beginning of the journey was promising enough. . . . River boats remain Borneo's preferred means of transport. In most places, there is no choice because there are no roads or airports. So we hop a water taxi down the Sarawak River, then a tired old longboat back upstream—a sort of mood-setting exercise for the exotica to come. . . .

> Sure enough, around the next bend stands what for Sarawak's 1.5 million residents, most of them villagers, is a pinnacle of exotica that looks as if it got lost on the way to Houston. It is called the Sarawak Plaza Shopping Complex—10 stories of offices and shops, plus a parking garage and an adjacent Holiday Inn. It is the newest of five such shopping complexes in Kuching.
>
> Since school is out, Sarawak Plaza is bustling with a species of teenager known in suburban America as the "mall rat." Young men—ethnic Chinese, Malays, Ibans—wear baggy trousers and shirts, and their hair is slicked back with styling mousse. Girls with four shades of color between their eyelids and brows flit up and down escalators and in and out of music and video shops (you can rent this year's Oscar-winning "Platoon" for two days at $1.20). . . .
>
> Here we are later in Kapit's only air-conditioned bar, and the town's hot spot, with yesterday's phone call from Anaheim still ringing in our ears. . . . Spend a week in darkest Borneo searching for the edge of civilization and what you find these days are computers and jogging shoes, blue jeans and the latest episode of "L. A. Law". . . . We are confessing failure to a local friend. But he is having trouble hearing because a Malay-Philippino rock band, called D-Illusions and as flat as the draft beer, is belting out a charming 20th-century lyric, "Gimme money, that's what I want."

SOURCE: J. P. Sterba, "Even Deep in Borneo, Civilization Intrudes In All Its Splendor," *Wall Street Journal* (May 5, 1987), p. 1. Reprinted by permission of *Wall Street Journal,* copyright © Dow Jones & Company, Inc., 1987. All Rights Reserved.

market for razor blades in developed countries is stagnant, Gillette is targeting Third World countries. "The opportunities on the blade side really lie in new geography," stated Roderick Mills, Executive Vice-President for Gillette's international business. "In the Third World, there's a very high proportion of people under 15 years old. All those young men are going to be in the shaving population in very short time," he added.[9]

2. To gain competitive advantages, corporations can seek low-cost production facilities in locations close to raw materials and/or cheap labor. They can widen their channels of distribution and access to new technology through joint ventures. Both General Electric and Société Nationale d'Étude et de Construction de Moteurs d'Aviation (SNECMA), the French engine maker, benefited from their joint venture, the forming of CFM International to produce and sell jet engines to airlines.[10]

3. In addition, to secure raw material resources, companies can engage in the worldwide exploration for, and the processing, transportation, and marketing of raw materials. For years, the major rubber companies have owned rubber plantations in Southeast Asia. Oil companies have, of course, gone international for the same reason.

There are a number of **disadvantages,** however, to international expansion. For one thing, the strategic management process is far more complex for a multinational than for a domestic firm. Dymsza lists six limitations to international expansion.[11]

First, the multinational company faces a multiplicity of political, economic, legal, social, and cultural environments as well as a differential rate of change in them.

Second, there are complex interactions between a multinational firm and the multiplicity of its national environments because of national sovereignties, widely disparate economic and social conditions, as well as other factors.

Third, geographical distance, cultural and national differences, variations in business practices, and other differences make communications difficult between the parent corporation and its subsidiaries.

Fourth, the degree of significant economic, marketing, and other information required for planning varies a great deal among countries in availability, depth, and reliability. Furthermore, in any given host country, modern techniques for analyzing and developing data may not be highly developed. For example, an international corporation may find it difficult and expensive to conduct the effective market research essential for business planning.

Fifth, analysis of present and future competition may be more difficult to undertake in a number of countries because of differences in industrial structure and business practices.

Sixth, the multinational company is confronted not only with different national environments but also with regional organizations such as the European Economic Community, the European Trade Area, and the Latin American Free Trade Area, all of which are achieving various degrees of economic integration. The United Nations and specialized international organizations such as the International Bank for Reconstruction and Development, the International Finance Corporation, and the General Agreement on Tariffs and Trade (GATT) may also affect its future opportunities.

The Multinational Corporation

The multinational corporation is a very special type of international firm. Any U.S. company can call itself "international" if it has a small branch office in, say, Juarez or Toronto. An **international company** is one that engages in any combination of activities from exporting/importing to full-scale manufacturing in foreign countries. The **multinational corporation,** in contrast, is a highly developed international company with a deep worldwide involvement, plus a global perspective in its management and decision making. A more specific definition of an MNC is suggested by Dymsza:[12]

1. Although a multinational corporation may not do business in every region of the world, its decision makers consider opportunities throughout the world.

2. A considerable portion of its assets are invested internationally. One authority suggests that a firm becomes global when 20% of its assets are in other countries. Another suggests that the point is reached when operations in other nations account for at least 35% of the corporation's total sales and profits.

3. The corporation engages in international production and operates plants in a number of countries. These plants may range from assembly to fully integrated facilities.

4. Managerial decision making is based on a worldwide perspective. The international business is no longer a sideline or segregated activity. International operations are integrated into the corporation's overall business.

Porter proposes that multinationals operate in world industries that vary on a continuum from multi-domestic to global.[13] **Multi-domestic industries** are specific to each country or group of countries. This type of international industry is a collection of essentially domestic industries, like retailing and insurance. The activities in an MNC's subsidiary in this type of industry is essentially independent of the activities of the MNC's subsidiaries in other countries. In each country the MNC tailors its products or services to the very specific needs of consumers in that particular country. **Global industries,** in contrast, operate worldwide with only small adjustments made by MNCs for country-specific circumstances. A global industry is one in which an MNC's activities in one country are significantly affected by its activities in other countries. MNCs produce products or services in various world locations and sell them with only minor adjustments all over the world. Examples of global industries are commercial aircraft, television sets, semi-conductors, copiers, automobiles, and watches.

10.2

STRATEGY FORMULATION

As described in Chapter 1, the strategic management process includes strategy formulation, implementation, and evaluation and control. In order to formulate strategy, the top management of a multinational corporation must scan both the external environment for opportunities and threats, and the internal environment for strengths and weaknesses.

Scanning the External International Environment

The dominant issue in the strategic-management process of a multinational corporation is the external environment. The type of relationship an MNC can have with each factor in its task environment varies from one country to another and from one region to another. International societal environments vary so widely that a corporation's internal environment and strategic management process must be very flexible. Cultural trends in West Germany, for example, have resulted in the inclusion of worker representatives in corporate strategic planning. Differences in the sociocultural, economic, political-legal, and technological aspects of societal environments strongly affect the ways in which an MNC conducts its marketing, financial, manufacturing, and other functional activities. Some of the variables to be monitored in the various international societal environments are listed in Table 10.1.

Sociocultural Forces

Different sociocultural norms and values have important effects on an MNC's activities. For example, some cultures accept bribery and payoffs as a fact of life, whereas others punish them heavily. In Nigeria the accepted "dash"

TABLE 10.1
Some Important Variables in International Societal Environments

SOCIOCULTURAL	ECONOMIC	TECHNOLOGICAL	POLITICAL-LEGAL
Customs, norms, values	Economic development	Regulations on technology transfer	Form of government
Language	Per capita income		Political ideology
Demographics	Climate	Energy availability/cost	Tax laws
Life expectancies	GNP trends	Natural resource availability	Stability of government
Social institutions	Monetary and fiscal policies	Transportation network	Government attitude toward foreign companies
Status symbols		Skill level of workforce	
Life-style	Unemployment level	Patent-trademark protection	Regulations on foreign ownership of assets
Religious beliefs	Currency convertibility		
Attitudes toward foreigners	Wage levels	Information-flow infrastructure	Strength of opposition groups
Literacy level	Nature of competition		Trade regulations
	Membership in regional economic associations		Protectionist sentiment
			Foreign policies
			Terrorist activity
			Legal system

(money under the table) ranges from 15% of a multibillion dollar contract to a few naira to get a hotel operator to place a phone call.

Most countries differentiate between "lubrication" or "grease" payments, made to minor officials to expedite the execution of their duties, and large-scale "whitemail" bribes, intended to hide either a violation of the law or an illegal contribution designed to influence government policy. In some countries grease payments are viewed by their citizens as an entitlement—necessary income to supplement low public salaries. Because the dividing line between these two forms of extra payment is indistinct, an MNC must carefully monitor each country's norms and ensure that its actions are in line with local practice. Ethics tend to become pragmatically bound to situations, and the top managers of MNCs may find themselves open to charges of being amoral.

In less developed countries (LDCs), most of the working population can be illiterate. A result is likely to be a shortage of skilled labor and supervisors. Manufacturing facilities that mesh with the technical sophistication of the work force must be designed. If U.S. managers are used in LDCs, they must be aware of the wide variance in working practices around the world and totally familiar with those in the country in which they are stationed. For example, it is common in Europe for employees to get added compensation according to the number of their family members or because of unpleasant working conditions. Finnish paper mill workers get a "sauna premium" for missing baths when they are asked to work on Sunday. Fiji Island miners receive a daily half-hour "sex break" to fulfill their marital obligations.[14] Other examples abound.

Differences in language and social norms will affect heavily the marketing mix for a particular country. Product presentation, packaging, distribution channels, pricing, and advertising must be attuned to each culture. For example, Western cosmetic firms such as Max Factor, Revlon, and Avon have had little success in selling their usual products in Japan. Certain cultural factors affect their sales: in Japan perfume is hardly used; suntans are considered ugly; and bath oil is impractical in communal baths.[15] In contrast, Mr. Donut franchise shops are very successful in Japan, even though there is no coffee and doughnut custom there. Doughnuts are presented as a snack rather than as a breakfast food and located near railroad stations and supermarkets. All the signs are in English in order to appeal to the Western interests of the Japanese.

Even if a product is desired by the public, the literal translation of a product's name and slogan can ruin sales. For example, Pepsi Cola's "Come alive" jingle was translated into German as "Come alive out of the grave."[16] When General Motors introduced its Nova model into Latin America, it believed the name would translate well. Nova means constellation in Spanish. Nevertheless, people began to pronounce it "no vá," which in Spanish means "it does not go."[17] When translated into Spanish, an advertisement for ink by the Parker Pen Company gave the false impression that the product helped prevent pregnancy.[18]

Religious beliefs can also make a significant impact on a country's business practices. For example, to conform with Islamic law, banks in Pakistan stopped paying interest to depositors. The alternative is a profit-sharing and loss-sharing system. Sudan and Iran are also moving toward a totally Islamic banking system.[19] In Japan, each time Mazda manufactures a new car model, a Shinto priest clad in traditional white robe, sandals, and black lacquered hat conducts "honorable purification" rites on the new product with top management in attendance.[20]

Economic Forces

The type of economic system in a country can strongly affect the kind of relationship an MNC can establish with a host country. The managers of an MNC based in a free-market capitalistic country may have difficulty understanding the regulations affecting trade with a centrally planned socialistic country. Licensing, acquisition, and joint ventures may be restricted severely by such a host country. In addition, in most countries inflation and currency exchange rates create further difficulties for an MNC. In Bolivia, for example, the inflation rate during 1985 was 25,000%! After being frozen by the government for a year, prices rose at an annual rate of 545% in Brazil during 1987. Following prices, Brazilian interest rates surged to more than 700%, creating a serious problem for business. An MNC's financial policy in an economy subject to rapid inflation must be altered to protect the firm against inflationary losses. Cash balances must be minimized. Credit terms must be restricted. Prices must be constantly watched. In addition, balance of payments problems in a host country can lead to formal currency devaluations, as occurred in Italy in 1985 and in Mexico throughout the 1980s. Informal currency devaluations, resulting from the "floating" currency-exchange rate, took place in the United States, as well as in some other countries, during the mid-1980s. Such a devaluation leads to an MNC's taking large losses in terms of the assets and profits of its subsidiary in the devaluating country. In addition, a socialistic country may control the prices of the products sold by the MNC in that country but may increase the price of the raw materials it sells to the MNC. This results in a severe profit squeeze as the host government attempts to pass the burden of inflation to "rich" multinational corporations.

Because of these and other economic problems throughout the world, an MNC must be prepared to engage in countertrade and in hedging its foreign currency. **Countertrade** is a modern form of bartering that ranges from relatively simple barter transactions to intricate arrangements that can involve many nations and goods as well as complex financing and credits. Because less developed countries are often unable to pay cash for needed goods, exchanging goods and services is becoming increasingly attractive for them. From 1976 to 1984, countertrade grew from an estimated 2% to 33% of world commerce. For example, Sorimex, a Renault subsidiary, accepts coffee, phosphates, and other commodities in exchange for autos, in agreements with such countries as Colombia, Tunisia, Turkey, Egypt, Rumania, and the People's Republic of China. Almost one-fifth of General Electric's $4 billion in exports in one year were under countertrade contracts. Banks now have countertrade divisions to turn commodities into cash for the bank's commercial customers.[21] Multinational corporations must also deal with fluctuating exchange rates by *hedging* their foreign-currency exposures in the forward foreign-exchange market in which currencies are bought and sold for delivery at specific dates. For example, if a U.S.-based multinational is scheduled to receive 100 million German marks in exchange for machine tools one year from today, it may lose money if the dollar rises in value in relation to that of the mark. Although the 100 million marks is worth 30 million U.S. dollars today, it might be worth only 25 million U.S. dollars next year. To avoid this risk, an MNC may choose to sell marks for dollars in the forward market for delivery in one year. This hedge "locks in" the MNC's dollar revenue at 30 million U.S. dollars regardless of currency fluctuations.

Political-Legal Forces

The system of laws and public policies governing business formation, acquisitions, and competitive activities constrains the strategic options open to a multinational company. It is likely that a particular country will specify guidelines for hiring, firing, and promoting people; it might also mandate employment ratios of "foreigners" to its citizens and restrict management's prerogatives regarding unions. In addition, there are likely to be government policies dealing with ownership, licensing, repatriation of profits (profits leaving the host country for the MNC's home country), royalties, importing, and purchasing. Beyond these, there are likely to be both some sentiment for the establishment of tariff barriers to keep out foreign goods and some strong negative feeling about foreign control by an MNC of the host country's assets.

There are many examples of countries expropriating and nationalizing foreign as well as domestic holdings. In 1981, for example, France, under socialist leader François Mitterand, ordered a number of foreign-owned firms (among them, Honeywell-Bull Computers, ITT-France, and Rouseel-Uclaf Drugs) to sell a large percentage of their stock to the French government. Other countries have passed laws forbidding foreign nationals (including MNCs) from having majority control of firms in key industries. Mexico and India restricted foreign ownership during the 1970s. Canada passed legislation in 1981 requiring U.S. energy companies operating in Canada to sell a majority of their stock to Canadian owners by 1990. Responding to Malaysia's requirement that Malaysians have majority control of rubber plantations, Uniroyal sold its profitable rubber plants to a Malaysian company in 1984 and left the country.[22] A more old-fashioned approach took place in Peru in 1985 when President Perez's police, carrying submachine guns, surrounded the headquarters of HNG/InterNorth Inc.'s Belco Petroleum Corporation and simply took the Omaha energy company's Peruvian assets, worth $400 million.[23]

By the mid-1980s two international trends were evident. One was the desire by a number of countries to sell to private interests previously state-owned firms and to welcome the presence of foreign-owned MNCs. Similar to President Reagan's deregulation of government agencies, this **denationalization** or **privatization** of state-owned corporations was taking place in Canada, Japan, and most Western European nations. Great Britain, for example, sold the assets of Jaguar automobiles and 51% of British Telecom, the telecommunications monopoly. From 1980 to 1988, more than fifty-six state-owned companies from every continent, with total value of more than $90 billion, were sold to private shareholders. Another 2,000 candidates, ranging from Britain's electricity industry and much of France's insurance business, to sugar mills in Mexico and steel mills in Bangladesh, were marked for sale during the early 1990s.[24] Experts predict that state-owned enterprises that become multinational will be increasingly privatized, whether formally or informally. The trend will continue because apart from purely national public services, all state-owned enterprises must expand internationally in order to survive in the increasingly global environment. They cannot compete successfully in other countries if they are forced to follow inefficient home-country government policies and regulations rather than economically-oriented international practices.[25]

The second international trend was an increasing amount of trade barriers, local content regulations, and other **protectionist measures,** designed to help domestic industry compete with foreign competition. Although tariffs world-wide were significantly less during the 1980s than they had been in the 1950s, they remained a favorite defense against imports in developing countries. Taiwan, for example charged a 65% fee on imported autos. Brazil added a 105% tariff to imported wine and sausage. The developed countries often do the same. In an attempt to protect U.S. pasta makers and to retaliate for the Common Market's discrimination against U.S. lemons and oranges, President Reagan in 1985 increased the tariff from about 1/10 cent to some 10 cents per pound on the price of European noodles. The quota has become very popular as a way to protect home industry without resorting to tariffs. For example, under polite but firm pressure from the European Community, the Japanese agreed to limit their shipments of quartz watches, hi-fi equipment, and computer-controlled machine tools to Europe. Japan, in turn, strictly limited its imports of leather, beef, and citrus fruits. Other protectionist measures are setting product standards at such a level that few foreign products will be acceptable for sale (a favorite in Japan), requiring that government procurement give preference to that nation's own industry (heavily used in the U.S. and France for "national security"), and outright government subsidies to companies in particular industries to help them compete in the international market with artificially lower prices (used worldwide to support local agriculture). Local content regulations, to force foreign companies to manufacture within a particular country at least a part of every product that they sell there, are being generated worldwide. Mexico, for example, requires its six foreign-car manufacturers to use locally produced parts and material equal to half of each vehicle's value. There are examples like these for most nations in the world. Such protectionist and nationalistic tendencies serve to short-circuit the basic logic underlying the economic concept of **comparative advantage** (see Illustrative Example 10.2); the results are higher prices for consumers and inefficient domestic industries.

In order to introduce some stability into international trade, a number of countries have formed alliances and negotiated mutual cooperation agreements. One such agreement is the General Agreement on Tariffs and Trade (GATT) established in 1948 by twenty-three countries. This agreement was formed to create a relatively free system of trading, primarily through the reduction of tariffs. It provides a forum for the negotiating of mutual reductions in trade restrictions. By 1987, ninety-four nations were contracting parties to the GATT. Although the General Agreement covers around 80% of world trade in merchandise, it does not cover a growing trade in services, agriculture, textiles, and investment and capital flows.[26] An example of a political/trade alliance is the European Economic Community (Common Market), which agreed not only to reduce duties and other trade restrictions among member countries, but also to have a common tariff against non-member countries. This provision was a major factor in encouraging firms from nonmember countries, such as the United States, to locate some manufacturing and marketing facilities inside the EEC to avoid tariffs.

There are also trade associations, such as the Organization of Petroleum Exporting Countries (OPEC), the International Tin Council, and the International Cocoa Organization, which attempt to stabilize commodity supplies and prices to the benefit of their member nations.

Technological Forces

As mentioned in Chapter 4, the question of technology "transfer" has become an important issue in international dealings. Most less developed countries welcome multinational corporations into their nation as conduits of advanced technology and management expertise. They realize that not only will local labor be hired to work for the firm, but also that the MNC will have to educate the work force to deal with advanced methods and techniques. Reich, in his book *The Next American Frontier,* argues that production technologies are rapidly moving from the developed to the developing nations of the world.[27] Countries such as Korea, Hong Kong, Taiwan, Singapore, Brazil, and Spain, which specialized in the 1960s in simple products like clothing and toys, are now mass producing technologically complex products like automobiles, televisions, and ships. At the same

ILLUSTRATIVE EXAMPLE 10.2

The Basics of Absolute and Comparative Advantage in International Trade

Suppose a country presently produces 1 million bushels of corn and 5 million bushels of beans each year. Its people desire more corn. Should it simply plant more corn and less beans? This seems like a reasonable solution until one notes that the soil and water are much better for growing beans than for corn. Each acre planted can produce twice as much bean crop as corn. It takes the same amount of work, and the seeds, fertilizer, and other costs are the same for the farmers regardless of the crop planted. Suppose that the neighboring country has different soil and on every acre planted is able to produce twice as much corn as beans.

The concept of *absolute advantage* in international trade suggests that when both countries are considered, the first country has advantage over the second country in producing beans, but the second has advantage over the first in producing corn. The logical conclusion is that the first country should specialize in producing beans (where it has absolute advantage) and the second should plant only corn (where it also has absolute advantage). The result would be that the first country would produce 7 million bushels of beans each year and *no* corn (with the 2 to 1 advantage of beans to corn, the 1 million bushels of corn would be replaced by 2 million bushels of beans). The reverse would be true in the second country. If the countries are able to trade freely with each other, both countries will be able to have more corn and beans if they each specialize in the crop with which there is advantage, than if both countries try to produce both crops.

Therefore, in answer to the question posed earlier, if a country wants more corn but has an absolute advantage in the production of beans, it should plant more beans. The excess beans can be exported to another country in exchange for more corn than the first country could ever produce with the same resources.

What happens, however, when the first country can produce more corn *and* beans per acre planted than can its neighboring country? Is there any benefit to trade? According to the concept of *comparative advantage,* it still makes sense to specialize as long as the first country is able to grow more of one crop than another crop per acre planted. As an analogy, suppose the best architect in town also happens to be the best carpenter. Would it make sense for him to build his own house? Certainly not, because he can earn more money per hour by devoting all his time to his job as an architect even though he has to employ a carpenter less skillful than himself to build the house. In the same manner, the first country will gain if it concentrates its resources on the production of that commodity it can produce most efficiently. It will earn enough money from the export of that commodity to still import what it needs from its less efficient neighbor country.

SOURCE: J. D. Daniels and L. H. Radebaugh, *International Business: Environments and Operations,* 4th ed. (Reading, Mass.: Addison-Wesley, 1987), pp. 121–129.

time, the less developed countries of Malaysia, Thailand, the Philippines, Sri Lanka, and India have taken over the production of clothing, toys, and the like. With Korea and Taiwan on its heels technologically, Japan reduced its steelmaking capacity and began orienting itself in the 1980s beyond consumer electronics toward telecommunications.

Political-legal considerations become important when aerospace firms, with their heavy dependence on government contracts, want to transfer the technology that they developed for military purposes into profitable commercial products sold internationally. General Electric, for example, had a great deal of difficulty forming a joint venture with the French national engine firm SNECMA in the early 1970s. The venture involved the sharing of jet engines developed specifically for the prototype of the B-1 bomber. Although the U.S. federal government refused, for political reasons, to put the B-1 bomber into production, it did not like the idea of GE's selling such advanced technology to another country.[28] The U.S. government has similar fears of semiconductor technology being sold to countries behind the Iron Curtain. The Coordinating Committee for Multilateral Export Controls (Cocom), composed of the fifteen members of the North Atlantic Treaty Organization (NATO) minus Spain and Iceland plus Japan, compiles lists of items that cannot be sold to Communist countries without its approval. This control has created a number of problems for MNCs wishing to sell high-technology products to China.[29]

Another technological issue raised in international trade is the determination of the appropriate technology for use in production plants located in host countries. For example, labor-saving devices (robots, for instance) that are economically justifiable in highly developed countries where wage rates are high, can be more costly than labor-intensive types of production in less developed countries with high unemployment and low wage rates. The knowledge of technology might be so low in a country that the MNC is tempted, to gain operating leverage, to employ very few local people and automate the plant as much as possible. The host country's government, however, faced with massive unemployment, could strongly desire a labor intensive plant.[30] The basic question an MNC might face is whether the benefits to be gained by modifying technologies for the unique conditions of each country are worth the costs that must be incurred.

Assessing International Opportunities and Threats

In searching for an advantageous market or manufacturing location, a multinational corporation must gather and evaluate data on strategic factors in a large number of countries and regions. Because of its global perspective, an MNC might use comparative advantage to its benefit, by making machine parts in Brazil, assembling them as engines in Germany, installing the engines in auto bodies in Italy, and shipping completed cars to the United States for sale. This strategy serves to reduce the risk to the MNC of operating in only one country, but exposes it to a series of smaller risks in a greater number of countries. Therefore, multinational corporations must be able to deal with political and economic risk in many diverse countries and regions.

Some firms, such as American Can Company, develop an elaborate computerized system to rank investment risks. Smaller companies can hire outside consultants like Chicago's Associated Consultants International or Boston's Arthur D. Little, Inc. to provide political risk assessments. Among the many systems that exist to assess political and economic risks are the Political System Stability Index, the Business Environment Risk Index,

Business International's Country Assessment Service, and Frost and Sullivan's World Political Risk Forecasts.[31] (For a summary of Frost and Sullivan's risk index, see the January/February, 1987, issue of *Planning Review*.)[32] Regardless of the source of data, a firm must develop its own method of assessing risk. It must decide upon the most important factors from its point of view and assign weights to each. An example of such a rating method is depicted in Table 10.2.

Scanning the Internal Environment

Any corporation desiring to move into the international arena will need to assess its own strengths and weaknesses. A corporation's chances for success are enhanced if it has or can develop the following capabilities:

1. **Technological lead.**   An innovative approach or a new product or a new process gives one a short-term monopolistic position.

2. **A strong trade name.**   If a well-known product has snob appeal, a higher profit margin can cover initial entry costs.

3. **Advantage of scale.**   A large corporation has the advantage of low unit costs and a financial base strong enough that it can weather setbacks.

4. **A scanning capability.**   An ability to search successfully and efficiently for opportunities will take on greater importance in international dealings.

5. **An outstanding product or service.**   A solid product or service is more likely to have staying power in international competition.

6. **An outstanding international executive.**   The presence of an executive who understands international situations and can develop a core of local executives who can work well with the home office, is likely to result in the building of a strong and long-lasting international organization.[33]

Evaluating Mission and Objectives

Upon assessing its internal strengths and weaknesses and the opportunities and threats present in the international environment, a business corporation must decide upon its level of commitment to national and international markets. Not every firm needs to become a multinational corporation to be successful. Not every MNC needs to aim for high market share throughout the world to be profitable. James Leontiades proposes that a company can take one of four basic approaches, as depicted in Figure 10.1, regarding international competition within an industry; the selection of an approach is based upon a company's **market share objective** and its desired **scope of operations:**[34]

- **Global high share.** As mentioned earlier in this chapter, a global industry is characterized by MNCs having global objectives and a worldwide coordination of resources in interdependent markets. A company desiring global high share in an industry should follow an overall low cost

TABLE 10.2

Example of Weighted Rating of Investment Climate

Factors Listed in Order of Importance	COUNTRY A			COUNTRY B		
	(1) Assigned Weights Considering Importance of Adverse Developments	(2) Rating of Factor from 0 (Completely Unfavorable) to 100 (Completely Favorable)	(3) Weighted Rating (Column 1 × Column 2)	(1) Assigned Weights Considering Importance of Adverse Developments	(2) Rating of Factor from 0 (Completely Unfavorable) to 100 (Completely Favorable)	(3) Weighted Rating (Column 1 × Column 2)
1. Possibility of expropriation.	10	90	900	10	55	550
2. Possibility of damage to property from rebellion or war.	9	80	720	9	50	450
3. Remission of earnings.	8	70	560	8	50	400
4. Governmental restrictions of foreign business compared to domestic-owned enterprise.	8	70	560	8	60	480
5. Availability of local capital at reasonable cost.	7	50	350	7	90	630
6. Political stability.	7	80	560	7	50	350
7. Repatriation of capital.	7	80	560	7	60	420
8. Currency stability.	6	70	420	6	30	180
9. Price stability.	5	40	200	5	30	150
10. Taxes on business (including any discriminatory provisions).	4	80	320	4	90	360
11. Problems of dealing with labor unions.	3	70	210	3	80	240
12. Government investment incentives.	2	0	0	2	90	180
TOTAL WEIGHTED RATING OF INVESTMENT CLIMATE			5,360			4,390

SOURCE: W. A. Dymsza, *Multinational Business Strategy* (New York: McGraw-Hill Book Co., 1972), p. 90. Copyright © 1972 by McGraw-Hill, Inc. Reprinted by permission.

FIGURE 10.1
Four Basic Approaches to International Competition

MARKET SHARE OBJECTIVE

		High	Low
SCOPE OF OPERATIONS	Global	Global High Share	Global Niche
	National	National High Share	National Niche

Source: Adapted from J. C. Leontiades, *Multinational Corporate Strategy* (Lexington, Mass.: Lexington Books, 1985), p. 53. Reprinted by permission.

strategy by placing its many operations in those countries where costs are lowest and by using economies of scale. Large MNCs such as IBM, Ford, Philips, and Sony take this approach.

- **Global niche.** Because relatively few companies will have the resources to pursue a global high share objective, most developing multinational corporations will attempt to gain global competitive advantage through specialization of product or market. Using a differentiation competitive strategy, such a corporation might produce a particular type of product or service that global high share MNCs cannot afford to produce. To grow globally, Schlumberger has, for example, offered a variety of specialized services to the oil and computer industries. A company can also follow a focus strategy to satisfy a particular market segment that exists in small numbers in many countries. Rolls Royce automobiles, for example, produces automobiles for the very wealthiest people throughout the world.

- **National high share.** Rather than compete in an international arena for which they are unprepared, many companies choose to concentrate on their domestic market. These firms can be very successful as long as their particular industry remains multi-domestic (in Porter's terms) as compared to global. National barriers to entry are crucial to the preservation of national high share. These barriers, which can range from tariffs to quotas to transportation and communication impediments as well as differences in taste, refer to anything that obstructs the corporation's freedom to transfer and coordinate resources across national borders. Examples of these multi-domestic industries, which exist in every country but are generally unattractive to global competitors, are retailing, distribution, insurance, consumer finance, and caustic chemicals.[35] Norfolk Southern Railroad is a very successful transportation company in the process of achieving national high share in the United States.

- **National niche.** To close off their markets from national high share and global competitors, national niche companies can take advantage of specialization on a national scale. Food (such as barbecue sauce in the U.S.), clothing, and some small-scale handicraft industries often allow a company to achieve a national niche.

If a multinational corporation chooses to achieve global high share, it must be prepared to establish a significant presence in the three developed areas of the world known collectively as **the triad.** Coined by Kenichi Ohmae, Managing Director of the Tokyo office of McKinsey & Company, the three markets of Japan, North America, and Western Europe now form a single market with common needs.[36] Arguing that consumers' behavior is influenced more by their educational background and disposable income than by ethnic characteristics, Ohmae proposes that strategic managers of MNCs must treat the inhabitants of the triad as a single race of consumers with shared needs and aspirations.

Focusing on the triad is essential for an MNC pursuing global high share, according to Ohmae, because close to 90% of all high-value-added, high-technology manufactured goods are produced and consumed in North America, Western Europe, and Japan. Ideally, a company should have a significant presence in each of these regions so that it can produce and market its products simultaneously in all three areas. Otherwise, it will lose competitive advantage to triad-oriented MNCs. No longer can an MNC develop and market a new product in one part of the world before it exports it to other developed countries. According to Ohmae, the previously used "cascade" model of product distribution by stages is being replaced by the "sprinkler" model of simultaneous production and marketing. A personal experience of Ohmae's shows how much of a global village the world has become:

> Recently, . . . when I was showing off my very thin Casio calculator, which fits inside my visiting card case, a Dutchman smiled and pulled out his own, and pointed out that it was even thinner. The latest Casio had been launched simultaneously in all regions of the triad, so that it reached certain parts of the Netherlands faster than a local shop in Japan.[37]

International Portfolio Analysis

To strengthen a firm's competitive position, strategic planning seeks to match markets with products and other corporate resources. Because most multinational corporations manufacture and sell a wide range of products, it is necessary, when management is formulating strategy, to keep track of the country's attractiveness as well as the product's strength. Nevertheless, there is a strong tendency for top management in MNCs to plan around either products or markets, but not both simultaneously.[38]

To aid international strategic planning, Harrell and Kiefer have shown how portfolio analysis can be applied to international markets. As depicted in Fig. 10.2, each axis summarizes a host of data concerning the attractiveness of a particular country and the competitive strength of a particular product.

A **country's attractiveness** is composed of its market size, the market rate of growth, the extent and type of government regulation, and economic and political factors. A product's **competitive strength** is composed of its market share, product fit, contribution margin, and market support. The two scales form the axes of the matrix in Fig. 10.2. Those products falling in the upper left generally should receive funding for growth, whereas products in the lower right are prime for "harvesting," or divesting. Those products falling on the lower left to upper-right diagonal require selective funding strategies. Those falling in the upper-right block require additional funding if the product is to contribute in the future to the firm's profits. Joint ventures or divestitures would be most appropriate if cash is limited. Those falling in the center and lower left blocks are probably good candidates for "milking." They can produce strong cash flows in the short run.[39]

Portfolio analysis might not be useful, however, to those MNCs pursuing

FIGURE 10.2
Matrix for Plotting Products by Country

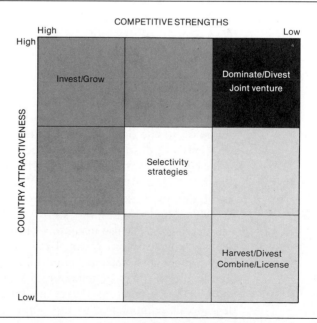

Source: G. D. Harrell and R. O. Kiefer, "Multinational Strategic Market Portfolios," *MSU Business Topics* (Winter 1981), p. 7. Reprinted by permission.

global high share via an overall low-cost competitive strategy. For those MNCs catering to the triad countries, portfolio analysis might be useful only in their considerations of Third World locations. In discussing the importance of global industries, Porter argues against the use of Harrell and Kiefer's recommended portfolio analysis on a country by country basis:

> In a global industry, however, managing international activities like a portfolio will undermine the possibility of achieving competitive advantage. In a global industry, a firm must in some way integrate its activities on a worldwide basis to capture the linkage among countries.[40]

Developing International Strategies

Depending upon its situation and its mission and objectives, a multinational corporation can select from a number of strategic options the most appropriate methods for it to use in entering a foreign market or establishing manufacturing facilities in another country.

Exporting

Exporting is a good way to minimize risk and to experiment with a specific product; it can be conducted in a number of ways. An MNC could choose to handle all critical functions itself, or it could contract these functions to an export management company. To operate in a country such as Japan, which has a series of complex regulations, an MNC could use the services of an agent or distributor.

Licensing

Under a *licensing* agreement, the licensing firm grants rights to a firm in the host country to produce and/or sell a product. The licensee pays compensation to the licensing firm in return for technical expertise. This is an especially useful strategy if the trademark or brand name is well known, but the MNC does not have sufficient funds to finance its entering the country directly. Domino's Pizza, Inc., for example, gave Ernest Higa in 1985 the sole rights to market Domino's pizza in Japan for a share of the receipts. In 1986, Higa's first three stores made more than $1 million in sales.[41] Anheuser-Busch is also using this strategy to produce and market Budweiser beer in Great Britain, Japan, Israel, Australia, Korea, and the Philippines. This strategy also becomes important if the country makes entry via investment either difficult or impossible. Examples are Japan and Eastern European countries. There is always the danger, however, that the licensee might develop its competence to the point that it becomes a competitor to the licensing firm.

Joint Ventures

Joint ventures are very popular with MNCs. Companies often form joint ventures to combine the resources and expertise needed for the development of new products or technologies.[42] The corporation engages in international ownership at a much lower risk. A joint venture may be an association between an MNC and a firm in the host country or a government agency in that country. A quick method of obtaining local management, it also reduces the risks of expropriation and harassment by host country officials. Some of the joint ventures that U.S. firms have made with foreign partners are listed in Table 10.3.

When more than two organizations participate in a joint venture, it is sometimes referred to as a **consortium.** For example, Airbus Industrie, the European producer of jet airplanes, is a consortium owned by four partners from four countries: Aerospatiale of France (37.9%), Messerschmitt-Bokkow-Blohm of West Germany (37.9%), British Aerospace Corp. (20%), and Construcciones Aeronauticas S. A. of Spain (4.2%). Disadvantages of joint ventures include loss of control, lower profits, probability of conflicts with partners, and the likely transfer of technological advantage to the local partner. Joint ventures typically are meant to be temporary, especially by the Japanese, who view them as a way to rectify a competitive weakness until they can achieve long-term dominance in the partnership.[43] For an example of an international joint venture by CSX Corporation, see the Integrative Case at the end of the chapter.

TABLE 10.3
Some International Joint Ventures

Joint Venture	U.S. PARENT	FOREIGN PARTNER	PRODUCTS
New United Motor Mfg.	General Motors	Toyota (Japan)	Subcompact cars
National Steel	National Intergroup	Nippon Kokan (Japan)	Steel
Siecor	Corning Glass Works	Siemens (Germany)	Optical cable
Honeywell/ Ericsson Development	Honeywell	L. M. Ericsson (Sweden)	PBX systems
Himont	Hercules	Montedison (Italy)	Polypropylene resin
GMFanuc Robotics	General Motors	Fanuc (Japan)	Robots
International Aero Engines	United Technologies	Rolls-Royce (Britain)	Aircraft engines

SOURCE: "Are Foreign Partners Good for U.S. Companies?" *Business Week* (May 28, 1984), p. 59. Reprinted from the May 28, 1984 issue of *Business Week* by special permission. Copyright © 1984 by McGraw-Hill, Inc.

Acquisitions

If an MNC wishes to keep total control of its operations, it might want to start a business from scratch or acquire a firm already established in the host country. An *acquisition* has merits because assets can be bought in their entirety rather than on a piecemeal basis. Synergistic benefits can result if the MNC acquires a firm with strong complementary product lines and a good distribution network. Nestlé S. A. of Switzerland, for example, purchased BeechNut (baby foods), Libby, McNeill and Libby (fruit juices), Stouffer (hotels and frozen dinners), Ward-Johnson (candy), Hills Brothers (coffee), and Carnation (evaporated milk) to complement its successful Nescafé, Quik, Nestea, and L'Oreal consumer products. In some countries, however, acquisitions can be difficult to arrange because of a lack of available information about potential candidates. Government restrictions on ownership, such as Canada's requirement that all energy corporations in Canada be controlled by Canadians, also can discourage acquisitions. It can be possible, however, for an MNC to have control of a foreign enterprise even though the MNC cannot attain more than 49% of the ownership. One way is to maintain control over some asset required by the foreign firm. Another device is to separate equity into voting and nonvoting stock so that the minority MNC investor has a majority of the voting stock.

Green-Field Development

If a corporation does not want to buy another firm's existing facilities via acquisition, it may choose a *green-field development,* or the building of a manufacturing facility from scratch. This is usually a far more complicated and expensive operation than acquisition, but it allows the MNC more freedom in designing the plant, choosing suppliers, and hiring a work force. An Italian semiconductor manufacturer, SGS-Ates Componenti Elettronici S. p. A., selected this strategy. According to its Vice-President of Marketing, Richard Pieranunzi: "To find a company that exactly matched our needs would be difficult. And we didn't want to buy other people's problems."[44]

Production Sharing

In a term coined by Peter Drucker, the process of *production sharing* combines the higher labor skills and technology available in the developed countries with the lower-cost labor available in developing countries. Since 1970, U.S. imports under production-sharing arrangements have been increasing at a rate of more than 20% per year.[45] Among the multinational corporations using this strategy are Texas Instruments, RCA, Honeywell, General Electric, and GTE. By locating assembly plants, called *maquiladoras,* in Ciudad Juarez and Tijuana, Mexico, and packaging plants across the border in Texas, these firms are able to take advantage of Mexico's low labor costs. This opportunity was a result of the Mexican government's relaxation of its laws against foreign ownership of factories and its reduction of import taxes on raw materials.

Management Contracts

A large multinational corporation is likely to have a large amount of management talent at its disposal. *Management contracts* offer a means through which an MNC may use part of its personnel to assist a firm in a host country for a specified fee and period of time. Such arrangements are common when a host government expropriates part or all of an MNC's holdings in its country. The contracts allow the MNC to continue to earn some income from its investment and keep the operations going until local management is trained. Management contracts are also used by a number of less developed countries that have the capital but neither the labor nor the managerial skills required to utilize available technology.

Turnkey Operations

Turnkey operations are typically contracts for the construction of operating facilities in exchange for a fee. The facilities are transferred to the host country or firm when they are complete. The customer is usually a government agency of, say, an Eastern European or Middle Eastern country that has decreed that a particular product must be produced locally and under its control. MNCs that perform turnkey operations are frequently industrial equipment manufacturers that supply some of their own equipment for the project and that commonly sell to the host country replacement parts and maintenance services. They thereby create customers as well as future competitors.

Subcontract Arrangements

MNCs might find that, in times of national fervor in the less developed countries, facilities that mine and process raw materials are prime targets for expropriation. Therefore, an MNC can *contract* with a foreign government or local firm to trade raw materials for certain resources belonging to the MNC. For example, several oil-producing countries have made arrangements with oil firms to let the firms take all exploration and development risks in exchange for a share of the sales of the oil produced.

10.3

STRATEGY IMPLEMENTATION

To be effective, international strategies must be implemented in concurrence with national and cultural differences. Among the many considerations of an MNC, three of the most important are (1) selecting the local partner for a joint venture or licensing arrangement, (2) organizing the firm around the most appropriate structure, and (3) encouraging global rather than national management practices.

Partner Selection

Joint ventures and licensing agreements between a multinational company and a local partner in a host country are becoming increasingly popular as a means by which an MNC can gain entry into other countries, especially less developed countries.[46] National policies as well as the complexity of the host country's market often make these the preferred strategies for the balancing of a country's attractiveness against financial risk. The key to the successful implementation of these strategies is the selection of the local partner. In Fig. 10.3, Lasserre proposes a model describing the many variables to be considered by both sides when they are assessing a partnership. Each party needs to assess not only the strategic fit of each company's project strategy, but also the fit of each company's respective resources. Lasserre contends that this process requires a minimum of one to two years of prior contacts between both parties.[47] The fact that joint ventures tend to have a high rate of costly failures suggests that few multinationals use such a careful selection process.[48]

Organizational Structure

Stages of MNC Development

Rarely, if ever, do multinational corporations suddenly appear as full-blown worldwide organizations. They tend to go through three common evolutionary stages, both in their relationships with widely dispersed geographic markets and in the manner in which they structure their operations and programs.

STAGE 1: INITIAL ENTRY The "parent" corporation is attracted to a particular market in another country and seeks to test the potential of its products in this market with minimal risk. The firm thus introduces a number of product lines into the market through home-based export programs, licensing agreements, joint ventures, and/or through local commercial offices. The product divisions at headquarters continue to be responsible for all functional activities.

STAGE 2: EARLY DEVELOPMENT Success in Stage 1 leads the parent corporation to believe that a stronger presence and broader product lines are needed for it to fully exploit its advantage in the host country. The parent company establishes a local operating division or company in the host country, such as Ford of Britain, to better serve the market. The product line is expanded. Local manufacturing capacity is established. Managerial

FIGURE 10.3
Assessing Partners to Implement Joint Venture and Licensing Strategies

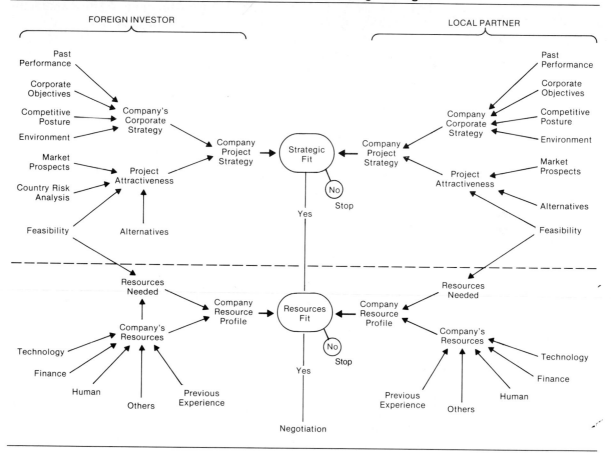

Source: P. Lasserre, "Selecting a Foreign Partner for Technology Transfer," *Long Range Planning* (December 1984), p. 45. Copyright © 1984 Pergamon Press, Ltd. Reprinted by permission.

functions (product development, finance, marketing, etc.) are organized locally. As time goes by, other related businesses are acquired by the parent company so that the base of the local operating division is broadened. As the subsidiary in the host country successfully develops a strong regional presence, it achieves greater autonomy and self-sufficiency.

STAGE 3: MATURITY As the parent corporation becomes aware of the success of its subsidiaries in other countries and the skills of its local managers, it consolidates operations under a regional management organization. It increases the amount of attention given to a wide range of investment opportunities, such as mergers and acquisitions. Although the regional or local company continues to maintain ties with the parent corporation and the product divisions in the home country, it tends to enjoy relative autonomy in terms of local policy-setting and managerial practices. As was the case with the North American Philips Corporation, originally an affiliate of N. V. Philips' Gloeilampenfabrieken, a subsidiary may become a totally separate company with local shareholders and publicly traded stock.[49] Table 10.4 summarizes some of the structural arrangements possible in each stage of MNC development.

Even though most international and multinational corporations move through these stages in their involvement with host countries, any one corporation can be at different stages simultaneously, with different products

TABLE 10.4
International Activity and Structure

Stage	ACTIVITIES OF COMPANY	ORGANIZATION RESPONSIBLE FOR INTERNATIONAL ACTIVITIES	EXECUTIVE IN CHARGE
1	Exports directly and indirectly, but trade is minor.	Export department.	Export manager, reporting to domestic marketing executive.
	Exports become more important.	Export division.	Division manager.
2	Company undertakes licensing and invests in production overseas.	International division.	Director of international operations, usually vice-president.
	International investments increase.	Sometimes international headquarters company as wholly owned subsidiary [of domestic parent company].	President, who is vice-president in parent company.
3	International investments substantial and widespread; diversified international business activities.	Global organizational structure by geographic areas, product lines, functions, or some combination. Also worldwide staff support.	No single executive in charge of international business.

SOURCE: Adapted from W. A. Dymsza, *Multinational Business Strategy* (New York: McGraw-Hill Book Company, 1972), p. 22. Copyright © 1972 by McGraw-Hill, Inc. Reprinted by permission.

in different markets. An example of corporate diversity in international operations is Hewlett-Packard. In the beginning of its international activity, the company exported its products. It used its own staff to oversee exports to Canada, and export management companies (export intermediaries operating on a buy-and-sell basis and providing financing for export shipments) to oversee exports to other countries. These exports were then sold in both cases to middlemen abroad. As sales expanded, Hewlett-Packard took over the exporting functions, opened its own sales office in Mexico, purchased a warehousing facility in Switzerland, organized a wholly owned manufacturing subsidiary in West Germany, and entered into a partly owned venture in Japan.[50]

Centralization versus Decentralization

A basic dilemma facing the globally oriented multinational corporation is how to organize authority centrally, so that it operates as a vast interlocking system that achieves synergy, and at the same time decentralize authority, so that local managers can make the decisions necessary to meet the demands of the local market or host government.[51] To deal with this problem, MNCs tend to structure themselves either along product groups or geographic areas. They may even combine both in a matrix structure.

Typically, multinational corporations do not organize themselves around business functions, such as marketing or manufacturing, unless they are in an extractive raw-materials industry. Basic functions are thus subsumed under either product or geographic units.[52] Two examples of the usual international structures are Nestlé and American Cyanamid. Nestlé's structure is one in which significant power and authority have been decentralized to geographic entities. This structure is similar to that depicted in Fig. 10.4, in which each geographic set of operating companies has a different group of products. In contrast, American Cyanamid has a series of product groups with worldwide responsibilities. To depict Cyanamid's structure, the geographical entities in Fig. 10.4 would have to be replaced by product groups or strategic business units.

The product-group structure enables the company to introduce and manage a similar line of products around the world. The geographic-area structure, in contrast, allows a company to tailor products to regional differences and to achieve regional coordination. Philips, the Dutch electronics firm, recently switched from a geographical structure, oriented to local needs, to a product structure, oriented to global needs. The company's production facilities were small and high-cost because they were designed only for regional markets. The switch to a product structure was believed by top management to be crucial if Philips were to compete effectively with the Japanese MNCs. "We are still weak," stated Dick Snijders, a Director of Corporate Finance at Philips, "because our emphasis is still too much on the national, and we need to achieve much greater economies of scale."[53]

FIGURE 10.4
Geographic Area Structure*

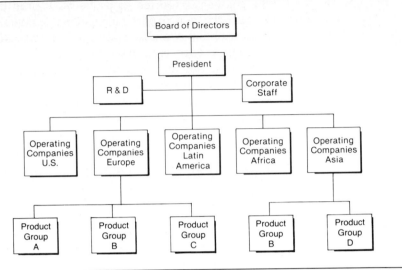

*Note: Because of space limitations, product groups for only Europe and Asia are shown here.

A survey of thirty-seven large, U.S.-based multinational corporations in various industries revealed that 43% used an international division; 35% were organized according to product group; 14% were structured around geographic areas; 5% used a functional structure; and 3% utilized the matrix structure. The international division is much more commonly used by U.S.-based MNCs than European-based MNCs; this is probably a result of the size difference between the domestic markets of the typical U.S.-based and the typical Swiss or British MNC.[54]

Management Practices

As is true of most people from any developed society, managers tend to believe that what works well in their society will work well anywhere. Thus, someone well-schooled in the virtues of MBO, participative decision making, theory Y practices, job enrichment, and management science will have a tendency to transplant these practices without alteration to foreign nations. Unfortunately, just as products often need to be altered to appeal to a new market, so too do most management practices.

In a study of forty different cultures, Hofstede found that he could explain the success or failure of certain management practices on the basis of four cultural dimensions: *power distance, uncertainty avoidance, individualism/ collectivism,* and *masculinity/femininity.*[55] He points out that management by objectives (MBO) has been the single most popular management technique "made in U.S.A." It has succeeded in Germany because the idea of replacing the arbitrary authority of the boss with the impersonal authority of mutually agreed-upon objectives fits the small power-distance and strong uncertainty-avoidance that are dimensions in the German culture. It has failed in France, however, because the French are used to large power distances—to accepting orders from a highly personalized authority. This French cultural dimension goes counter to key aspects of MBO: the small power distance between superior and subordinate, and impersonal, objective goal-setting. This same cultural dimension explains why the French, for whom vertical authority lines are very important, are significantly more reluctant than Americans to accept the multiple authority structures of project management or matrix organization.[56]

Because of these cultural differences, managerial style and practices must be tailored to fit the particular situations in other countries. Most multinational corporations therefore attempt to fill executive positions in their subsidiaries with well-qualified citizens of the host countries. More than 95% of all managers employed by Unilever are "nationals" of the country in which they work.[57] IBM follows a similar policy. This policy serves to placate nationalistic governments and to better attune management practices to the host country's culture. Another approach to staffing the managerial positions of multinational corporations is to use people with an "international" orientation regardless of their country of origin or host country assignment. This approach allows for more promotion opportunities than does Unilever's policy but it can result in a greater number of misunderstandings and conflicts with the local employees and with the host country's government. In addition, it is estimated that anywhere from 25 to 40% of *expatriate* managers (people from a country other than the host country) fail to adjust to the host country's social and business environment.[58] This failure is costly in terms of management performance, operations efficiency, and customer relations. The average cost to the company of repatriating an executive and the family exceeds $100,000.[59] Consequently, to improve their chances of success, multinational corporations are putting more emphasis on intercultural training for those managers being sent on an assignment in a foreign country.[60]

10.4

EVALUATION AND CONTROL

As MNCs increase the scope of their activities around the world, timely information becomes even more important for effective evaluation and control. In evaluating the activities of its international operations, the MNC should consider not only return on investment and other financial measures, but also the effects of its activities on the host country.

Transborder Data Flows

Multinational corporations are increasingly relying on transborder data flow (TDF) and international data networks to coordinate their international operations and control their subsidiaries. TDF, the electronic movement of data across national boundaries, has been made possible by the rapid growth and convergence of new technologies, such as telecommunications and computers. A survey of eighty-nine MNCs concluded that these companies were already dependent on international data flows for their foreign operations and will become even more so in the future. Transborder data flow appears to be a major information-systems issue in multinational corporations. More and more countries are taking steps to control the flow of data across their borders and thus handicap an MNC in its evaluation and control function.[61]

Financial Measures

The three most widely used techniques for international performance evaluation are return on investment, budget analysis, and historical comparisons. In one study, 95% of the corporate officers interviewed stated that they use the same evaluation techniques for foreign and domestic operations. Rate of return was mentioned as the single most important measure.[62] The use of ROI, however, can cause problems when it is applied to international operations: "Because of foreign currencies, different rates of inflation, different tax laws, and the use of transfer pricing, both the net income figure and the investment base may be seriously distorted."[63]

Authorities in international business recommend that the controls used by a globally oriented MNC be different from those used by a multi-domestic MNC.[64] The *multi-domestic MNC* should use loose controls with its foreign units. The management of each geographic unit should be given considerable operational latitude, but be expected to meet some performance targets. Because profit and ROI measures are often unreliable in international operations, it is recommended that the MNC's top management in this instance emphasize budgets and nonfinancial measures of performance, such as market share, productivity, public image, employee morale, and relations with the host country government, to name a few.[65] Multiple measures should be used to differentiate between the worth of the subsidiary and the performance of its management.

An MNC with a *global perspective*, however, needs tight controls over its many units. In order to reduce costs and gain competitive advantage, it is trying to spread the manufacturing and marketing operations of a few fairly uniform products around the world; therefore, its key strategic and operational decisions must be centralized. Its environmental scanning must include research not only into each of the national markets in which the MNC competes, but also into the "global arena" of the interaction between markets. Foreign units are thus evaluated more as cost centers, revenue centers, or expense centers, than as investment or profit centers, because MNCs with a global, high-share perspective do not often make the entire product in the country in which it is sold.

MNC/Host Country Relationships

As multinational corporations grow and spread across the world, nations find themselves in a dilemma. Most countries, especially the less-developed ones, want to have the many benefits an MNC can bring: technology transfer, employment opportunities, tax revenues, and the opportunity that domestic business corporations could be built in partnership with powerful and well-connected foreign-based companies. These countries also fear the problems an MNC can bring. Having welcomed an MNC with tax benefits and subsidies of various types, the host country can find itself in a double bind regarding the repatriation of profits. It can either allow the MNC to export its profits to corporate headquarters—thereby draining the nation of potential investment capital, or it can allow the MNC to send home only a small portion of its profits—thereby making the host country unattractive to other MNCs. For example, research reveals that between 1960 and 1968, profits sent to the United States from Latin America by MNCs exceeded new investment there by $6.7 billion.[66] Host countries also note that MNCs' technology transfer to less-developed countries seldom increases their exports. MNCs also have a tradition of placing business values above the cultural values of the host country.[67] For example, an MNC's need to continue manufacturing operations in order to meet a deadline from the home office may conflict with a country's desire to honor a special event by declaring a holiday.

Given the pros and cons of the multinational corporation's presence in the world, Fayerweather proposes four basic relationships that an MNC can assume with a host country. They range from the positive, *contributing* to the country's development, to the negative, *undermining* the basic culture of the country.[68]

Contributory Relationships _____

An MNC can act to directly augment or contribute to the goals or achievement of a host nation without any negative effect. In this relationship both the MNC and the local partner (if any) positively help each other as well as their respective countries. Occidental Petroleum's agreement in 1985 with the Bank of China Trust and Consultancy Company and the state-run China National Coal Development Corporation, to develop one of the world's largest open-pit coal mines, has the potential to help all three partners in the relationship plus both countries.[69]

Reinforcing Relationships

The actions of an MNC can reinforce the goals or achievement of a host nation but still tend to have some negative side-effects. This is a somewhat less than ideal relationship. The MNC invests heavily in the country's development and might build the transportation and communication systems so necessary for economic development. Nevertheless, the MNC sends all its profits to its headquarters and its emphasis on its own cultural values sometimes conflicts with the host country's values. This is probably the type of relationship existing between the U.S.-based MNCs that are production-sharing in Mexico and the Mexican government.

Frustrating Relationships

Actions of an MNC can challenge the goals of the nation or impede its immediate functioning in ways to which the nation cannot respond effectively, so that its government is frustrated. Nestlé's aggressive marketing of baby formula to mothers in less-developed countries is an example of this type of relationship. In countries in which breast-feeding is more nutritious and healthier for babies than bottle-feeding (because of the poor quality of water and sanitary conditions), the use of Nestlé's baby formula contributed to babies' malnutrition and other sickness. Because many LDC governments were unable to deal with the situation, church groups from the developed countries plus the United Nations put enough pressure on Nestlé to cause it to stop its aggressive marketing practices in the LDCs.[70]

Undermining Relationships

The effect of an MNC can be to reduce the basic logic (in terms of norms, values, and philosophy) of a nation, so that its functioning is weakened or undermined. MNCs' development of oil resources in the Middle Eastern countries caused a clash between traditional Moslem values and Western values; this clash probably contributed to the Iranian revolution and to disruptions in other Moslem countries. The resulting antagonism from such a relationship is reflected in the following comment by a Third World representative:

> Poor countries have often been swindled out of a decent return for their produce in the name of market mechanism, deprived of their economic independence, seduced by imported life styles, foreign value systems, irrelevant research designs—all in the name of freedom of choice.[71]

To the extent that an MNC fails to contribute to or reinforce the functioning of a host country, it might find its assets expropriated and its home-country management team asked to leave. Those corporations that go to less-developed countries to locate and extract needed raw materials but see the host countries only as something to manipulate and use get pulled into a particular cycle.

> *First,* they are welcomed by the host country as a source of foreign currency, a major employer, a means of upgrading the country's skills, a stimulant to the economy, and a catalyst to attract other investors. *Second,* after a few years, pressure increases on the firm to process in addition to only extracting the material. This often leads to a second phase of investment by the company and more benefits to the country. *Third,* the company is now sufficiently dependent to be vulnerable to a request to have local participation in ownership, either through private parties or directly by the host government. *Fourth,* nationalization advances to a takeout stage after more years of evolving relationships, usually involving compensation for assets and some arrangement of management. *Fifth,* recalling that the primary reason for the original investment was a source of materials, and recognizing that government-owned operations are almost always inefficient, the company is forced to pay increasing prices and turns to alternative sources if they exist.[72]

SUMMARY AND CONCLUSION

A knowledge of international considerations is becoming extremely important to the proper understanding of the strategic-management processes in large corporations. Just as North American firms are becoming more involved every year with operations and markets in other countries, imports and subsidiaries from other countries are becoming more a part of the American landscape. International corporations have been transforming themselves slowly into multinational corporations (MNCs) with a global orientation and flexible management styles.

The dominant issue in the strategic-management process of a multinational corporation is the effects of widely different external environments on the firm's internal activities. A firm's top management must therefore be well schooled in the national differences in sociocultural, economic, political-legal, and technological environmental variables. Data-search procedures and analytical techniques must be used in assessments of the many possible investment opportunities and their risks in world business. Once top management believes that the corporation has the requisite internal qualifications to become multinational, it must then determine the appropriate set of strategies for entering and investing in potential host countries. These may vary from simple exportation, to the formation with other companies of very complex consortiums. The corporation's product portfolio must be constantly monitored for strengths and weaknesses.

Attention must also be paid to the selection of the most appropriate local partner, organizational structure, and management system for a worldwide enterprise. An overall system of control and coordination must be balanced against a host country's need for local flexibility and autonomy. An MNC should use a series of performance indicators so that return on investment, budget analysis, and historical comparisons can be viewed in the context of a strategic audit of operations in the host country. Above all, the top management of a multinational corporation has the responsibility to ensure that the MNC contributes to and reinforces the functioning of the host nation, rather than frustrating or undermining its government and culture.

DISCUSSION QUESTIONS

1. What differentiates a multinational corporation from an international corporation?

2. If the basic concepts of absolute and comparative advantage suggest free trade as the best route to prosperity for all nations, why do so many countries use protectionist measures to keep out imports?

3. Should MNCs be allowed to own more than half the stock of a subsidiary based in a host country? Why or why not?

4. Should the United States allow unrestricted trade between corporations in the United States and communist countries? Why or why not?

5. Discuss the pros and cons of using portfolio analysis in international strategic analysis.

6. There are many disadvantages to the joint venture (loss of control, lower profits, probability of conflicts with partners, and the likely transfer of technological advantage to a partner), plus its typical temporary nature; so why is it such a popular strategy?

7. What are the advantages and disadvantages of using a product-group structure as compared to a geographical-area structure in a multinational corporation?

8. What is the overall impact of multinational corporations on world peace? How do they help? How do they hinder?

9. As discussed in the Integrative Case at the end of this chapter, what are the pros and cons of this joint venture for each of the three involved companies?

NOTES

1. B. D. Henderson, *New Strategies for the New Global Competition* (Boston: Boston Consulting Group, 1981), p. 1.

2. *International Financial Statistics Yearbook,* Vol. LX (Washington, D.C.: International Monetary Fund, 1987), pp. 116–117.

3. *International Financial Statistics Yearbook,* pp. 698–699.

4. D. J. Teece, *The Competitive Challenge* (Cambridge, Mass.: Ballinger Publishing Co., 1987), p. 1.

5. A. Kates, "They Find Bargains in Our Stocks," *USA Today* (January 19, 1988), p. 1B.

6. J. Castro, P. Stoler, and F. Ungeheuer, "The Canadians Came Calling," *Time* (November 17, 1986), p. 68.

7. M. McLuhan, *Understanding Media: The Extensions of Man* (New York: McGraw-Hill Paperbacks, 1965).

8. M. Schrage and D. A. Vise, "Murdock, Turner Launch Era of Global Television," *Washington Post* (August 31, 1986), p. H1.

9. D. Wessel, "Gillette Keys Sales to Third World Tastes," *Wall Street Journal* (January 23, 1986), p. 33.

10. S. Carey and U. Gupta, "GE and CFM Get $2 Billion Order For Airbus Engines," *Wall Street Journal* (July 29, 1987), p. 12.

11. Adapted from W. A. Dymsza, *Multinational Business Strategy* (New York: McGraw-Hill, 1972), pp. 50–51.

12. Dymsza, pp. 5–6.

13. M. E. Porter, "Changing Patterns of International Competition," *California Management Review* (Winter 1986), pp. 9–40. Also in *The Competitive Challenge,* ed. D. J. Teece

(Cambridge, Mass.: Ballinger Publishing Co., 1987), pp. 27–57.

14. J. D. Daniels and L. H. Radebaugh, *International Business: Environments and Operations,* 4th ed. (Reading, Mass.: Addison-Wesley Publishing Co., 1987) p. 766.

15. Daniels and Radebaugh, p. 628.

16. D. Ricks, M. Y. C. Fu, and J. S. Arpan, *International Business Blunders* (Columbus, Ohio: Grid, Inc., 1974).

17. Daniels and Radebaugh, p. 640.

18. D. A. Ricks and V. Mahajan, "Blunders in International Marketing: Fact or Fiction," *Long Range Planning* (February 1984), pp. 78–82.

19. "Banks in Pakistan To Stop Paying Interest in 1985," *Wall Street Journal* (June 18, 1984), p. 23.

20. S. Chang, "The Gods and the U.A.W. Are Smiling: Mazda's New Boss Plans To Make Cars, and Jobs, for Yanks," *People* (February 18, 1985), pp. 90–91.

21. R. T. Grieves, "Modern Barter," *Time* (June 11, 1984) p. 48.
D. B. Yoffie, "Profiting from Countertrade," *Harvard Business Review* (May–June 1984), pp. 8–12, 16.

22. "Uniroyal Sells a Unit for Over $71 Million to Malaysian Concern," *Wall Street Journal* (December 24, 1984), p. 12.

23. J. Ryser and C. A. Robbins, "Garcia Dusts Off An Old Ploy: Expropriation," *Business Week* (January 13, 1986), p. 50.

24. R. I. Kirkland, Jr., "The Death of Socialism," *Fortune* (January 4, 1988), p. 65.

25. J. P. Anastassopoulos, G. Blanc, and P. Dussage, *State-Owned Multinationals* (Chichester, England: John Wiley & Sons, 1987), pp. 180–181.

26. P. Choate and J. Linger, "Tailored Trade: Dealing With the World As It Is," *Harvard Business Review* (January-February 1988), pp. 86–93.

27. R. B. Reich, *The Next American Frontier* (New York: Times Books, 1983).

28. G. W. Weiss, Jr., "The General Electric-SNECMA Jet Engine Development Program" (Boston: *Intercollegiate Case Clearing House,* no. 9-380-739, 1980).

29. J. Mark, "High-Tech Exports to China Still Being Delayed, Despite Eased Rules, U.S. Firms Finding," *Wall Street Journal* (January 3, 1985), p. 16.

30. R. Stobaugh and R. T. Wells, Jr., *Technology Crossing Borders* (Boston: Harvard Business School Press, 1984), p. 4.

31. T. N. Gladwin, "Assessing the Multinational Environment for Corporate Opportunity," in W. D. Guth (ed.), *Handbook of Business Strategy* (Boston: Warren, Gorham and Lamont, 1985), pp. 7.28–7.41.

32. W. D. Coplin and M. K. O'Leary, "World Political/Business Risk Analysis For 1987," *Planning Review* (January/February 1987), pp. 34–40.

33. Y. N. Chang and F. Campo-Flores, *Business Policy and Strategy* (Santa Monica, Calif.: Goodyear Publishing, 1980), pp. 602–604.

34. J. Leontiades, "Going Global—Global Strategies vs. National Strategies," *Long Range Planning* (December 1986), pp. 96–104.

35. Porter, (1987), pp. 29–30.

36. K. Ohmae, "The Triad World View," *Journal of Business Strategy* (Spring 1987), pp. 8–19.

37. Ohmae, p. 12.

38. G. D. Harrell and R. O. Kiefer, "Multinational Strategic Market Portfolios," *MSU Business Topics* (Winter 1981), p. 5.

39. Harrell and Kiefer, p. 8.

40. M. Porter, (1986), p. 12.

41. K. Graven, "Tokyo Takeout: Family In Japan Plays Big Role Importing Fast Food From U.S.," *Wall Street Journal* (March 3, 1987), p. 1.

42. J. S. Harrison, "Alternatives to Merger-Joint Ventures and Other Strategies," *Long Range Planning* (December 1987), p. 80.

43. V. Pucik and N. Hatvany, "Management Practices in Japan and Their Impact on Business Strategy," in R. Lamb (ed.), *Advances in Strategic Management,* Vol. I (Greenwich, Conn.: Jai Press, 1983), p. 124.

44. S. P. Galante, "Foreign Semiconductor Firms Try New Strategy in U.S.," *Wall Street Journal* (August 23, 1984), p. 20.

45. K. P. Power, "Now We Can Move Office Work Offshore To Enhance Output," *Wall Street Journal* (June 9, 1983), p. 30.

46. P. Lasserre, "Selecting a Foreign Partner for Technology Transfer," *Long Range Planning* (December 1984), pp. 43–49.

47. Lasserre, pp. 48–49.

48. W. H. Davidson, "Creating and Managing Joint Ventures in China," *California Management Review* (Summer 1987), p. 77.

49. R. L. Drake and L. M. Caudill, "Management of the Large Multinational: Trends and Future Challenges," *Business Horizons* (May-June 1981), pp. 84–85.

50. J. D. Daniels, E. W. Ogram, Jr., and L. H. Radebaugh, *International Business: Environments and Operations,* 2nd ed. (Reading, Mass.: Addison-Wesley, 1979), p. 359.

51. Stobaugh and Wells, pp. 16–17.

52. J. Garland and R. N. Farmer, *International Dimensions of Business Policy and Strategy* (Boston: Kent Publishing Co., 1986), pp. 98–102.

53. G. Turner, "Inside Europe's Giant Companies: Cultural Revolution at Philips," *Long Range Planning* (August 1986), p. 14.

54. J. D. Daniels, R. A. Pitts, and M. J. Tretter, "Organizing for Dual Strategies of Product Diversity and International Expansion," *Strategic Management Journal* (July-September 1985), pp. 223–237.

55. G. Hofstede, "The Cultural Relativity of Organizational Practice and Theories," in *International Business Knowledge: Managing International Functions in the 1990s,* ed. W. A. Dymsza and R. G. Vambery (New York: Praeger Press, 1987), pp. 309–323.

G. Hofstede, "Motivation, Leadership, and Organization: Do American Theories Apply Abroad?" *Organizational Dynamics* (Summer 1980), pp. 42–63.

G. Hofstede, "National Cultures in Four Dimensions: A Research-Based Theory of Cultural Differences among Nations," *International Journal of Management and Organization* (Spring-Summer 1983), pp. 46–74.

G. Hofstede, "The Cultural Relativity of the Quality of Life Concept," *Academy of Management Review* (July 1984), pp. 389–398.

56. G. Inzerilli and A. Laurent, "Managerial Views of Organization Structure in France and the USA," *International Studies of Management and Organization* (Spring-Summer 1983), p. 113.

57. W. C. Kim and R. A. Mauborgne, "Cross-Cultural Strategies," *Journal of Business Strategy* (Spring 1987), p. 30.

58. M. Mendenhall and G. Oddou, "The Dimensions of Expatriate Acculturation: A Review," *Academy of Management Review* (January 1985), pp. 39–47.

59. N. J. Adler, *International Dimensions of Organizational Behavior* (Boston: Kent Publishing Company, 1986), p. 220.

60. P. C. Earley, "Intercultural Training For Managers: A Comparison of Documentary and Interpersonal Methods," *Academy of Management Journal* (December 1987), pp. 685–698.

For more information on dealing with intercultural differences see R. E. Axtell, *Do's and Taboos Around the World*

(Janesville, Wisconsin: The Parker Pen Company, 1985); and P. R. Harris and R. T. Moran, *Managing Cultural Differences,* 2nd ed. (Houston: Gulf Publishing Co., 1987).

61. R. Chandran, A. Phatak, and R. Sambharya, "Transborder Data Flows: Implications for Multinational Corporations," *Business Horizons* (November–December 1987), pp. 74–82.

62. S. M. Robbins and R. B. Stobaugh, "The Bent Measuring Stick for Foreign Subsidiaries," *Harvard Business Review* (September-October 1973), p. 82.

63. Daniels and Radebaugh, pp. 673–674.

64. W. R. Fannin and A. F. Rodrigues, "National or Global?—Control vs. Flexibility," *Long Range Planning* (October 1986), pp. 84–188.

65. A. V. Phatak, *International Dimensions of Management* (Boston: Kent Publishing Co., 1983) p. 139.
Daniels and Radebaugh, p. 674.

66. K. Paul and R. Barbato, "The Multinational Corporation in the Less Developed Country: The Economic Development Model versus the North-South Model," *Academy of Management Review* (January 1985), p. 9.

67. P. Wright, "MNC-Third World Business Unit Performance: Application of Strategic Elements," *Strategic Management Journal* (July-September 1984), pp. 231–240.

68. Adapted from J. Fayerweather, *International Business Strategy and Administration* (Cambridge, Mass.: Ballinger Publishing, 1978), p. 124.

69. "U.S. Oil Firm, China Sign Pact For Giant Mine," *Des Moines Register* (June 30, 1985), p. 3A.

70. J. E. Post, "Assessing the Nestlé Boycott," *California Management Review* (Winter 1985), pp. 113–131.

71. M. Ul Haq, *The Poverty Curtain: Choices for the Third World* (New York: Columbia University Press, 1976) as quoted by Wright, p. 232.

72. F. T. Haner, *Business Policy, Planning and Strategy* (Cambridge, Mass.: Winthrop Publishers, 1976), p. 441.

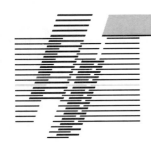

INTEGRATIVE CASE

CSX CORPORATION FORMS INTERNATIONAL JOINT VENTURE

When U.S. Lines Inc. declared bankruptcy in December 1986, industry observers wondered what would become of the firm's twelve giant container ships—often called "superfreighters" or "econships." With the shipping industry suffering from overcapacity in trans-Atlantic shipping, the sale of these twelve ships could only make the glut worse and cut shipping rates even further.

Sea-Land, a unit of CSX Corporation, agreed in February 1988 to purchase all twelve ships for $160 million from the creditors of U.S. Lines. Rather than keep the ships only for its own use, Sea-Land reached an agreement with two other companies to share the superfreighters. Sea-Land's management planned to use all twelve of the ships in trans-Atlantic service between the U.S. and Europe in a space-sharing arrangement with P & O Containers (Trans Freight Lines) Ltd. of the United Kingdom and Nedlloyd Lijnen B.V. of the Netherlands. The superfreighters were to replace twenty-three smaller vessels that the three companies had operated in the Atlantic and would boost their combined capacity less than 4%. The ships were to fly the U.S. flag and operate with U.S. crews.

Industry observers praised the joint venture as a way to improve efficiency in trans-Atlantic shipping. "Hopefully it should take some pressure off rates by boosting the efficiency of the carriers through economies of scale," said Donald Aldridge, a Senior Vice President of the U.S. unit of Hapag Lloyd AG, a West German shipping company. Sea-Land's purchase of the ships and the three companies' sharing agreement were in part defensive measures to keep the giant containerships out of the hands of low-cost competitors who could have started a rate war. "If some Mickey

Mouse operator had bought these ships, anything could have happened," said Frits van Riet, President of the U.S. unit of Nedlloyd, the Dutch company sharing the superfreighters with Sea-Land.

SOURCE: D. Machalaba, "Sea-Land Will Buy 12 Superfreighters Idled by U.S. Lines Inc. for $160 Million," *Wall Street Journal* (February 9, 1988), p. 8.

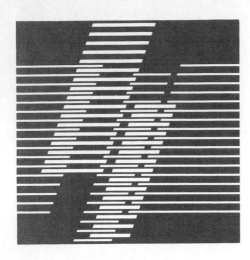

CHAPTER 11

STRATEGIC ISSUES IN NOT-FOR-PROFIT ORGANIZATIONS

STRATEGIC MANAGEMENT MODEL

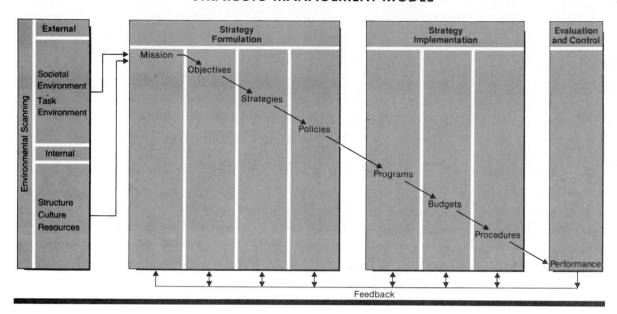

T raditionally, studies in strategic management have dealt with profit-making firms to the exclusion of nonprofit or governmental organizations. The little existing empirical research suggests that not-for-profit organizations are in the initial stage of using strategic management.[1] From their study of 103 not-for-profit organizations, Unterman and Davis conclude: "Not only have not-for-profit organizations failed to reach the strategic management stage of development, but many of them have failed to reach even the strategic planning stages that for-profit enterprises initiated 15 to 20 years ago."[2] Nevertheless, an increasing number of not-for-profits, especially hospitals and colleges, are concerned with strategic issues and strategic planning, even though their use of it might be only an informal process.

A knowledge of not-for-profit organizations would be important even if there were no other reason than the fact that they employ over 25% of those working in the United States and own approximately 15% of the nation's private wealth.[3] Private nonprofit organizations, in particular, represent 5.2% of all corporations, partnerships, and proprietorships in the United States, receive 3.5% of all revenue, and hold about 4.3% of the total assets of business firms. During the 1970s, nonprofit firms increased both in total number and revenues *faster* than did profit-making firms.[4] It is estimated that over one-third of the world's gross product is generated by "non-market" corporations (which include state-owned corporations and regulated utilities).[5] In the United States alone, in addition to various federal, state, and local government agencies, there are about 10,000 not-for-profit hospitals and nursing homes, 4,600 colleges and universities, over 100,000 private and public elementary and secondary schools, almost 350,000 churches and synagogues, plus many thousands of charities and service organizations.[6]

The first ten chapters of this book dealt primarily with the strategic management of profit-making corporations. Scholars and practitioners are concluding, however, that many strategic management concepts and techniques can be successfully adapted to not-for-profit organizations.[7] The purpose of this chapter is, therefore, to highlight briefly the major differences between the profit-making and the not-for-profit organization, so that the effects of their differences on the strategic management process are seen.

11.1

CATEGORIES OF ORGANIZATIONS

All profit-making and not-for-profit organizations can be grouped into four basic categories. In some instances, it is difficult to clearly state where one category leaves off and another begins: "The wide and growing involvement of government in all aspects of life has caused a convergence or blurring of the various sectors."[8] Four categories are as follows:

1. **Private for-profit** businesses depend on the market economy to generate the means of their survival. (These range from small businesses to major corporations.)

2. **Private quasi-public** organizations are created by legislative authority and given a limited monopoly to provide particular goods or services to a population subgroup. (These are primarily public utilities.)

3. **Private nonprofit** organizations operate on public goodwill (donations, contributions, and endowments or government stipends), but are constituted outside the authority of governmental agencies or legislative bodies.

4. **Public** agencies of the government (federal, state, and local) are constituted by law and authorized to collect taxes and provide services.[9]

Typically, the term **not-for-profit** includes private nonprofit corporations (such as hospitals, institutes, private colleges, and organized charities) as well as public governmental units or agencies (such as welfare departments, prisons, and state universities). Regulated public utilities are in a grey area somewhere between profit and not-for-profit. They are profit making and have stockholders, but take on many of the characteristics of the not-for-profit organization, such as a greater dependence on rate-setting government commissions than on customers.

11.2

WHY NOT-FOR-PROFIT?

The not-for-profit sector of the American economy is becoming increasingly important for a number of reasons. *First,* society desires certain goods and services that profit-making firms cannot or will not provide. These are referred to as "public" or "collective" goods because people who might not have paid for the goods also receive benefits from them. Paved roads, police protection, museums, and schools are examples of public goods. A person cannot use a private good unless she or he pays for it. Generally once a public good is provided, however, anyone can partake of it.

Second, a private nonprofit firm tends to receive benefits from society that a private profit-making firm cannot obtain. Preferred tax status to nonstock corporations is given in section 501(c)(3) of the United States Internal Revenue Code in the form of exemptions from corporate income taxes. Private nonprofit firms also enjoy exemptions from various other state, local, and federal taxes. Under certain conditions these firms also benefit from the tax deductibility of donors' contributions and membership dues. In addition, they qualify for special third-class mailing privileges.[10] These benefits are allowed because private nonprofit organizations are typically service organizations, which are expected to use any excess of revenue over costs and expenses to either improve service or reduce the price of their service. This service orientation is reflected in the fact that not-for-profit organizations do not use the term *customer* to refer to the consumer or recipient of the service. The recipient is typically referred to as a patient, student, client, case, or simply "the public."

11.3

IMPORTANCE OF REVENUE SOURCE

The feature that best differentiates not-for-profit organizations from each other as well as from profit-making corporations is their source of income.[11] The profit-making firm depends upon revenues obtained from the sale of its goods and services to customers. Its source of income is the customer who buys and uses the product, and who typically pays for the product when it is received. Profits result when revenues are greater than the costs of making and distributing the product, and are thus a measure of the corporation's **effectiveness** (a product is valued because customers purchase it for use) and **efficiency** (costs are kept below selling price).

The not-for-profit organization, in contrast, depends heavily on dues, assessments, or donations from its membership, or on funding from a sponsoring agency such as the United Way or the federal government. Revenue, therefore, comes from a variety of sources—*not* just from sales to customers/clients. It can come from people who do not even receive the services they are subsidizing. Such charitable organizations as the American Cancer Society and CARE are examples. In another type of not-for-profit organization—such as unions and voluntary medical plans—revenue comes mostly from the members, the people who receive the service. Nevertheless, the members typically pay dues *in advance* and must accept later whatever service is provided whether they want it or not, whether it is what they expected or not. The service is often received long after the dues are paid. Therefore, some members who have paid into a fund for many years leave the organization or die without having received services, whereas newcomers may receive many services even though they have paid only a small amount into it.

Therefore, in profit-making corporations, there is typically a simple and direct connection between the customer or client and the organization. The organization tends to be totally dependent on sales of its products or services to the customer for revenue, and is therefore extremely interested in pleasing the customer. As shown in Fig. 11.1, the profit-making organization (organization A) tries to influence the customer to continue to buy and use its services. By either buying or not buying the item offered, the customer, in turn, directly influences the organization's decision-making process.

In the case of the typical not-for-profit organization, however, there is

FIGURE 11.1

The Effects of Sources of Revenue on Patterns of Client–Organization Influence

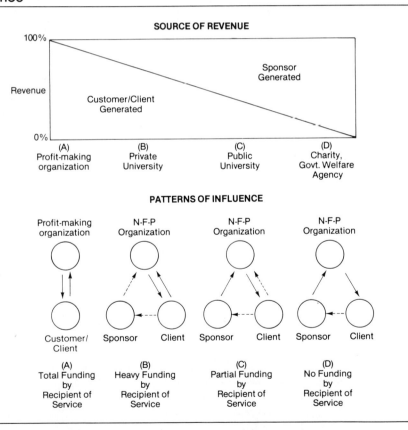

Source: Thomas L. Wheelen and J. David Hunger, "The Effect of Revenue upon Patterns of Client–Organization Influence." Copyright © 1982 by Wheelen and Hunger Associates. Reprinted by permission.

likely to be a very different sort of relationship between the organization providing and the person receiving the service. Because the recipient of the service typically does not pay the entire cost of the service, outside sponsors are required. In most instances, the sponsors receive none of the service but provide partial to total funding of the needed revenues. As indicated earlier, these sponsors can be the government (using taxpayers' money) or charitable organizations, such as the United Way (using voluntary donations). As shown in Fig. 11.1, the not-for-profit (NFP) organization can be partially dependent on sponsors for funding (organizations B and C) or totally dependent on the sponsors (organization D).

The pattern of influence on the organization's strategic decision making derives from its sources of revenue. As shown in Fig. 11.1, a private university (organization B) is heavily dependent on student tuition and other client-generated funds, for around 71% of its revenue.[12] Therefore, the students' desires are likely to have a stronger influence (as shown by an unbroken line) on the university's decision making than are the desires of the various sponsors, such as alumni and private foundations. The sponsors' relatively marginal influence on the organization is reflected by a broken line. In contrast, a public university (depicted in Fig. 11.1 as organization C) is more heavily dependent on outside sponsors, such as a state legislature, for revenue funding. Student tuition and other client-generated funds form a small percentage (typically only 37%) of total revenue. Therefore, the university's decision making is heavily influenced by the sponsors (unbroken line) and only marginally influenced directly by the students (broken line). In the case of organization D in Fig. 11.1, however, the client has no direct influence on the organization because the client pays nothing for the services received. In this type of situation, the organization tends to measure its effectiveness in terms of sponsor satisfaction. It has no real measure of its efficiency other than its ability to carry out its mission and achieve its objectives within the dollar contribution it has received from its sponsors. In contrast to other organizations in which the client contributes a significant proportion of the needed revenue, this type of not-for-profit organization (D) actually might be able to increase the amount of its revenue by heavily lobbying its sponsors while reducing the level of its service to its clients!

Regardless of the percentage of total funding generated by the client, the client may attempt to indirectly influence the not-for-profit organization through the sponsors. This is depicted by the broken lines connecting the client and the sponsor in organizations B, C, and D in the figure. Welfare clients or prison inmates, for example, may be able to indirectly improve the services they receive if they pressure government officials with letters to legislators or, even, by rioting. And students at public universities can lobby state officials for student representation on governing boards.

The key to understanding the management of a not-for-profit organization is thus learning who pays for the delivered services. If the recipients of the service pay only a small proportion of the total cost of the service, it is likely that top management will be more concerned with satisfying the needs and desires of the funding sponsors or agency than those of the people receiving the service. As previous studies indicate, acquisition of resources can become an end in itself.[13]

11.4

CONSTRAINTS ON STRATEGIC MANAGEMENT

Because not-for-profit organizations are truly different from profit-making organizations, there are a number of characteristics peculiar to the former that constrain its behavior and affect its strategic management. Newman and Wallender list the following five constraining **characteristics:**

1. Service is often intangible and hard to measure. This difficulty is typically compounded by the existence of multiple service objectives developed in order to satisfy multiple sponsors.

2. Client influence may be weak. Often the organization has a local monopoly, and payments by customers may be a very small source of funds.

3. Strong employee commitment to professions or to a cause may undermine their allegiance to the organization employing them.

4. Resource contributors—notably fund contributors and government—may intrude upon the organization's internal management.

5. Restraints on the use of rewards and punishments may result from characteristics 1, 3, and 4.[14]

It is true that a number of these characteristics can be found in profit-making as well as in not-for-profit organizations. Nevertheless, as Newman and Wallendar state, the ". . . frequency of strong impact is much higher in not-for-profit enterprises. . . ."[15] As a result, the strategic-management process for any given situation will be different in a not-for-profit organization than in the typical profit-making corporations discussed in earlier chapters.

Impact on Strategy Formulation

The long-range planning and decision making affected by the listed constraining characteristics, serve to add at least four **complications** to strategy formulation.

1. **Goal conflicts interfere with rational planning.** Because the not-for-profit organization typically lacks a single clear-cut performance criterion (such as profits), divergent goals and objectives are likely.[16] This divergence is especially likely if there are multiple sponsors. Differences in the concerns of various important sponsors can prevent top management from stating the organization's mission in anything but very broad terms, if they fear that a sponsor who disagrees with a particular, narrow definition of mission might cancel its funding. In such organizations it is the reduced influence of the clients that **permits** this diversity of values and goals to occur without a clear market check.

2. **An integrated planning focus tends to shift from results to resources.** Because not-for-profit organizations tend to provide services that are hard to measure, they rarely have a net "bottom line." Planning, therefore, becomes more concerned with resource inputs, which can easily be measured, than with service, which cannot. Goal displacement, therefore, becomes even more likely that it is in business organizations.

3. **Ambiguous operating objectives create opportunities for internal politics and goal displacement.** The combination of vague objectives and a heavy concern with resources allows managers considerable leeway in their activities. Such leeway makes possible political maneuvering for personal ends. In addition, because the effectiveness of the not-for-profit organization hinges on the satisfaction of the sponsoring group, there is a tendency for management to ignore the needs of the client while focusing on the desires of the powerful sponsor. This problem is compounded by the fact that boards of trustees are often selected not on the basis of their managerial experience, but on the basis of their ability to contribute money, raise funds, and work with politicians. Their lack of interest in overseeing management is reflected in an overall board-meeting attendance rate of only 50%, compared to 90% for boards of directors of business corporations. Board members of not-for-profit organizations therefore tend to ignore the task of determining strategies and policies—leaving this to the paid (and sometimes unpaid) executive director.[17]

4. **Professionalization simplifies detailed planning but adds rigidity.** In those not-for-profit organizations in which professionals hold important roles (as in hospitals or colleges), professional values and traditions can prevent the organization from changing its conventional behavior patterns to fit new service missions tuned to changing social needs. This rigidity, of course, can occur in any organization that hires professionals. The strong service orientation of most not-for-profit organizations, however, tends to encourage the development of static professional norms and attitudes.

Impact on Strategy Implementation

The five constraining characteristics affect how a not-for-profit organization is organized in both its structure and job design. Three **complications,** in particular, can be highlighted.

1. **Decentralization is complicated.** The difficulty of setting objectives for an intangible, hard-to-measure service mission complicates the delegation of decision-making authority. Important matters are therefore often centralized, and low-level managers are forced to wait until top management makes a decision. Because of the heavy dependence on sponsors for revenue support, the top management of a not-for-profit organization must always be alert to the sponsors' view of an organizational activity. This necessary caution leads to "defensive centralization," in which top management retains all decision-making authority so that low-level managers cannot take any actions to which the sponsors may object.

2. **Linking pins for external–internal integration become important.** Because of the heavy dependence on outside sponsors, a special need arises for people in "buffer" roles to relate to both inside and outside groups. This role is especially necessary when the sponsors are diverse (revenue comes from donations, membership fees, and federal funds), and the service is intangible (for instance, a "good" education) with a broad mission and multiple shifting objectives. The job of a "Dean for External Affairs," for example, consists primarily of working with the school's alumni and raising funds.

3. **Job enlargement and executive development can be restrained by professionalism.** In organizations that employ a large number of professionals, managers must design jobs that appeal to prevailing professional norms. Professionals have rather clear ideas about which activities are, and which are not, within their province. Enriching a nurse's job by expanding his or her decision-making authority for drug dosage, for example, can cause conflict with medical doctors who believe that such authority is theirs alone. In addition, a professional's promotion into a managerial job might be viewed as a punishment rather than as a reward.

Impact on Evaluation and Control

Special **complications** arising from the constraining characteristics also affect how behavior is motivated and performance is controlled. Two problems, in particular, are often noticed.

1. **Rewards and penalties have little or no relation to performance.** When desired results are vague and the judgment of success is subjective, predictable and impersonal feedback cannot be established. Performance is judged either intuitively ("You don't seem to be taking your job seriously") or on the basis of those small aspects of a job that can be measured ("You were late to work twice last month").

2. **Inputs rather than outputs are heavily controlled.** Because its inputs can be measured much more easily than outputs, the not-for-profit organization tends to focus more on the resources going into performance than on the performance itself.[18] The emphasis is thus on setting maximum limits for costs and expenses. Because there is little to no reward for meeting these standards, people usually respond negatively to controls.

11.5

TYPICAL RESPONSES TO CONSTRAINTS

Not-for-profit organizations tend to deal with the complications resulting from constraining characteristics in a number of ways. Although these responses may occur in profit-making organizations as well, they are more typical of not-for-profit organizations.

Select a Dynamic and Forceful Leader

One approach, which is also used in profit-making firms at times, is to appoint a strong leader to the top management position: "The leader has personal convictions about the values to be used in decision making and either has enough power to make important choices, or is so influential that her or his values are accepted by others who make decisions."[19] This manager thus can force a change in the organizational mission and objectives without antagonizing the sponsors; this leader can also direct changes in the organizing and controlling of activities. Father Theodore Hesburgh, past President of Notre Dame University, had enormous influence in shaping the strategic direction of his university. "The very essence of leadership is you have to have a vision," Hesburgh stated. "It's got to be a vision you articulate clearly and forcefully on every occasion. You can't blow an uncertain trumpet."[20] The danger with relying primarily on this approach, however, is that change can occur only from the top down. Rather than accepting the normal risks inherent in making an important decision, low-level managers "play it safe" and either wait for guidance from above to indicate which way "the wind is blowing" or pass the decision upward in the hierarchy.

Develop a Mystique

To integrate the organization's efforts toward the successful accomplishment of its goals, it can develop a "mystique" that dominates the enterprise and attracts sponsors. A strong conviction shared by all employees, as well as the sponsors, about the importance of a particular mission or service objective can also motivate employees to produce unusually high performance and client satisfaction. This sense of mission typically focuses on providing a unique service to a highly visible client group, such as mentally retarded children. Once established, the mystique sets the character and values that decision makers and others are expected to follow. Thus it is similar to the corporate culture discussed earlier. One danger in using mystique to focus activities and to motivate performance is that the mission can move far afield from that desired by the sponsoring groups.

Generate Rules and Regulations

The described constraints can force people in not-for-profit organizations to be concerned more with pleasing the sponsors than with achieving a mission of satisfying the client, and top management's response to this misdirection of efforts might be to generate rules and regulations regarding activities with the client. Minimum standards may be developed regarding the number of contact hours spent with each client, the number of reports completed, and/or the "proper" method of working. The danger inherent in this approach is that it tends to emphasize form over substance and to confuse looking good and keeping busy with actual performance. Goal displacement develops and feeds upon itself. "Burnout" develops among dedicated employees who might believe that they are being forced to spend too much energy fighting the system rather than helping the client.

Appoint a Strong Board

A board of directors or trustees can help ensure vigilance in setting and monitoring the objectives of the organization. To the extent that the board actively represents the sponsors and special interest groups that determine the organization's revenues, it has a great deal of power: "The potential for control by some not-for-profit boards far exceeds that of the boards of a corporation which represents only the owners."[21] In performing as watchdog over the organization, the board can demand clear-cut, measurable objectives and a mission of client satisfaction. The danger with this approach, however, is that the board might get too involved in operational activities. The board might involve itself not only with strategic matters, but also with operational matters such as hiring, directing, and developing the budget.[22] Nevertheless, like the boards discussed in Chapter 3, not-for-profit boards can range in their degree of involvement in strategic management, from the passive phantom or figurehead boards to the active catalyst type.[23]

Establish Performance-Based Budgets

A fifth approach to dealing with complications in a not-for-profit organization is to institute an information system that ties measurable objectives to budgeted line items. One such system is the *planning, programming, budgeting system* (PPBS) developed by the U.S. Department of Defense. It assists not-for-profit administrators in choosing among alternative programs in terms of resource use. It includes five steps:

1. Specify objectives as clearly as possible in quantitative, measurable terms.
2. Analyze the actual output of the not-for-profit organization in terms of the stated objectives.
3. Measure the cost of the particular program.
4. Analyze alternatives and search for those that have the greatest effectiveness in achieving the objectives.
5. Establish the process in a systematic way so that it continues to occur over time.[24]

Another system is *zero base budgeting* (ZBB). It is a planning process that requires each manager to justify budget requests in detail for each year that a budget is constructed. This procedure serves to avoid the development of annual budgets that are simply based upon the previous year's budget plus a certain percentage of increase. ZBB forces a manager to justify the use of money for old established programs as well as for new ones. The system requires three steps:

1. Identify each activity with a program so that input relates to output.
2. Evaluate each activity by systematic analysis.
3. Rank all programs in order of performance.[25]

Zero base budgeting has been used by the U.S. Department of Agriculture since 1971 and has been employed in nearly a dozen state and local governments as well as other federal agencies, and in over one hundred business firms.[26] Its main value is to tie inputs with outputs and to force managers to set priorities on service programs. It is also a very useful adjunct to MBO, which is being adopted by an increasing number of not-for-profit organizations.

The danger with emphasizing performance-based budgets is that members of an organization become so concerned with justifying the existence of pet programs that they tend to forget about the effects of these programs on achieving the mission. The process can become very political. It gives the appearance of rational decision making, but it can be just another variant of trying to please the sponsors and looking good on paper.[27]

11.6

POPULAR NOT-FOR-PROFIT STRATEGIES

Because the typical mission of the not-for-profit organization is to satisfy an unmet need of a segment of the general public, its objective becomes one of satisfying that need as much as is possible. If revenues exceed costs and expenses, the not-for-profit therefore is likely to use the surplus (otherwise known as "profit") to expand or improve its services. If, however, revenues are less than costs and expenses, strong pressures from both within and without the organization often prevent it from reducing its services. To the extent that management is able to find new sponsors, all may be well. For many not-for-profits, however, there is an eventual limit to contributions with no strings attached. The organization is thus painfully forced to reject contributions from sponsors who wish to alter a portion of the organization's basic mission as a requirement of the contribution.

Because of various pressures upon them to provide more services than the sponsors and clients can pay for, not-for-profit organizations are developing strategies to help them meet their desired service objectives. Two popular strategies are *strategic piggybacking* and *interorganizational linking*.

Strategic Piggybacking

Coined by Nielsen, the term **strategic piggybacking** refers to the development of a new activity for the not-for-profit organization that would generate the funds needed to make up the difference between revenues and expenses.[28] The new activity is related typically in some manner to the not-for-profit's mission, but its purpose is to help subsidize the primary service programs. In an inverted use of portfolio analysis, top management invests in new, safe *cash cows* to fund its current cash-hungry stars, question marks, and dogs.

Although this strategy is not a new one, it has become very popular in the 1980s. As early as 1874, for example, the Metropolitan Museum of Art retained a professional to photograph its collections and to sell copies of the prints. Profits were used to defray the museum's operating costs. Surpluses generated from the sale of food, wine, liquor, and tickets to the Boston Pops performances help support the primary mission of the Boston Symphony Orchestra—the performance of classical music. More recently, various income-generation ventures have appeared under various auspices, from the Girl Scouts to UNICEF, and in numerous forms, from small gift shops to vast real estate developments. The Small Business Administration, however, views this activity as "unfair competition."[29] The Internal Revenue Service advises that a not-for-profit that engages in a business "not substantially related" to the organization's exempt purposes may jeopardize its tax-exempt status, particularly if the income from the business exceeds approximately 20% of total organizational revenues.[30]

Although strategic piggybacks can help not-for-profit organizations self-subsidize their primary missions and better utilize their resources, according to Nielsen, there are several potential negative effects.[31] First, the revenue-generating venture could actually lose money—especially in the short run. Second, the venture could subvert, interfere with, or even take over the primary mission. Third, the public, as well as the sponsors, could reduce their contributions because of negative responses to such "money-grubbing activities" or because of a mistaken belief that the organization is becoming self-supporting. Fourth, the venture could interfere with the internal operations of the not-for-profit organization.

Edward Skloot, President of the New York consulting firm New Ventures, suggests that a not-for-profit organization have five resources before it begins a revenue-earning activity:[32]

1. **Something to sell.** The organization should assess its resources to see if people might be willing to pay for a good or service closely related to the organization's primary activity.

2. **Critical mass of management talent.** There must be enough available people to nurture and sustain an income venture over the long haul.

3. **Trustee support.** If the trustees have strong feelings against earned-income ventures, they could actively or passively resist commercial involvement.

4. **Entrepreneurial attitude.** Management must be able to combine an interest in innovative ideas with businesslike practicality.

5. **Venture capital.** Because it often takes money to make money, engaging in a joint venture with a business corporation can provide the necessary start-up funds as well as the marketing and management support. For example, Massachusetts General Hospital receives $50

million from Hoechst, the West German chemical company for biological research, in exchange for exclusive licenses to develop commercial products from particular research discoveries. The Children's Television Workshop, in partnership with Anheuser-Busch, developed a theme park for young children in Langhorne, Pennsylvania.

Interorganizational Linking

A major strategy often used by not-for-profit organizations to enhance their capacity to serve clients or to acquire resources is developing cooperative ties with other organizations.[33] Not-for-profit hospitals are increasing their use of this strategy as a way to cope with increasing costs and declining revenues. Services can be purchased and provided more efficiently through cooperation with other hospitals than if they were done for one hospital alone. Currently, close to one-third of all nongovernmental not-for-profit hospitals in the United States are part of a *multihospital system,* defined as "two or more acute care hospitals owned, leased, or contract-managed by a corporate office."[34] By belonging to a system, a formerly independent hospital can hope to benefit in terms of staff utilization and management efficiency.

A few of the largest hospital cooperatives are American Healthcare Systems, Inc., an alliance of 1,000 hospitals; Voluntary Hospitals of America, Inc., a league of 480 hospitals; and Consolidated Catholic Health Care, Inc., an alliance of 19 Catholic hospital systems representing 301 institutions. These cooperatives not only pool their members' purchasing orders to reduce costs, they also develop for-profit ventures and access capital markets through investor-owned subsidiaries. Don Arnwine, Chairman of Voluntary Hospitals of America, commented on this trend: "It is time we in the not-for-profit sector got off our duffs and competed."[35]

SUMMARY AND CONCLUSION

Strategic management in not-for-profit organizations is in its initial stages. Approaches and techniques, such as MBO, which work reasonably well in profit-making corporations, are being tried in a number of not-for-profit organizations. Nevertheless, private nonprofit and public organizations differ in terms of their sources of revenue and thus must be treated differently. The relationship between the organization and the client also is more complicated in these organizations. Moreover, not-for-profit organizations have certain constraining characteristics that affect their strategic-management process. These characteristics cause variations in the ways that managers in not-for-profit organizations formulate and implement strategic decisions. Not-for-profit organizations therefore are more likely than profit-making corporations to look for dynamic and forceful leaders who can pull together various constituencies, to develop a mystique about their activities, to generate many rules and regulations regarding the client, to appoint a strong board of directors/trustees to represent sponsoring agencies and special interest groups, and to develop performance-based budgets. As increasing numbers of not-for-profit organizations find it difficult to generate from sponsors the funds they need to achieve key service objectives, they are turning to *strategic piggybacking* and *interorganizational linking* strategies.

Not-for-profit organizations form an important part of society. It is therefore important to understand their reason for existence and their differences from profit-making corporations. The lack of a profit motive often results in vague statements of mission and unmeasurable objectives. This, coupled with a concern for funding

from sponsors, can cause a lack of consideration for the very client the organization was designed to serve. Programs that have little or no connection with the organization's mission can develop. Nevertheless, it is important to remember that not-for-profit organizations usually are established to provide goods and services judged valuable by society, that profit-making firms cannot or will not provide. It is dangerous to judge their performance on the basis of simple economic considerations, because they are designed to deal with conditions under which profit-making corporations could not easily survive.

DISCUSSION QUESTIONS

1. Are not-for-profit organizations less efficient than profit-making organizations? Why or why not?

2. Do you agree that the source of revenue is the best way to differentiate between not-for-profit and profit-making organizations as well as among the many kinds of not-for-profit organizations? Why or why not?

3. Is client influence always weak in the not-for-profit organization? Why or why not?

4. Why does the employment of a large number of people who consider themselves to be professionals complicate the strategic management process? How can this also occur in profit-making firms?

5. How does the lack of a clear-cut performance

measure, such as profits, affect the strategic management of a not-for-profit organization?

6. What are the pros and cons of *strategic piggybacking?*

7. In the past, a number of profit-making businesses such as city bus lines and railroad passenger services have changed their status to not-for-profit as governmental agencies took them over. Recently, however, a number of not-for-profit organizations in the U.S. have been converting to profit-making. For example, more than 20 of the 115 nonprofit Health Maintenance Organizations (HMOs) formed with federal money have converted to for-profit status.[36] Why would a not-for-profit organization want to change its status to profit-making?

NOTES

1. M. S. Wortman, Jr., "Strategic Management: Not-for-Profit Organizations," *Strategic Management,* eds. D. E. Schendel and C. W. Hofer (Boston: Little, Brown, 1979), pp. 353–381.

M. S. Wortman, Jr., "Strategic Management in Voluntary and Nonprofit Organizations: Reality, Prescriptive Behavior and Future Research," in M. Moyer (ed.), *Managing Voluntary Organizations* (Toronto, Ontario: York University, 1983), pp. 146–167.

J. E. Freed, "Relationships Among Indicators of Institutional Viability and Variables Associated with Planning Processes in Small, Independent Liberal Arts Institutions" (unpublished Ph.D. dissertation, Iowa State University, 1987), p. 103.

2. I. Unterman and R. H. Davis, "The Strategy Gap in Not-For-Profits," *Harvard Business Review* (May-June 1982), p. 30.

3. G. Rudney, "The Scope and Dimensions of Nonprofit Activity," in *The Nonprofit Sector: A Research Handbook,* ed. W. W. Powell (New Haven: Yale University Press, 1987), p. 56.

C. P. McLaughlin, *The Management of Nonprofit Organizations* (New York: John Wiley & Sons, 1986), p. 4.

4. D. R. Young, *If Not For Profit, For What?* (Lexington, Mass.: D. C. Heath, Lexington Books, 1983), p. 9.

5. J. Ruffat, "Strategic Management of Public and Non-Market Corporations," *Long Range Planning* (April 1983), p. 74.

6. U. S. Bureau of the Census, *Statistical Abstract of the United States: 1987,* 107th ed. (Washington, D.C., 1986).

7. I. Unterman and R. H. Davis, *Strategic Management of Not-For-Profit Organizations* (New York: Praeger Press, 1984), p. 2.

8. M. D. Fottler, "Is Management Really Generic?" *Academy of Management Review* (January 1981), p. 2.

9. Fottler, p. 2.

10. J. G. Simon, "The Tax Treatment of Nonprofit Organizations: A Review of Federal and State Policies," in *The Nonprofit Sector: A Research Handbook,* ed. W. W. Powell (New Haven: Yale University Press, 1987), pp. 67–98.

11. B. P. Keating and M. O. Keating, *Not-For-Profit* (Glen Ridge, N.J.: Thomas Horton & Daughters, 1980), p. 21.

12. "Revenues and Expenditures of Colleges and Universities, 1981–82," *The Chronicle of Higher Education* (April 4, 1984), p. 14.

13. D. Mott, *Characteristics of Effective Organizations* (San Francisco: Harper & Row, 1972) as reported by H. L. Tosi, Jr. and J. W. Slocum, Jr., "Contingency Theory: Some Suggested Directions," *Journal of Management* (Spring 1984), p. 11.

The contention that the pattern of environmental influence on the organization's strategic decision making derives from the organization's source(s) of income agrees with the work of Emerson, Thompson, and Pfeffer and Salancik. See R. E. Emerson, "Power-Dependence Relations," *American Sociological Review* (February, 1962), pp. 31–41; J. D. Thompson, *Organizations In Action* (New York: McGraw-Hill, 1967), pp. 30–31; and, J. Pfeffer and G. R. Salancik, *The External Control of Organizations: A Resource Dependence Perspective* (New York: Harper & Row, 1978), p. 44.

14. W. H. Newman and H. W. Wallender, III, "Managing Not-For-Profit Enterprises," *Academy of Management Review* (January 1978), p. 26.

15. Newman and Wallender, p. 27. The following discussion of the effects of these constraining characteristics is taken from Newman and Wallender, pp. 27–31.

16. P. C. Nutt, "A Strategic Planning Network for Non-Profit Organizations," *Strategic Management Journal* (January-March 1984), p. 57.

17. Unterman and Davis (1984) p. 174.

18. R. M. Kanter and D. V. Summers, "Doing Well While Doing Good: Dilemmas of Performance Measurement in Nonprofit Organizations and the Need for a Multiple-Constituency Approach," in *The Nonprofit Sector: A Research Handbook,* ed. W. W. Powell (New Haven: Yale University Press, 1987), p. 163.

19. Newman and Wallender, p. 27.

20. E. Bowen and B. Dolan, "His Trumpet Was Never Uncertain," *Time* (May 18, 1987), p. 68.

21. Keating and Keating, p. 130.

22. E. H. Fram, "Changing Expectations for Third Sector Executives," *Human Resource Management* (Fall 1980), p. 9.

23. For more information on the boards of not-for-profit organizations, see C. N. Waldo, *A Working Guide for Directors of Not-For-Profit Organizations* (New York: Quorum Books, 1986); C. A. Anderson and R. N. Anthony, *The New Corporate Directors* (New York: John Wiley & Sons, (1986), pp. 193–220; and R. D. Hay, *Strategic Management of Non-Profit Organizations* (Santa Barbara, California: Kinko's Publishing Group, 1986), pp. 4.1–4.18.

24. Keating and Keating, pp. 140–141.

25. Keating and Keating, pp. 143–144.

26. S. M. Lee and J. P. Shim, "Zero-Base Budgeting—Dealing with Conflicting Objectives," *Long Range Planning* (October 1984), p. 103.

27. M. W. Dirsmith, S. F. Jablonsky, and A. D. Luzi, "Planning and Control in the U.S. Federal Government: A Critical Analysis of PPB, MBO, and ZBB," *Strategic Management Journal* (October-December 1980), pp. 303–329.

E. E. Chaffee, "The Link between Planning and Budgeting," Working Paper, National Center for Higher Education Management Systems, Boulder, Colorado, October 1981, pp. 12–13.

28. R. P. Nielsen, "SMR Forum: Strategic Piggybacking—A Self-Subsidizing Strategy for Nonprofit Institutions," *Sloan Management Review* (Summer 1982), pp. 65–69.

R. P. Nielsen, "Piggybacking for Business and Nonprofits: A Strategy for Hard Times," *Long Range Planning* (April 1984), pp. 96–102.

29. "When Should the Profits of Nonprofits Be Taxed?" *Business Week* (December 5, 1983), p. 191.

30. E. Skloot, "Should Not-For-Profits Go Into Business?" *Harvard Business Review* (January-February 1983), p. 21.

31. R. P. Nielsen, "Piggybacking Strategies for Nonprofits: A Shared Costs Approach," *Strategic Management Journal* (May-June 1986), pp. 209–211.

32. Skloot, pp. 20–24.

33. K. G. Provan, "Interorganizational Cooperation and Decision Making Autonomy in a Consortium Multihospital System," *Academy of Management Review* (July 1984), pp. 494–504.

34. *Directory of Multihospital Systems* (Chicago: American Hospital Association, 1980).

35. T. Mason, "Lifesaving Partnerships For Nonprofit Hospitals," *Business Week* (August 26, 1985), p. 84.

36. D. Wellel, "As HMOs Increasingly Become Big Businesses, Many of Them Convert to Profit-Making Status," *Wall Street Journal* (March 26, 1985), p. 4.

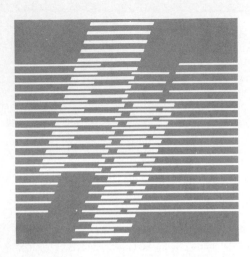

CHAPTER 12

STRATEGIC ISSUES IN ENTREPRENEURIAL VENTURES AND SMALL BUSINESSES

STRATEGIC MANAGEMENT MODEL

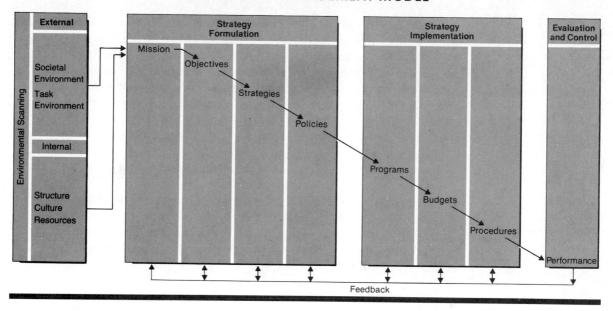

Studies in strategic management have typically dealt with the large, established business corporation to the virtual exclusion of the small business firm. Robinson and Pearce point out in their review of small firm strategic planning that "the state of knowledge pertinent to the strategic management of small and growing firms is woefully inadequate."[1] Except in those instances of an entire industry heavily composed of small entrepreneurial companies that capture the public imagination (like the computer software industry), the strategic management of small firms is rarely considered and rarely discussed in the business press or academic community. There is a tendency to treat these companies as if they were just a smaller version of larger companies and to apply standard strategic management concepts and techniques to their situation. This "little big business" orientation can be a serious mistake. For example, single product companies cannot readily apply portfolio analysis to their situation. Because a large number of small businesses and entrepreneurial ventures have only one product or product line, portfolio theory has little, if any, relevance to their strategy formulation process.

Small business cannot be ignored, however, when strategic management is discussed. Around 99% of the 17 million businesses in the U.S. employ fewer than 100 persons. Small business accounts for approximately half of all U.S. employment. Over 80% of all new jobs created in the U.S. between 1960 and 1985, were created by small businesses. Well over 60% of this total were created by new ventures. Between 1980 and 1988, three million jobs were lost in the Fortune 500 companies while 17 million jobs were created by small businesses.[2] Research reveals that not only do small firms spend almost twice as much of their R&D dollars on fundamental research as do large firms, but also that small companies are responsible for a high proportion of innovations in products and services.[3] For example, 43% of the awards for process and product innovation given over a six-year period by *Food Processing* magazine went to companies with less than $10 million in sales.[4]

Despite the overall success of small businesses, however, every year tens of thousands of small companies go out of business. Even in the best of times a firm has only a 50% chance of survival during its first five years.[5] As shown in Table 12.1, the causes of small business failure (depending upon the study cited) range from inadequate accounting systems to inability to cope with growth. The underlying problem appears to be an overall lack of strategic management—beginning with an inability to formulate a strategy to reach the customer, and ending with a failure to develop a system of evaluation and control to keep track of performance.

TABLE 12.1
Causes of Small Business Failure According to Various Studies

	A GOVERNMENT ANALYSIS	A LARGE ACC'T FIRM	DUN AND BRADSTREET STUDY	BANK OF AMERICA
Inadequate acct'g systems	x	x		
Poor location	x			
Lack of marketing skills	x			
Lack of a capital budget		x		
Inadequate provision for contingencies		x		
Lack of management skills		x		
Excessive inventory		x		
Incompetency			x	
Lack of experience			x	
Neglect			x	
Fraud			x	
Disaster			x	
Poor recordkeeping				x
Reckless money management				x
Lack of formal planning				x
Insufficient marketing talents				x
Indifferent employees				x
Inability to cope with growth				x

SOURCE: M. J. Stanford, *New Enterprise Management* (Reston, Va.: Reston Publishing Company, 1982), p. 4. Courtesy of American Institute of Certified Public Accountants.

Some of the strategic issues that are present in a small, developing company as well as in a large, established firm are:

- What goods or services are to be produced?
- Who is the customer?
- What sources of supply will be used?
- Where will the business be located?
- How much capital is required?
- How will the goods or services be produced?

These are only a few of the many possible strategic decisions with which managers must cope. The small business entrepreneur, however, usually faces them alone. Often defined as a person who organizes and manages a business undertaking, who assumes risk for the sake of a profit, the *entrepreneur* is the ultimate strategic manager. He or she makes all the strategic as well as operational decisions. All three levels of strategy—corporate, business, and functional—are the concerns of this founder and owner-manager of a company.

For these, among other reasons, it is important to understand how strategic management is practiced in small and developing companies as contrasted with large established corporations.

12.1

DIFFERENCE BETWEEN SMALL BUSINESS AND ENTREPRENEURIAL VENTURES

The United States Small Business Administration categorizes a business as small for the purpose of loan qualification if it fits the following criteria:

1. It is **independently** owned and operated.
2. It is not **dominant** in its field.
3. If in **manufacturing,** it has an average employment of no more than 250 employees or a relatively small size within the specific industry (up to 1,500 employees under some circumstances).
4. If in **wholesaling,** its annual sales are no more than $9.5–$22 million, depending on the industry.
5. If in **retailing** or **service,** its annual receipts are no more than $2–$8 million, depending on the industry.
6. If in **construction,** its average annual receipts cannot exceed $9.5 million for the three most recently completed fiscal years for general construction. For special trade construction, the average annual receipts cannot exceed $1 or $2 million for the three most recently completed fiscal years, depending on the industry.
7. If in agriculture, its annual receipts are no more than $1 million.[6]

Although there is considerable overlap between "small business" and "entrepreneurship," the concepts are different. The **small business firm** is defined as any business that is independently owned and operated, not dominant in its field, and does not engage in innovative practices. The **entrepreneurial venture,** in contrast, is any business with primary goals of profitability and growth and can be characterized by innovative strategic practices.[7] The basic difference between the small business firm and the entrepreneurial venture, therefore, lies not in the type of goods or services provided, but in their fundamental views toward growth and innovation. A high percentage of both small businesses and entrepreneurial ventures fit into the first stage of corporate development and the organizational life-cycle, as discussed in Chapter 8. Although all businesses begin life as entrepreneurial ventures and must grow to survive, many owners choose to stabilize their businesses at a particular size of operations and remain indefinitely in either Stage I (entrepreneurial) or II (functional). The primary goal of such a company changes from growth in order to survive, to stability in order to satisfy key needs of the owners/investors, such as lifetime employment for family members or a desire to keep total control in the hands of the entrepreneur.

12.2

USE OF STRATEGIC MANAGEMENT

Sexton, an authority on entrepreneurship, proposes that strategic planning is more likely to be present in an entrepreneurial venture than in the typical small business firm:

> Most firms start with just a single product. Those oriented toward growth immediately start looking for another one. It's that planning approach that separates the entrepreneur from the small-business owner.[8]

The reasons often cited for the apparent lack of strategic management practices in many small business firms are four-fold:

1. **Not enough time.** Day-to-day operating problems take up the time necessary for long-term planning.

2. **Unfamiliar with strategic management.** The small business's CEO may be unaware of strategic management concepts or view them as irrelevant to the small business situation.

3. **Lack of skills.** Small-business managers often lack the skills necessary to begin the strategic decision making process and do not have or wish to spend the money necessary to import trained consultants.

4. **Lack of trust and openness.** Many small-business owner/managers are very sensitive regarding key information about the business and are thus unwilling to share strategic planning with employees or outsiders. For this reason, boards of directors are often composed only of close friends and relatives of the owner/manager—people unlikely to provide an objective viewpoint or professional advice.[9]

Value of Strategic Management

Although many small companies do not use it, strategic management is being practiced by a growing number of small business and entrepreneurial companies. Research shows that strategic planning is strongly related to small business financial performance. For example, a study of 265 entrepreneurs of dry cleaning businesses revealed that firms that had engaged in strategic planning for more than five years significantly outperformed, in terms of revenue growth and net profits, those firms with less than five years of experience in strategic planning.[10] Another study of 135 small businesses in six different industries concluded that firms that engaged in strategic planning had greater increases in both sales and profits over a three-year period than did non-planners.[11]

Degree of Formality in Strategic Planning

Research generally concludes that the strategic planning process should be far more informal in small companies than it is in large corporations.[12] Some studies have even found that too much formalization of the strategic planning process can result in reduced performance![13] It is possible that a heavy emphasis on structured, written plans can be dysfunctional to the small entrepreneurial firm because it detracts from the very flexibility that is a benefit of small size. Nevertheless, there is some evidence that a certain degree of formality and structure in the strategic management process can be very beneficial to the small and developing company. In the study of dry cleaning firms mentioned earlier, companies with written plans (resulting from an analysis of internal strengths and weaknesses, and external opportunities and threats) had higher sales and profits than did those firms with strictly intuitive plans developed by the entrepreneur or no planning process at all. The study concluded that *the process of strategic planning, not the plan itself, was a key component of business performance.*[14]

A study of 220 of the fastest-growing, privately-held companies in the U.S. ranked by *INC.* magazine provided further evidence that some formality in strategic planning is needed as the company grows:

- While one-half of the *INC.* companies did not have a "formal" business plan at start-up, the majority adopted some form of strategic planning once the company was in operation.
- As the companies' sales volume grew, the planning processes became more formal, structured, and participatory. These processes were, however, much less sophisticated than those used by larger corporations.
- The strategic planning activity was more short-run-oriented than that conducted by large corporations.[15]

These observations suggest that new entrepreneurial ventures begin life in Mintzberg's *entrepreneurial mode* of strategic planning (explained in Chapter 6), and move toward the *planning mode* as the company becomes established and wants to continue its strong growth. If, after becoming successfully established, the entrepreneur instead chooses stability over growth, the venture moves more toward the *adaptive mode* so common to many small businesses.

Usefulness of Strategic Management Model

The descriptive model of strategic management, which was presented in Chapter 1 in Figure 1.3 and which prefaces each chapter in the book, is also relevant to entrepreneurial ventures and small businesses. As does the large corporation, the small company must go through (1) strategy formulation, (2) strategy implementation, and (3) evaluation and control. Using an assessment of the company's external and internal environments, top management (often just the CEO/entrepreneur) must first decide the company's mission, objectives, strategies, and policies, and then implement them with the appropriate programs, budgets, and procedures, so that the company's performance meets or exceeds expectations. This basic model holds for both an established small company and a new entrepreneurial venture. As the research mentioned earlier concluded, small and developing companies increase their chances of success if they make a serious attempt to work through the strategic issues imbedded in the strategic management model. The terms used in the process are relatively unimportant. The key is to focus on what's important—that set of managerial decisions and actions that determines the long-run performance of the company. The following list of informal questions can be more useful to a small company than are the more formal terms used by large corporations.

FORMAL	INFORMAL
Define mission	What do we stand for?
Set objectives	What are we trying to achieve?
Formulate strategy	How are we going to get there? How can we beat the competition?
Determine policies	What sort of ground rules should we all be following to get the job done right?
Establish programs	How should we organize this operation to get what we want done as cheaply as possible with the highest quality possible?
Prepare pro-forma budgets	How much is it going to cost us and where can we get the cash?
Specify procedures	In how much detail do we have to lay things out, so that everybody knows what to do?
Determine performance measures	What are those few key things that will determine whether we make it or not? How can we keep track of them?

Usefulness of Strategic
Decision-Making Process

As mentioned in Chapters 2 and 6, one way in which the strategic management model can be made action-oriented is to follow the strategic decision-
making model presented in Figs. 2.2 and 6.1. The eight steps presented in
that model are just as appropriate for small companies as they are for large
corporations. Unfortunately, the process does not fit new entrepreneurial
ventures. It makes no sense to begin the process with an evaluation of
current performance results if the company has not yet started. Likewise,
an entrepreneurial venture has no current mission, objectives, strategies,
and policies to be evaluated. It must develop new ones out of a comparison
of its external opportunities and threats to its potential strengths and weaknesses. Consequently we propose in Figure 12.1 a modified version of the
strategic decision-making process; this version more closely suits the new
entrepreneurial business.

The *strategic decision-making process for new ventures* is composed of the
following eight interrelated steps:

1. **Development of the basic business idea**—a mix of products and/or services
   having target customers and/or markets. The idea can be developed
   from a person's experience or it can be generated in a moment of
   creative insight.

2. **A scanning of the external environment, to locate strategic factors** in the
   societal and task environments that pose opportunities and threats. The
   scanning should focus particularly on market potential and resource
   accessibility.

3. **A scanning of the internal strategic factors** relevant to the new business.
   The entrepreneur should objectively consider personal assets, areas of
   expertise, abilities, and experience, in terms of the organizational needs
   of the new venture.

4. **Analysis of the strategic factors,** in light of the current situation. The
   venture's potential strengths and weaknesses must be evaluated in light
   of opportunities and threats.

5. **Decision point.** If the basic business idea appears to be a feasible
   business opportunity, the process should be continued. Otherwise, further development of the idea should be canceled unless the strategic
   factors change.

6. **Generation of a business plan** specifying how the idea will be transformed
   into reality. See Table 12.2 for the suggested contents of a strategic
   business plan. The proposed venture's mission, objectives, strategies,
   and policies, as well as its likely board of directors (if a corporation)
   and key managers, should be developed. Key internal factors should be
   specified and performance projections generated. The business plan is
   the last step of a new venture's strategy formulation; it serves as a
   vehicle through which financial support is obtained from potential investors and creditors.[16]

FIGURE 12.1
Strategic Decision-Making Process for New Ventures

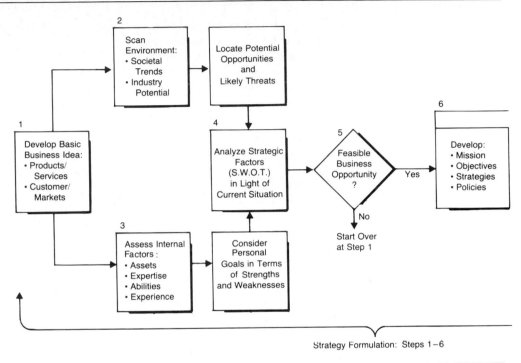

Source: Adapted from Thomas L. Wheelen and Janiece L. Gallagher, *Entrepreneurship and Strategic Management* (New York: McGraw-Hill, 1990). Developed by Thomas L. Wheelen and Charles E. Michaels, Jr. Copyright © 1987 by Thomas L. Wheelen and Janiece L. Gallagher. Reprinted by permission.

7. **Implementation of the business plan,** via the use of action plans and procedures.

8. **Evaluation of the implemented business plan,** through comparison of actual performance against projected performance results. This step leads to step 1(b) of the strategic decision-making process as shown in Figures 2.2 and 6.1. To the extent that actual results are less than or greatly exceed the anticipated results, the entrepreneur needs to reconsider the company's current mission, objectives, strategies and policies, and possibly formulate strategic changes to the original business plan.

12.3

ISSUES IN STRATEGY FORMULATION

A fundamental reason for differences in strategy formulation between large and small companies lies in the relationship between owners and managers.[17] The CEO of a large corporation has to consider and balance the varied needs of the corporation's many stakeholders. The CEO of a small business,

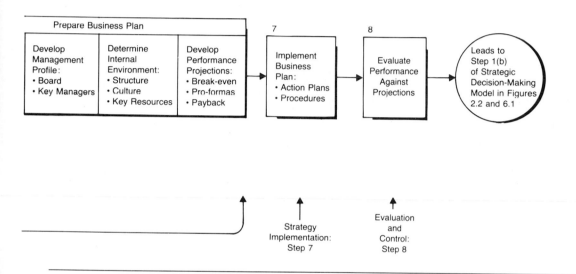

TABLE 12.2

Contents of a Strategic Business Plan for an Entrepreneurial Venture

I. Table of Contents	X. Human Resources Plan
II. Executive Summary	XI. Ownership
III. Nature of the Business	XII. Risk Analysis
IV. Strategy Formulation	XIII. Timetables and Milestones
V. Market Analysis	XIV. Strategy Implementation—Action Plans
VI. Marketing Plan	
VII. Operational Plans—Service/Product	XV. Evaluation and Control
	XVI. Summary
VIII. Financial Plans	XVII. Appendixes
IX. Organization and Management	

SOURCE: Adapted from Thomas L. Wheelen and Janiece L. Gallagher, *Entrepreneurship and Strategic Management* (N.Y.: McGraw-Hill, 1990). Copyright © 1988 by Thomas L. Wheelen. Reprinted by permission.

however, is very likely to also be the owner—the company's primary stake-holder. Personal and family needs can thus strongly affect the company's mission and objectives and can overrule other considerations. For example, large corporations often choose growth strategies for their many positive side-effects for management as well as for the stockholders. A small company may, however, choose a stability strategy because the entrepreneur is inter-ested mostly in generating employment for family members, providing the family a "decent living," and in being "the boss" of a firm small enough that he/she can manage it comfortably. "Thus in order to understand the goals of a small organization, it is first necessary to understand the moti-vations of the owner since the two are indistinguishable, certainly in the early days of the firm's start-up."[18]

The basic S.W.O.T. analysis is just as relevant to small businesses as it is to larger ones. As mentioned earlier, portfolio theory is not often relevant to small companies because many of them have only one product or product line. The greatest strength and weakness of the small firm, at least in the beginning, lies with the entrepreneur—the owner/manager of the business. The entrepreneur is *the* strategic manager, the source of product/market knowledge, and the dynamo that energizes the company. That is why the internal assessment of a new venture's strengths and weaknesses focus in Figure 12.1 on the personal characteristics of the founder—his/her assets, expertise, abilities, and experience. Just as an entrepreneur's strengths can be the key to company success, personal weaknesses can be a primary cause of failure. For example, the reason for the failure of many small retail businesses is the founders' lack of knowledge of retailing skills.[19]

Environmental scanning in small businesses is much less sophisticated than in large corporations. The business is usually too small to justify hiring someone to only do environmental scanning or strategic planning. Top managers, especially if they are the founders, tend to believe that they know the business and can follow it better than anyone else. A study of 220 small, rapid-growth companies reveals that the typical approach to strategic plan-ning includes an analysis of competition (carried out by 60% of the com-panies), identification of customer requirements (74%), development of detailed resource-allocation plans (65%), analysis of operational strengths and weaknesses (76%), consideration of contingency plans (86%), allowance for control and feedback (70%), and procedures for implementation (86%). Approximately two-thirds of the companies surveyed focus their planning activities in the marketing area, around 20% concentrate on plans for operations, and only 4% focus their planning in the financial area. The majority of the CEOs are actively and personally involved in all phases of the planning process, but especially in the setting of objectives. Only 15% of the companies use a planning officer or form a planning group to assist in the planning process. In the rest of the firms, operating managers who participate in strategic planning only provide input to the CEO, who then formulates the plan.[20]

Sources of Innovations

Drucker, in his book *Innovation and Entrepreneurship*, proposes the existence of seven sources for innovative opportunity that should be monitored by those interested in starting an entrepreneurial venture, either within an established company or as an independent small business.[21] The first four sources of innovation lie within the industry itself. The last three arise in the societal environment. These seven sources are:

1. **The Unexpected.** An unexpected success, an unexpected failure, or an unexpected outside event, can be a symptom of a unique opportunity. For example, at a time in the 1950s when Japanese television manufacturers marketed their products only to affluent people in the cities, Matsushita, a small, undistinguished company, noted that a sizable number of their sets were being bought by farmers who were supposedly too poor to afford TVs. Instead of ignoring this fact as other manufacturers did, Matsushita began to sell their televisions door-to-door in the country. The company soon grew to become a major multinational corporation known for its Panasonic and National brands.

2. **The Incongruity.** A discrepancy between reality and what everyone assumes it to be, or between what is and what ought to be, can create an innovative opportunity. For example, in the 1950s the ocean-going freighter business was believed to be dying. It was assumed that it would be replaced by air freight, to be used for all shipments except bulk commodities. The cost of ocean freight was going up partially because of congestion and pilferage in many ports. To concentrate on competing with air, the industry had emphasized the use of faster, more economical ships using less crew. But loading and unloading problems still overcame any savings. In 1966, however, a new company called Sea-Land Corporation solved the problem: it introduced containerized shipping. Goods could now be packed into large, secure containers at the shipper's warehouse and loaded quickly onto specially-designed containerships. This system reduced time in port and cut costs by 60%. Sea-Land grew to become a dominant force in trans-oceanic shipping and eventually became part of CSX Corporation.

3. **Innovation based on process need.** When a weak link is evident in a particular process, but people work around it instead of doing something about it, an opportunity is present to the person or company willing to supply the "missing link." For example, when a pharmaceutical company's salesman named William Connor decided to start his own business, he looked for a need that was not being fulfilled. Eye surgeons at that time dreaded cutting a particular ligament when they were doing cataract surgery. Unfortunately, the doctors had no choice but to do so. Connor noted that a specific enzyme was known to easily dissolve this particular ligament, but it was not used because it could not be stored for more than a few hours. Through trial and error, Connor found a preservative that would make the enzyme usable. Within a year all eye

surgeons were using his patented compound. Twenty years later, Connor sold his company, Alcon Laboratories, to a multinational company for a substantial amount.

4. **Changes in industry or market structure.** A business is ready for an innovative product, service, or approach to the business, when the underlying foundation of the industry or market shifts. In 1954, George E. Johnson noted that blacks in the United States wanted to be able to straighten their naturally coarse, thick hair so that they would have more flexibility in hair styling. Even though black consumers were becoming recognized as an important market segment, no established hair care or cosmetics company was interested at the time in developing hair care products specifically for them. Seeing a strong need in a developing market, George Johnson formed what was soon to become the largest manufacturer of personal grooming products for black consumers in the world—Johnson Products Company.

Deregulation in the U.S. and privatization around the world in the 1980s also created innovative opportunities that were used by firms like Texas Air. Small, non-union, entrepreneurial rail lines were born in the U.S., as major unionized rail companies dropped what had been for them unprofitable lines of track. See Illustrative Example 12.1 for one such entrepreneurial venture, the tiny Delaware Otsego Railroad.

5. **Demographics.** Changes in the population's size, age structure, composition, employment, level of education, and income, can create innovative opportunities. One typical example has been the impact of the WW II "baby boomers" on the U.S. economy in particular. As this large bulge in the U.S. population ages, its interests dominate the marketplace. For example, when this group was in its twenties during the 1970s, products appealing to young adults, such as skiing, beer, rock music, and X-rated movies (to name a few), became very popular. As this group moved into their 30s during the 1980s, their interests shifted to those products and services that would help them balance their developing family and career interests. Day-care centers, family-oriented resorts, and physical fitness centers became popular. The beer-consumption pattern changed from the drinking of cheap beer by the pitcher to the drinking of imported or specialty beers by the glass. Wine coolers replaced six packs. As this group ages, expect increasing interest in health care, cultural activities, travel, and financial security.

6. **Changes in perception, mood, and meaning.** Innovative opportunities can develop when a society's general assumptions, attitudes, and beliefs change. For example, people's feelings about eating have been shifting from "feeding" (getting down necessary sustenance in the easiest, simplest, and cheapest way) to "dining" (eating gourmet foods in a gracious atmosphere). Because of this shift, gourmet cookbooks and special sections in supermarkets have become very popular. In another example, as families in the developed countries choose to have fewer children, parents tend to spend the same amount on one child as they might have spent on two. Thus baby-carriage manufacturers are able to keep up their sales in dollars while their sales in units drop; they emphasize high-

ILLUSTRATIVE EXAMPLE 12.1

Delaware Otsego Railroad Takes Advantage of Industry Changes and Becomes a Key Small Business in the Northeast

When deregulation in the U.S. changed the competitive environment for railroads, three rail companies emerged as dominant in the Eastern U.S.—Conrail, CSX, and Norfolk Southern. Only one of these, Conrail, had track to New York City. When CSX bought Sea-Land in 1986 and became a global transportation company, it found that ocean-going container ships were using the United States continent as a "land bridge" between the Atlantic and Pacific Oceans; this alternative was cheaper than use of the Panama Canal. To provide rail transportation to and from the west coast for its Sea-Land container traffic, CSX needed access to New York City. To obtain this access, however, CSX had to pay Conrail, a serious rival for containerized traffic, a high fee for the use of its tracks to New York.

Walter Rich saw opportunity in this situation. As the President and CEO of Delaware Otsego Corporation (parent of the small New York, Susquehanna, and Western Railway), he had stitched together unused rail trackage and formed a rail system from New York City to Warwick, New York, and from Binghamton, New York, to Jamesville and Utica, New York. Because he needed track to connect Warwick with Binghamton (his track was in terrible condition), he convinced Conrail in 1982 to grant him rights to use Conrail's track between the two cities. When Sea-Land

failed to reach an acceptable agreement with Conrail on price and terminals, Mr. Rich took advantage of his local freight agreement to break Conrail's monopoly position into New York City. He offered Sea-Land a better deal. Rich's line was able to make a good profit on the traffic even though it had to pay high fees to Conrail. Labor costs were 50% lower than Conrail's because Rich's line was non-union and thus able to operate with smaller crews and less costly work rules.

In 1987 Rich decided to renovate his own decrepit 70-mile stretch of hilly, curvy track between Binghamton and Warwick to avoid Conrail's high fee. Analysts saw it as an audacious but preposterous move. "He's running trains on a Burma Road. The route is long, slow, has stiff gradients, no signals and numerous grade crossings," stated one expert. Nevertheless, Rich was able to proceed partially because of the support of connecting railroads (CSX and Norfolk Southern) eager to find a non-Conrail route to New York City. "We're like a fly on the back of an elephant," confesses Mr. Rich. He went on to say, however, that "within five years we will be very important."

SOURCE: D. Machalaba, "Delaware Otsego Refuses To Be Shunted," *Wall Street Journal* (October 12, 1987), p. 6.

quality products with high prices. This move is aided by the trend to two-career families and a high level of divorce—causing parents to spend money instead of time on their children. This trend created a huge market for "educational" products, such as personal computers. Witness the rapid development of Apple Computer—an entrepreneurial success story.

7. **New knowledge.** Advances in scientific and nonscientific knowledge can create new products and new markets. Advances in two different areas can sometimes be integrated to form the basis of a new product. For example, simultaneous developments in computers, communication, and office equipment are being merged to form one new set of products that are able to do what three or more different products did before.

New software firms emerge weekly as new programs are needed to take advantage of technological advancements in computer hardware.

Drucker further proposes **five principles of innovation,** which can help the entrepreneur to take advantage of a source of innovation.[22]

- Begin with an analysis of the opportunities.
- Analyze the opportunity to see if people will be interested in using the innovation. Remember that few people were interested in buying a computer until "user-friendly" software was developed.
- To be effective, the innovation must be simple and clearly focused on a specific need. The "Post-It" note pad was a huge success because, once people saw the removable, self-stick notes in action, they could readily find many uses for the product.
- Effective innovations start small. By appealing to a small, limited market, a product or service requires little money and few people to produce and sell it. As the market grows, the company has time to fine-tune its processes and stay ahead of the emerging competition.
- Aim at market leadership. If an innovation does not aim at leadership in the beginning, it is unlikely to be innovative enough to successfully establish itself. Leadership here can mean dominating a small market niche.

Factors Affecting a New Venture's Success

According to Hofer and Sandberg, there are three factors that have a substantial impact on a new venture's performance. In order of importance, they are (1) *the structure of the industry entered,* (2) *the new venture's business strategy,* and (3) *behavioral characteristics of the entrepreneur.*[23]

Industry Structure

Research shows that the chances for success are greater for those entrepreneurial ventures that enter rapidly changing industries than for those that enter stable industries. In addition, prospects are better in industries that are in the early, high-growth stages of development. There is often less intense competition. Fast market growth also allows new ventures to make a certain number of mistakes without serious penalty. New ventures also increase their chances of success when they enter markets in which they can erect entry barriers to keep out competitors.

PIMS data reveals that a new venture is more likely to be successful entering an industry in which one dominant competitor has a 50% or more market share, than entering an industry in which the largest competitor has less than 25% market share. To explain this phenomenon, Hofer and Sandberg point out that when an industry has one dominant firm, the remaining competitors are relatively weak and are easy prey for an aggressive entrepreneur. To avoid direct competition with a major competitor, the new venture can focus on a market segment that is being ignored.

Two product characteristics of the industry also have a significant impact on a new venture's success. First, a new venture is more likely to be successful when it enters an industry with heterogeneous (different) products than when it enters one with homogeneous (similar) products. In a heterogeneous industry, a new venture can differentiate itself from competitors with a unique product or, by focusing on the unique needs of a market segment, it can find a market niche. Second, a new venture is, according to PIMS data, more likely to be successful if the product is relatively unimportant to the customer's total purchasing needs, than if it is important. Customers are more likely to experiment with a new product if the costs are low and product failure will not create a problem.

Business Strategy

According to Hofer and Sandberg, the key to success in new-venture strategy is (1) to differentiate the product from other competitors in meaningful areas of quality and service and (2) to focus the product on customer needs in a segment of the market, so that a dominant share of that part of the market is achieved. This guideline is in agreement with those of other authorities who argue that a small company cannot successfully follow an overall low-cost strategy because it cannot achieve the economies of scale available to large corporations. Therefore, Porter's focus and differentiation strategies are the most attractive alternatives to small companies who recognize their size and marketing "muscle" limitations.[24] (See the discussion of Michael Porter's competitive strategies in Chapter 7.) Adopting guerrilla-warfare tactics, these companies go after opportunities in market niches too small to justify retaliation from the market leaders.[25] Like the Delaware Otsego Railroad in Illustrative Example 12.1, such a company can operate quite successfully as a "fly on the back of an elephant."

To continue its growth once it has found a niche, the entrepreneurial firm can emphasize continued innovation and pursue natural growth in its current markets. It can expand into related markets in which the company's core skills, resources, and facilities offer the keys to further success. See Illustrative Example 12.2 for one example of such an entrepreneurial company.

Entrepreneurial Characteristics

Hofer and Sandberg propose four behavioral factors as being key to a new venture's success:[26]

1. Successful entrepreneurs are able to identify potential venture opportunities better than are most people. They focus on opportunities—not on problems—and try to learn from failure.

The Successful Use of a Differentiation Strategy by a Small Business: Gold Ribbon Concepts

Stephen and David Spencer had been reasonably successful operating a car radio and installation shop called Spencer Sound Systems, which they had started in 1978 in Iowa City, Iowa. After a couple years of barely breaking even, they began earning a healthy profit by installing expensive car stereo equipment—systems sometimes costing $10,000 to $20,000. Soon, they began selling home stereo equipment and moved to a bigger building.

In 1982, the Spencer brothers noticed an innovative opportunity. They began putting most of the company's profits into the development of gold ribbon speakers. The idea of using ribbons in loud speakers, instead of the usual voice coils and cone diaphragms, was not new. Technicians had been experimenting with ribbon designs since the 1920s. Never before, however, had anyone tried to make speaker ribbons with gold.

During the next three years, the brothers spent nearly $1 million on the project before finding their patented technique for making 1-inch-wide gold ribbons on a membrane thinner than a human hair. Combined with other materials, the gold ribbons form what the Spencers call a "transducer" which is then placed inside a padded cabinet. The transducer costs $800 and is sold to serious audiophiles who wish to build their own cabinets. A finished speaker, called *The Gold,* costs between $3,150 and $7,000.

The speakers have been praised by international stereo magazines. While their product was still under development in 1985, the Spencer brothers were honored at the International Consumer Electronics Trade Show in Chicago. Buyers have come from all over the world to buy the Spencers' version of "high-end" stereo. More than 60% of the first shipment in 1986 was sent to customers in Oslo, Hong Kong, Bangkok, Tokyo, and Sydney. These customers tend to be males earning $30,000–$40,000 annually who like to spend their money on the very best stereo equipment. "Most of our customers are very, very technically oriented," said Stephen Spencer, the 33-year-old Chief Executive of Gold Ribbon Concepts, the speaker side of the Spencer brothers' business.

The Spencers intend to keep plowing profits back into research and development. They plan to create new cabinet designs and gold ribbon car stereo speakers. They may even be able some day to take their speakers home to enjoy. "We are selling them too fast," smiled Stephen. "There haven't been enough for us."

SOURCE: M. Murray, "Audiophiles Strike Gold in Coralville," *Des Moines Register* (January 5, 1986), p. 1.

2. Successful entrepreneurs have a sense of urgency that makes them action-oriented. They have a high need for achievement, which motivates them to turn their ideas into action.

3. Successful entrepreneurs have a detailed knowledge of the key factors needed for success in the industry and have the physical stamina needed to put their lives into their work.

4. Successful entrepreneurs seek outside help to supplement their skills, knowledge, and abilities. Through their enthusiasm, they are able to attract key investors, partners, creditors, and employees. As mentioned in Illustrative Example 8.2, Mitch Kapor of Lotus Development did not hesitate to bring in Jim Manzi as president, because Manzi had the managerial skills that Kapor lacked.

In summarizing their conclusions regarding factors affecting the success of entrepreneurial ventures, Hofer and Sandberg propose guidelines in Table 12.3.

12.4

ISSUES IN STRATEGY IMPLEMENTATION

The implementation of strategy in a small business involves many of the same issues, mentioned in Chapter 8, that concern a large corporation. Programs, budgets, and procedures to make the strategy action-oriented must be developed and used. Resources must be organized so that the work can be done efficiently and effectively; the proper people must be selected for key jobs; and employees' efforts need to be directed toward task accomplishment and coordinated so that the company achieves its objectives and fulfills its mission. The major difference between the large and small company is *who* must implement the strategy. In a large corporation, the implementors are often a very different group of people from those who formulated the strategy. In a small business, the formulators of the strategy are usually the ones to implement it. It is for this reason that the imaginary line between strategy formulation and implementation often becomes blurred in most small businesses.

TABLE 12.3
Some Guidelines for New Venture Success

- Focus on industries facing substantial technological or regulatory changes, especially those with recent exits by established competitors.
- Seek industries whose smaller firms have relatively weak competitive positions.
- Seek industries that are in early, high-growth stages of evolution.
- Seek industries in which it is possible to create high barriers to subsequent entry.
- Seek industries with heterogeneous products that are relatively unimportant to the customer's overall success.
- Seek to differentiate your products from those of your competitors in ways that are meaningful to your customers.
- Focus such differentiation efforts on product quality, marketing approaches, and customer service—and charge enough to cover the costs of doing so.
- Seek to dominate the market segments in which you compete. If necessary, either segment the market differently or change the nature and focus of your differentiation efforts to increase your domination of the segments you serve.
- Stress innovation, especially new product innovation, that is built on existing organizational capabilities.
- Seek natural, organic growth through flexibility and opportunism that builds on existing organizational strengths.

SOURCE: C. W. Hofer and W. R. Sandberg, "Improving New Venture Performance: Some Guidelines for Success," *American Journal of Small Business* (Summer 1987), pp. 17 and 19. Copyright © 1987 by C. W. Hofer and W. R. Sandberg. Reproduced by permission.

Stages of a Small Business's Development

The implementation problems of a small business change as the company grows and develops over time. Just as the strategic decision-making process for entrepreneurial ventures is different from that of established businesses, so do the managerial systems in small companies often vary from those of large corporations. Those variations are based upon their stage of development. The stages of corporate development and the organizational life-cycle discussed in Chapter 8 suggest that all small businesses are either in Stage I or trying to move into Stage II. These models imply that all successful new ventures eventually become Stage II, functionally organized companies. This is not always true, however. In attempting to clearly show how small businesses develop, Churchill and Lewis propose five *sub-stages* of small business development: (a) Existence, (b) Survival, (c) Success, (d) Take-off, and (e) Resource Maturity.[27] (See Table 12.4.) A review of these stages shows in more detail how a company can move through its entrepreneurial Stage I into a functionally-oriented, professionally-managed Stage II of existence.

A. Existence

At this point, the entrepreneurial venture faces the problems of obtaining customers and delivering the promised product or service. The organizational structure is a simple one—like that shown in Figure 5.1 of Chapter 5. The entrepreneur does everything and directly supervises subordinates. Systems are minimal. The owner *is* the business.

TABLE 12.4
Sub-stages of Small Business Development*

A. Existence
B. Survival
C. Success
    1. Disengagement
    2. Growth
D. Take-off
E. Resource Maturity

SOURCE: N. C. Churchill and V. L. Lewis, "The Five Stages of Small Business Growth," *Harvard Business Review* (May–June 1983), pp. 30–50.

*NOTE: These are actually sub-stages within the stages of development discussed in Chapter 8. Thus, small business Stages A through D are really sub-stages of Stage I, entrepreneurial management; whereas Stage E is the first sub-stage of Stage II, functional management. Refer to Table 8.2.

B. Survival

Those ventures able to satisfy a sufficient number of customers enter this sub-stage. The rest of the ventures close when the owners run out of start-up capital. Those reaching the survival stage are concerned about generating the cash flow needed to repair and replace capital assets as they wear out, and to finance the growth to continue satisfying the market segment it has found. At this point in the young company's life, it can be plagued by "problems of prosperity." It is unable to comfortably finance or manage its growth, but it must satisfy an increasing number of customers or else lose them to a competitor.

At this sub-stage, the organizational structure is still simple, but it probably has a sales manager or general foreman to carry out the well-defined orders of the owner. A major problem of many small businesses at this sub-stage is finding a person who is qualified to supervise the business when the owner can't be present but who is still willing to work for a very modest salary. Entrepreneurs usually attempt to use family members rather than to hire an outsider, who lacks the entrepreneur's dedication to the business and (in the words of one owner-manager) "steals them blind." A company that remains in this sub-stage for a long time, will earn marginal returns on invested time and capital (with lots of psychic income!) and eventually go out of business when "mom and pop" give up or retire.

C. Success

By this point the company's sales have reached a level such that the firm is not only profitable, but has sufficient cash flow to reinvest in the business. They key issue at this sub-stage is whether the company should be used as a platform for growth, or as a means of support for the owners as they completely or partially disengage from the company. The company is in transition to a functionally structured organization, but still relies on the entrepreneur for all key decisions.

C(1). DISENGAGEMENT The company can now successfully follow a stability strategy and remain at this sub-stage almost indefinitely—provided that environmental change does not destroy its niche or poor management reduce its competitive abilities. By now functional managers have taken over some duties of the entrepreneur. A few staff members—usually a controller in the office and a scheduler in the work area—become part of the company's management. The company at this sub-stage may be incorporated, but it still is primarily owned by the founder or founder's family. Consequently, the board of directors is either a rubber stamp for the entrepreneur or a forum for family squabbles. Growth strategies are not pursued, because either the market niche will not allow growth or because the owner is content with a company of the size he/she can still manage comfortably. For example, Fritz Maytag, the owner/manager CEO of Anchor Brewing Company, deliberately chooses to keep his company small.[28]

C(2). GROWTH Like the Spencer brothers in Illustrative Example 12.2, the entrepreneur risks all available cash and the established borrowing power of the company in financing further growth. Strategic as well as operational planning is extensive and deeply involves the owner. Managers with an eye to the company's future rather than for its current situation are hired. It is in this sub-stage that the company avoids creeping bureaucratization and returns to being a risky entrepreneurial venture. Top management begins to view its own role as that of a blocking back in football (eliminating obstacles) rather than that of the quarterback (calling all the plays).[29] The emphasis now is upon teamwork rather than upon the entrepreneur's personal actions and energy.

D. Take-Off

The key problems in this sub-stage are how to grow rapidly and how to finance that growth. The entrepreneur must learn to delegate to the specialized managers who now form the top management of the company. A functional structure for the organization should now be solidly in place. Operational and strategic planning heavily involves the hired managers, but the company is still dominated by the entrepreneur's presence and stock control. Vertical and horizontal growth strategies are being seriously considered as the firm's management debates when and how to grow. This is the point at which the entrepreneur either rises to the occasion of managing the transition from a small to a large company, or recognizes personal limitations, sells his/her stock for a profit, and leaves the firm. The composition of the board of directors changes, from dominance by friends and relatives of the owner, to a large percentage of outsiders with managerial experience, who can help the owner during the transition to a professionally managed company. The biggest danger facing the firm in this sub-stage is the owner's desire to stay in total control as if it were still an entrepreneurial venture, even though he/she lacks the managerial skills necessary to run an established corporation. As pointed out in Chapter 8 in Illustrative Example 8.2, both Steve Jobs of Apple Computer and Mitch Kapor of Lotus Development realized their limitations and brought in someone else to manage the transitions of their firms. William Norris of Control Data, in contrast, had to be forced out.

E. Resource Maturity

It is at this point that the small company has adopted most of the characteristics of an established, large company. It may still be a small- to medium-sized company, but it is recognized as an important force in the industry and a possible candidate for the Fortune 500 someday. The greatest concerns of a company at this sub-stage are (1) controlling the financial gains brought on by rapid growth, and (2) retaining its flexibility and entrepreneurial spirit. The company has now arrived. In the terms of the stages of corporate development and the organizational life cycle discussed in Chapter 8, the company has become a full-fledged Stage II functional corporation.

Transfer of Power and Wealth in Family Businesses

Small businesses are often family businesses. Even though the founders of the companies are the primary forces in starting the entrepreneurial ventures, their needs for personal help and financial assistance will cause them to turn to family members who can be trusted, over unknown outsiders of questionable integrity, who will demand more salary than the enterprise can afford. Sooner or later the founder's spouse and children are drafted into business operations either because (1) the family standard of living is directly tied to the business, or (2) the entrepreneur is in desperate need of help just to staff the operation. The children are guaranteed summer jobs and the business changes from dad's or mom's company to "our" company. The family members are extremely valuable assets to the entrepreneur because they are often also willing, to help the business succeed, to put in long hours at low pay. Even though the spouse and children might have no official stock in the company, they know that they will somehow share in its future and perhaps even inherit the business.

Churchill and Hatten propose that family businesses go through four sequential phases from the time in which the venture is strictly managed by the founder, to the time in which the next generation takes charge.[30]

1. **Owner-managed business.** This is the point that begins at start-up and continues to the entrance of a family member into the business on a full-time basis. Family considerations influence but are not yet a directing part of the firm. At this point, the founder (entrepreneur) and the business are one.

2. **Training and development of new generation.** The children begin to learn the business at the dining table during early childhood and then through part-time and vacation employment. The company is still dad's or mom's, but the children now begin to think of themselves as a small part of the company. The family and the business become one. A key value develops: What's good for the business is good for the family and vice-versa. Just as the entrepreneur ego-identified with the business earlier, the family now begins to identify itself with the business.

3. **Partnership between generations.** At this point, a son or daughter of the founder has acquired sufficient business and managerial competence so that he or she can be involved in key decisions for at least a part of the company. The entrepreneur's offspring has to gain respect from the

firm's employees and other managers and show that he or she can do the job right. Otherwise, the rest of the employees will ignore "Junior" and only pay attention to the founder. Another issue is the willingness of the founder to share authority with the son or daughter. Even the founder may not have sufficient confidence in the child's ability to make company decisions. Consequently, a common tactic taken by sons and daughters in family businesses is to take a job in a large, established corporation in either the same industry or in an industry similar to that of the family business. With a few years of experience in a large respected firm, the son or daughter can return to the family as a successful manager in his/her own right. By that time, the founder might be more willing to view the child as a competent business person.

4. **Transfer of Power.** Instead of the founder's being forced to sell the company when he or she can no longer manage the business, the founder has the option in a family business of turning it over to the next generation as part of their inheritance. Often the founder moves to the position of chairman of the board and promotes one of the children to the position of CEO. This allows the founder to still have an interest in the firm, but not operating responsibility. Unfortunately, some founders cannot resist meddling in operating affairs and unintentionally undermine the leadership position of the son or daughter. Henry Ford I, for example, used his position as Board Chairman to contradict decisions made by his son, the President—Edsel Ford. Because of this intervention, Ford Motor Company floundered through the 1930s until it almost went bankrupt. To avoid this problem, strong-willed entrepreneurs will sell portions of their stock in the company for retirement income. They will make a big ceremony of turning over the reins of power and take an extended vacation. Some will even use the money to start a new venture of their own, to keep their mind occupied and away from what is now someone else's company.

12.5

ISSUES IN EVALUATION AND CONTROL

As a means by which the corporation's implementation of strategy can be evaluated, the control systems of large corporations have evolved over a long period of time, in response to pressures from the environment (particularly the government). Conversely, the entrepreneur creates what is needed as the business grows. Because of a personal involvement in decision making, the entrepreneur has little need for a detailed reporting system.[31] Thus, the founder who has little understanding of accounting and a shortness of cash might employ a bookkeeper instead of an accountant. A formal personnel function might never appear because the entrepreneur lumps it with simple bookkeeping and uses a secretary to handle personnel files. As an entrepreneurial venture becomes more established, it will develop more complex evaluation and control systems, but they are often not the kind used in large corporations and are probably used for different purposes.

Financial statements, in particular, tell only half the story in small, privately-owned companies. The formality of the financial reporting system in such a company is usually a result of pressures from government tax agencies, not from management's desire to have an objective evaluation and control system. Because balance sheets and income statements are not always what they seem, standard ratios such as return on assets and debt/equity are unreliable. Levin and Travis provide five reasons why owners, operators, and outside observers should be wary of using standard financial methods to indicate the health of a small, privately-owned company.[32]

- **The line between debt and equity is blurred.** In some instances, what appears as a loan is really an easy-to-retrieve equity investment. The entrepreneur in this instance doesn't want to lose his/her investment if the company fails. Another condition is that retained earnings seldom reflect the amount of internal financing needed for the company's growth. This account may merely be a place in which cash is left so that the owner can avoid double taxation. To avoid other taxes, owner/managers may own fixed assets that they lease to the corporation. The equity that was used to buy those assets is really the company's equity, but it doesn't appear on the books.

- **Life-style is a part of financial statements.** The life-style of the owner and the owner's family is often reflected in the balance sheet. The assets of some firms include beach cottages, mountain chalets, and automobiles. In others, plants and warehouses that are used for company operations are not shown because they are held separately by the family. Income statements may not reflect how well the company is operating. Profitability is not so important in decision making in small, private companies as it is in large, publicly-held corporations. For example, spending for recreation or transportation and paying rents or salaries above market rates to relatives put artificially high costs on the books of small firms. One privately-held dry cleaning establishment has never made much profit in its years of existence, but has provided the owner with a comfortable living and the owner's children with good paying jobs so that they could go to college. The business might appear to be poorly managed to an outsider, but the owner is acting rationally. The owner/manager wants dependable income or its equivalent with the least painful tax consequences. Because the standard profitability measures like ROI are not useful in the evaluation of such a firm, Levin and Travas recommend return on current assets as a better measure of corporate productivity.[33]

- **Standard financial formulas don't always apply.** Following practices that are in contrast to standard financial recommendations, small companies will often use short-term debt to finance fixed assets. The absence of well-organized capital markets for small businesses, along with the typical banker's resistance to making loans without personal guarantees, leaves the private owner little choice.

- **Personal preference determines financial policies.** Because the owner is often the manager of the small firm, dividend policy is largely irrelevant. Dividend decisions are based not on stock price (which is usually unknown because the stock is not traded), but on the owner's life-style and the trade-off between taking wealth from the corporation and double taxation.

- **Banks combine personal and business wealth.** Because of the large percentage of small businesses that go bankrupt every year, banks' loan officers are reluctant to loan money to a small business unless the owner also provides some personal guarantees for the loan. In some instances, part of the loan may be composed of a second mortgage on the owner's house. If the owner does not want to succumb to this pressure by lenders to include the owner's personal assets as part of the collateral, the owner/manager might be willing to pay high interest rates for a loan that does not put their family's assets at risk.

SUMMARY AND CONCLUSION

Entrepreneurial ventures and small businesses are managed far more informally than are the large, established business corporations discussed elsewhere in this book. Some of the more popular strategic-management concepts and techniques, like portfolio analysis, are not very useful to the typical small-business manager or entrepreneur. As Mintzberg pointed out in Chapter 6, small, rapidly growing companies tend to follow the entrepreneurial mode of strategy formulation—characterized by bold moves and intuitive decisions. The time frame is oriented to the short-run. Once the company has opened its doors, management's concerns are for operations, not for strategic planning. The usual rationale for not engaging in formal strategic management is: "Why should I develop a five-year plan when I don't even know if I'm going to be in business next year?"

Research in this area does support the conclusion that small firms which engage in strategic management outperform those which do not. This does not mean, however, that formal procedures are necessary. *The process of strategic planning, not the plan itself, appears to be a key component of business performance.* The strategic management model that was introduced in Chapter 1 and is used to introduce every chapter in this book is just as useful to small and entrepreneurial companies as it is to large business corporations and not-for-profit organizations. Even the strategic decision-making process discussed in Chapters 2 and 6 is valuable to existing small businesses. A few adjustments have been made to the model so that it can be applied to new entrepreneurial ventures, as shown in Figure 12.1.

This chapter presented some issues in strategy formulation that apply to new ventures and small businesses. S.W.O.T. analysis is very useful, but environmental scanning can be much more informal than that performed in large corporations. Peter Drucker proposes seven sources of innovation, which should be carefully monitored by any prospective entrepreneur. Hofer and Sandberg conclude from their research that a new venture's success is largely determined by (1) the industry's structure, (2) the venture's business strategy, and (3) the behavioral characteristics of the entrepreneur.

Although the implementation process for small and entrepreneurial businesses is similar to that used by large corporations, there are some important differences. The primary difference is that in small businesses the person(s) who formulates strategy is usually also responsible for developing implementation plans and carrying them out. Consequently, small business managers tend to make little distinction between formulation and implementation. The stages of growth and development for a small business are also very different from those presented in Chapter 8. Between Stages I and II are five distinct substages that characterize many small companies. The implementation of strategy is also different for those many small companies (and for a few large ones as well) that are privately-held, family businesses. The next generation must always be considered in decisions concerning the staffing of key positions and the company's organization for future growth.

Evaluation and control in small businesses and entrepreneurial ventures is quite different from that practiced by most large, publicly-held corporations. For the small operator, the procedures are far less formal and usually result more from the owner/manager's preferences and government taxation policies than from any strategic considerations. Businesses are often run on a cash basis and have minimum reporting procedures. Again, the rationales often given for what appear to be slip-shod accounting and financial practices

is (1) secrecy (the owner-manager wants to keep everything in his/her head so that neither competitors nor tax people can understand the business), and (2) a lack of concern about the future because of current concerns for survival. For these and other reasons, owners, operators, and outside observers should be wary of using standard evaluation methods to measure the health of a small, privately-owned company.

In conclusion, this chapter provides the reader with a basic understanding of the differences between large corporations and small businesses in terms of their use of strategic management. Entrepreneurs and top managers of other small businesses live in a very different kind of world from that occupied by their counterparts in large corporations. These managers have few resources to draw upon and operate with the knowledge that the difference between success and bankruptcy can be their personal willingness to risk all their possessions on a dream.

DISCUSSION QUESTIONS

1. What are some arguments for and against the use of strategic management concepts and techniques in a small or entrepreneurial business?

2. If the owner/manager of a small company asked you for some advice concerning the introduction of strategic planning, what would you tell the person?

3. In terms of strategic management, how does a new venture's situation differ from that of an ongoing small company?

4. How should a small company engage in environmental scanning? To what aspects of the environment should management pay most attention?

5. What considerations should small-business entrepreneurs keep in mind when they are deciding if a company should follow a growth or a stability strategy?

6. From a small company's point of view, what is the difference between a differentiation and a focus competitive strategy?

7. How does being family-owned as compared to publicly-owned affect the firm's strategic management?

8. What are the pros and cons of using a standard financial reporting system in a small business?

NOTES

1. R. B. Robinson, Jr. and J. A. Pearce, II, "Research Thrusts in Small Firm Strategic Planning," *Academy of Management Review* (January 1984), p. 128.

2. *The State of Small Business: A Report to the President* (Washington, D.C.: U.S. Government Printing Office, 1987), pp. 12–20 and *ABC World News Tonight* (May 6, 1988).

C. W. Hofer and W. R. Sandberg, "Improving New Venture Performance: Some Guidelines for Success," *American Journal of Small Business* (Summer 1987), pp. 11–12.

3. *The State of Small Business: A Report to the President,* p. 117.

4. T. Hall, "When Food Firms Merge, Effects Reach Into

Aisles of Supermarkets," *Wall Street Journal* (June 13, 1985), p. 29.

5. B. C. Vaught and F. Hoy, "Have You Got What It Takes To Run Your Own Business?" *Business* (July-August 1981), p. 2.

6. *The State of Small Business: A Report to the President* (Washington, D.C.: U.S. Government Printing Office, 1985).

7. J. W. Carland, F. Hoy, W. R. Boulton, and J. A. C. Carland, "Differentiating Entrepreneurs from Small Business Owners: A Conceptualization," *Academy of Management Review* (April 1984), p. 358.

8. S. P. Galante, "Counting On A Narrow Market Can Cloud Company's Future," *Wall Street Journal* (January 20, 1986), p. 17.

9. Robinson and Pearce, p. 129.

10. J. S. Bracker and J. N. Pearson, "Planning and Financial Performance of Small, Mature Firms," *Strategic Management Journal* (November-December 1986), pp. 503–522.

11. R. Ackelsberg and P. Arlow, "Small Businesses Do Plan and It Pays Off," *Long Range Planning* (October 1985), pp. 61–67.

12. Robinson and Pearce, p. 130.

13. R. B. Robinson, Jr. and J. A. Pearce II, "The Impact of Formalized Strategic Planning on Financial Performance in Small Organizations," *Strategic Management Journal* (July-September 1983), pp. 197–207.
Ackelsberg and Arlow, pp. 61–67.

14. Bracker and Pearson, p. 512.

15. J. C. Shuman and J. A. Seeger, "The Theory and Practice of Strategic Management in Smaller Rapid Growth Firms," *American Journal of Small Business* (Summer 1986), pp. 7–18; and J. C. Shuman, J. D. Shaw, and G. Sussman, "Strategic Planning in Smaller Rapid Growth Companies," *Long Range Planning* (December 1985), pp. 48–53.

16. For information on preparing a business plan, see S. R. Rich and D. E. Gumpert, "How to Write a Winning Business Plan," *Harvard Business Review* (May-June 1985), pp. 156–163 and C. M. Baumback, *How to Organize and Operate a Small Business* (Englewood Cliffs, N.J.: Prentice-Hall, 1988), pp. 109–112.

17. S. Birley and D. Norburn, "Small vs. Large Companies: The Entrepreneurial Conundrum," *Journal of Business Strategy* (Summer 1985), pp. 81–87.

18. Birley and Norburn, p. 82.

19. Birley and Norburn, p. 83.

20. Shuman and Seeger, p. 14.

21. P. F. Drucker, *Innovation and Entrepreneurship* (New York: Harper and Row, 1985), pp. 30–129.

22. Drucker, pp. 133–136.

23. Hofer and Sandberg, pp. 12–23.

24. P. Wright, "A Refinement of Porter's Strategies," *Strategic Management Journal* (January-February 1987), pp. 93–101.
H. W. Fox, "Strategic Superiorities of Small Size," *SAM Advanced Management Journal* (Winter 1986), pp. 14–21.

25. Birley and Norburn, p. 84.
K. R. Harrigan, "Guerrilla Strategies For Underdog Competitors," *Planning Review* (November 1986), pp. 4–11, 44–45.

26. Hofer and Sandberg, p. 22.

27. N. C. Churchill and V. L. Lewis, "The Five Stages of Small Business Growth," *Harvard Business Review* (May-June 1983), pp. 30–50.

28. F. Maytag, "The Joys of Keeping the Company Small," *Harvard Business Review* (July-August 1986), pp. 6–14.

29. H. H. Stevenson and J. C. Jarillo-Mossi, "Preserving Entrepreneurship As Companies Grow," *Journal of Business Strategy* (Summer 1986), p. 17.

30. N. C. Churchill and K. J. Hatten, "Non-Market-Based Transfers of Wealth and Power: A Research Framework for Family Businesses," *American Journal of Small Business* (Winter 1987), pp. 51–64.

31. Birley and Norburn, p. 85.

32. R. I. Levin and V. R. Travis, "Small Company Finance: What the Books Don't Say," *Harvard Business Review* (November-December 1987), pp. 30–32.

33. Levin and Travas, p. 31.

SUBJECT INDEX

406